*The Spirit and Christ in the New Testament
and Christian Theology*

Max Turner

The Spirit and Christ in the New Testament and Christian Theology

ESSAYS IN HONOR OF MAX TURNER

Edited by

I. Howard Marshall, Volker Rabens & Cornelis Bennema

WILLIAM B. EERDMANS PUBLISHING COMPANY
GRAND RAPIDS, MICHIGAN / CAMBRIDGE, U.K.

© 2012 Wm. B. Eerdmans Publishing Co.
All rights reserved

Published 2012 by
Wm. B. Eerdmans Publishing Co.
2140 Oak Industrial Drive N.E., Grand Rapids, Michigan 49505 /
P.O. Box 163, Cambridge CB3 9PU U.K.

Library of Congress Cataloging-in-Publication Data

The Spirit and Christ in the New Testament and Christian theology:
essays in honor of Max Turner / edited by I. Howard Marshall,
Volker Rabens & Cornelis Bennema.
    p.   cm.
Includes index.
ISBN 978-0-8028-6753-7 (pbk.: alk. paper)
1. Bible. N.T. — Criticism, interpretation, etc. 2. Bible. N.T. — Theology.
3. Jesus Christ — Biblical teaching. I. Turner, Max, 1947-
II. Marshall, I. Howard. III. Rabens, Volker, 1971-
IV. Bennema, Cornelis, 1964-

BS2361.3.S65 2012
231′.3 — dc23

                                2012002495

www.eerdmans.com

Contents

Contributors	viii
Abbreviations	xiii
Editors' Foreword	xiv
An Introduction to Max Turner *Steve Walton*	xvi
"The Lord, the Giver of Life": The Gift of the Spirit as Both Life-giving and Empowering *James D. G. Dunn*	1
The Spirit, Simeon, and the Songs of the Servant *John R. Levison*	18
Whose Spirit? The Promise and the Promiser in Luke 12:12 *Steve Walton*	35
The Persecuted Prophets: A Mirror Image of Luke's Spirit-Inspired Church *Robert P. Menzies*	52

Contents

"Was It Not Necessary for the Messiah to Suffer These Things and Enter into His Glory?" The Significance of Jesus' Death for Luke's Soteriology *Joel B. Green*	71
The Giving of the Spirit in John 19–20: Another Round *Cornelis Bennema*	86
Is Faith in Christ Without Evidence Superior Faith? A Re-examination of John 20:29 *D. A. Carson*	105
Apollos and the Ephesian Disciples: Befores and Afters (Acts 18:24–19:7) *Conrad Gempf*	119
Power from In Between: The Relational Experience of the Holy Spirit and Spiritual Gifts in Paul's Churches *Volker Rabens*	138
Divine Spirit and Human Spirit in Paul in the Light of Stoic and Biblical-Jewish Perspectives *Desta Heliso*	156
Ephesians and Divine-Christology *Chris Tilling*	177
Salvation's Bath by the Spirit: A Study of Titus 3:5b-6 in Its Canonical Setting *Robert W. Wall*	198
The Spirit in Hebrews: No Longer Forgotten? *Steve Motyer*	213
New Jerusalem and the Conversion of the Nations: An Exercise in Pneumatic Discernment (Rev. 21:1–22:5) *John Christopher Thomas*	228

Moses as "God" in Philo of Alexandria:
A Precedent for Christology? 246
   Richard Bauckham

Jesus and the Spirit in Biblical and Theological Perspective:
Messianic Empowering, Saving Wisdom, and the Limits
of Biblical Theology 266
   Mark L. Strauss

Cyril of Alexandria and the Incarnation 285
   Anthony N. S. Lane

"By the Washing of Regeneration and Renewal
in the Holy Spirit": Towards a Pneumatological
Theology of Justification 303
   Veli-Matti Kärkkäinen

Towards a Theology of Togetherness —
Life through the Spirit 323
   Graham McFarlane

Creative Reason and the Spirit: Identifying, Evaluating,
and Developing Paradigms of Pneumatology 336
   André Munzinger

List of Publications by Max Turner 356

List of Published PhD Dissertations
by Max Turner's Research Students 361

Index of Authors 363

Contributors

RICHARD BAUCKHAM is Professor Emeritus of New Testament Studies at the University of St. Andrews, UK. He is the author of *Jesus and the Eyewitnesses: The Gospels as Eyewitness Testimony* (Grand Rapids: Eerdmans, 2006) and *Jesus and the God of Israel: God Crucified and Other Studies on the New Testament's Christology of Divine Identity* (Milton Keynes: Paternoster/Grand Rapids: Eerdmans, 2008).

CORNELIS BENNEMA is Associate Professor of New Testament at the South Asia Institute of Advanced Christian Studies, Bangalore, India. He is the author of *The Power of Saving Wisdom: An Investigation of Spirit and Wisdom in Relation to the Soteriology of the Fourth Gospel* (Tübingen: Mohr Siebeck, 2002), *Excavating John's Gospel: A Commentary for Today* (Delhi: ISPCK, 2005; repr. Eugene: Wipf & Stock, 2008), and *Encountering Jesus: Character Studies in the Gospel of John* (Milton Keynes: Paternoster, 2009).

D. A. CARSON is Research Professor of New Testament at Trinity Evangelical Divinity School, Deerfield, Illinois, USA. Among his works are *The Gospel according to John*, Pillar New Testament Commentary Series (Leicester: IVP/Grand Rapids: Eerdmans, 1991), (with D. J. Moo) *An Introduction to the New Testament*, 2nd ed. (Grand Rapids: Zondervan, 2005), and *Commentary on the New Testament Use of the Old*, ed. with G. K. Beale (Grand Rapids: Baker Academic, 2007).

JAMES D. G. DUNN is Emeritus Lightfoot Professor of Divinity at the University of Durham, UK. His books include *Baptism in the Holy Spirit*

(Philadelphia: Westminster Press, 1970), and *Jesus and the Spirit* (London: SCM Press, 1975). He has completed two volumes of a trilogy on *Christianity in the Making*: Vol. 1. *Jesus Remembered* (Grand Rapids: Eerdmans, 2003); Vol. 2. *Beginning from Jerusalem* (Grand Rapids: Eerdmans, 2009), and is working on the third.

CONRAD GEMPF is Lecturer in New Testament at London School of Theology, UK. He is the editor of Colin Hemer's *The Book of Acts in the Setting of Hellenistic History* (Tübingen: Mohr Siebeck, 1989), and editor and contributor to the multi-volume *Acts in Its First Century Settings* series (Grand Rapids: Eerdmans, 1993-1996).

JOEL B. GREEN is Professor of New Testament Interpretation and Associate Dean for the Center for Advanced Theological Studies at Fuller Theological Seminary, Pasadena, California, USA. His books include *1 Peter* in the Two Horizons Commentary on the New Testament series (Grand Rapids: Eerdmans, 2007), *Methods for Luke,* ed. J. B. Green (Cambridge: Cambridge University Press, 2010), and *Practicing Theological Interpretation: Engaging Biblical Texts for Faith and Formation* (Grand Rapids: Baker Academic, 2011).

DESTA HELISO is Director of the Ethiopian Graduate School of Theology, Addis Ababa, Ethiopia. He is the author of *Pistis and the Righteous One: A Study of Romans 1:17 against the Background of Scripture and Second Temple Jewish Literature* (Tübingen: Mohr Siebeck, 2007) and "Enoch as the Son of Man: Contextual and Christological Considerations," *Swedish Missiological Themes* 98 (2010): 141-55.

VELI-MATTI KÄRKKÄINEN is Professor of Systematic Theology at Fuller Theological Seminary, Pasadena, California, USA, and Docent of Ecumenics, University of Helsinki, Finland. Among his works are *One with God: Salvation as Deification and Justification* (Collegeville: Liturgical Press, 2004), *Trinity and Religious Pluralism: The Doctrine of the Trinity in Christian Theology of Religions* (Aldershot: Ashgate, 2004), and *Global Dictionary of Theology,* ed. with W. A. Dyrness (Downers Grove: IVP, 2008).

ANTHONY N. S. LANE is Professor of Historical Theology at London School of Theology, UK. He is the author of *Justification by Faith in Catholic-Protestant Dialogue: An Evangelical Assessment* (London: T&T

Clark, 2002), *A Concise History of Christian Thought* (London: T&T Clark/ Grand Rapids: Baker Academic, 2006), and *A Reader's Guide to Calvin's Institutes* (Grand Rapids: Baker Academic, 2009).

JOHN R. LEVISON is Professor of New Testament at Seattle Pacific University, Seattle, Washington, USA. He is the author of *The Spirit in First Century Judaism* (Leiden: Brill, 1997), *Return to Babel: Global Perspectives on the Bible*, ed. with Priscilla Pope-Levison (Louisville: Westminster John Knox Press, 1999), and *Filled with the Spirit* (Grand Rapids: Eerdmans, 2009).

I. HOWARD MARSHALL is Professor Emeritus of New Testament at the University of Aberdeen, UK. Among his publications are (in collaboration with Philip H. Towner) *A Critical and Exegetical Commentary on the Pastoral Epistles*, International Critical Commentary (Edinburgh: T&T Clark, 1999), W. F. Moulton and A. S. Geden, *Concordance to the Greek New Testament*, ed. I. H. Marshall, 6th ed. fully revised (London: T&T Clark, 2002), and *New Testament Theology: Many Witnesses, One Gospel* (Downers Grove: IVP, 2004).

GRAHAM MCFARLANE is Senior Lecturer in Systematic Theology at London School of Theology, UK. He is the author of *Why Do You Believe What You Believe About the Holy Spirit?* (Carlisle: Paternoster Press, 1998), *Christ and the Spirit* (Carlisle: Paternoster Press, 1999), and *Why Do You Believe What You Believe About Jesus?* (Carlisle: Paternoster Press, 2000).

ROBERT P. MENZIES is Director of Synergy, a rural service organization located in Kunming, China. Among his works are *Empowered for Witness: The Spirit in Luke–Acts* (London: T&T Clark, 2004 [orig. 1994]), (with W. W. Menzies) *Spirit and Power: Foundations of Pentecostal Experience* (Grand Rapids: Zondervan, 2000), and *The Language of the Spirit: Interpreting and Translating Charismatic Terms* (Cleveland: CPT Press, 2010).

STEVE MOTYER is Program Leader for Theology & Counselling and Lecturer in New Testament and Hermeneutics at London School of Theology, UK. He is the author of *Israel in the Plan of God* (Leicester: IVP, 1989), *Your Father the Devil? A New Approach to John and 'the Jews'* (Carlisle: Paternoster, 1997), and a popular commentary *Discovering Hebrews* (Leicester: IVP, 2005).

ANDRÉ MUNZINGER is Research Fellow at the Institute for Hermeneutics at the University of Bonn, Germany. He is the author of *Discerning the Spirits: Theological and Ethical Hermeneutics in Paul* (Cambridge: Cambridge University Press, 2007), "Vernunft und Religion: Zur Ermöglichung interkultureller Koexistenz" (unpublished Habilitationsschrift, University of Bonn, 2012), and various articles on the ethics of development and globalization.

VOLKER RABENS is Research Scholar of the Käte Hamburger Kolleg "Dynamics in the History of Religions" and Lecturer in New Testament at the University of Bochum, Germany. His publications include *The Holy Spirit and Ethics in Paul: Transformation and Empowering for Religious-Ethical Life* (Tübingen: Mohr Siebeck, 2010), and *"Trading Religions": Religious Formation, Transformation and Cross-Cultural Exchange between East and West*, ed. with Peter Wick (Leiden: Brill, forthcoming 2012).

JOHN CHRISTOPHER THOMAS is Clarence J. Abbott Professor of Biblical Studies at Pentecostal Theological Seminary, Cleveland, Tennessee, USA, and Director of the Centre for Pentecostal and Charismatic Studies at Bangor University, Bangor, Wales, UK. He is the author of *Footwashing in John 13 and the Johannine Community* (Sheffield: JSOT Press, 1991), *The Devil, Disease, and Deliverance: Origins of Illness in New Testament Thought* (Sheffield: Sheffield Academic Press, 1998), and *The Spirit of the New Testament* (Leiden: Deo Publishing, 2005).

MARK L. STRAUSS is Professor of New Testament at Bethel Seminary, San Diego, USA. He is the author of *The Davidic Messiah in Luke–Acts: The Promise and Its Fulfillment in Lukan Christology* (Sheffield: Sheffield Academic Press, 1995); *Four Portraits, One Jesus: An Introduction to Jesus and the Gospels* (Grand Rapids: Zondervan, 2007), and *How to Read the Bible in Changing Times: Understanding and Applying God's Word Today* (Grand Rapids: Baker, 2011).

CHRIS TILLING is Tutor in New Testament Studies at St Mellitus College and St Paul's Theological Centre, London, UK. He is the author of *Paul's Divine Christology* (Tübingen: Mohr Siebeck, forthcoming 2012), and several articles on themes ranging from Paul, the historical Jesus, to the relationship between science and theology.

Contributors

ROBERT W. WALL is Paul T. Walls Professor of Scripture and Wesleyan Studies at Seattle Pacific University, Seattle, Washington, USA. His publications include *Community of the Wise: The Letter of James,* The New Testament in Context (London: Continuum, 1997), "The Acts of the Apostles" in *The New Interpreter's Bible,* ed. L. E. Keck (Nashville: Abingdon Press, 2002), vol. 10, pp. 1-370, and *The Catholic Epistles and Apostolic Traditions,* ed. with Karl-Wilhelm Niebuhr (Waco: Baylor University Press, 2009).

STEVE WALTON is Professor of New Testament at London School of Theology, UK. He is the author of *Leadership and Lifestyle: The Portrait of Paul in the Miletus Speech and 1 Thessalonians* (Cambridge: Cambridge University Press, 2000) and (with D. Wenham) *Exploring the New Testament.* Volume 1: *The Gospels and Acts,* 2nd ed. (London: SPCK/Downers Grove: IVP, 2011).

Abbreviations

The abbreviations in this book are taken from *The SBL Handbook of Style for Ancient Near Eastern, Biblical, and Early Christian Studies,* ed. Patrick H. Alexander et al. (Peabody: Hendrickson, 1999). The following abbreviations are used in addition.

CMT	*Currents in Mission and Theology*
DBSJ	*Detroit Baptist Seminary Journal*
JBTh	*Jahrbuch für biblische Theologie*
JEPTA	*Journal of the European Pentecostal Theological Association*
JPT	*Journal of Pentecostal Theology*
JTI	*Journal of Theological Interpretation*
NZSTh	*Neue Zeitschrift für Systematische Theologie und Religionsphilosophie*
ThGespr	*Theologisches Gespräch*
ZFWU	*Zeitschrift für Wirtschafts- und Unternehmensethik*
ZNT	*Zeitschrift für Neues Testament*

Editors' Foreword

This is a *Festschrift* to celebrate Max Turner's sixty-fifth birthday. When we were searching for a suitable publisher for this project a few years ago, Jon Pott, Vice-President and Editor-in-Chief of the Wm. B. Eerdmans Publishing Company, stated that Eerdmans would be happy to publish the *Festschrift* to honor the occasion. We gladly accepted. It quickly became apparent that Max's friends and colleagues at London School of Theology (LST) warmly supported the project, and this was backed up by colleagues further afield who respect Max for his scholarship and wish to share in honoring him. At the same time we felt that such a volume should be united by more than a common desire to honor Max. Two principal areas in which Max has worked focus on the work of Jesus Christ and the Holy Spirit in the New Testament, with the implications of this for the life of the church today. A volume that picks up these themes and uses Max's work as the launching pad for further investigation of these topics would be of considerable value to students and scholars alike. We thus aimed to strike out in fresh directions rather than repeat what previous studies have done. As a result, this *Festschrift* contains contributions from Max's colleagues at LST and the wider academy, as well as his former students (many of whom now belong to the latter category). It focuses on the areas of the Spirit and Christ, both in the New Testament and in aspects of Christian theology, with topics that are relevant for the church worldwide today.

From the beginning we were greatly encouraged by the willingness of Jon Pott to commit Eerdmans to the publication of the volume and want to thank his colleagues and himself for their efficient han-

Editors' Foreword

dling of the process and the quality of the resulting publication. We want to express our immense gratitude to the scholars who have contributed to this volume. Thanks are due to Lucy, Max's wife, for her help with regard to personal details of Max's career, and to Steve Walton, a long-standing friend of Max, who ably wrote up the story and impact of Max's life. At some stage it was agreed to let Max know what was in store for him so that he might have the pleasure of anticipation as well as the joy of reception. That time has now come, and the occasion of the LST graduation ceremony on 30 June 2012 commended itself to all concerned as the ideal venue for the presentation of the volume. With it we express our best wishes to him for good health and for further fruitful scholarship and service to the Lord.

I. HOWARD MARSHALL
VOLKER RABENS
CORNELIS BENNEMA

An Introduction to Max Turner

Steve Walton

Professor Martin Maximillian Barnaby Turner — known to all as Max — is a remarkable person, whom we are delighted to honor in this volume. He combines a brilliant mind, an energetic character, a warm heart, and a generous spirit, held together by a deep Christian faith.

Max grew up in Cyprus, where his father worked as a head teacher, before the family returned to the UK in his teens. He gained a scholarship to read Natural Sciences at Trinity Hall, Cambridge, and took Parts IA and IB of the Medical Sciences Tripos, intending to pursue a medical career. However, his life changed when he met thoughtful Christians among his fellow-students in Cambridge, and he became a Christian there. A key figure in his conversion was fellow-student Hugh Williamson, now Regius Professor of Hebrew at Oxford — "the other place," as Cambridge people always refer to it. After a striking experience of hearing God audibly say, "Feed my sheep," Max switched to Part II of the Theology Tripos, graduating in 1970. Following a year teaching Chemistry in Kent and Zambia, he returned to Cambridge in 1971 to pursue a PhD. Much of his early Christian experience had been among Pentecostals, and so it was natural for him to research on the Holy Spirit in Luke and Acts. The Spirit has remained a key theme for his subsequent research, writing, and teaching, and Max is now one of the world's leading scholars on the Spirit in the New Testament.

Max the Lecturer and Supervisor

At the end of Max's three years of research in Cambridge, London Bible College (LBC — now London School of Theology, LST) was looking for a librarian who would also do some lecturing. Max was one of the first non-alumni to be appointed to the LBC faculty, and he brought great energy and an orderly mind to the task. When he eventually gave up the role of librarian as he moved fully into lecturing, the library was much better run than the one which he had inherited.

Max rapidly developed a reputation as a thorough and precise teacher with an encyclopedic knowledge. He is never satisfied — in himself or in others — with superficial knowledge or understanding, but always wants to press on to greater depth and greater clarity. He thus worked long hours to master the material he taught, and the quality and depth of his teaching were deeply appreciated.

Max's reputation spread, and in 1986 he was given the opportunity to be Lecturer in New Testament Exegesis at Aberdeen University for five years. He and the family moved north, and he had five happy years in the Aberdeen Divinity Faculty at King's College. There he began to supervise research students, and inculcated into them his own enthusiasm and scholarly thoroughness.

Max is a fine supervisor of research students and has enabled and encouraged at least 18 PhD students and several MTh students to successful completion: most have had their theses published, often in prestigious monograph series. One former research student describes Max's style of supervision as "learning to swim." He writes: "Max is the swimming instructor, telling his students (while they are still on dry ground) how they should move their arms and legs and where to swim to. Then he would throw us into the pool and tell us to do it. . . . Besides Max's expert probing into the subject material, he would also teach us how to go about research — a skill for life." This may sound daunting, but Max's track record is that it works, and works well. The good number of his former research students now teaching around the world in universities, seminaries, and theological colleges bears testimony to his success.

Max's scholarship, teaching and supervision were recognized in 1994, when — after his move back to LBC — he was made Senior Lecturer in New Testament Studies by LBC and Brunel University, and then in 1998 when he became LBC's first Professor — a singular honor.

An Introduction to Max Turner

He became Professor Emeritus on his retirement in 2011, and continues to contribute actively to research supervision.

Max the Contributor

On his return to LBC in 1991, Max was appointed Director of Research, and applied his great energy to the college's vision to become a centre for postgraduate research. He inherited about half a dozen research students and in a matter of a few years the research department was transformed into a burgeoning and lively research community of greater size than many university theology research departments. Max built relationships with the Council for National Academic Awards (CNAA), who validated LBC's research degrees in the early years, including developing a one-year research degree, the Master of Theology, which attracted numerous students.

Through a personal link with Joel Green at Asbury Theological Seminary, Kentucky, USA, Max also made academic connections which allowed supervisors outside LBC to supervise research degrees through LBC. This connection grew and developed to embrace other American institutions and supervisors, and increased the global ministry of LBC.

Max's contribution to LBC was further recognized in 1996, when he was appointed Vice-Principal for Academic Affairs by the Principal, Derek Tidball. He served in this role for eight years, including being a key link in LBC's relationship with Brunel University, which became LBC's validating university when the CNAA closed in 1993. He brought all his characteristic energy to this role and worked hard at encouraging faculty colleagues in their own research and writing, in their teaching, and in their own development to be the best that they could be.

Max the Scholar, Author, and Editor

Max published a string of important articles on the Spirit arising from his PhD research in scholarly journals. His period in Aberdeen saw him, with strong encouragement from Professor Howard Marshall, begin working towards two very substantial books which cemented his reputation as one of the finest scholars on the Spirit in the New Testament. While in Aberdeen, he published further articles which were the precursors of these two books.

Power from on High: The Spirit in Israel's Restoration and Witness in Luke-Acts[1] is a major scholarly study of Luke's understanding of the Spirit and presents Max's mature thinking on the topic, developed from its roots in his PhD research. It is rightly recognized as a major treatment of the theme and indispensable to serious work on the topic.

The Holy Spirit and Spiritual Gifts — Then and Now[2] was written as a textbook for third-year British undergraduates, but goes well beyond what would be expected in such a book. There Max discusses the testimony of the major New Testament authors (Luke, John, Paul) about the Spirit, and engages sympathetically, thoughtfully and critically with debates about the Spirit in the modern Christian scene. This book offers a thought-through alternative to classical Pentecostalist and cessationist views of the Spirit and it has rightly been highly influential, rooting the thinking and practice of the contemporary charismatic renewal movement in the Bible.

Both of these books show Max engaging in scholarly controversy with clarity and graciousness. It is notable that his major dialogue partners, such as Jimmy Dunn, Bob Menzies, and Gordon Fee, are also personal and valued friends, and that he maintains warm relationships with these people.

These books were not Max's first foray into book authorship, for he had already co-authored the important *Linguistics and Biblical Interpretation* with Peter Cotterell (then a faculty colleague at LBC, later Principal),[3] a book which provides an accessible and thorough "way in" to the significance of linguistics for biblical scholarship. He also co-edited two *Festschriften*, for his Aberdeen colleague Howard Marshall and his LBC colleague Peter Cotterell.[4] With Joel Green he later pio-

---

1. Sheffield: Sheffield Academic Press, 1996 (reprinted, with corrections, 2000).

2. Carlisle: Paternoster, 1996. A revised edition was published as: *The Holy Spirit and Spiritual Gifts in the New Testament Church and Today* (Peabody: Hendrickson, 1997), and a further revised edition as: *The Holy Spirit and Spiritual Gifts — Then and Now* (Carlisle: Paternoster, 1999).

3. London: SPCK, 1989/Downers Grove: IVP, 1988.

4. Joel B. Green and Max Turner, eds., *Jesus of Nazareth: Lord and Christ: Essays on the Historical Jesus and New Testament Christology*, FS I. Howard Marshall (Carlisle: Paternoster/Grand Rapids: Eerdmans, 1994); Antony Billington, Tony Lane, and Max Turner, eds., *Mission and Meaning: Essays Presented to Peter Cotterell* (Carlisle: Paternoster, 1995).

neered a new kind of New Testament commentary series, the Two Horizons series, which aims to develop the interface between New Testament Studies and constructive theology — their co-edited volume of 2000 is the precursor of the series,[5] and the first volumes suggest a rich and stimulating vein of fresh thinking is entering the academic and Christian world.

Max's scholarly work led to recognition. He was elected a member of the *Studiorum Novi Testamenti Societas* in 1998 and a Fellow of the Royal Society of Arts in 1999. He was Drumwright Lecturer at the South Western Baptist Theological Seminary in 2001 and Beeson International Scholar-in-Residence at Asbury Theological Seminary in 2002. He has lectured in a number of countries and is greatly appreciated for his depth of knowledge, insight, and understanding.

Max the Person and Pastor

It would be all too easy for a person's head to be turned by such attention and recognition, but Max has never lost his enthusiasm for teaching and equipping others for Christian ministry and service in many spheres. He was ordained and served as minister of North Bushey Free (Baptist) Church from 1976, teaching and preaching there and elsewhere on a regular basis.

His students — undergraduate and postgraduate — speak of his personal care, thoughtfulness, generosity, and support for them. Not a few of his students have been rock climbing or hill walking with him, sharing his love of the outdoors; during his time in Aberdeen he "bagged" 167 Munros (mountains in Scotland over 3000 feet).

Max is also a much loved husband to Lucy, father to Abby and Duncan, and grandfather to Isaac. He is far from a one-dimensional scholar, but seeks to live a full life which is lived "more abundantly" (John 10:10) in love and response to Christ, who captured his heart while a student. We give thanks to God for him and wish him and Lucy many more happy and productive years to come.

---

5. Joel B. Green and Max Turner, eds., *Between Two Horizons: Spanning New Testament Studies and Systematic Theology* (Grand Rapids: Eerdmans, 2000).

"The Lord, the Giver of Life": The Gift of the Spirit as Both Life-giving and Empowering

James D. G. Dunn

Much of the recent debate about the Holy Spirit and the gift of the Spirit has focused on the distinction between the life-giving Spirit and the charismatic Spirit or Spirit of prophecy. This is understandable since within the early Judeo-Christian perception of the Spirit both aspects are prominent, and usually in different circumstances. Consequently in the debate occasioned by the classic Pentecostal conception of baptism in the Spirit as a separate work of the Spirit subsequent to and distinct from the Spirit's soteriological or life-giving work, any distinction between the life-giving Spirit and the charismatic or empowering Spirit is grist to the mill. It was on the basis of such a distinction that resolution has traditionally been sought with regard to the Acts accounts of the first Pentecost and as a solution to the puzzle of Samaria in Acts 8. For earlier generations (and centuries) it was natural to assume that the first disciples had already received the life-giving Spirit during their time with Jesus, and only at Pentecost received the Spirit empowering for witness (Acts 1:8). In particular, if John's Gospel can be neatly slotted into the fuller history of Luke, then it can be readily argued that such a passage as John 13:10 or 15:3 indicates that the disciples were already "born again" (3:5), so that the subsequent Pentecostal outpouring of the Spirit can be readily distinguished as the giving of the charismatic Spirit (Acts 2:4).[1] And in Acts 8 we have what is probably the classic instance where such a distinction seems to be required and

---

1. As noted in my *Baptism in the Holy Spirit*, 2nd ed. (London: SCM Press, 2010), pp. 38-39, 173.

to make best sense. The Samaritans had both believed and been baptized in the name of the Lord Jesus (8:12), and yet "the Spirit had not come upon any of them" (8:16); it was through the subsequent laying on of Peter's and John's hands that "they received the Holy Spirit" (8:17). So, for example, Calvin inferred that the Samaritan believers were "regenerate" and "endued with the Spirit of adoption" as a result of Philip's ministry. What they subsequently experienced through the laying on of Peter's and John's hands were "excellent graces of the Spirit."[2] In my *Baptism*, chapter 5, I noted a fair number of similar expositions, from both Catholic and Protestant commentators. And not surprisingly it is the same distinction between soteriological Spirit and empowering Spirit (two distinct works of the same Spirit) which provided the launch-pad for the most impressive recent attempt to maintain the validity of a Pentecostal reading of Acts.[3] It is this passage especially which is regarded by those critical of the main thesis of my *Baptism* as its Achilles' heel.[4] Max Turner has, of course, been heavily involved in the debate[5] and it is a pleasure both to contribute to his *Festschrift* and to use the opportunity to return once more to issues with which we have both been engaged for several decades, and in increasing agreement.[6]

Here I simply want to restate and reinforce my older conviction, which I share with Max, that the action of the Spirit cannot be so neatly separated into distinct categories — that life-giving and empowering are two aspects of the same action of the Spirit, since both are aspects of the same Spirit, aspects of, as we might say, the Spirit's character, outworkings of the Spirit's presence. If a single word can sum up

---

2. J. Calvin, *The Acts of the Apostles,* ed. D. W. Torrance and T. F. Torrance (Edinburgh: Oliver and Boyd, 1965), pp. 235-36.

3. R. P. Menzies, *The Development of Early Christian Pneumatology* (Sheffield: JSOT Press, 1991).

4. E.g. H. Ervin, *Conversion-Initiation and the Baptism in the Holy Spirit* (Peabody: Hendrickson, 1984), pp. 25-40; R. Stronstad, *The Charismatic Theology of St Luke* (Peabody: Hendrickson, 1984), pp. 63-65; R. P. Menzies, "Luke and the Spirit: A Reply to James Dunn," *JPT* 4 (1994): 120-22.

5. Particularly *Power from on High: The Spirit in Israel's Restoration and Witness in Luke-Acts* (Sheffield: Sheffield Academic Press, 1996), where he already questions the separation of the soteriological work of the Spirit from the Spirit's empowering for mission (pp. 433-38); the present paper is an attempt to strengthen the main thrust of his thesis.

6. Most recently in *JPT* 19 (2010): 3-43.

the action of the Spirit and sign of the Spirit's presence, it is *vitality*. Vitality does not denote simply life, but also the expression of that life in movement and activity — "vitality" in its dictionary equivalents of "animation, liveliness, and ability to perform its functions." The church which lacks visible signs of vitality may lack the life of the Spirit, and in any case will be in need of the re-vitalizing work of the Spirit. As one who first approached this whole issue out of an interest in and concern for Christian renewal or revival, I stand four-square with Pentecostals on that point.

1. The *Ruach* (רוח) of Life

To begin with we should remind ourselves of the range of meaning embraced by the term "spirit," both in Hebrew (רוח) and in Greek (πνεῦμα). In its early usage, the common element which allows the same word to be used for "wind," "breath," and "spirit" seems to be a sense that in each case the movement of air is involved — "wind" as רוח experienced with some force; "breath" as essentially a similar movement in every-day living; and "spirit" in effect identified with that breath of life.[7] In two of the most vivid Spirit passages in the Bible full play is made of this range of meaning. In the great vision of dry bones of Ezekiel 37, Ezekiel, confronted with a valley full of corpses, is called upon to

> Prophesy to the breath (רוח), prophesy, son of man, and say to the breath (רוח), "Thus says the Lord God: Come from the four winds, O breath (רוח), and breathe upon these slain that they may live." Ezekiel continues: "I prophesied as he commanded me, and the breath (רוח) came into them, and they lived, and stood on their feet, a vast multitude" (Ezek. 37:9-10).

And in John 3:8 Jesus says to Nicodemus,

> The wind (πνεῦμα) blows where it chooses, and you hear the sound of it, but you do not know where it comes from or where it goes. So it is with everyone who is born of the Spirit (πνεῦμα).

---

7. S. Tengström, "רוח," *TDOT*, 13:368, 372-79.

In fact, from these two passages, one would be justified in inferring that *life is the most fundamental mark of the Spirit*. After all, it is the primary function attributed to the Spirit in the creation narrative: "the Lord God formed man from the dust of the ground, and breathed into his nostrils the breath of life; and the man became a living being" (Gen. 2:7).[8] Although רוח is not used here, it is clearly the same imagery (רוח = breath, spirit) which is in mind. Human "spirit" is the breath of God. So, for example,

- Genesis 6:17 — the flood will destroy "all flesh in which is the breath (רוח) of life";
- Job 33:4 — "the Spirit of God has made me, and the breath of the Almighty gives me life";
- Psalm 104:29-30 — "when you take away their breath, they die and return to the dust. When you send forth your Spirit, they are created; and you renew the face of the ground."

The vision of Ezekiel makes the same assumption: the Lord God says, "I will cause רוח to enter you, and you shall live" (Ezek. 37:5).

In the light of such passages, we should not hasten to make a sharp distinction between human spirit and divine Spirit. If the Spirit of God is what gives life, if the breath of God is what makes man a living soul (נפש), then the life-force in human beings, that which relates them directly to God (the spirit, or spiritual dimension which they inhabit), is the Spirit of God. This emphasis has rightly been brought to the fore recently by John Levison, who makes the case that in pre-Christian biblical and Jewish literature the life-principle and the Spirit of God were understood to be one and the same, the human spirit as holy spirit.[9] This is a salutary reminder, when we are discussing whether clear distinctions can be made between the different functions of the divine Spirit, that the common ground of "life," life from God, has to be a given from the start.

This line of thought leads to another aspect which should not be missed: that the Spirit is the creator of life, that is, of all life. The fact

---

8. The role of the רוח in the first creation narrative (Gen. 1:2) is unclear; possibly "a wind (רוח) swept over the face of the waters" (NRSV), or "the Spirit of God hovered over the surface of the water" (REB); "either as an element of chaos or, more likely, as God's creative energy" (*TDOT,* 13:381).

9. J. R. Levison, *Filled with the Spirit* (Grand Rapids: Eerdmans, 2009).

"The Lord, the Giver of Life"

that Genesis 6:17 does not make a distinction between human and animal life, and the presence of the רוח from the beginning of creation (Gen. 1:2), means that any sharp distinction between the creator Spirit and the soteriological Spirit has equally to be rethought. The Spirit as the life-giver is one of the points at which Judeo-Christian theology can see itself as contributing a crucial insight to the understanding of the world in which we live. The amazing life-force which so dominates the reality which we all experience — the extraordinary fecundity of created life, the superabundance of sperm and seed which ensures that generation follows generation, the tenacity with which life clings to arid desert or vertical cliff-face or the deepest depths of ocean, the apparently arbitrary mutation which modifies species and produces ever new variations, the rich bio-diversity of the planet — all that can be seen as the divine life-force, the expression of the רוח of God still sweeping over the face of creation, still bringing into existence what had not existed before, still bringing life to where there was none. If we want to recognize the Spirit of God in creation, we need hardly look beyond the evidence of *life*. And as humankind has found too often in the past, when we distinguish spiritual life too sharply from human life and from the breath of life which animates all living things, then the spirituality is deformed and we begin to lose touch with the Creator God and Spirit.[10]

A third aspect brings us back nearer to our main concern, to the integral interaction of life and vitality. For the life-force in a human being is not constant. The רוח of the individual can faint (Pss. 77:3; 142:3; 143:4, 7), can be broken (Job 17:1; Ps. 51:17; Prov. 15:13; 18:14) or be crushed (Ps. 34:18), can in effect be lost to that person — "there was no more spirit in her" (1 Kgs. 10:5; 2 Chr. 9:4); but it can also be revived (Gen. 45:27; Judg. 15:19; 1 Sam. 30:12). This perception of human life is not far removed from two other perceptions which are more directly related to the רוח of God — the gifted individual, whose gift is attributed to the divine Spirit, as in the case of Bezalel, "filled with divine spirit, with skill, intelligence, and knowledge in every kind of craft" (Exod. 35:31), or Joshua, "full of the spirit of wisdom" (Deut. 34:9), or Daniel, acknowledged as one who was endowed with a spirit of the holy gods (Dan. 4:8-9, 18; 5:11-12, 14). The divine life-force in these individuals expressed it-

---

10. A similar point could be drawn from the readiness of OT writers to speak of wind as the רוח of YHWH, just as the breath of life is the Spirit of God (*TDOT*, 13:381-83).

self in special character and gift, but not as "a *donum superadditum*,"[11] more as an expression of the divine life-force in a gifted character, much as the same life force also causes some flowers to grow in gorgeous color, or some birds to have beautiful plumes. We even have to question whether we should make a clear distinction between the gifted individual and the charismatically endowed leader. Certainly, Gideon, Samson and the others were given their heroic leadership qualities by the Spirit coming upon them (e.g. Judg. 3:10; 6:34; 14:19). But Saul, equally distinguished as a charismatic leader (1 Sam. 11:6), lost his leadership quality when "the Spirit of the Lord departed" from him (16:14). How different was the case of the Spirit of the Lord rushing upon Samson (Judg. 14:6) from the case of the Spirit of the Lord "stirring" him (13:25)? The coming of the Spirit upon a person could also be described as the revitalizing of the person's spirit, the replugging of the person into the divine life-force. The point is simply an extension or application of Levison's insight: that the life-force in a person, evidence of the divine breath vivifying a person, should not be too easily distinguished from the gifts which a person has or the divine enablings that a person may experience in particular situations. It may rightly all be attributed to the one Spirit of God.

In short, when scripture speaks about the s/Spirit it speaks about life. And not just about life as a context for other things, as the background for other activities, but life as vitality, life as expressing that divine breath, life as gifted and manifesting the divine character of that life. The manifestations of that divine life can be very varied, as are the manifestations of all created life; but the manifestations are not something other than that life, they are simply manifestations of that life. So there is a basic flaw in a distinction between different functions of the Spirit, as between the soteriological Spirit and the charismatic Spirit or Spirit of prophecy, which neglects that each function is an expression of the life-giving Spirit. For we are not dealing with two distinct Spirits. The Spirit of life is the soteriological Spirit, is also the Spirit of prophecy, the revitalizing life of one and the same Spirit, and the revitalized life of the human spirit expressing their conjoint vitality in the particular expressions of prophecy. Particular expressions of that life/Spirit may be very vivid and heightened

---

11. I use Menzies' phrase (as in *Development*, pp. 48, 316); Menzies largely ignores the close link between the Spirit and life and the key texts discussed here.

and temporary, may be described (understandably) as the Spirit coming upon or inspiring for a particular purpose. But is it best expressed as a *donum superadditum*? For it is not a different Spirit which is in view in these passages, and not essentially different from the indwelling Spirit bubbling up in the vitality which is the divine life/Spirit in a person.

2. The Life-Giving πνεῦμα

All this can be inferred from the basic Hebrew understanding of the divine רוח which the first Christians inherited. But it becomes particularly clear in the New Testament's own talk of the divine πνεῦμα. Although most of the New Testament references are either to the divine Spirit or to the human spirit, the fact that in a number of cases it is unclear whether the πνεῦμα is one or the other (e.g. 1 Cor. 14:15), divine Spirit or human spirit, reinforces Levison's point. Gordon Fee's rendering of πνεῦμα in these cases as "S/spirit" makes the same point.[12] The point may simply be that in experiencing the πνεῦμα, the individual who has the experience is typically unable to distinguish divine Spirit from human spirit. And, theologically speaking, justifiably so. For the inability to make that distinction is another reminder that the πνεῦμα is the continuum between the divine and the human. Which is also why, existentially, it is often so difficult, as we shall see, to make a distinction between Christ and the Spirit of Christ, precisely because it is the mediatorial role, the bridging or inter-linking role of Christ/the Spirit which is in view. A quick review of the strong association in many New Testament texts between the Spirit and "life" will reinforce the point being made.

Most striking, of course, is the explicit designation of the Spirit as "the life-giving Spirit," the "life-giver" — the basis of the Nicene creedal confession which provides the title of this essay. The verb occurs in the New Testament eleven times, all but one (1 Pet. 3:18) referring to the soteriological work of the Spirit.[13] In three cases the text ex-

12. G. Fee, *God's Empowering Presence: The Holy Spirit in the Letters of Paul* (Peabody: Hendrickson, 1994), pp. 24-26.

13. Interestingly, in view of the reflections in the first part of this essay, although the NT does not speak about the Spirit in reference to created life, Paul does use the imagery of the life of nature to illustrate how he understands the resurrection of the body

plicitly refers to God as the one who gives life (John 5:21; Rom. 4:17; 8:11). But the same thought, God as the life-giver, is implied in other references (1 Cor. 15:22, 45; Gal. 3:21); and talk of the Son as the one who "makes alive" (John 5:21) belongs to the same line of thought. What is interesting for us, however, is the way the same authors speak explicitly of the Spirit as the one who "gives life":

- John 6:63 — "it is the Spirit that makes alive; the flesh is of no value";[14] in the present text, as following on the strong emphasis in 6:51-56 on the absolute necessity of eating/crunching the flesh of the Son of Man, with the strong implication that the passage is an elaboration of the words of institution at the Last Supper,[15] it is hard to escape the implication that 6:63 is an attempt to warn against an overemphasis on the sacrament; it is not the flesh (and blood) itself which gives life, it is the Spirit.[16]
- Romans 8:11 — "If the Spirit of him who raised Jesus from the dead dwells in you, he who raised Christ from the dead will give life to your mortal bodies as well, through his Spirit which dwells in you"; in a passage where indwelling Christ and indwelling Spirit are evidently alternative ways of describing the same relationship (8:9-11), the life-giving power of resurrection is attributed to God through the Spirit, and it is conceived as a divine work from within rather than an acting on the body of death from without.[17]
- 1 Corinthians 15:45 — "'The first man (Adam) became a living soul' (Gen. 2:7), the last Adam life-giving s/Spirit"; should we translate "*a* life-giving spirit"? In biblical thought there is only one life-giving Spirit, the Spirit of God. So even if we want to

---

— like a seed sown in the autumn (and dying), only to "be made alive/come to life" in the spring (1 Cor. 15:36).

14. NRSV translates "the flesh is useless."

15. See, e.g., R. E. Brown, *The Gospel according to John (i–xii)*, Anchor Bible 29 (New York: Doubleday, 1966), pp. 287-91.

16. John 6:63 is of a piece with 3:6 — "What is born of the flesh is flesh, and what is born of the Spirit is Spirit."

17. Similarly in 2 Cor. 4:16–5:5 the resurrection is understood as the end-point of the process of outer nature wasting away and inner nature being renewed day by day (4:16), as both a re-clothing and as "the mortal swallowed up by life" (5:4), the Spirit being the first installment and guarantee (5:5).

avoid the thought that in resurrection Jesus *became* the Spirit,[18] it is clear enough that Paul did not share that concern here (otherwise he would have expressed himself differently). As Jesus was identified with divine Wisdom (e.g. 1 Cor. 8:6; Heb. 1:3), and by John as the incarnate Word (John 1:14),[19] so here the resurrected Jesus seems to be identified with the Spirit. That may be an overstatement of what Paul otherwise expresses by using equivalent phrases (as in Rom. 8:9-11), or by identifying the Spirit as the Spirit of Christ (Rom. 8:9; Gal. 4:6; Phil. 1:19), but he does not flinch from saying what he does here,[20] and, for our purposes, it is important to note that the identification is with the life-giving Spirit.

- 2 Corinthians 3:6 — the "new covenant" is "not of the letter but of the s/Spirit; for the letter kills, but the Spirit makes alive"; the defining feature of the old covenant was the law, here depicted as understood too superficially (as "letter"); the defining feature of the new covenant was the Spirit, the life-giving Spirit. That it is not the law as such which Paul denigrates here should be clear, since his whole language and imagery are drawn from the prophets who looked for the reality of the law to be written in the heart, for a new heart, from which true obedience would come. It is this imagery on which Paul draws, in talking of the Spirit writing on tablets of human hearts (3:3) and of the *"new* covenant" (Jer. 31:31-34; Ezek. 11:19; 36:26-27). Again the thought is of a new life which expresses itself in an enabling to do what had not been done before. Paul cherishes the same thought in Romans 7:6 and 8:4.[21]

---

18. "Became" is clearly implied in the second half of the verse, which is constructed to parallel the first half:

> first Adam became εἰς living soul
> last Adam εἰς life-giving Spirit.

19. Further detail in my *Christology in the Making*, 2nd ed. (London: SCM Press, 1989), chs. 6 and 7.

20. 2 Cor. 3:17 is usually taken in the same way: "the Lord is the Spirit," where "the Lord" is understood to be the Lord Jesus, though I think the intention was rather to identify "the Lord" of Exod. 34:34 as the divine presence encountered when someone converted (3:16); discussion in *Christology*, pp. 141-49.

21. The parallel between 2 Cor. 3:6 and the "life-making" of Gal. 3:21 should be more noted than is usually the case. The point of Gal. 3:21 was to remind readers/audiences that God did not intend the law to be life-giving; the law's function was different

James D. G. Dunn

3. The Spirit and Life

The correlation between s/Spirit and life extends further than the particular term ("to give life/make alive"). Again this is clearest in John and Paul.

- John 3:3-6 — no one can enter the kingdom of God without being born of the Spirit.
- 4:10-14 — Jesus offers to the woman of Samaria "living water," which he elaborates as the water which will become in those who drink it "a spring of water bubbling up into eternal life." The intention is to evoke the imagery of the life-giving Spirit, as 7:38-39 makes clear.
- 7:38-39 — ". . . as the scripture said, 'Out of his belly shall flow rivers of living water.' This he (Jesus) said about the Spirit, which those who believed in him were to receive; for the Spirit was not yet (given), because Jesus was not yet glorified."

The imagery used in the last two passages is striking. "Living" water is water which is moving; certainly not still and stagnant, but also not just still and calm. The imagery, particularly in John 4:14, is of vitality, of an active spring bubbling up and pouring forth. This is the life-giving work of the Spirit, active and activating; not a tranquil pond, but a running stream, like a brimming channel bringing life-giving water to seeds just sown and tender shoots. This is what John, and the other New Testament writers, understood by the life given and sustained by the Spirit.

- Romans 8:2 — "the law of the Spirit of life in Christ Jesus has set you free from the law of sin and death."

Many find it next to impossible that Paul should describe the law as "the law . . . of life," that is, should attribute life to the law. And Galatians 3:21 (n. 21 above) underlines the difficulty in attributing such a thought to Paul. In that case the preference is to see a play on νόμος, that is, that Paul did not refer to the law in this case, but used the term

---

— to show the people how to live as the covenant people, that is "by (doing) them" (3:12). Life-giving was the function of the Spirit.

in the sense of "principle."[22] I think such an exegesis misses the important thrust of the passage, running from 7:6-8:13. In a passage which should be regarded as a defense of the law (7:7), Paul shows that the real problem for humankind is the power of sin and the weakness of the flesh (7:8-11, 13-14). It is sin which abuses and perverts the law from its true purpose (of expressing God's will). Since the outcome of such travesty is death, Paul can summarize the plight of humankind, and of the law, by reference to "the law of sin and death"; it is very difficult, in my view, to avoid the implication that the phrase is Paul's summary of the exposition of 7:7-13. The great resolution of the problem for Paul is that God has done through Christ what the law could not do, because of the weakness of the flesh (8:3). Paul could even regard this act of Christ as a liberating of the law from the power of sin and death, to become the law of the Spirit of life (8:2). That is, the Spirit enabled the believer to do what he lamentably failed to do without the Spirit; despite knowing and wanting to do God's will, sin and flesh incapacitated him (7:14-24); but now, (the law of) the Spirit of life had set him free from (the law of) sin and death (8:2), and enabled those who "walked according to the Spirit" to fulfill what the law required (8:4) — the very thing that had been impossible without the Spirit.

- Romans 8:6 — "The flesh's way of thinking is death, but the Spirit's way of thinking is life."
- Romans 8:13 — "If you live according to the flesh, you will certainly die; but if by the Spirit you put to death the deeds of the body, you will live."
- Galatians 5:25 — "If we live by the Spirit, let us also follow the Spirit."
- Galatians 6:8 — "Those who sow to their own flesh shall from the flesh reap corruption; but those who sow to the Spirit shall from the Spirit reap eternal life."

All these make clear that for Paul the life given by the Spirit was not a static life, a life simply being sustained by the Spirit. It was much more — a life being lived in active discipleship. This is not a Christian

---

22. Particularly H. Räisänen, "The 'Law' of Faith and the Spirit," in *Jesus, Paul and Torah* (Sheffield: Sheffield Academic Press, 1992), pp. 48-68; otherwise my *Beginning from Jerusalem* (Grand Rapids: Eerdmans, 2009), pp. 903-4 n. 186.

life understood as requiring something more than had already been received, another Spirit, another endowment by the Spirit. This was how the life of the Spirit, the life given by the Spirit, expressed itself. The alternative was not a quiescent, (simply) regenerating Spirit requiring the empowering or charismatic Spirit as a kind of supplement, or as booster rocket to ensure a sustainable orbit. The alternative is laid out by Paul in Romans 8:5-8 and 12-13 much more starkly: the alternative to the Spirit and life is the flesh and death; the alternative to active life is not inactive life, but an existence devoted to the flesh and in the grip of sin and death.

- 1 Corinthians 12:13 — "In one Spirit we were all baptized into one body . . . and were all given to drink of one Spirit."

This is the passage in Paul which takes up most clearly the water imagery for the Spirit used by the prophets (Isa. 32:15; 44:3; Joel 2:28-29) and evoked so vividly in John's Gospel. The word "life" is not used here, but it is clearly presupposed in the imagery of a person/land dying of thirst being given to drink the water of life. The triple emphasis on "one" is a reminder that the unity of the church (in this case the church in Corinth) was wholly dependent on the Spirit, wholly the expression of the shared life given by the Spirit, wholly the effect of the church members sharing in the same Spirit. More striking for a modern audience is the fact that Paul only here uses the phrase "baptized in Spirit." However that phrase can be understood when it is used elsewhere, here it is clear beyond doubt that for Paul it was by being baptized in the one Spirit that a person became a member of the one body of Christ. What is also clear, but needs more emphasis, is the fact that the phrase and verse (12:13) occur as an integral part of Paul's description of the charismatic body of Christ. Paul evidently did not think of those who were already members of the church (in Corinth) as having been only baptized in the Spirit (to become members), and then subsequently receiving particular gifts (χαρίσματα) for ministry in the church. The implication is clear that the baptizing of individuals into the church was into functioning membership, dynamic membership (1:4-7). Paul did not think of some members as without charisms, or as awaiting some charismatic gift. Gifts had been given to each, to all (12:7, 11). Members were organs of Christ's body on earth/in Corinth and Rome, each with its function/πρᾶξις (Rom. 12:4). Χάρισμα means basically the manifestation of χάρις (grace). No member was, almost by definition, without grace (Rom. 3:24; 5:15, 17, 20; 1 Cor. 1:4-5). But χάρις received inevitably manifested itself in and as χάρισμα.[23] So the life of the Spirit, the life given by the Spirit, manifested itself in a living community, in grace-conveying ministry, as well as in a life of active discipleship.

4. The Empowering Life of the Spirit

In the light of all the above, better sense can be made of the puzzle of Pentecost and the puzzle of Samaria, on which so much has hung in the ongoing debate regarding the Pentecostal Spirit to which Max Turner as a student of the New Testament has made such an important contribution.

If we take John's Gospel first, two things need to be said. One is that whatever should be made of John 3:5; 13:10 and 15:3, it is clear that John himself did not regard the disciples of Jesus as having already drunk of the water of life during Jesus' pre-resurrection ministry. The point is explicitly expressed in John 7:39: the imagery of the Spirit as rivers of living water referred to the future — "the Spirit, which those who believed in him were to receive; for the Spirit was not yet (given), because Jesus was not yet glorified." As is generally recognized, John uses the verb "glorified" to refer to the whole eternal-life-effecting climax of Jesus' mission — not just his post-resurrection exaltation to heaven, but also his uplifting on the cross, his resurrection, and his ascension.[24] John clearly regarded these as a theological unity, and told his version of the story of Jesus using the language of "glorification" to bring home the point.

John can even say that "the Spirit was not yet." Such an extreme statement could hardly be intended to mean that the Spirit did not yet exist. It must mean that the Spirit had not become part of the disciples' experience — "was not yet" so far as they were concerned. This completely undermines any argument that, of course, in John's view the disciples of Jesus must have been "born again" during the course of Jesus' mission in Galilee and Jerusalem. John is clear: those who believed

---

23. See further my *The Theology of Paul the Apostle* (Grand Rapids: Eerdmans, 1998), pp. 319-23, 553-54 and n. 116 (in some disagreement with Max).

24. Brown, *John*, pp. 145-46, 470-71, 503-4.

in Jesus were yet to experience the life given by the Spirit, the rivers of living water.

The point is put beyond doubt by John's description of the evening of resurrection Sunday, when Jesus "breathed on them (the disciples) and said to them, 'Receive the Holy Spirit'" (20:22). What is sometimes missed at this point is the deliberate evocation of Genesis 2:7, by John's use of the verb "breathed" (ἐνεφύσησεν).[25] For that verb is used only twice to denote the divine creative breath in the Greek version of the Hebrew Bible. First in Genesis 2:7 — God "breathed (ἐνεφύσησεν) into the nostrils (of Adam) the breath of life; and the man became a living being." Second in Ezekiel 37:9 in Ezekiel's great vision of an exiled Israel as a valley of dry bones, where, as already noted, Ezekiel is instructed to prophesy: "Come from the four winds, O breath (or wind or Spirit) and breathe (ἐμφύσησον) upon these slain, that they may live." It could hardly be clearer that what John had in view is the breath/Spirit of life.[26] In depicting this scene (John 20:19-23) with just this language there can be little doubt that John intended his readers/audiences to understand this event as the new creation — Jesus giving the Spirit of new creation life to the disciples as God gave old creation life to Adam in the beginning.

Nor should we ignore the fact that 20:22 is the meat in the middle of a sandwich. For Jesus precedes his breathing of new life into the disciples by saying, "As the Father has sent me, so I send you" (20:21). And having said, "Receive the Holy Spirit," Jesus continues, "If you forgive the sins of any, they are forgiven them; if you retain the sins of any, they are retained" (20:23). In other words, *the life-giving breath was also the commissioning of the disciples for mission, the bestowing on them of ministry.* This is why John 20:22 is often referred to as the "Johannine Pentecost," because in John's telling of the story of Jesus this event was equivalent to the Pentecost of Luke's Acts. We should probably infer that this compressing of what in Acts were events separated by several weeks was also part of John's theological insistence that the gift of the Spirit was part of the same soteriological climax and unity as crucifixion, resurrection,

---

25. But observed by Max in *The Holy Spirit and Spiritual Gifts — Then and Now* (Carlisle: Paternoster, 1996), ch. 6; C. Bennema, "The Giving of the Spirit in John's Gospel — A New Proposal?" *EvQ* 74 (2002): 195-213; R. P. Menzies, "John's Place in the Development of Early Christian Pneumatology," in *The Spirit and Spirituality: Essays in Honour of Russell P. Spittler*, ed. W. Ma and R. P. Menzies (London: T&T Clark, 2004), pp. 41-52.

26. I drew attention to this in *Baptism*, p. 180.

and ascension. The giving of the life-creating Spirit was the immediate and direct consequence of Jesus' passion.[27] But even if someone wants to insist on the chronological distance between John 20:22 and Pentecost (even though the attempt to dovetail John and Acts together as though they were documents of the same character is a dubious procedure), the key fact which remains is that for John himself there was no distance or distinction between the disciples' reception of the life-giving Spirit and their commissioning, empowering, and equipping for mission and ministry. Their reception of the life-giving Spirit was their commissioning.

So far as Acts is concerned the chief point is that Luke is the classic example of a New Testament writer who saw the coming of the Spirit into a life as both soteriological and as empowering. He certainly perceives an endowing by or bubbling up of the Spirit on more than one occasion; he uses the imagery of being "filled with the Spirit" for a particular occasion (Acts 2:4; 4:8, 31; 9:17; 13:9, 52). But the initial entry of the Spirit into the life and experience of a person he describes in a variety of ways: they were "baptized in the Holy Spirit" (Acts 1:5; 11:16), "the Holy Spirit came upon" them (1:8; 19:6), the Spirit was "poured out" on them (2:17, 18, 33; 10:45), they "received the Holy Spirit" (2:38; 8:15, 17, 19; 10:47; 19:2), they were "given the Holy Spirit" (5:32; 8:18; 11:17; 15:8), and "the Holy Spirit fell upon" them (8:16; 10:44; 11:15). All these refer to a first action of the Spirit in and upon the recipients. Luke does not speak of a second action of the Spirit, subsequent to the first, with any of these terms. And that first action Luke clearly understands as both soteriological and empowering.

- According to Acts 11:16-17, Peter refers to the first disciples' own experience of the Spirit at Pentecost as God giving them the Spirit "when we believed in the Lord Jesus Christ." The integration of belief and the gift of the Spirit was such that Peter is presented as taking it for granted that the same was true also of the experience of Pentecost: Pentecost may not have been when they first believed in Jesus, but it was when their belief was granted the

27. John makes the same point earlier in his description of Jesus' passion: in 19:30, the dying Jesus (literally) "handed over the Spirit" — not language normally used to describe death, but used regularly to describe the passing on of something to someone else; and in 19:34, John describes blood and water coming out from the side of the crucified Jesus — the nearest thing that John provides to a fulfillment of 7:38-39.

response that Peter/Luke assumed to be the norm. And that experience was certainly an empowering one, a being baptized in the Spirit (1:5).

- The gift of the Spirit implied in Acts 2:38-47 was directly linked with forgiveness of sins (2:38), and manifested in the κοινωνία (2:42), sharing of possessions, worship and successful evangelism which followed (2:43-47). None of that required another bestowal of the Spirit; it was evidently the direct and immediate result of the giving of the Spirit with forgiveness of sins.
- Paul's reception of the Holy Spirit (9:17) is clearly associated both with his commissioning (9:15-16; 26:16-18) and with his baptism, having his sins washed away, calling on the name of the Lord Jesus (22:16).
- The sequence of the offer of forgiveness of sins (10:43) and salvation (11:14), followed immediately by the outpouring of the Spirit on Cornelius and his companions (10:44; 11:15), implies that the gift of the Spirit was what brought the offer to effect. This implication is confirmed by the response of the Jerusalem brothers when told that the Caesareans had been thus baptized in the Spirit: "Then God has given even to the Gentiles repentance into life" (11:17-18), "life-giving repentance" (REB); it was the gift of life (not just of repentance) that the Jerusalem believers recognized, the vitality of the Spirit manifested by the recipients' speaking in tongues and praise (10:45-46). Similarly in 15:7-9 the Caesareans believing, their reception of the Spirit, and their hearts being cleansed by faith are all presented as alternative ways of describing the same event.[28]
- When Paul encounters the Ephesian disciples, his question to them assumes that the gift of the Spirit is God's response to belief: "Did you receive the Holy Spirit when you believed?" (19:2). As implied also in 11:17, the commitment of belief results in the gift of the Spirit, whose coming upon those who (believe and) are baptized is again (as in 10:45-46) manifested in their speaking in tongues and prophesying (19:6).

---

28. Contra Menzies, *Development*, pp. 266-67; in 15:7-9 the gift of the Spirit (15:8) is the ham in the sandwich of their believing (15:7) and their heart-cleansing faith (15:9); cf. Turner, *Power*, pp. 380-87.

"The Lord, the Giver of Life"

In the light of this basic feature of Luke's understanding of the Spirit, we can make better sense of the otherwise puzzling account of the Samaritans. For Luke evidently did not think of any of the characters in his narrative as *having* the Spirit *prior to* the Spirit "coming upon" them, *prior to* their being baptized in the Spirit. Luke evidently did not think of the Spirit entering a life quietly prior to the more visible "crash, bang, wallop" of the reception of the Spirit (as he describes it). Despite Calvin, there is *no* thought in Acts that the Samaritans were "regenerate" and "endued with the Spirit of adoption" as a result of Philip's ministry. On the contrary, Luke's point could hardly be clearer: "the Spirit had *not yet* fallen upon them" (8:16), the Spirit had not yet been given and received (8:15, 17-19);[29] "they had *only* been baptized in the name of the Lord Jesus" (8:16). Here too, Luke presumably thought of this initial gift of the Spirit as both life-giving and empowering.

So, let us not diminish the full importance of the New Testament's understanding of the Spirit as "the giver of life." In the New Testament passages reviewed above that life could never be conceived as a passive or unconscious life. It is the character of the Spirit that the life thus given is vitality, a life that liberates, energizes, empowers, and expresses itself in a wide variety of forms all indicative of the fact that the Spirit is *life!*

---

29. To speak of this as "a supplementary gift" (Menzies, *Development*, p. 258) diminishes the importance that Luke places on it. Contrast Turner: For Luke "Acts 8.17 describes the Samaritans' first and only reception of 'the promise of the Spirit'" (*Power*, p. 369).

The Spirit, Simeon, and the Songs of the Servant

John R. Levison

Max Turner has disclosed the qualities of the Holy Spirit in Luke-Acts with sustained and stunning perspicacity. I have often leaned on — or rather leaned *into* — his able interpretations, his reliable judgments, his meticulous attention to textual detail, his mastery of the secondary literature. There is little I have to add to the exegetical *gravitas* that characterizes his scholarship, yet I am compelled by the tenor and tack of his scholarship — and the occasion of this *Festschrift* — to linger over the Holy Spirit in Luke-Acts. To honor Max's enduring contribution to our understanding of the Holy Spirit in Luke-Acts, I offer here reflections on a poignant passage from Luke's Gospel: Simeon's Song.

Genuine appreciation, so as not to be disingenuous, should be accompanied by critique, so let me draw our attention to one such particular point: in his monumental monograph, *Power from on High: The Spirit in Israel's Restoration and Witness in Luke-Acts*, Max Turner may have underestimated the forcefulness and nuance of Simeon and his song in Luke 2:25-35. The chapter in which he interprets Luke 2:25-35 begins boldly, even brashly: "Like a blast of joyful trumpets, Lk. 1.5–2.52 sounds a theological fanfare to herald the themes which will make more measured and stately progress through the rest of Luke-Acts."[1] The note that is played in the story of Simeon, however, is dull and monotonous, even muted, in Turner's treatment.

Turner notices first that the permanent endowment of the

---

1. Max Turner, *Power from on High: The Spirit in Israel's Restoration and Witness in Luke-Acts* (Sheffield: Sheffield Academic Press, 1996), p. 140.

The Spirit, Simeon, and the Songs of the Servant

Spirit, as it rests upon Simeon (2:25), though "rare in Judaism," is not unique in the literature of the rabbis. The revelation by the Holy Spirit that Simeon would see the messiah before his death (2:26) "corresponds to the majority of intertestamental and rabbinic cases which largely pertain to foreseeing some important future salvation-historical circumstance." Finally, "the description of Simeon in 2.27 as coming into the temple 'in the Spirit' . . . is barely more distinctive." Even if this means that the Spirit enabled Simeon's recognition of the child as the promised messiah or "afforded the revelation that is the basis of the oracular speech in 2.29-32, 34-35 . . . these activities are still within the traditional range of prototypical gifts of the Spirit of prophecy [in Judaism]."[2]

Simeon is no more distinctive when he is compared, in two respects, with the experience of the Holy Spirit in the church. First, even though the verb Luke chooses for "reveal" is unique in the LXX and Luke-Acts, "the general idea of someone receiving charismatic revelation through the Spirit (as in 2.26) is commonplace." Second, the use of the preposition, "upon," is unlike the more typical use of "fullness" words to signify the continuing presence of the Holy Spirit in Luke-Acts. "It is thus possible," Turner suggests, "that his [Luke's] language here deliberately contrasts Simeon's experience of the Spirit as a lesser one compared with Christian experience (though it may simply be due to his source)." Turner is even able to dismiss the "possible deliberate parallel" which lies in the salient observation that the occurrence of the Spirit with "upon" is found in the story of Simeon and the proclamation of Jesus at Nazareth (Luke 4:18). This parallel is unconvincing because "the choice of terminology in Jesus' case is really determined by the Old Testament passage he cites (Isa. 61.1-2) — a passage that goes on to qualify what is meant by the Spirit being 'upon' Jesus in such a way as to emphasize the *unique* character of Jesus' endowment (rather than its 'typical' nature)."[3]

In Turner's defense, he attempts in this chapter of *Power from on High* to make the important point that all but one (1:35) of the experiences of the Spirit in Luke 1–2 "quite clearly fall within the scope of what a contemporary Jew might recognize as 'the Spirit of prophecy.'"[4]

---

2. All citations in this paragraph are from Turner, *Power*, p. 149.
3. All citations in this paragraph are from Turner, *Power*, p. 150.
4. Turner, *Power*, p. 147. By this he means that Luke gives no sign that he is "con-

He is certainly successful in this. Yet the promise of "a blast of joyful trumpets" goes flat in the case of Simeon and his song. The story of his inspiration, notwithstanding the staccato of three references to the Spirit in quick succession, is, Turner intimates, uninspiring. The praise Simeon raises is a mirror of Jewish hopes for Israel's restoration. His experience is a reflection of experiences of the Spirit among the rabbis. This is not a negative evaluation, Turner would tell us, I think, because it is essential that these chapters at the start of Luke's Gospel find their home in Early Judaism.

Yet I cannot help but feel that Turner has proven this thesis at Simeon's expense. To redress the balance, I hope to recapture some of the "theological fanfare" of Simeon and his song when his presence is unconstrained by a particular thesis, however sound it may be. We will even discern in Simeon's song startling traces of other songs, ancient songs composed half a millennium earlier.

1. Simeon, the Servant, and a Vision for Israel

Our story begins in the Jewish temple, though not among the hustle of priests and the din of the Pharisees' discussion of Torah, but at the seemingly insignificant fringes of Jewish life, in the world of widows and very old men. The scene is prompted by the appearance of peasant parents from Galilee who are so poor that they cannot afford the offering of sheep for purification after the mother gives birth; this peasant couple brings only two turtle doves (Lev. 12:1-8). Yet the simplicity of their offering cannot keep others from gathering to celebrate the occasion — not elite priests and influential Pharisees, but socially insignificant types, including a very old man.

The usual facts about the old man, Simeon, are left out. His family relationships, such as whose son he was, are not even identified. Yet he is described with unusually lavish language. "Now there was a man in Jerusalem whose name was Simeon; this man was righteous and devout, looking forward to the consolation of Israel, and the Holy Spirit rested on him. It had been revealed to him by the Holy Spirit that he

---

sciously accommodating Simeon's experience either to specifically Old Testament (rather than ITP [the Intertestamental Period]) pneumatology or to the experience of Jesus and the Church" (*Power*, p. 150).

would not see death before he had seen the Lord's messiah. Guided by the Spirit, Simeon came into the temple . . ." (Luke 2:25-27). This old man, though invisible to the powers-that-be, was inspired.

When Simeon sees the peasants' child, he takes the baby — this is one of the most poignant details in early Christian literature — in his arms and praises God: "Master, now you are dismissing your servant in peace, according to your word; for my eyes have seen your salvation, which you have prepared in the presence of all peoples, a light for revelation to the Gentiles and for glory to your people Israel" (Luke 2:28-32). This exclamation, though it seems extemporaneous and unplanned, is actually deliberate and drenched in the dream of Isaiah 40–55. These sixteen chapters of prophetic poems were probably written during the dire days of Babylonian exile, when Israel was weary to the bone, mired in hopelessness. Into the dark of national defeat, a nameless prophet flashed the brilliance of the expectation that God's people were on the cusp of liberation.

Simeon's short speech, tendered to the peasant parents more than five hundred years later, combines words that reach deep into the vision of Isaiah 40–55. His anticipation of "the consolation of Israel," of comfort for his people, weighs like an anchor that connects this otherwise unmoored and unknown old man to one of the most glorious words of hope in all of antiquity — words memorialized in Handel's *Messiah:* "Comfort ye, comfort ye, my people, saith your God." These are the words that open the curtain of hope in Isaiah 40–55: "Comfort, O comfort my people, says your God. Speak tenderly to Jerusalem, and cry to her that she has served her term, that her penalty is paid, that she has received from the LORD's hand double for all her sins" (Isa. 40:1-2).[5]

Yet the roots of Simeon's song spread more broadly, for Simeon understands that the advent of the baby is the inauguration of the liberation which this prophet of the exile had announced.[6] The first word of the *nunc dimittis,* an apparently superfluous "now" (Luke 2:29), rivets his prayer to the words, "but now," in Isaiah 43:1 and 44:1, both of which mark a sharp contrast between Israel's old guilt and ways (42:18-

---

5. On consolation, see also Isa. 49:13; 51:3; 57:18; 61:2. See further D. Bock, *Luke,* Baker Exegetical Commentary on the New Testament (Grand Rapids: Baker, 1994), vol. 1, p. 238.

6. R. Tannehill (*Luke* [Nashville: Abingdon, 1996], p. 72) refers to "the pervasive influence of Isaiah on this passage [Luke 2:33-40]."

25 and 43:22-28) and the new word of God that will shape Israel's future.[7] Simeon's use of the neuter, σωτήριον (Luke 2:30), rather than the more usual feminine noun, σωτηρία, is reminiscent of Isaiah as well. It occurs, slightly later in Luke 3:6, with a quotation of Isaiah 40:5, then in Acts 28:28 in a lengthy citation of Isaiah 6. Simeon's belief that salvation will be "a light for revelation to the nations" is rooted in Isaiah 42:6, "I have given you as . . . a light to the nations," as well as Isaiah 49:6, "It is too light a thing that you should be my servant to raise up the tribes of Jacob and to restore the survivors of Israel; I will give you as a light to the nations, that my salvation may reach to the end of the earth."[8] Simeon's belief that this salvation is also "for glory to your people Israel" is rooted in Isaiah 46:13, "I bring near my deliverance, it is not far off, and my salvation will not tarry; I will put salvation in Zion, for Israel my glory." The "salvation" that "you [God] have prepared in the presence of all nations," which Simeon sees in front of him, is rooted in Isaiah 52:10, which imagines that "The LORD has bared his holy arm before the eyes of all the nations; and all the ends of the earth shall see the salvation of our God."[9]

Simeon's praise resurrects the expansive vision of Isaiah 40–55. His vast vision of God's salvation for the nations grows from the soil of an ancient Israelite vision that is no less vast, a vision that has shaped his eager expectation of salvation. If Jerusalem will be comforted, if glory will come to Israel and salvation to Zion, it will be through someone who will offer salvation to all peoples and light to all nations. That someone, of course, is the baby in Simeon's arms.

2. The Servant, Simeon, and Lifelong Learning

While Israel eked out its meager existence in the parched sands of exile, the prophet who composed the poetry of Isaiah 40–55 spoke out with a

---

7. G. Grogan, "The Light and the Stone: A Christological Study in Luke and Isaiah," in *Christ the Lord: Studies in Christology presented to Donald Guthrie*, ed. H. Rowdon (Leicester: IVP, 1982), p. 154. Grogan's illuminating article ("Light," pp. 151-67), in a bit of serendipity, occurs directly before Max Turner's article, "The Spirit of Christ and Christology," in the same *Festschrift* (pp. 168-90).

8. Isa. 49:6 is quoted in Acts 13:47 in reference to the extension of Christ's ministry to the Gentiles through the apostles. See Grogan, "Light," pp. 157-58, and Acts 26:17-18.

9. See also Isa. 60:1-3, 5.

promise of the Spirit from God's mouth to Israel's ears. Israel should stop fear in its tracks because:

> I will pour water on the thirsty land, and streams on the dry ground; I will pour my Spirit upon your descendants, and my blessing on your offspring. They shall spring up like a green tamarisk, like willows by flowing streams. This one will say, "I am the LORD's," another will be called by the name of Jacob, yet another will write on the hand, "The LORD's," and adopt the name of Israel. (Isa. 44:3-5)

In this unlikely promise, the nation will once again be vitalized, not this time by birth, by the process of being fruitful and multiplying, as in the Bible's opening poem (Gen. 1:26-28) and the days of slavery in Egypt (Exod. 1:7), but by attraction, by gathering others, *foreigners,* into the beleaguered nation. The claim, "I am the LORD's" in Isaiah 44:5 and the adoption of the name of Israel are the words of converts to Israelite faith, newly minted citizens who adopt their new land. The hope of Judah in this promise, then, rests less in the replenishment of Israel's numbers with physical descendants than in the work of the Spirit among those who have not yet come to faith. The untamed torrents of the Spirit, the outpouring of the Spirit just a few lines earlier, in Isaiah 44:3, are not limited to the boundaries of Israel; they overflow to nations that have yet to profess faith in Israel's God. This is a remarkable reversal of Israel's situation: although this small nation is nearly extinguished, reduced in exile to little more than the Egyptian slaves they once were, its future lies in the Spirit's ability to renew and refresh, so that believers in other nations will willingly enslave themselves to Israel's God, writing on their hands, "The LORD's," and adopting the name of Israel.

At the heart of hope in Isaiah 40-55 lies a pivotal person, whom the exilic author of Isaiah 40-55 calls the servant.[10] It is never clear

---

10. The so-called servant songs consist of Isa. 42:1-4; 49:1-6; 50:4-9 and 52:13–53:12. Bernhard Duhm during the late nineteenth century first isolated them and suggested that they were originally independent compositions which were later interpolated into Isa. 40-55. Apart from the question of whether these texts were originally independent of Isaiah, scholars continue to debate how closely they are related to one another in the present context. For a brief and helpful introduction, see J. Blenkinsopp, *Isaiah 40-55: A New Translation with Introduction and Commentary,* Anchor Bible 19A (New York: Doubleday, 2002), pp. 76-81.

whether this servant is an individual, the prophet himself, the nation of Israel, a faithful remnant within Israel, or some combination of these.[11] It is clear that this servant is inspired by the Spirit. What is also clear is that this person is not an anointed king, promised by Isaiah of Jerusalem centuries earlier, during whose messianic reign the lion would lie down with the lamb (Isa. 11:1-9). Nor is the servant a famed political leader, like the Persian ruler Cyrus, whom the prophet calls a messiah, an anointed one (Isa. 45:1). The singular qualification of the servant, in God's mind, is that he is, simply put, inspired:

> Here is my servant, whom I uphold, my chosen, in whom my soul delights; I have put my Spirit upon him; he will bring forth justice to the nations. He will not cry or lift up his voice, or make it heard in the street; a bruised reed he will not break, and a dimly burning wick he will not quench; he will faithfully bring forth justice. He will not grow faint or be crushed until he has established justice in the earth; and the coastlands wait for his teaching [*torah*]. (Isa. 42:1-4)

The scope of this vision is breathtaking, extending, as it does, to include nations at a distance. The servant, who cannot be identified with any particular historical figure of the exilic era, is being introduced to an audience that expands to the coastlands and eagerly awaits his teaching. As "a light to the nations" (Isa. 42:6), this servant has a vocation that aligns perfectly with God's, as it is expressed later: "Listen to me, my people, and give heed to me, my nation; for a teaching [*torah*] will go out from me, and my justice for a light to the nations. I will bring near my deliverance swiftly, my salvation has gone out and my arms will rule the nations; the coastlands wait for me, and for my arm they hope" (Isa. 51:4-5). The gist of this vision is clear: teaching *(torah)* will extend to the four corners of the earth, and justice will reach a crowd of human beings beyond Israel's borders.

---

11. Based upon the reference to Jacob in Isa. 49:5, some argue that the servant is Israel, or a remnant within Israel. Understood as an individual, the servant has been variously identified as Moses, Cyrus (see Isa. 45:1), a royal figure (based upon Isa. 11:1-9), or a prophetic figure. Those who do not see a taut relationship between the so-called servant songs are able to offer multiple identities. For an excellent discussion of possible identifications, see J. Goldingay, *The Message of Isaiah 40–55: A Literary-Theological Commentary* (London: T&T Clark, 2005), pp. 149-54.

The Spirit, Simeon, and the Songs of the Servant

How does the servant receive this *torah*? How does the Spirit rest upon him? In a fascinating autobiographical glimpse, the servant describes how he grasps what to say: "the Lord GOD has given me the tongue of a disciple [one who is taught], that I may know how to sustain the weary with a word. Morning by morning God wakens — wakens my ear to listen as those who are taught. The Lord GOD has opened my ear, and I was not rebellious, I did not turn backward" (Isa. 50:4-5). The servant, in this snippet, offers a peek into the mechanics of inspiration. The Hebrew noun למוד (disciple), is related to the Hebrew verb למד, which occurs countless times to describe teaching and training, such as when parents are commanded, "*Teach* them to your children, talking about them when you are at home and when you are away, when you lie down and when you rise" (Deut. 11:19; cf. 4:1, 5).

The servant's ability to know what to say, therefore, is not due to ecstatic impulses — to inspiration untrammeled by the tasks of learning. Nor do the works come in the spontaneity of the moment, void of preparation. God *teaches* the servant as parents teach their children. The word למוד (disciple) even suggests devotion to a particular teacher. When Isaiah wants to preserve his teaching, for example, he turns his written word over to his protégés: "Bind up the testimony," he says, "seal the teaching [*torah*] among my disciples [בְּלִמֻּדָי]" (Isa. 8:16).

What has the servant of Isaiah 40–55 learned on a day-to-day basis? What does he teach? Justice at home. Justice abroad. Justice, plain and simple. God has called the servant in justice, taken him by the hand and given him as "a light to the nations, to open the eyes that are blind, to bring out the prisoners from the dungeon, from the prison those who sit in darkness" (Isa. 42:6-7). The servant, in short, embodies for all nations what Isaiah, centuries earlier, urged his own nation to do: to "learn [לִמְדוּ] to do good; seek justice, rescue the oppressed, defend the orphan, plead for the widow" (Isa. 1:17).

The servant, however, cannot beat his hearers over the head with a demand for justice. He needs to learn "how to sustain the weary with a word" (Isa. 50:4) because Israel is exhausted, depleted by Babylonian captivity. His hearers are weary, worn, and they need to become acquainted again with "the everlasting God, the creator of the ends of the earth who does not *grow weary* or faint, whose understanding is unsearchable, who gives power to the *weary*, and strengthens the powerless. Even youths will *be weary* and faint, and the young will fall exhausted; but those who wait for the LORD shall renew their strength, they shall mount up with wings like eagles, they shall run and not faint, they shall walk and not *be weary* (Isa. 40:28-31).

These are magnificent words of reassurance, yet they do not reassure with a vacuous promise. The servant's words are not an oral hug, comfort for comfort's sake. They are tied at the hip to a demand for justice, to a future that is anything but comfortable — a destiny of equity, not for Israel alone, but for the whole of the world. The servant may not be a potentate, a king, an emperor, therefore, but his words are no less effective and forceful than their military swords and spears and foot-soldiers. Daily the servant waits for instruction. Every morning he turns his ear to God so that he can be taught a word of comfort for the young men who have fallen exhausted, for the young women who have fainted, not just to make them feel better, comforted, *comfortable,* but to urge them to join in the grand human march to justice, to equity even at the coastlands.

Compare this belief that inspiration arises from the soil of learning with the view of Elihu, one of Job's hapless companions. The youthful Elihu cannot wait for his elders to be quiet because he has an answer for Job. Elihu knows that "it is the spirit in a mortal, the breath of the Almighty that makes for understanding" (Job 32:8). When the dam bursts, Elihu floods the silence:

> And am I to wait, because they do not speak,
> because they stand there, and answer no more?
> I also will give my answer; I also will declare my opinion.
> For I am full of words; the spirit within me lays siege
> > works against me.
> My heart is indeed like wine that has no vent;
> Like new wineskins, it is ready to burst.
> I must speak, so that I may find relief;
> I must open my lips and answer.
>
> (Job 32:16-20)

Shaking with impatient rage — this is how Elihu depicts the impact of the Spirit within him. The verb he chooses to describe the Spirit's effect (צוק) is used elsewhere of enemies' *bringing on* a siege which results in such desperate straits that the Israelites will eat the flesh of their sons and daughters (Deut. 28:53, 55, 57).[12] The verb is used more collo-

---

12. Jeremiah describes such a siege, which will *afflict* Jerusalem (19:9), and Isaiah

quially of the relentless nagging of Delilah that finally drives Samson to divulge the meaning of a riddle (Judg. 14:17) and the mystery of his hair (16:16). Something visceral occurs here.

The Spirit, claims Elihu, tumbles out of his mouth, across his tongue, taking shape in the words that fill him — not just any words, but words that will be full of wisdom (32:18). Elihu is confident, but he is also misguided. He has no wisdom to offer Job. Not a whit. Not even wit. Elihu offers Job only self-serving clichés and egocentric assertions, without a smidgeon of sensitivity.

The inspiration of the servant in Isaiah 40–55 is altogether different in all sorts of ways from Elihu's.

- The servant waits patiently, morning by morning. Every day. Compare this with Elihu, whose patience evaporates because he has to listen to others for a while.
- The servant listens with the ear of a disciple, למוד, of one who is eager to learn, למד, to receive God's teaching. Elihu is his own teacher, the unfortunate source of his own trite insight. He is not, like the servant, a learner.
- The servant listens in order to sustain the weary with a word. Elihu offers censure and callous advice but nothing to sustain Job with a word.
- The servant offers a vision of the world turned toward justice. Elihu offers self-serving clichés.

The supposed Spirit in Elihu contrasts as well with Simeon and the Spirit. Elihu is a model of how the Spirit is thought to produce irrepressible physical symptoms and inspired words. Simeon's experience is altogether different because his inspired words arise from his thorough knowledge of a profound portion of a prophetic book, Isaiah 40–55. Simeon is prepared to identify the child because he is mentally alert — and not mentally inert — to Isaiah's vision of a God who will comfort and rescue Jerusalem by offering salvation and light, not just to them,

---

surprises with the image that God will *distress* — besiege — Jerusalem, as David had besieged it, and that "there shall be moaning and lamentation . . . siege works against you" (29:2-3). Yet, imagines Isaiah, the many nations who fight against Jerusalem, "who *distress* her," will evaporate (Isa. 29:7). A later prophet in the line of Isaiah criticizes Israel for cowering before the fury of the *oppressor* who is bent on destruction (51:13).

but to all the nations — including, in Simeon's day, not the Babylonians but the Romans, who have power over every road and ruler and regulation.[13]

This old man is ready, though not because he has fallen into an emotional tizzy or experienced the physical sensation of the Holy Spirit's urging. This old man is ripe, ready to reveal the inevitability of salvation and to lift this peasant son in his arms because the whole of his being is saturated by the prophetic vision of Isaiah 40-55. Simeon is inspired, in other words, because he is vigilant, because he has studied the poignant prophecies of Isaiah 40-55, which he now sees taking shape in a very young Galilean boy who will be a light to the nations, who will offer salvation to all the world's peoples.

3. The Servant, Simeon, and Suffering

And this is the rub. Consolation, Simeon's people would receive. Yet he does not only offer inspired insight that is rife with the fragrance of roses, though it does exude a pungent whiff of dissent. While Mary and Joseph marvel at what Simeon has said about their baby, he speaks a second time, this time more briefly, more hauntingly, and only to Mary:

> This child is destined for the falling and the rising of many in Israel, and to be a sign that will be opposed so that the inner thoughts of many will be revealed — and a sword will pierce your own soul too. (Luke 2:34-35)

Simeon realizes that Jesus will arouse hostility. The simultaneous rising and falling of many, the division that Jesus will catalyze, the chasm that will erupt — these signal the inevitability of opposition. Some in

---

13. Grogan ("Light," p. 167) captures this coalescence of the Spirit and the study of Isaiah: "Simeon's ministry recognizes its [Isaiah's] relevance to the messianic child, and involves a particular understanding of the nature of that child, of the vocation to which he was called, of the blessed results of that vocation, and of the importance of a right attitude to him. All this seems to have been based, not simply, if at all, on some direct revelation from heaven, but on a deep Spirit-guided study of Isaiah's prophecies. Those prophecies presented one who was a royal child and suffering Servant, Lord of hosts and God's anointed, salvation, light and glory, sanctuary and stumbling-stone, at once the epitome of divine consolation and the object of man's scornful rejection, with divine significance both for the Gentiles and for Israel."

The Spirit, Simeon, and the Songs of the Servant

Israel will follow Jesus. Others will not. This is a puzzle, however, that Simeon presents without solving it. We cannot look in the back of the book for answers to why Simeon's tone has changed and his message shifted so dramatically. We can, however, glance once again in the front of the book. The question which the change in Simeon, from praising the baby to warning his mother, raises finds its answer in the person of the servant, and the servant's fate, in Isaiah 40–55. Here is where we are able to apprehend the contours of Jesus' destiny.

The servant's vocation in Isaiah 40–55 is a magnificent vision of justice: bringing teaching to non-Israelites along the coastlines and light to distant nations. What is so unsettling is that this imagined world, this inspired vocation, will cost the servant his life.

The hues of suffering are already evident, though muted, in some of the earlier musings about the servant, including a lovely, detailed portrait spoken by God:

> Here is my servant, whom I uphold, my chosen, in whom my soul delights; I have put my Spirit upon him; he will bring forth justice to the nations. He will not cry or lift up his voice, or make it heard in the street; a bruised reed he will not break, and a dimly burning wick he will not quench; he will faithfully bring forth justice. He will not grow faint or be crushed until he has established justice in the earth; and the coastlands wait for his teaching. (Isa. 42:1-4)

Woven into this portrait of inspired perseverance is the subtle but unmistakable presence of pain and anguish. This is evident enough in the line, "He will not grow *faint* or be *crushed until* . . ." He will not arrive at the finish line as the triumphant victor but as the nearly vanquished teacher. Failure, weariness, exhaustion — these accompany the servant. Further, the verb, *cry out,* in the line, "he will not cry [out] or lift up his voice . . ." refers throughout the book of Isaiah to cries of anguish, such as in the prediction that "you shall cry [out] for pain of heart, and shall wail for anguish of spirit" (Isa. 65:14; see also 19:20; 33:7). The servant will not give outward expression to anguish, will "not cry or lift up his voice, or make it heard in the street." This servant will not give up or give in, will not scream in anguish or bring anguish to others in the process. This servant will persist, on the edge of fainting and the crush of his vocation, "until he has established justice in the earth; and the coastlands wait for his teaching" (Isa. 42:1-4).

The Spirit here is the source of the servant's persistence. Yet this comes with a price, with the need to be upheld, with an experience of anguish to which he will not give an outlet. Nor does the Spirit dispel self-doubt. The servant is filled with self-doubt and asks whether "I have labored in vain, I have spent my strength for nothing and vanity" (Isa. 49:4).

Not all that the servant experiences, however, is personal. There will be a more horrific price to pay than anguish, exhaustion, and self-doubt. The servant has apparently ignited fiery opposition. "The Lord GOD has opened my ear, and I was not rebellious, I did not turn backward. I gave my back to those who struck me, and my cheeks to those who pulled out the beard; I did not hide my face from insult and spitting" (Isa. 50:5-6). The servant's knees, however, do not buckle at the onslaught of such vitriol; he sets his face like flint to the task ahead and, with a word play on the Hebrew root כלם, contends that he can endure "insults" (כְּלִמּוֹת) yet not "be ashamed" (נִכְלָמְתִּי) (Isa. 50:6-7).

The servant's enemies, however, are not satisfied with blows to the back and tearing out his beard. He will also be despised, rejected, a man of sorrows and acquainted with sickness, one from whom others hide, despised, of no account, struck down, afflicted, wounded, crushed, punished, oppressed, afflicted, dumb like a lamb before the slaughter, cut off from the living, stricken for the sin of God's people, buried with the wicked, crushed with pain, anguished, poured out to death, counted among transgressors — and all of this although he never took up violence, although he had never uttered a single dishonest or disingenuous word (Isa. 52:13–53:12).

Despite such intense opposition, unimaginable humiliation, and dire physical pain, the only weapon the inspired servant takes up is the spoken word, the tongue of a disciple, teaching that reaches to the coastlands. In a moment of self-reflection, he claims that God "made my mouth like a sharp sword . . . God made me a polished arrow" (Isa. 49:2). The spoken word, the ability to teach, is the inspired servant's only weapon against the brutality of his opponents.

Why then does the servant's message prove so troubling to some in Israel? Why does the servant's teaching lead straight to his death? Perhaps because, in Isaiah 40–55, in which the servant features prominently, the Spirit comes increasingly to be associated with other than the patriotic pulse of Israel. The Spirit will be poured out upon converts who will claim the name of the LORD, and the coastlands wait for the servant's teaching. This is a remarkably expansive vision, particularly if these chapters are dated, as they often are, toward the end of Babylonian exile in the mid-500s BCE. Here is a community that has paid its penalty, served its term, paid double for all its sins (Isa. 40:2). Here is a nation that has been devastated, whose young men have fallen headlong (40:27-31). Here is a nation that has every cause to turn inward, to insulate itself from the pervasive pain that is perpetrated by political powers. Yet from this community arises a servant upon whom God's Spirit rests, a light to the nations, for whose teaching the coastlands can scarcely wait.

Any prophet who faced exile and devastation could justifiably have responded to national disaster with a call for revenge or a plea for violent resistance. These sensibilities peer from the words of Habakkuk and Nahum. Yet this expectation never materializes in the book of Isaiah, where the inspired servant reaches the coastlands with teaching rather than weapons and war-mongering. In no single line of the book that bears the name of Isaiah is the Spirit associated with anything more powerful than the spoken word. If the nations are to be conquered, they will be vanquished by the sort of teaching for which they eagerly wait, to which they will voluntarily bind themselves by writing God's name on their hands. These nations, apparently, will be persuaded rather than pursued, taught rather than trounced by the expansion of God's people.

At the core of the conflict between the servant and his Israelite brothers and sisters lies the magnanimity of this message. Good news to the oppressing enemy, a light to the nations, cannot have been met with a flurry of Israelite cheers, at least not by an audience whose grandparents had been slaughtered by a single, relentless foreign nation, Babylon. The conviction that the servant's teaching extends beyond the narrow compass of Israel's battered and beaten survivors to bring salvation to the powerful nations who walk in darkness can hardly have been understood by devoted patriots in Israel as part and parcel of the message of comfort the servant ought to bring. These are a weary people, worn down by the demise of Jerusalem, exhausted by the bullying of brash nations around them. Can they be expected to imagine a future when the descendants of Abraham and Sarah would include, on equal footing, the descendants of those who murdered their grandparents?

When, five hundred years later, Simeon holds the peasant child in his arms, he recognizes God's salvation, prepared in the face of all peoples, a light to the nations, and the glory of God's people Israel. He also sees the hostility Jesus will raise; many will stumble and many rise because of him. Simeon is not just making a good guess about Jesus. Nor is he in some sort of ecstatic state in which the Spirit has stripped him of his faculties and foisted insight into his mouth. There is something else going on here. Simeon is prepared, poised for the redemption of Israel. He is sure about the reassurance of Israel that is woven into Isaiah 40–55. His words, peppered as they are by the language of Isaiah 40–55, also reveal that he understands the nature of this reassurance. It will be universal and global, and precisely that international quality will cut against the grain of many in Israel. So he speaks to Mary, and to Mary alone, warning the mother about her young son's fate. Destined to take on the part of the servant, Jesus will bring revelation to the nations through his inspired teaching. He will simultaneously seal his fate. Those Israelites who fall on his account will, in the end, rise against him, tearing out his beard, battering his back, and slaughtering the soon-to-be silent teacher.

4. The Servant, Simeon, and Robust Inspiration

Simeon's song, and the prophetic vision that suffuses it, is a profoundly moving portrait of the Spirit that has the potential to shatter complacency and to dispel ignorance. Simeon is a figure of epic inspiration, though we know nothing else about him — except that he was a student of the book of Isaiah. His story and his song, set in the context of those chapters from Isaiah that shaped him, offer vital insight into the nature of the Holy Spirit and witness.

The Spirit and Study

Simeon models the symbiosis that exists between the Spirit and study. It is obvious from what he says that Simeon has studied tirelessly and become intimately familiar with the vision of Isaiah 40–55. He is the model of inspiration that rises from the soil of study, of immersion in ancient texts with an eye toward that single significant inspired moment when all that he has studied, all of the knowledge that has shaped him, combusts as he recognizes — perhaps just this once — the open-handed, expansive, and certainly unexpected salvation of God, as surprising as a baby carried to the temple by his peasant parents. In this commitment to study, Simeon brings his life into line with the text he has studied. The servant, too, had listened to God morning by morning, had learned, had adopted the vision of justice that Isaiah centuries before him had demanded of God's people. Simeon and the servant together provide a model of inspiration that is rooted in study.

The Spirit and Inspired Words

Simeon speaks under the compulsion of inspiration, predicting the fate of Jesus and teaching Mary about the impact this will have upon her. Speech delivered under the force of the Spirit, of course, was the rule rather than the exception in the early church, as Luke told the story. Yet Simeon's experience of the Holy Spirit is also reminiscent of the servant himself, whom God inspired, whose teaching would reach the coastlands. Simeon may not have reached the coastlands, at least not yet, but his teaching did. And there is even an interpretation of Acts 15:14, in which Simeon, at the Council in Jerusalem, "related how God first looked favorably on the Gentiles, to take from among them a people for his name." The ability to relate what had happened among the Gentiles is an indication that Simeon, perhaps the Simeon who had held the baby in his arms, had reached the coastlands, had visited Caesarea, the coastal city in which the Spirit had been poured out upon the Gentiles (Acts 10:44).

The Spirit and an Expansive Vision

Certainly Simeon speaks about the fate of Israel, the glory of God's people. His words, however, carry the peasant parents far beyond the horizon of Israel. Like the servant long before, the Spirit impels Simeon to understand that, though the nexus of God's salvation is Israel, the scope of God's salvation encompasses the nations. Neither Simeon nor the servant offers a word to weary patriots, or rabid ones. Their words take those with ears to hear to the heart of God's promise to the ancestors, to Abraham and Sarah, who were told that Israel would be a blessing to the nations. Israel will not rise if the nations around it fall.

The Spirit and Suffering

The expansive, inspired vision of the servant of Isaiah 40–55, and of Jesus the servant, will, Simeon knows, raise hostility, so he warns the young mother: "This child is destined for the falling and the rising of many in Israel, and to be a sign that will be opposed. . . ." The primary gift of the Spirit, both for the servant and Simeon long after him, is quiet teaching — yet not the sort of teaching that fails to raise the hackles of their hearers. The authentic work of the Spirit is disturbingly preoccupied with the well-being of those outside of our borders, and it is this disequilibrium, this uncompromising expansiveness, that leads the servant, and Jesus after him, to personal anguish, to the torment of having his beard torn out and his back beaten, and to an early and ignominious death.

There is a salient line that the servant uses to describe his inspiration: "God made my mouth like a sharp sword" (Isa. 49:2). This is an unexpected image in the mouth of a quiet, anguished, expansive servant. And it emerges once more in the quiet words of an old man to a young woman: "and a sword will pierce your own soul too" (Luke 2:35). It already has — the sword has pricked her skin — in the word that her baby would become "a sign that would be opposed."[14] There, at two ends of life and the edge of respectability, an old man and a young woman share a word that is rooted in an ancient vision — a vision that would shape the destiny of the peasants' son.

---

14. The primary scriptural referent may be LXX Ezek. 14:17, although this does not exclude an allusion to Isa. 49:2, particularly in light of how pervasive Isaiah is in the story and song of Simeon. See Grogan, "Light," pp. 163-64. See also Zech. 13:7.

Whose Spirit? The Promise and the Promiser in Luke 12:12

Steve Walton

The nature of the Holy Spirit's presence and work among the early believers is a key feature of the "newness" of the Christian community's life, and has been freshly recognized as such in scholarship in the last forty years, not least through the fine work of Max Turner.[1] This essay explores a somewhat neglected promise by Jesus concerning the Spirit's role (Luke 12:12). There Jesus assures his disciples that when they are persecuted, the Spirit will give specific help to them, and we shall suggest that this promise entails implications about Jesus' relationship with the Spirit — implications which are explicated more fully in Acts.

Our discussion proceeds in three main stages. First, we shall consider Jesus' specific promise of help by the Spirit in Luke 12:12 and seek to exegete it in its immediate and wider Lukan contexts. Secondly, we shall consider other promises of the Spirit's enabling in the Old Testament and Second Temple Jewish literature, as a basis for comparison with Luke 12:12. Thirdly, we shall reflect on Acts 2:33 and consider the christological implications of reading Luke 12:12 with this key verse on the relation of Christ and the Spirit.

---

1. Particularly Max Turner, *Power from on High: The Spirit in Israel's Restoration and Witness in Luke-Acts* (Sheffield: Sheffield Academic Press, 1996); Max Turner, *The Holy Spirit and Spiritual Gifts — Then and Now*, rev. ed. (Peabody: Hendrickson, 1998/Carlisle: Paternoster, 1999). I am delighted to offer this essay in Max Turner's honor, for I have had the privilege of having him as a senior colleague for the last twelve years at London School of Theology. I have learned much from him, including through having the fun of team-teaching on the Spirit with him, and have greatly valued his encouragement in my own work.

Steve Walton

1. The Promise of Luke 12:12

This saying by Jesus in Luke comes in teaching about the importance of public confession of Jesus (12:8-10) and particularly in the context of trials before the authorities (12:11a). This teaching is addressed in the first instance to his disciples (12:1b) with the crowd overhearing (12:1a). In such a setting, Jesus assures his disciples that the Spirit will teach them what to say (12:12) and thus that they need not worry in advance about how to defend themselves (12:11b). There are a number of parallel passages to this section in the synoptic Gospels which we shall consider, in order to identify Luke's specific message, before turning to exegete Luke's text in more detail (see the appendix for the parallel texts).

1.1. *Luke's Sayings and the Synoptic Parallels*

Luke 12:8-9 parallels Matthew 10:32-33, but no parallel is found in Mark. Matthew's location of this saying in a different context to Luke may suggest that both Luke and Matthew have received the content of the saying about blasphemy against the Spirit as a "free" tradition which lacked context, or that the traditions they utilized placed the saying in different contexts, or that one placed the saying in its traditional place and the other relocated it.[2] It is likely that a travelling preacher such as Jesus re-used teaching material on numerous occasions, as well as giving his disciples teaching to repeat in their teaching (e.g. Luke 9:2; 10:1, 9), and so the latter is not at all impossible.[3]

Matthew 12:31-32 and Mark 3:28-29 parallel Luke 12:10, but in the different context of Jesus responding to the accusation that he casts out demons by Beelzebul (Mark 3:22; Matt. 12:24; cf. Luke 11:15). This difference of context is frequently suggested to indicate that, in

---

2. For the latter possibility, see Robert H. Stein, *Luke*, New American Commentary 24 (Nashville: Broadman, 1992), p. 345 n. 90.

3. See, e.g., James D. G. Dunn, *Jesus Remembered*, Christianity in the Making, vol. 1 (Grand Rapids: Eerdmans, 2003), pp. 239, 243; Darrell L. Bock, *Luke*, Baker Exegetical Commentary on the New Testament (Grand Rapids: Baker Academic, 1996), vol. 2, pp. 1130-31; cf. Bauckham's argument that Jesus expected his disciples to learn his teaching in order to pass it on (Richard Bauckham, *Jesus and the Eyewitnesses: The Gospels as Eyewitness Testimony* [Grand Rapids: Eerdmans, 2006], pp. 280-86).

the tradition which Luke used, 12:10 did not originally belong with 12:8-9.[4]

There are parallels to Luke 12:12 in the other synoptic Gospels (Matt. 10:19-20; Mark 13:11) and Luke himself has an interesting parallel (21:12-15; cf. Matt. 24:9-13). There are clear similarities and differences among these four passages: (i) all are placed in a context of trial, although there is considerable variation in the specified authorities; (ii) structurally, Luke 12, Matthew 10, and Mark 13 begin with a generalizing ὅταν ("whenever") clause, whereas Luke 21 does not, for this seems to refer to a *specific* time of trials; (iii) Jesus calls his disciples not to worry (μὴ μεριμνήσητε/προμεριμνᾶτε) in advance in Luke 12, Mark 13, and Matthew 10, whereas Luke 21 simply specifies that the disciples must not prepare (μὴ προμελετᾶν) in advance; (iv) Luke 12, Matthew 10, and Mark 13 mention the Spirit as the one who will give the disciples words to say (although Matthew alone specifies that it is the Father's Spirit), whereas Luke 21 says that Jesus himself will give them words to speak; (v) Luke alone (in 12:11 and 21:14) uses the language of "defence" (ἀπολογέομαι), a word found only in these passages in Luke and only here in the Gospels, although it is also used in Acts in forensic contexts.[5]

This combination of similarities and differences prompts Bovon to propose that Luke follows Q in 12:11-12 and his *Sondergut* in 21:14-15, whereas Matthew 10:19-20 follows Mark 13:11.[6] Whether or not we agree with Bovon's proposal, we may affirm that some kind of relationship among these texts is likely, whether literary or oral or some combination of the two, and that it is likely that the material is traditional and likely to go back to Jesus.[7] Such a conclusion is supported by the presence of a sufficiently large body of Gospel material in which Jesus

---

4. E.g., I. Howard Marshall, *The Gospel of Luke: A Commentary on the Greek Text*, New International Greek Text Commentary (Exeter: Paternoster, 1978), p. 510; Joseph A. Fitzmyer, *Luke*, Anchor Bible 28B (Garden City: Doubleday, 1985), vol. 2, p. 962. François Bovon, *Das Evangelium nach Lukas*, Evangelisch-Katholischer Kommentar zum Neuen Testament (Neukirchen-Vluyn: Neukirchener Verlag, 1996), vol. 2, p. 260 notes the view that the saying in Luke 12:10 circulated in two versions, that found in Mark 3:28-29 and a Q version found in Luke 12:10.

5. Acts 19:33; 24:10; 25:8; 26:1-2, 24; the only other New Testament uses are Rom. 2:15; 2 Cor. 12:19.

6. Bovon, *Lukas*, vol. 2, p. 265; he also notes that Mark 13:9 is paralleled in Matt. 10:17-18.

7. E.g., the tradition is multiply attested in different Gospel sources.

speaks of persecution to come and of the role of the Spirit.[8] Marshall summarizes accurately, "The claim that the saying in its Marcan form is 'naturally of Christian origin' (Pesch, 132) is arbitrary; there is no reason why Jesus should not have spoken of persecution or of the Spirit."[9]

1.2. Focusing on Luke's Sayings

It is the distinctively Lukan promise that the Spirit/Jesus will give words (12:12; 21:15) which commands our attention here. Various features of these sayings require comment.

First, Matthew and Mark have Jesus call the disciples to speak on the basis that they will be given what to say by the Spirit, using an explanatory γάρ ("for") clause (Matt. 10:20; Mark 13:11). Luke's γάρ clause introduces the reason they should not *worry*, rather than an explanation of why they should *speak*. Matthew and Mark also say that *the Spirit will be speaking* through the disciples,[10] whereas Luke portrays *the Spirit as teaching* them what to say. While we should not drive too deep a wedge between Luke and the other synoptics here, there is a difference of emphasis. Fitzmyer nicely observes:

> Jesus . . . promises that the Spirit of God, which has been depicted thus far in the Lucan story as the source of Jesus' own power (3:22; 4:1, 14, 18; 10:21), will also be the source of strength and eloquence in the disciples when they are called upon to defend themselves and their mission. . . . Human helplessness and inarticulateness will give way to the strength and eloquence that comes from God's Spirit.[11]

Secondly, it is noticeable that the Spirit will *teach* (διδάξει) the disciples what to say, a statement unique in the synoptic Gospels (although cf. John 14:26). This striking expression parallels Jesus' own

---

8. E.g., persecution: Matt. 10:16//Luke 10:3; Matt. 5:11-12//Luke 6:22-23 (see C. G. Kruse, "Apostle," in *DJG*, pp. 27-33 esp. p. 32; James A. Kelhoffer, *Persecution, Persuasion and Power: Readiness to Withstand Hardship as a Corroboration of Legitimacy in the New Testament* [Tübingen: Mohr Siebeck, 2010], ch. 9); Spirit: Mark 1:10//Luke 3:22//Matt. 3:16 (see M. M. B. Turner, "Holy Spirit," in *DJG*, pp. 341-51; Turner, *Power*, chs. 6-9, 11).

9. Marshall, *Gospel*, p. 769.

10. Matthew makes this explicit: ἐν ὑμῖν (10:20).

11. Fitzmyer, *Luke*, vol. 2, p. 965.

ministry of teaching,[12] and thus portrays the Spirit as one who will perform at least some of Jesus' functions in the future (again, cf. John 14:26; 15:26; 16:13-14). Turner resists the theological move which deduces the personhood of the Spirit from the predication of verbs of personal action by the Spirit on the ground that, in line with Jewish figurative usage of "Spirit" language, such uses "could simply be shorthand for '*God*, as Spirit (or "by his Spirit"), said . . . ,' etc."[13] However, to assert that the Spirit will *teach* may go beyond this, given that the personal activity of teaching is such a feature of Jesus' ministry (and see the discussion below of the parallel in Luke 21:14-15), and that there does not appear to be any clear rabbinic or earlier Jewish example which specifically predicates *teaching* (rather than other forms of Spirit-inspired speech) of the Spirit of God.[14] The Matthean parallel is suggestive here, for Matthew names the Spirit as "the Spirit *of the Father*," thus making clear that it is not simply God *as Spirit* who will teach — if that were so, "of the Father" would be superfluous.[15]

Thirdly, the promise given is specific to the situation of judicial trial before authorities (Luke 12:11; 21:12), and thus stands alone among the promises of the Spirit to the disciples in the synoptic Gospels in being situation-specific. Other Spirit-promises (granted that there are not many) are more general, concerning the role of the Spirit in equipping the disciples as witnesses to Jesus (notably Luke 24:49). Jesus' assurance of the Spirit's help in judicial trials is fulfilled in the trials of believers in Acts, where Luke draws attention to the Spirit filling Peter and John when they respond to the charges against them in the Sanhedrin (Acts 4:8), and also Stephen on trial (Acts 7:51, 55; cf. 6:9-10).[16]

---

12. Luke 4:15, 31; 5:3, 17; 6:6; 13:10, 22, 26; 19:47; 20:1, 21, 39; 23:5.
13. Turner, *Holy Spirit*, pp. 170-72, quoting p. 172.
14. There are examples of humans teaching who are enabled or sent by the Spirit (e.g. 4Q381.4; CD 2.12), but this is not the same as the Spirit actually teaching.
15. I owe this observation to Dr Cornelis Bennema.
16. Both Fitzmyer (*Luke*, vol. 2, p. 966) and Bock (*Luke*, vol. 2, p. 1144) draw attention to the immediacy of the promise (ἐν αὐτῇ τῇ ὥρᾳ, "in that very hour," v. 12) and compare Philo's retelling of the angel's instruction to Balaam: "Go on in the journey in which you have set out, for you shall do no good to those who have sent for you, and you must say what I prompt you, without any thoughts of your own, finding utterance, as I will guide the organs of your speech in the way that shall be just and expedient, for I will direct your words, predicting all that shall happen through the agency of your tongue, though you yourself understand nothing of it" (*Mos.* 1.274). Philo goes on to tell how "the prophetic spirit entered" Balaam (προφητικοῦ πνεύματος ἐπιφοιτήσαντος, 1.277) with

Fourthly, the parallel promises in Luke 12:12 and 21:14-15 are suggestive for the relationship of Jesus and the Spirit. Both relate the promise of aid during trials to the instruction not to prepare a defence in advance, both use the rare ἀπολογέομαι ("I defend"), and both explain the basis of this statement with a γάρ ("for") clause. However, the one providing the aid in 12:12 is the Spirit, whereas in 21:15 it is Jesus himself (emphatic ἐγώ, "I myself"). This theme develops and expands in Acts, for while often it is the Spirit who empowers and leads the disciples in witness (Acts 4:8-12; 6:10; 8:29; 10:19; 13:2-4), sometimes it is Jesus (Acts 7:55-56; 9:4-5, 10-16; 18:9-10; 22:7-10, 17-21; 23:11; 26:14-18).[17] It is thus hard to agree with Green, if his implication is that it is *only* by the Spirit that Jesus will be present to his disciples:

> . . . Jesus thus portends his continual presence with the disciples even as they face the tribunal, following his death; only with the onset of Acts we understand fully that he will be present to the community of his followers by means of the Holy Spirit poured out among them.[18]

Buckwalter points to an interesting parallel: in the Old Testament, action by YHWH from heaven is described in similar terms to action by the Spirit, and YHWH is not limited to appearing on earth *as or by* the Spirit; in Luke-Acts, action by *the exalted Jesus* from heaven is described in similar terms to action by the Spirit, and again, Jesus is not limited to appearing on earth *as or by* the Spirit.[19] It is thus plausible that the parallel actions of Jesus and the Spirit in empowering and enabling speech when the disciples are on trial (in Luke 12 and 21) entail a relationship of Jesus in relation to the Spirit which is similar to that of YHWH and the Spirit.[20] Not only that, but the ability of the exalted Jesus to be present with disciples in different times and places when they are on trial shows Jesus (and the Spirit) to have the same multi-

---

the result that he prophesied (θεσπίζει, 1.278). However, this is not strictly parallel, since it is about prophetic inspiration, rather than inspiration when on trial.

17. See discussion, Douglas Buckwalter, *The Character and Purpose of Luke's Christology* (Cambridge: Cambridge University Press, 1996), pp. 197-204.

18. Joel B. Green, *The Gospel of Luke*, New International Commentary on the New Testament (Grand Rapids: Eerdmans, 1997), p. 737.

19. Buckwalter, *Character*, ch. 8.

20. Buckwalter, *Character*, pp. 203-4.

locational ability as YHWH.[21] We shall explore this theme further below in relation to Turner's reading of Acts 2:33.

2. Comparing Other Promises of the Spirit

We turn next to consider other promises of the Spirit's aid or coming in the Old Testament and Second Temple Jewish literature in order to assess how distinctive this Lukan promise is.[22] Since the Lukan promise of the Spirit's aid in the specific circumstance of being on trial is unique in the synoptic Gospels in being given for a particular situation, we are seeking passages which promise the Spirit's enabling *in a particular defined set of circumstances,* in the manner of Luke 12:12 and parallels, rather than more general promises of the Spirit's help.

We note first that the Spirit's work in these sources frequently focuses on enabling speech, in tune with the Spirit's character as the "Spirit of prophecy."[23] Thus, in the Old Testament, the Spirit enables prophecy (Num. 11:25; 1 Sam. 10:10), speaks through David (2 Sam. 23:2), and wisdom and God's counsel come from the Spirit (Wis. 9:17). As Turner has shown,[24] the Spirit also enables invasive charismatic praise (1 Sam. 19:20-23; cf. *Tg. Ps.-J.* 1 Sam. 19.20, 23; 10.6, 10), as well as brings charismatic wisdom and revelation.

2.1. *Old Testament*

Four Old Testament books contain promises of the Spirit coming which may inform our discussion: Joel 2:28-32 (LXX 3:1-5); Isaiah 44:3; Ezekiel 11:19-20; 36:26-27; 37:14; Zechariah 12:10.

The promise in Joel is famously taken up in Peter's Pentecost speech (Acts 2:16-21). In its original context in Joel, the promise will be fulfilled "after these things" (μετὰ ταῦτα), a somewhat vague phrase, re-

---

21. Stein, *Luke,* pp. 518-19. He goes on to suggest that we should therefore "describe Jesus as possessing an *essence* different from others" (p. 519, his italics).
22. I gratefully acknowledge the use of a database of such references prepared by Max Turner and shared with successive MA classes on the Holy Spirit and Spiritual Gifts at London School of Theology.
23. See the fine discussion in Turner, *Power,* ch. 3.
24. Turner, *Power,* ch. 3.

placed in Peter's speech by "in the last days" (ἐν ταῖς ἐσχάταις ἡμέραις, Acts 2:17).[25] Thus, although the content of the promise is reasonably clear — the Spirit will produce prophetic manifestations, both verbal and visual — the timing of the promise is unspecific. It is not that Joel prophesies that in a particular set of circumstances God will pour out the Spirit in this way; it is simply that at some future time (undefined, from Joel's perspective), God will do this. Peter's speech identifies the pentecostal outpouring as signalling the time of fulfillment, but it gives no indication that anyone in advance of Pentecost would have expected its fulfillment then. Menzies notes the citations of Joel 2:28 in *Deuteronomy Rabbah* 6.14; *Midrash Psalms* 14.6; *Midrash Haggadol Genesis* 140; *Numbers Rabbah* 15.25, all of which are either vague about the timing of the fulfillment of Joel's promise, or relate it to the world to come (which for our purpose amounts to the same thing).[26] While many of these documents were edited later, Menzies rightly argues that these passages probably reflect first-century Jewish hopes accurately, because of: (i) parallels in the Dead Sea Scrolls (1QS 3.13-4.26); (ii) the presence of a belief of the withdrawal of the Spirit in the first century and its tension with these texts; and (iii) the likelihood that such passages would be suppressed in the light of later Christian claims, rather than being created when Christian claims became more well-known.[27]

The oracle in Isaiah 44 is similarly vague about time: it is simply the descendants of those whom the prophet addresses who will receive the blessings in 44:3-5. Goldingay and Payne note that the imaginative style of speech "makes even less evident its relationship with concrete socio-political realities,"[28] further weakening any sense of YHWH promising the coming of the Spirit in a particular set of circumstances. In addition, the oracle may allow רוח to be interpreted as "breath" rather than "s/Spirit,"[29] thus making the nature of the promise less clear cut

---

25. Turner, *Power*, p. 270, considers this substitution as functioning to identify the gift of the Spirit as eschatological, and believes it to be traditional (rather than Lukan).

26. Robert P. Menzies, *Empowered for Witness: The Spirit in Luke-Acts* (Sheffield: Sheffield Academic Press, 1994), pp. 95-97, including translations.

27. Menzies, *Empowered*, pp. 97-98.

28. John Goldingay and David F. Payne, *A Critical and Exegetical Commentary on Isaiah 40–55*, International Critical Commentary (London: T&T Clark, 2006), vol. 1, p. 320; cf. Claus Westermann, *Isaiah 40–66: A Commentary*, Old Testament Library (London: SCM Press, 1969), pp. 135-36.

29. Goldingay and Payne, *Isaiah 40–55*, vol. 1, p. 324.

for our discussion. It is thus interesting that the Targum interprets the text in a way that resolves the ambiguity: "For just as waters are provided on the land of a thirsty place, and flow on the dry ground, so I will bestow my Holy Spirit upon your sons, and my blessing upon your sons' sons" (*Tg. Isa.* 44.3). However, even this interpretive paraphrase is vague about the timing of this intervention by YHWH in his people's fortunes.

The Ezekiel passages promise that YHWH will give a new heart and a new s/Spirit to his people which will enable them to keep his laws. Ezekiel 11:19-20 and 36:26-27 are located in a time when YHWH restores them to the land after exiling them (11:17; 36:24). Ezekiel 37:14 is part of the vision of the valley of dry bones and pictures the restoration of the people in terms of resurrection — God's Spirit will revivify the people. The rabbis understood the promise of 36:26 to be about the time when God will remove the "evil inclination" (רעי) and replace it with a heart of flesh; they did not characteristically speak of this as the work of the Spirit.[30] Thus *Targum Jonathan Ezekiel* 36.25-27 reads:

> And I will forgive your sins, as though you had been purified by the waters of sprinkling and by the ashes of the heifer sin-offering, and you shall be cleansed of all your defilements, and from your idols I will cleanse you. And I will give you a faithful heart, and I will put a faithful spirit deep inside you, and I will demolish the wicked heart, which is as hard as stone, from your flesh; and I will give you a heart that is faithful before Me, to do My will. And My holy spirit will I put deep inside of you and I will act so that you shall walk in my statutes and keep my laws and observe them.

In any case, however these Ezekiel passages are interpreted as to their content, it is clear that they are not promises about the coming of the Spirit in a specified historical situation — the tendency is to interpret them eschatologically.

Zechariah 12:10 occurs following a prophecy about YHWH giving victory to Jerusalem against surrounding pagan armies (12:1-9, esp. vv. 2, 3b, 9). Then (perhaps as the beginning of a new oracle, running from 12:10 to 13:1)[31] comes the promise of YHWH pouring out "a s/Spirit of

---

30. See the discussion in Turner, *Power*, pp. 130-31; Menzies, *Empowered*, pp. 95-96.
31. So, e.g., George L. Klein, *Zechariah*, New American Commentary 21B (Nashville: Broadman & Holman, 2008), p. 362.

compassion and supplication" (LXX: "a s/Spirit of grace and compassion"). LXX differs significantly from MT in this passage, for the Hebrew is very difficult,[32] but in either version the text is vague about the circumstances in which YHWH will do this. Nothing in the situation — or in any of the Old Testament texts we have considered — seems to be connected to the promise of the s/Spirit in any way similar to what we have seen in the synoptic Gospels.

2.2. Second Temple Jewish Literature

Three representative passages which contain explicit promises of the Spirit's work in people are worth considering here, from Philo, the Dead Sea Scrolls, and *Midrash Tanḥuma*.

1QS 4.20-23 and *Midrash Tanḥuma Addition* to חקת both look to a future time when God will take the "evil impulse" from people and replace it by Holy Spirit:

> Then God will purify all the doings of man by his truth and purge a part of mankind. He will utterly destroy the spirit of deceit from them and cleanse his flesh by a holy spirit from all ungodly acts. He will sprinkle upon it a spirit of truth like water of purification, from all the abominations of falsehood and (from) being polluted by a spirit of impurity, so that the upright ones may achieve insight in the knowledge of the Most High and the wisdom of the sons of heaven, and the perfect in way become wise. For those has God chosen for an eternal covenant, and theirs is all the glory of Adam without deceit.... Until now the spirits of truth and deceit struggle in the heart of man. (1QS 4.20-23)

> Concerning this the Wise say: The one who does not look at another's wife, the evil impulse has no power over him. In the world to come the Holy One, blessed be he, will take the evil impulse from us and place in us his Holy Spirit, as it is written: "I will remove the heart of stone from your flesh and I will put my Spirit in you" (Ezek. 36:26-27) (*Midr. Tanḥ. Addition* to חקת).

---

32. See Christopher Tuckett, "Zechariah 12:10 and the New Testament," in *The Book of Zechariah and Its Influence*, ed. Christopher Tuckett (Aldershot: Ashgate, 2003), pp. 111-21, esp. pp. 113-15.

Schäfer notes that the Midrash looks to life in the world to come.³³ A similar conclusion concerning 1QS 4.20-23 is likely, for 1QS 3.12–4.25 seems to be a brief discussion of the "two spirits" (of truth and deceit) which closes with "For God has established the two spirits in equal measure until the determined end, and until the Renewal . . ." (1QS 4.25), pointing to an eschatological future in the world to come.³⁴ Thus these texts look forward to God sending the Spirit to change people's hearts, but do not envisage this taking place within the present bounds of space and time.

Philo writes:

> For no pronouncement of a prophet is ever his own; he is an interpreter prompted by Another in all his utterances, when knowing not what he does he is filled with inspiration (καθ' ὃν χρόνον ἐνθουσιᾷ γεγονὼς ἐν ἀγνοίᾳ) as the reason withdraws and surrenders the citadel of the soul to a new visitor and tenant, the divine Spirit (τοῦ θείου πνεύματος), which plays upon the vocal organism and dictates the words which clearly express its prophetic message. (*Spec.* 4.49)

This statement focuses on the Spirit inspiring prophetic speech, and so might be thought similar to the situation of Luke 12:12 and parallels, where the Spirit enables the disciples on trial to speak appropriately. However, Philo's statement is reminiscent of John's portrait of the Spirit as being as sovereignly free as the wind blowing where it wills (John 3:8), and shares with that portrait the unlikelihood of the Spirit coming in particular, defined circumstances — a great contrast to Luke 12:12 and parallels.

2.3. John the Baptizer

Our third comparison is with the promise of the Spirit by John the baptizer, whom the Gospels consistently present as Jesus' forerunner, painted in prophetic colors. John promises that the Spirit will come

---

33. Peter Schäfer, *Die Vorstellung vom heiligen Geist in der rabbinischen Literatur* (Munich: Kösel-Verlag, 1972), p. 114.
34. For discussion of the "two spirits" in 1QS, see Cornelis Bennema, *The Power of Saving Wisdom: An Investigation of Spirit and Wisdom in Relation to the Soteriology of the Fourth Gospel* (Tübingen: Mohr Siebeck, 2002), pp. 87-89.

through the Coming One (Mark 1:8; Matt. 3:11-12; Luke 3:16-17).[35] Here is a clear promise from a prophetic figure of the Spirit's future coming, and a particular person will be the agent who baptizes with Spirit and fire. However, the promise is not linked to a particular set of circumstances when the Spirit's power will be available, by contrast with Luke 12:12 and parallels.

2.4. The Fourth Gospel

Finally, we note the Johannine promises that the Spirit will come to enable the disciples, which may be thought to parallel Luke's promises. Jesus promises that the Spirit will teach and remind the disciples of his own teaching (John 14:26), will testify about Jesus and (by implication) enable the disciples to testify about Jesus (John 15:26-27), and will continue teaching the disciples (John 16:14).[36] The first and third of these promises are rather general and unspecific concerning the occasion(s) on which the Spirit will perform such actions. The second, although given in the context of warnings about the world hating the disciples (John 15:18-25), is not as specific as the Lukan promise, which is that the Spirit will enable them to speak *when on trial*. John 15:26-27 is the closest parallel we have identified, but since (by common consent) John's Gospel post-dates Luke's, we may safely conclude that even this passage does not provide a precedent for the specific nature of Luke 12:12 and parallels, even if it may provide a (later) partial parallel.

3. Reading Acts 2:33 with Luke 12:12

At the risk of laboring the point, it seems clear in the passages from the Old Testament and other Second Temple Jewish sources, including interpretations of the Old Testament in the Targums, that the promise of Luke 12:12 and parallels is unprecedented in assuring a group of people that the Spirit will give them assistance in a particular type of setting

---

35. For discussion of these sayings, see Turner, *Power*, pp. 170-87; Menzies, *Empowered*, pp. 123-31; James D. G. Dunn, *Baptism in the Holy Spirit* (London: SCM Press, 1970), pp. 8-22.

36. See the lucid and helpful discussion of Bennema, *Power*, pp. 228-36.

in the future.[37] We therefore turn to consider Luke 12:12 and parallels in the context of the fuller picture of the Spirit's activity and roles in the book of Acts.

One of Max Turner's many important contributions to New Testament scholarship has been his careful reading of Acts 2:33.[38] This is a key verse for understanding Luke's view of the relation of the exalted Jesus to the Spirit, for it states that the exalted Jesus has received the Spirit from the Father and he — Jesus — now pours out "what you both see and hear." The latter phrase refers to the manifestations of the Spirit in the rush of the wind, the tongues of fire and the believers' xenolalic speech (Acts 2:2-4), and thus points to Jesus as the one who now pours out the Spirit.

The significance of this remarkable event can be discerned by asking who, in Second Temple Jewish understanding, pours out the Spirit. The answer is Yhwh and Yhwh alone: no other being in the universe has this ability, for God's Spirit *"was a way of speaking of the active* (usually self-revealing) *personal presence of the transcendent God himself."*[39] Luke has prepared for this point by the presence of "God declares" (λέγει ὁ θεός) in Acts 2:17. This phrase, not included in Luke's source text, Joel 2:28-32, makes it clear that it is God himself who is the speaker in the promise of the Spirit (Acts 2:17-21) — *God* will pour out the Spirit in the last days, not any human being or angel or other creature. So when Peter speaks in v. 33 to say that *Jesus himself* is the one who has poured out the Spirit in the events of Pentecost — not even that Jesus mediates the Spirit from Yhwh — this means that Jesus, exalted to God's right hand, is Lord of the Spirit and the Spirit is his "executive power."[40] The Spirit is now related to Jesus as the Spirit has been related to God: "God the Father grants Jesus *the same authority as himself* to pour out the Spirit."[41]

---

37. By common consent, John 14:26; 15:26-27 are written later than Luke, and so cannot be argued to be precedents for the saying in Luke 12:12 and parallels.

38. Turner, *Power*, pp. 275-79; Max Turner, "The Spirit of Christ and Christology," in *Christ the Lord: Studies in Christology Presented to Donald Guthrie*, ed. Harold H. Rowdon (Leicester: IVP, 1982), pp. 168-90, esp. pp. 175-84; Max Turner, "The Spirit of Christ and 'Divine' Christology," in *Jesus of Nazareth: Lord and Christ. Essays on the Historical Jesus and New Testament Christology*, ed. Joel B. Green and Max Turner (Carlisle: Paternoster/Grand Rapids: Eerdmans, 1994), pp. 413-36, esp. pp. 419-24, all summarized in what follows.

39. Turner, *Power*, p. 277 (his italics).

40. Turner, *Power*, p. 278; cf. Buckwalter, *Character*, pp. 194-96.

41. Buckwalter, *Character*, p. 195 (his italics); cf. *TDNT*, 6:405 (Jesus is "not a pneumatic, but the Lord of the Spirit").

We may thus go on (with Turner) to observe that another key part of the Joel quotation is fulfilled by Jesus. Joel speaks of people calling "on the name of the Lord" (Joel 2:32; Acts 2:21), and it is made clear that the Lord on whom they are now to call is Jesus (Acts 2:36)[42] and thus that they are to be baptized in the name of Jesus (Acts 2:38). This conclusion chimes in with the exalted Jesus' ability to pour out the Spirit — he is now to be placed in the same category as Yhwh.

Let us then consider Luke 12:12 in the light of this reading of Acts 2:33. In Luke 12:12, Jesus makes it clear that the Spirit will give aid to the disciples when they are in the specific situation of being hauled before the authorities on trial, and we have observed that the specific nature of this promise goes beyond anything we have seen in the Old Testament or Second Temple Jewish expectation. Read in the light of Acts 2:33, this promise goes beyond the ability of prophets to declare the mind of Yhwh, for here Jesus promises what the Spirit will do (and do regularly — recall the introduction of the promise with the generalizing ὅταν "whenever") in a specific context. Thus Luke 12:12 hints at the picture of Jesus as Lord of the Spirit in Acts.

The parallel saying in Luke 21:14-15 takes this argument a step further, for there it is *Jesus* who will assist his disciples to speak when on trial. Taking this saying with Luke 12:12 and Acts 2:33, we may observe that Luke is weaving a nexus of connections which places Jesus in the same role in relation to the Spirit as Yhwh, for Jesus himself will assist the disciples by the Spirit, just as Yhwh helps his people by his Spirit. In the context of first-century Judaism, this is a remarkable claim — Jesus the Lord of the Spirit stands alongside Yhwh in aiding his followers.[43]

4. Conclusion

We have seen, then, that the promise in Luke 12:12 is remarkable in several respects. First, it is very unusual in being situation-specific, promising the aid of the Spirit to disciples whenever they are on trial before

---

42. With, e.g., Ernst Haenchen, *The Acts of the Apostles* (Oxford: Blackwell, 1971), pp. 179, 186.

43. The (later) partial parallel we noted above in John's Gospel contains similar assumptions about Jesus' relation to the Spirit, but while those assumptions are commonly recognized by students of John, they are not generally recognized by students of Luke.

the authorities. Secondly, it is paralleled by a further saying (Luke 21:14-15) where Jesus promises that he himself will give similar aid to his disciples in the same situation. Thirdly, when read with Acts 2:33 in context, Luke 12:12 portrays Jesus as having the same relation to the Spirit as Yhwh himself, and contributes to our picture of Luke's portrait of Jesus as one who saves as Yhwh saves, aids as Yhwh aids, and in his exalted state can be present as widely as Yhwh can — wherever his people need his help in defending their Lord before the authorities.

Appendix: Comparison of the Texts of the Sayings[44]

Luke 21	Luke 12	Mark	Matthew
	vv. 8-9 Λέγω δὲ ὑμῖν, πᾶς ὃς ἂν ὁμολογήσῃ ἐν ἐμοὶ ἔμπροσθεν τῶν ἀνθρώπων, καὶ ὁ υἱὸς τοῦ ἀνθρώπου ὁμολογήσει ἐν αὐτῷ ἔμπροσθεν τῶν ἀγγέλων τοῦ θεοῦ· ὁ δὲ ἀρνησάμενός με ἐνώπιον τῶν ἀνθρώπων ἀπαρνηθήσεται ἐνώπιον τῶν ἀγγέλων τοῦ θεοῦ.		10:32-33 Πᾶς οὖν ὅστις ὁμολογήσει ἐν ἐμοὶ ἔμπροσθεν τῶν ἀνθρώπων, ὁμολογήσω κἀγὼ ἐν αὐτῷ ἔμπροσθεν τοῦ πατρός μου τοῦ ἐν [τοῖς] οὐρανοῖς· ὅστις δ' ἂν ἀρνήσηταί με ἔμπροσθεν τῶν ἀνθρώπων, ἀρνήσομαι κἀγὼ αὐτὸν ἔμπροσθεν τοῦ πατρός μου τοῦ ἐν [τοῖς] οὐρανοῖς.
	And I tell you, everyone who acknowledges me before others, the Son of Man also will acknowledge before the angels of God; 9 but whoever denies me before others will be denied before the angels of God.		Everyone therefore who acknowledges me before others, I also will acknowledge before my Father in heaven; but whoever denies me before others, I also will deny before my Father in heaven.

44. English translations are from NRSV. Underlining indicates agreement or near-agreement in wording; double underlining indicates agreement or near-agreement among some of the texts; highlighting indicates agreement in a particular verb choice.

Steve Walton

Luke 21	Luke 12	Mark	Matthew
	v. 10 Καὶ πᾶς ὃς ἐρεῖ λόγον εἰς τὸν υἱὸν τοῦ ἀνθρώπου, ἀφεθήσεται αὐτῷ· τῷ δὲ εἰς τὸ ἅγιον πνεῦμα βλασφημήσαντι οὐκ ἀφεθήσεται.	3:28-29 Ἀμὴν λέγω ὑμῖν ὅτι πάντα ἀφεθήσεται τοῖς υἱοῖς τῶν ἀνθρώπων τὰ ἁμαρτήματα καὶ αἱ βλασφημίαι ὅσα ἐὰν βλασφημήσωσιν· ὃς δ' ἂν βλασφημήσῃ εἰς τὸ πνεῦμα τὸ ἅγιον, οὐκ ἔχει ἄφεσιν εἰς τὸν αἰῶνα, ἀλλὰ ἔνοχός ἐστιν αἰωνίου ἁμαρτήματος.	12:31-32 Διὰ τοῦτο λέγω ὑμῖν, πᾶσα ἁμαρτία καὶ βλασφημία ἀφεθήσεται τοῖς ἀνθρώποις, ἡ δὲ τοῦ πνεύματος βλασφημία οὐκ ἀφεθήσεται. καὶ ὃς ἐὰν εἴπῃ λόγον κατὰ τοῦ υἱοῦ τοῦ ἀνθρώπου, ἀφεθήσεται αὐτῷ· ὃς δ' ἂν εἴπῃ κατὰ τοῦ πνεύματος τοῦ ἁγίου, οὐκ ἀφεθήσεται αὐτῷ οὔτε ἐν τούτῳ τῷ αἰῶνι οὔτε ἐν τῷ μέλλοντι.
	And everyone who speaks a word against the Son of Man will be forgiven; but <u>whoever blasphemes against the Holy Spirit will not be forgiven</u>.	Truly I tell you, people will be forgiven for their sins and whatever blasphemies they utter; but <u>whoever blasphemes against the Holy Spirit can</u> never <u>have forgiveness</u>, but is guilty of an eternal sin.	Therefore I tell you, people will be forgiven for every sin and blasphemy, but blasphemy against the Spirit will not be forgiven. 32 Whoever speaks a word against the Son of Man will be forgiven, but <u>whoever speaks against the Holy Spirit will not be forgiven</u>, either in this age or in the age to come.

Whose Spirit?

Luke 21	Luke 12	Mark	Matthew
vv. 12-15 Πρὸ δὲ τούτων πάντων ἐπιβαλοῦσιν ἐφ' ὑμᾶς τὰς χεῖρας αὐτῶν καὶ διώξουσιν, παραδιδόντες εἰς τὰς συναγωγὰς καὶ φυλακάς, ἀπαγομένους ἐπὶ βασιλεῖς καὶ ἡγεμόνας ἕνεκεν τοῦ ὀνόματός μου· ἀποβήσεται ὑμῖν εἰς μαρτύριον. θέτε οὖν ἐν ταῖς καρδίαις ὑμῶν μὴ προμελετᾶν ἀπολογηθῆναι· ἐγὼ γὰρ δώσω ὑμῖν στόμα καὶ σοφίαν ᾗ οὐ δυνήσονται ἀντιστῆναι ἢ ἀντειπεῖν ἅπαντες οἱ ἀντικείμενοι ὑμῖν.	vv. 11-12 Ὅταν δὲ εἰσφέρωσιν ὑμᾶς ἐπὶ τὰς συναγωγὰς καὶ τὰς ἀρχὰς καὶ τὰς ἐξουσίας, μὴ <u>μεριμνήσητε πῶς ἢ τί ἀπολογήσησθε ἢ τί εἴπητε· τὸ γὰρ ἅγιον πνεῦμα</u> διδάξει ὑμᾶς ἐν αὐτῇ τῇ ὥρᾳ ἃ δεῖ εἰπεῖν.	13:11 καὶ <u>ὅταν</u> ἄγωσιν ὑμᾶς παραδιδόντες, <u>μὴ προμεριμνᾶτε τί λαλήσητε, ἀλλ' ὃ ἐὰν δοθῇ ὑμῖν ἐν ἐκείνῃ τῇ ὥρᾳ τοῦτο λαλεῖτε· οὐ γάρ ἐστε ὑμεῖς οἱ λαλοῦντες ἀλλὰ τὸ πνεῦμα τὸ ἅγιον.</u>	10:19-20 <u>ὅταν</u> δὲ παραδῶσιν ὑμᾶς, <u>μὴ μεριμνήσητε πῶς ἢ τί λαλήσητε· δοθήσεται γὰρ ὑμῖν ἐν ἐκείνῃ τῇ ὥρᾳ τί λαλήσητε· οὐ γὰρ ὑμεῖς ἐστε οἱ λαλοῦντες ἀλλὰ τὸ πνεῦμα τοῦ πατρὸς ὑμῶν τὸ λαλοῦν ἐν ὑμῖν.</u>
But before all this occurs, they will arrest you and persecute you; they will hand you over to synagogues and prisons, and you will be brought before kings and governors because of my name. This will give you an opportunity to testify. So make up your minds not to prepare your defense in advance; for I will give you words and a wisdom that none of your opponents will be able to withstand or contradict.	<u>When</u> they bring you before the synagogues, the rulers, and the authorities, <u>do not worry about how</u> you are to defend yourselves or what you are to say; <u>for the Holy Spirit</u> will teach you at that very hour what you ought to say.	<u>When</u> they bring you to trial and hand you over, <u>do not worry</u> beforehand <u>about what</u> you are to say; but <u>say whatever is given you at that time, for it is not you who speak,</u> but <u>the Holy Spirit</u>.	<u>When</u> they hand you over, <u>do not worry about how</u> you are to speak or what you are to say; <u>for what you are to say will be given to you at that time; for it is not you who speak, but the Spirit of your Father</u> speaking through you.

51

The Persecuted Prophets:
A Mirror Image of Luke's
Spirit-Inspired Church

Robert P. Menzies

I consider it a distinct privilege to be able to contribute to this work honoring my friend and, in many respects, mentor, Max Turner. Max's initial years of service at the University of Aberdeen overlapped with mine, a fact for which I will always be grateful. Of course, he was the instructor, I, the student. During this period I grew to appreciate Max not only as a brilliant scholar, but also as a highly committed Christian brother. Max has deep roots in the Pentecostal movement and, while he has blessed the broader Christian community through his ministry of teaching and writing, he has never forgotten this heritage. He, like few others, has engaged and stimulated Pentecostal scholars in our efforts to clarify the role of the Holy Spirit in the New Testament, and Luke-Acts in particular. I have benefited greatly from Max's scholarship, his friendship, and his encouragement through the years. Although we have often disagreed in print and at times Max may have felt like one of the persecuted prophets described in my essay, these conversations reflect our similar roots, interests, and perspectives. They also reflect my respect for a gifted and dedicated servant of the Lord.

Some time ago house church leaders from two different church groups in China met together in my home in southwest China. It was fascinating watching how they interacted with each other. They asked each other three key questions. It was apparent that these three questions touched upon matters they viewed as significant and foundational for church leadership. First, they asked about their conversion experience. Second, they wanted to know about their call to ministry. Finally, they asked about their experience of persecution (or, more spe-

The Persecuted Prophets

cifically, their time in prison). Their conversion, their call, and their suffering — these were the marks of a true minister.

I could not help but compare this list with the list of qualifications we generally look for in church leaders in the West. There was something very basic and compelling about their approach. It reminded me of Luke's perspective on ministry, particularly his portrait of the apostolic church as a community of prophets. In the book of Acts, the Christian prophets, like the prophets of Israel's past, are inspired by the Holy Spirit to declare God's message. As a result, they too suffer.[1]

This theme of "the persecuted prophets" can be traced throughout Luke's two-volume work. Luke frequently highlights the fact that the prophets of old suffered.[2] In one dramatic scene, Stephen, speaking to the Jewish leaders who opposed him, declares, "Was there ever a prophet your fathers did not persecute?" (Acts 7:52).[3] Ironically, Stephen himself suffers the fate of a prophet.

Of course Jesus, the prophet like Moses (Acts 3:22; 7:37), is the supreme example of a persecuted prophet. Luke, more than any other evangelist, highlights the fact that Jesus is a prophet.[4] Luke also stresses the necessity of Jesus' suffering, which was foretold by the prophets.[5] As the narrative unfolds, it becomes clear that Jesus' disciples will not only share his prophetic anointing, they will also share his suffering.[6] Persecution comes with the call. Like the prophets of old and the Prophet-Messiah, Christian prophets will also face persecu-

---

1. Accounts of persecution can be found in almost every chapter of the book of Acts. See for example Acts 4:3, 18-21; 5:18, 27-29, 40-41; 6:9-13; 7:54-60; 9:16, 23-25, 29. In fact, in Luke's perspective, those who do not suffer are viewed with suspicion. Note Luke 6:26 (unique to Luke): "Woe to you when all men speak well of you, for that is how their fathers treated the false prophets."

2. Luke 6:23, 26; 11:47-51; 13:31-35; Acts 7:51-53.

3. All English Scripture citations are taken from the NIV unless otherwise noted.

4. Luke 4:24; 7:16, 39; 13:33; 22:64; 24:19; Acts 3:22; 7:37.

5. Texts that specifically refer to Jesus' suffering as foretold by the prophets include Luke 16:31; 18:31-32; 24:25-27, 44-46; Acts 3:18; 7:52; 13:27; 26:22-23; cf. Acts 10:39-43; 28:23.

6. Paul S. Minear describes "Luke's two volumes as an account of the training of apprentice seers and exorcists" and then speaks of "a succession of prophets from Abel to Paul . . . linked together by divine purpose and human suffering" (*To Heal and To Reveal: The Prophetic Vocation According to Luke* [New York: The Seabury Press, 1976], pp. 148-49).

tion. Thus Paul and Barnabas declare, "We must go through many hardships to enter the kingdom of God" (Acts 14:22).

Numerous scholars have dealt with this significant Lukan theme.[7] Although it is obvious that persecution is a major theme in Luke-Acts, scholars remain divided concerning what this emphasis tells us about the community for which Luke writes and his purpose.[8] Does Luke write to encourage a church facing persecution? Scott Cunningham cautiously answers this question in the affirmative, but he acknowledges the complexity of the question: "One cannot argue that because there is persecution in Luke-Acts, therefore there must be persecution in the Lukan community."[9] Indeed, since Luke is writing a historical account — to be sure, history with a purpose, but history none-the-less — is it not possible that Luke records these dramatic events of persecution simply because they happened? While this is theoretically possible, in the following essay I will suggest that this is not the case. I will argue that the evidence is compelling and that it tells us that Luke does indeed write to encourage a church facing persecution.[10] Since Cunningham and, more recently, Martin Mittelstadt have

---

7. See the review of the literature in Scott Cunningham, *"Through Many Tribulations": The Theology of Persecution in Luke-Acts* (Sheffield: Sheffield Academic Press, 1997), pp. 23-41, and Martin W. Mittelstadt, *The Spirit and Suffering in Luke-Acts: Implications for a Pentecostal Pneumatology* (London: T&T Clark, 2004), pp. 12-28.

8. Scholars who view Luke's church and his purpose as strongly influenced by persecution include: G. Braumann, "Das Mittel der Zeit: Erwägungen zur Theologie des Lukasevangeliums," *ZNW* 54 (1963): 117-45; F. Schütz, *Der leidende Christus: Die angefochtene Gemeinde und das Christuskerygma der lukanischen Schriften* (Stuttgart: Kohlhammer, 1969); Robert J. Karris, "Missionary Communities: A New Paradigm for the Study of Luke-Acts," *CBQ* 41 (1979): 80-97; Cunningham, *"Through Many Tribulations"*; Mittelstadt, *The Spirit and Suffering*. Scholars who do not see persecution as an important issue for Luke and his community include: Robert Maddox, *The Purpose of Luke-Acts* (Edinburgh: T&T Clark, 1982); J. T. Sanders, *The Jews in Luke-Acts* (Philadelphia: Fortress Press, 1987); and C. K. Barrett, *The Acts of the Apostles: A Shorter Commentary* (London: T&T Clark, 2002), esp. pp. xxxv-xl.

9. Cunningham, *"Through Many Tribulations,"* p. 329.

10. That Luke writes for a Christian community is, in my mind, quite obvious (cf. Luke 11:13 and the two texts, Luke 10:1-16 and Acts 2:17-21, cited in this essay). This does not mean, however, that Luke has abandoned a concern for faithfully passing on historically reliable tradition. See Richard Bauckham, *Jesus and the Eyewitnesses: The Gospels as Eyewitness Testimony* (Grand Rapids: Eerdmans, 2006), on the limitations of form criticism (pp. 240-63) and on related assumptions concerning the communal nature of the formation of early gospel traditions (pp. 290-318). See also Paul Rhodes Eddy and Greg-

offered excellent overviews of the persecution theme, I will not seek to reduplicate their efforts.[11] Rather, in this short essay, I will seek to supplement their work by focusing on two important texts from Luke-Acts, the significance of which has been largely ignored by contemporary scholars engaged in this debate. These texts indicate that Luke viewed those in his community, all of them, as prophets called and (at least potentially) empowered to follow in the prophetic vocation modeled by Jesus and the apostolic community. Furthermore, these texts reveal Luke's intention to engage and encourage these readers. Since Luke makes it abundantly clear that the prophetic vocation includes suffering, these conclusions represent a definitive answer to our central question. Let us now turn to these key texts.

1. The Significance of the Seventy (Luke 10:1-16)

Luke's account of the Sending of the Seventy (Luke 10:1-16) is strategically located toward the beginning of Luke's travel narrative (Luke 9:51–19:27). In this section of his gospel, Luke deviates from his tendency to follow Mark's chronology and appropriate Markan material. He now utilizes almost exclusively material drawn largely from Q or other sources unique to his gospel. The journey begins with Luke's declaration, "Jesus resolutely set out for Jerusalem" (Luke 9:51). In the ensuing verses references to the journey abound (Luke 9:52, 57; 10:1, 38; 13:22; 14:25; 17:11). The portrait Luke generates is sharp and clear: Jesus, the eschatological prophet like Moses (Acts 3:22; 7:37; cf. Luke 4:18-19), embarks on a journey that will lead to Jerusalem and the inevitable fate of the prophet that awaits him there (cf. Luke 11:47-51; 13:34; Acts 7:52). This journey "on the way,"[12] which has its counterpart in Acts with the movement of the disciples from Jerusalem to "the ends of the earth" (Acts 1:8), takes on the character of a "mission."[13]

---

ory A. Boyd, *The Jesus Legend: A Case for the Historical Reliability of the Synoptic Jesus Tradition* (Grand Rapids: Baker Academic, 2007), for an evangelical perspective on the formation of the gospels; for their assessment of redaction criticism, see pp. 396-406.

11. See Cunningham, *"Through Many Tribulations,"* and Mittelstadt, *The Spirit and Suffering*.

12. For references to "the way" (ὁδός) see Luke 9:57; 10:4; 12:58; 18:35; Acts 9:2; 19:9, 23; 24:14, 22.

13. Keith J. Hacking, *Signs and Wonders, Then and Now: Miracle-working, Commissioning and Discipleship* (Nottingham: Apollos, 2006), p. 201.

Robert P. Menzies

All three synoptic Gospels record Jesus' words of instruction to the Twelve as he sends them out on their mission (Matt. 10:1-16; Mark 6:6-12; Luke 9:1-9). However, only Luke records a second, larger sending of disciples (Luke 10:1-16). In Luke 10:1 we read, "After this the Lord appointed seventy-two [some mss. read, 'seventy'] others and sent them two by two ahead of him to every town and place where he was about to go." A series of detailed instructions follow. Jesus warns the disciples that the journey will not be easy. They will face opposition, for he is sending them out "like lambs among wolves" (10:3).

The essential question that we must address centers on the number of disciples that Jesus sent out and its significance. The manuscript evidence is, at this point, divided. Some manuscripts read "seventy," while others list the number as "seventy-two." Bruce Metzger, in his article on this question, notes that the external manuscript evidence is evenly divided and internal considerations are also inconclusive. Metzger thus concludes that the number "cannot be determined with confidence."[14] More recent scholarship has largely agreed with Metzger, with a majority opting cautiously for the authenticity of "seventy-two" as the more difficult reading.[15] Although we cannot determine the number with confidence, it will be important to keep the divided nature of the manuscript evidence in mind as we wrestle with the significance of this text.

Most scholars agree that the number (for convenience, we will call it "seventy") has symbolic significance. A number of proposals have been put forward,[16] but only two deserve serious consideration. A ma-

---

14. Bruce Metzger, "Seventy or Seventy-Two Disciples?," *NTS* 5 (1959): 299-306 (quote, p. 306). See also the response of Sidney Jellicoe, "St Luke and the 'Seventy(-Two),'" *NTS* 6 (1960): 319-21.

15. All of the following scholars favor the "seventy-two" reading as original: Darrell L. Bock, *Luke 9:51–24:53*, Baker Exegetical Commentary of the New Testament (Grand Rapids: Baker Academic, 1996), p. 994; I. H. Marshall, *The Gospel of Luke: A Commentary on the Greek Text*, New International Greek Testament Commentary (Grand Rapids: Eerdmans, 1978), p. 415; Joel Green, *The Gospel of Luke*, New International Commentary on the New Testament (Grand Rapids: Eerdmans, 1997), p. 409; Robert C. Tannehill, *The Narrative Unity of Luke-Acts: A Literary Interpretation* (Philadelphia: Fortress Press, 1986), vol. 1, p. 233; Craig Evans, *Luke*, New International Biblical Commentary (Peabody: Hendrickson, 1990), p. 172. One exception to this general rule is John Nolland, who favors the "seventy" reading (*Luke 9:21–18:34*, Word Biblical Commentary 35B [Dallas: Word, 1993], p. 546).

16. For the various options see Metzger, "Seventy or Seventy-Two Disciples," pp. 303-4, and Bock, *Luke 9:51–24:53*, p. 1015.

The Persecuted Prophets

jority of scholars find the background for the reference to the "seventy" in the list of nations in Genesis 10, which in the Hebrew text numbers seventy and in the LXX, seventy-two.[17] The number "seventy" is then viewed as a symbolic anticipation of the mission of the church beyond Israel to the Gentile nations. The central reasons this position has been accepted by so many scholars are: (1) the theme of the Gentile mission is prominent in Acts and there are specific parallels between the instructions given to the seventy and the actual mission of the church as it is described in Acts (e.g., the importance of table fellowship, traveling in groups of two, and miracles of healing); and (2) the textual traditions for the table of nations (Hebrew: seventy; LXX: seventy-two) account nicely for the divided manuscript evidence.

As compelling as these arguments appear at first sight, I would suggest that the evidence points in another direction. The second proposal, adopted by a minority of scholars,[18] maintains that the background for the reference to the "seventy" is to be found in Numbers 11:24-30. This passage describes how the Lord "took of the Spirit that was on [Moses] and put the Spirit on the seventy elders" (Num. 11:25). This resulted in the seventy elders, who had gathered around the Tent, prophesying for a short duration. However, two other elders, Eldad and Medad, did not go to the Tent; rather, they remained in the camp. But the Spirit also fell on them and they too began to prophesy and continued to do so. When Joshua heard this news, he rushed to Moses and urged him to stop them. Moses replied, "Are you jealous for my sake? I wish that all the Lord's people were prophets and that the Lord would put his Spirit on them!" (Num. 11:29). The significance of the symbolism is thus found in the expansion of the number of disciples "sent out" into mission from the Twelve to the Seventy. The reference to the Seventy evokes memories of Moses' wish that "all the Lord's people

---

17. The following scholars favor this reading: Fred B. Craddock, *Luke* (Louisville: Westminster John Knox Press, 1990), pp. 144-45; R. Alan Culpepper, *The Gospel of Luke*, New Interpreter's Bible 9 (Nashville: Abingdon Press, 1995), p. 219; Nolland, *Luke 9:21–18:34*, p. 558; Marshall, *Luke*, p. 415; Evans, *Luke*, p. 169; Tannehill, *Luke*, p. 233; and Green, *Luke*, p. 412.

18. Susan R. Garrett, *The Demise of the Devil: Magic and the Demonic in Luke's Writings* (Minneapolis: Fortress Press, 1989), pp. 47-48, and Keith F. Nickle, *Preaching the Gospel of Luke: Proclaiming God's Royal Rule* (Louisville: Westminster John Knox Press, 2000), p. 114. Many scholars note this view as a possibility, but cautiously opt for the table of nations (Gen. 10) explanation.

were prophets," and, in this way, points ahead to Pentecost (Acts 2; cf. 2:17), where this wish is initially and dramatically fulfilled. This wish continues to be fulfilled throughout Acts as Luke describes the coming of the empowering Spirit of prophecy to other new centers of missionary activity, such as those gathered together in Samaria (Acts 8:14-17), Cornelius' house (Acts 10:44-48), and Ephesus (Acts 19:1-7). The reference to the Seventy, then, does not simply anticipate the mission of the church to the Gentiles; rather, it foreshadows the outpouring of the Spirit on all the servants of the Lord and their universal participation in the mission of God as end-time prophets (Acts 2:17-18; cf. 4:31).[19] In Luke's view, each member of the church is called (Luke 24:45-49; Acts 1:4-8/Isa. 49:6; cf. Luke 11:13) and promised the requisite power (Acts 2:17-21; cf. 4:31) to take up the prophetic vocation and engage in mission. Luke 10:1 anticipates the fulfillment of this reality.

The Numbers 11 proposal has a number of significant advantages over the Genesis 10 explanation. First, it should be noted that the Numbers 11 passage accounts for the two textual traditions underlying Luke 10:1. While the number of the elders is listed in Numbers 11:24-25 (cf. 11:16) as seventy, it is not entirely clear whether Eldad and Medad should be considered as part of the seventy or whether they are additions to the seventy. Thus, we can see why scribes would have been tempted to correct the "seventy" to "seventy-two," or vice versa. As we have noted, the Genesis 10 explanation also accounts for the two textual traditions. But neither the Hebrew nor the LXX text of Genesis 10 actually lists the number of nations as "seventy" or "seventy-two." This number must be inferred from a calculation of the names included in the text. It is true that Jewish tradition lists the number of princes and languages in the world as seventy-two (*3 En.* 17.8; 18.2-3; 30.2), yet how clear this association would have been for Luke's audience is uncertain. In short, the Numbers 11 proposal, with its explicit reference to "seventy" elders and a plausible explanation for scribal discrepancies, offers a clearer explanation of the textual tradition behind Luke 10:1.

Secondly, the Numbers 11 proposal finds explicit fulfillment in the narrative of Acts, whereas the Genesis 10 explanation does not. The fulfillment of Moses' wish in Numbers 11:29 is clearly described in Acts

---

19. Nickle, *Luke*, p. 117: "The 'Seventy' is the church in its entirety, including Luke's own community, announcing the in-breaking of God's royal rule throughout the length and breadth of God's creation."

2. Peter explains the Pentecost phenomena with reference to Joel's prophecy: "In the last days, God says. . . . Your sons and daughters will prophesy" (Acts 2:17).[20] By way of contrast, Acts "contains no hint that Luke thought of the Gentile nations as numbering seventy(-two)."[21] In fact, the list of nations that Luke actually gives (Acts 2:8-11) offers a far more restricted list of nations.

Thirdly, the verse that immediately follows the reference to the Seventy focuses on the great need for more missionaries: "The harvest is plentiful but the workers are few. Ask the Lord of the harvest, therefore to send out workers into his harvest field" (Luke 10:2). The call to pray specifically for more workers is particularly striking. This fits more closely with an emphasis on the universal nature of God's missionary call (all of God's people are called to engage in the mission) rather than an emphasis on a universal mission (to all people, including the Gentiles).

Fourthly, the Numbers 11 proposal ties into one of the great themes of Luke-Acts, the work of the Holy Spirit. Luke consistently presents the Spirit as the source of prophetic inspiration and, as such, as the driving force behind the mission of the church.[22] In Luke 11:9-13, by modifying his Q material (cf. Matt. 7:7-11), Luke returns to this great theme and challenges his church to pray for the gift of the Spirit. The repetitive nature of the prayer envisioned and the fact that this call to prayer is addressed to disciples (and thus clearly anticipates the post-Pentecost location of Luke's church) remind us that Luke has in mind here a prophetic anointing similar to that of Jesus described in Luke 4:18-19 (cf. Luke 3:21-22) and that of the early church described in Acts 2:17-21 (cf. Acts 2:1-4). This reference to the Holy Spirit in close proximity to the Sending of the Seventy passage further strengthens our argument. The significance of this connection is heightened further by the references to prayer that join the two passages together thematically (Luke 10:2; 11:1-13).

Finally, a number of recent scholarly studies have noted that in his travel narrative, Luke "presents Jesus as the prophet like Moses, on

---

20. The point is highlighted further with the insertion of the phrase καὶ προφητεύσουσιν ("and they will prophesy") into Joel's text (cf. Acts 2:18 and Joel 3:2 [LXX]).

21. Garrett, *Demise of the Devil*, p. 47.

22. See Robert P. Menzies, *The Development of Early Christian Pneumatology with Special Reference to Luke-Acts* (Sheffield: JSOT Press, 1991), pp. 114-279.

a journey to Jerusalem to effect a new Exodus for the people of God."[23] The stage is set in the Transfiguration account (Luke 9:28-36), where Moses, along with Elijah, appears in glorious splendor and speaks with Jesus (Luke 9:30-31). They speak of Jesus' ἔξοδον ("departure"), "which he was about to bring to fulfillment at Jerusalem" (Luke 9:31). We can also hear an echo of Deuteronomy 18:15, "The Lord your God will raise up for you a prophet like me from among your own brothers. You must listen to him [αὐτοῦ ἀκούσεσθε]," in the phrase, "Listen to him [αὐτοῦ ἀκούετε]," found in Luke 9:35. One need not accept in its entirety the thesis of C. F. Evans or David Moessner, both of whom suggest that Luke structures his travel narrative largely on the basis of the book of Deuteronomy, to recognize that an interest in Moses typology has influenced Luke's literary program in a significant way.[24] Certainly we should not miss the fact that the words "serpent" (ὄφις) and "scorpion" (σκορπίος) which appear together in Luke 10:19 are found together in the Old Testament (LXX) only in Deuteronomy 8:15. And Luke's redacted version of the Q saying found in Luke 11:20, "But if I drive out demons by the finger of God [ἐν δακτύλῳ θεοῦ], then the kingdom of God has come to you," echoes Exodus 8:19 (8:15 LXX), "The magicians said to Pharaoh, 'This is the finger of God' [δάκτυλος θεοῦ].''[25] Luke's narrative also explicitly depicts Jesus as "the prophet like Moses" (Acts 3:22; 7:37; cf. Deut. 18:15-19) who, like Moses before Pharaoh (Exod. 7:3), performs "signs and wonders" (σημεῖα καὶ τέρατα; Acts 2:19). These allusions to Moses and his actions collectively add considerable support to our suggestion that the symbolism for Luke's reference to the Seventy should be found in Numbers 11 rather than Genesis 10.

The cumulative evidence is compelling and leads us to conclude that Luke has indeed crafted his account of the Sending of the Seventy with the seventy elders of Numbers 11 and particularly Moses' wish that

---

23. Greg W. Forbes, *The God of Old: The Role of the Lukan Parables in the Purpose of Luke's Gospel* (Sheffield: Sheffield Academic Press, 2000), p. 329.

24. So also Edward J. Woods, *The "Finger of God" and Pneumatology in Luke-Acts* (Sheffield: Sheffield Academic Press, 2001), pp. 47-48. Note also C. F. Evans, "The Central Section of Luke's Gospel," in *Studies in the Gospels*, ed. D. E. Nineham (Oxford: Blackwell, 1957), pp. 37-53, and David P. Moessner, *Lord of the Banquet: The Literary and Theological Significance of the Lukan Travel Narrative* (Minneapolis: Fortress Press, 1989).

25. For arguments supporting the notion that Luke has altered the original Q reading, "Spirit of God," reflected in Matthew 12:28, see Menzies, *Development*, pp. 185-89.

"all the Lord's people were prophets" (Num. 11:29) in mind. In this way, Luke anticipates Pentecost, when Moses' wish begins to be fulfilled. But Luke clearly looks beyond Pentecost to the needs of his own church (cf. Luke 11:13).[26] Just as Moses' wish continues to be fulfilled throughout the narrative of Acts as Luke describes the establishment of new centers of missionary activity in Samaria (Acts 8:14-17), Cornelius' house (Acts 10:44-48), and Ephesus (Acts 19:1-7), so also Luke anticipates that Moses' wish will be fulfilled in the lives of those in his church (cf. Acts 2:17-21). The Sending of the Seventy foreshadows the outpouring of the Spirit upon all the Lord's people and their universal participation as end-time prophets in the mission of God. In Luke's view, every believer is called to take up Israel's prophetic vocation and be "a light to the nations" by bearing bold witness for Jesus (Acts 1:4-8; cf. Isa. 49:6). The Sending of the Seventy, then, represents a promise. It anticipates what is yet to come. Let us now examine the fulfillment of this promise.[27]

2. Pentecost as a Paradigm (Acts 2:17-21)

Every New Testament scholar worth his salt will tell you that Luke 4:16-30, Jesus' dramatic sermon at Nazareth, is paradigmatic for Luke's Gospel. All of the major themes that will appear in the gospel are foreshadowed here: the work of the Spirit; the universality of the gospel; the grace of God; and the rejection of Jesus. And this is the one significant point where the chronology of the Gospel of Luke differs from the

---

26. If, as I have argued, the Sending of the Seventy anticipates the prophetic mission that every post-Pentecost disciple of Jesus is called and empowered to carry forward, then is it not reasonable to assume that the instructions the Seventy receive from Jesus are intended by Luke to serve in large measure as a model for the missionary praxis of his church? I argue that a comparison of these commands with the mission of the early church as recorded in Acts suggests that this is the case. See R. Menzies, "The Sending of the Seventy and Luke's Purpose," in *Trajectories in the Book of Acts: Essays in Honor of John Wesley Wyckoff*, ed. Paul Alexander, Jordan D. Mays, and Robert Reid (Eugene: Wipf & Stock, 2010), pp. 87-113.

27. Karris suggests that while Luke employs a theology of "fulfillment of promises," he is not able to utilize it in a consistent manner: "For example, one must use a magnifying glass of superior quality to find this theology at work in Luke 9:51–19:44" ("Missionary Communities," p. 95). My analysis of Luke 10:1-16 reveals that Luke is more consistent than Karris had realized.

Robert P. Menzies

Gospel of Mark. Here Luke takes an event from the middle of Jesus' ministry and brings it right up front to inaugurate the ministry of Jesus. Luke does this because he understands that this event, particularly Jesus' recitation of Isaiah 61:1-2 and his declaration that this prophecy is now being fulfilled in his ministry, provides important insights into the nature of Jesus and his mission. This passage, then, provides us with a model for Jesus' subsequent ministry.

It is interesting to note that Luke provides a similar sort of paradigmatic introduction for his second volume, the book of Acts. After the coming of the Spirit at Pentecost, Peter delivers a sermon (Acts 2:14-41) that in many ways parallels that of Jesus in Luke 4. In his sermon, Peter also refers to an OT prophecy concerning the coming of the Spirit, this time Joel 2:28-32, and declares that this prophecy too is now being fulfilled (Acts 2:17-21). The message is clear: Just as Jesus was anointed by the Spirit to fulfill his prophetic vocation, so also Jesus' disciples have been anointed as end-time prophets to proclaim the word of God. The text of Joel 2:28-32 that is cited here, like the paradigmatic passage in Luke 4, also shows signs of careful editing on the part of Luke.

The text of Acts 2:17-21 reads:

[v. 17] *In the last days, God says,* . . . [Joel: "after these things"]
I will pour out my Spirit on all people.
Your sons and daughters will prophesy,
Your young men will see visions, . . . [Joel: these lines are inverted]
Your old men will dream dreams.
[v. 18] *Even* on *my* servants, both men and women, . . . [additions to Joel]
I will pour out my Spirit in those days,
And they will prophesy.
[v. 19] I will show wonders in the heaven *above*
And *signs* on the earth *below,*
Blood and fire and billows of smoke.
[v. 20] The sun will be turned to darkness and the moon to blood
Before the coming of the great and glorious day of the Lord.
[v. 21] And everyone who calls on the name of the Lord will be saved.
　　　　　(Acts 2:17-21; modification of Joel 2:28-32 italicized).

Luke carefully shapes this quotation from the LXX in order to highlight important theological themes. Three modifications are particularly striking:

First, in verse 17 Luke alters the order of the two lines that refer to young men having visions and old men dreaming dreams. In Joel, the old men dreaming dreams comes first. But Luke reverses the order: "Your young men will see visions, your old men will dream dreams" (Acts 2:17). Luke rearranges these two lines drawn from Joel so that the reference to "visions" precedes the comment about "dreams." A survey of Acts reveals that this alteration is not simply an insignificant stylistic change. This is not merely a whim or slip of the eye. On the contrary, this subtle shift is intentional. Luke gives the reference to "visions" pride of place in order to emphasize its importance. With this modification of the LXX, Luke highlights a theme that he sees as vitally important and which recurs throughout his narrative.

A survey of the key terms is instructive. First, we find that the terms associated with dreams and dreaming occur only here in the book of Acts. The term translated "shall dream" is a future passive of ἐνυπνιάζω. This verb occurs only here and in Jude 8 in the entire New Testament. The noun, ἐνύπνιον ("dream"), is found nowhere else in Acts or the rest of the New Testament. Clearly, Luke is not big on dreaming.[28]

Luke, however, loves to recount stories that refer to guidance through "visions." At first glance this may not appear to be the case. The noun translated "visions" in verse 17, ὅρασις, occurs four times in the New Testament and only here in Acts. The other three occurrences are all found in Revelation. But appearances are often misleading and this is the case here. Luke uses another term, a close cousin to ὅρασις, the neuter noun, ὅραμα, often and at decisive points in his narrative to refer to "visions." The noun ὅραμα occurs 12 times in the New Testament and 11 of these occurrences are found in the book of Acts.[29] Luke is, indeed, fond of visions. Although in Acts 2:17 Luke retains the language of the LXX, elsewhere in his narrative he employs his preferred, very similar term, to speak of "visions."

As I have noted, references to visions are not only plentiful in

---

28. Note how Luke describes revelatory experiences at night, which might have taken place during sleep, as "visions" and not "dreams" (e.g. Acts 16:9-10).

29. Acts 7:31; 9:10, 12; 10:3, 17, 19; 11:5; 12:9; 16:9, 10; 18:9; and then also in Matt. 17:9.

Luke's narrative, they also come at strategic moments.[30] Thus, Luke's alteration at this point appears to be theologically motivated. Of course, visions are not the only way that God guides the church in the book of Acts. Yet Luke's point is hard to miss: By linking the "visions" of Joel's prophecy (Acts 2:17) with the visions of the early church, Luke is in effect saying that in "these last days" — that period inaugurated with Jesus' birth and leading up to the Day of the Lord — the mission of the church must be directed by God, who will lead his end-time prophets in special and personal ways, including visions, angelic visitations, and the prompting of the Spirit, so that we might fulfill our calling to take the gospel to "the ends of the earth." In short, for Luke, the experience of the early church, a church that is supernaturally led by God, serves as a model for his church (and ours).

Second, with the addition of a few words in verse 19, Luke transforms Joel's text to read: "I will show wonders in the heaven *above*, and *signs* on the earth *below*." In this way, Luke consciously links the miracles associated with Jesus (notice the very first verse that follows the quotation from Joel: "Jesus . . . was a man accredited by God to you by miracles, wonders and signs," Acts 2:22) and the early church (e.g., 2:43) together with the cosmic portents listed by Joel (Acts 2:19-20). All are "signs and wonders" that mark the end of the age. For Luke, "these last days" — remember, Luke's church and ours are firmly rooted in this period — represents an epoch marked by "signs and wonders." Luke, then, is not only conscious of the significant role that miracles have played in the growth of the early church, he also anticipates that these "signs and wonders" will continue to characterize the ministry of the church to whom he writes.

Third and most important for our purposes, Luke inserts the phrase "And they will prophesy" into the quotation in verse 18. This insertion simply emphasizes what is already present in the text of Joel. The previous verse has already reminded us that this end-time outpouring of the Spirit of which Joel prophesies is nothing less than a fulfillment of Moses' wish "that all the Lord's people were prophets" (Num. 11:29). Acts 2:17 quotes Joel 2:28 verbatim: "I will pour out my Spirit on all people. Your sons and daughters will prophesy." Now, in verse 18, Luke echoes this refrain. Luke highlights the fact that the

---

30. For the strategic role of visions in the narrative of Acts see: Acts 9:10-12; 10:3, 17, 19; 11:5; 16:9-10; 18:9-10.

Spirit comes as the source of prophetic inspiration because this theme will dominate his narrative. It is a message that Luke does not want his readers to miss. The church in "these last days," Luke declares, is to be a community of prophets — prophets who are called to bring the message of "salvation to the ends of the earth" (Isa. 49:6). And now Luke reminds his readers that they also have been promised power to fulfill this calling. The Spirit will come and enable his church — Luke's and ours — to bear bold witness for Jesus in the face of opposition and persecution.

This theme of bold, prophetic witness is anticipated in Luke's Gospel. Jesus is anointed with the Spirit so that he might "preach the good news to the poor," so that he might "proclaim freedom for the prisoners" and "proclaim the year of the Lord's favor" (Luke 4:18-19). The parallels between Jesus' experience at the Jordan and that of the disciples at Pentecost are striking and should not be missed. Both occur at the beginning of the respective missions of Jesus and the early church, both center on the coming of the Spirit, both are described as a prophetic anointing in the context of a sermon that cites Old Testament prophecy. Through his careful shaping of the narrative, Luke presents Jesus, the ultimate prophet, as a model for all of his followers, from Pentecost onward. Luke's church has a mission to carry out, a message to proclaim.

This motif of bold, Spirit-inspired witness is also highlighted in the teaching of Jesus. Luke foreshadows events that will follow in his second volume by relating the important promise of Jesus recorded in Luke 12:11-12: "When you are brought before synagogues, rulers and authorities, do not worry about how you will defend yourselves or what you will say, for the Holy Spirit will teach you at that time what you should say."

Immediately after Pentecost, in the first story Luke recounts, we begin to see how relevant and important this promise of Jesus is for the mission of the church. Luke describes the dramatic story of Peter and John's encounter with a crippled beggar and the beggar's miraculous healing. A large crowd gathers, gaping at this marvelous event. The story builds to a climax as the Jewish leaders arrest Peter and John for preaching about the resurrection of Jesus. "You killed the author of life," Peter declares, "but God raised him from the dead. We are witnesses of this" (Acts 3:15). The Jewish leaders, upset with this turn of events, move in and arrest Peter and John. After spending the night in prison, Peter and John are called before the leaders and questioned. Peter is filled with the Holy Spirit and begins to bear bold witness for Jesus (Acts 4:8). Peter and John's courage is so striking that it leaves the Jewish leaders astonished and amazed. Finally, after deliberations, the leaders command the apostles to stop preaching about Jesus. But Peter and John reply with incredible boldness. They declare, "Judge for yourselves whether it is right in God's sight to obey you rather than God. We cannot help speaking about what we have seen and heard" (Acts 4:19-20).

This is merely the beginning of the persecution the end-time prophets must face. Very soon the apostles are again arrested. The Jewish leaders interrogate the apostles and angrily declare, "We gave you strict orders not to teach in this name [the name of Jesus].... Yet you have filled Jerusalem with your teaching" (Acts 5:28). Peter and the apostles incur the wrath of their opponents when they declare, "We must obey God rather than men! The God of our fathers raised Jesus from the dead.... We are witnesses of these things, and so is the Holy Spirit" (Acts 5:29-32). The apostles are flogged and warned not to speak about Jesus. But the beatings do not have their desired effect. The apostles rejoice that they have been "counted worthy of suffering" for Jesus and continue to proclaim "the good news that Jesus is the Messiah" (Acts 5:41-42).

The persecution intensifies. What began with warnings in Acts 4 and led to beatings in Acts 5, now extends to Stephen's martyrdom in Acts 7. Just as the apostles were strengthened by the Spirit to bear bold witness for Jesus, so also Stephen's witness unto death is inspired by the Spirit (Acts 6:10). In the midst of his sermon to his persecutors recorded in Acts 7, Stephen declares, "You always resist the Holy Spirit! Was there ever a prophet your fathers did not persecute?" (Acts 7:51-52). The powerful irony should not be missed, for this same crowd moves to kill Stephen, a man "full of the Holy Spirit" (Acts 7:55).[31] The witness of another prophet is rejected.

This pattern of bold, Spirit-inspired witness in the face of opposition continues with Paul, the dominant character in the latter portion of Acts. Paul is chosen by the Lord to take the gospel to the Gentiles.

---

31. Karris notes that in Acts 7:55-56 the promises of Luke 6:22-23 and 12:8 are fulfilled and concludes: "Luke 6:22-23 and 12:8 are meant for the edification of Luke's persecuted and harassed readers" ("Missionary Communities," p. 95).

We are told that his journey will not be easy. The Lord, speaking to Ananias, declares, "I will show him how much he must suffer for my name" (Acts 9:16). And suffer he does. Yet, in the face of mind-numbing opposition, Paul is guided and strengthened by the Holy Spirit. A trail of churches filled with believers who worship Jesus are left in his wake. The narrative of Acts ends with Paul in prison in Rome, where he "boldly and without hindrance" preached about Jesus (Acts 28:31).

Luke's motive in presenting these models of Spirit-inspired ministry — Peter, John, Stephen, and Paul, to name a few — should not be missed. Luke has more in mind than simply declaring to his church, "This is how it all began!" Certainly Luke highlights the reliability of the apostolic witness to the resurrection of Jesus. And he wants to be sure that we are all clear about their message, which is to be handed on from generation to generation, people group to people group, until it reaches "the ends of the earth." Yet Luke also narrates the ministry of these end-time prophets because he sees them as important models of missionary praxis that his church needs to emulate. These characters in Acts demonstrate what it truly means to be a part of Joel's end-time prophetic band and thus challenge Luke's readers to fulfill their calling to be a light to the nations. As they face opposition by relying on the Holy Spirit, who enables them to bear bold witness for Jesus no matter what the cost, these end-time prophets call Luke's church to courageously follow the path first traveled by our Lord.

Some dismiss the notion that Luke intended his narrative to serve as a model for the mission of his church. They insist that Luke wrote to provide his contemporaries with a record of the beginnings of the church so that they would know that the message about Jesus is reliable and that the origins of the church were indeed a part of God's divine plan. With these purposes in mind, they insist that Pentecost is a unique event that can never be repeated. The Holy Spirit inspired the apostles for their special function as eyewitnesses to the ministry and resurrection of Jesus (Acts 1:21-22). So also the Lord validated this apostolic preaching with signs and wonders unique to the early church. Although we are called to faithfully pass on the apostolic message, the missionary methods of the apostolic church, we are told, are unique and not paradigmatic for later generations.[32]

---

32. See, for example, Ben Witherington III, *The Acts of the Apostles: A Socio-Rhetorical Commentary* (Grand Rapids: Eerdmans, 1998), p. 132; Darrell Bock, *Acts,* Baker Exegetical

Yet two aspects of Luke's narrative call us to challenge this reductionistic perspective. First, it should be noted that Joel's promise, amplified in Acts 2:18, "and they shall prophesy," characterizes potentially every member of the church — young and old, men and women — in the period described as "the last days." According to Luke this epoch begins with the miraculous birth of Jesus and extends until his second coming, the climax of God's redemptive plan. This promise of prophetic power is thus applicable to Luke's church (and ours), not simply the apostles.

Additionally, this conclusion is supported by the fact that Luke's description of Spirit-inspired prophetic witnesses is not limited solely to those who are apostles in the Acts 1 sense of the word (that is, those who were with Jesus during his ministry and witnessed his resurrection and ascension, Acts 1:21-22). Luke repeatedly describes how the Spirit comes upon the entire community of believers and not just the apostles, first at Pentecost and then in response to prayer in the face of persecution. The latter account explicitly states, "they were all filled with the Holy Spirit and spoke the word of God boldly" (Acts 4:31). Although Peter, John, and the rest of the Twelve bear witness for Jesus, so also do others who are not a part of the apostolic band. Stephen, Philip, and Paul — none of whom qualify as apostles according to Acts 1:21-22 — they are all anointed and directed by the Spirit to bear bold witness for Jesus.[33] Indeed, this is precisely the message that Luke pre-

---

Commentary on the New Testament (Grand Rapids: Baker, 2007), *passim* (cf. Darrell Bock, *Luke*, IVP New Testament Commentaries [Downers Grove: IVP, 1994], pp. 189-90); and Hacking, *Signs and Wonders, passim*. Witherington highlights the "unique" nature of the Pentecostal outpouring of the Spirit, and Bock also fails to develop the theological implications of Acts 1-2 for the missionary praxis of the contemporary church (see my review of Bock's Acts commentary in *Pneuma* 30 [2008]: 349-50). Hacking argues that the miracles of Jesus and the apostles were not intended to serve as models for the post-apostolic church and that the commissioning accounts are relevant only to a select few (see my review of Hacking's book in *EvQ* 79 [2007]: 261-65).

33. This conclusion is supported by Roger Stronstad's insightful study, *The Prophethood of All Believers: A Study in Luke's Charismatic Theology* (Sheffield: Sheffield Academic Press, 1999). For a dissenting perspective, see Max Turner's two articles, "Does Luke Believe Reception of the 'Spirit of Prophecy' Makes All 'Prophets'? Inviting Dialogue with Roger Stronstad," *JEPTA* 20 (2000): 3-24; and "Every Believer as a Witness in Acts? — In Dialogue with John Michael Penney," *ATJ* 30 (1998): 57-71. Turner argues that only a select group is empowered for prophetic witness. Yet I would suggest that his discussion fails to adequately account for the Lukan texts cited above.

pares his readers to receive with his account of the Sending of the Seventy (Luke 10:1-16), and it is the message that he dramatically highlights through his summary of Peter's sermon: "In the last days, God says, I will pour out my Spirit on all people . . . and they will prophesy" (Acts 2:17-18).

3. Conclusion

Luke crafted his narrative, and particularly Luke 10:1-16 and Acts 2:17-21, in order to challenge his church to consider the nature of their prophetic calling. The call, Luke declares, comes to every follower of Jesus, young and old, male and female. The call comes first to the Twelve, then to the Seventy, and finally at Pentecost to "all the Lord's people." It is a call to follow Jesus down difficult and dangerous roads. Like the prophets of old and the Prophet like Moses, those who take up the call will suffer. However, this is a part of God's triumphant plan. Furthermore, Luke urges his church to remember: the Holy Spirit will direct your path and grant you the strength that you need to render faithful witness. The Holy Spirit will enable you to fulfill your calling to be a light to the nations.

I believe that it is imperative for those of us that live in a stable and affluent West to reconsider Luke's call. This is the case because it is especially easy for us to rationalize away our relative lack of boldness and power. Persecution has a way of reorienting one's vision. Our lack of experience in this regard may serve to constrict our vision. One Chinese house church leader who was no stranger to persecution put it this way, "When Chinese believers read the book of Acts, we see in it our own experience; when foreign Christians read the book of Acts, they see in it inspiring stories." His point was clear: our experience of opposition and persecution, or our lack of it, impacts how we read Luke's narrative.[34] Luke did not intend for his narrative to be read simply as a historical account of inspiring stories. He desired that his readers would find in his narrative a paradigm for their lives and mission.[35]

---

34. Luke Wesley argues this thesis with reference to the Chinese church in his book *The Church in China: Persecuted, Pentecostal, and Powerful* (Baguio: AJPS Books, 2004).

35. Of course our context will, to a large degree, determine the extent and nature of the opposition or persecution that we as Christians experience. Nevertheless, the

Robert P. Menzies

Does Luke write to encourage a church facing persecution? Luke's narrative makes little sense if his original audience had no experience of persecution. Why would Luke define the prophetic vocation in terms of suffering and then declare to his readers that they are a community of prophets, if their own experience contradicted the message? Given Luke's obvious literary skills and the careful way that he has crafted his narrative, surely it is more logical to conclude that Luke writes to a community facing persecution.[36] He writes to offer a battered community guidance and encouragement, and countless witnesses through the ages will agree that he has accomplished this goal.

---

challenging message of Luke and other NT authors (cf. Mark 10:30; John 15:18–16:4; and 2 Tim. 3:12) regarding persecution cannot be ignored.

36. I am in agreement with Karris, who posits that Luke wrote shortly after the destruction of Jerusalem and its Temple (around 75 CE) and that he wrote to "communities whose missionary work and daily existence are prone to danger and suffering — both from Jew and Gentile, but primarily from the Jewish synagogal authorities" ("Missionary Communities," p. 96).

"Was It Not Necessary for the Messiah to Suffer These Things and Enter into His Glory?" The Significance of Jesus' Death for Luke's Soteriology

Joel B. Green

From the early days of redaction criticism, during which it can be said that Luke began to be appreciated as a theologian in his own right, up to and including literary and narratological approaches to Luke's narrative, scholars have recognized Luke's dearth of interest in the soteriological significance of Jesus' suffering and death. Writing at the onset of modern study of Luke, for example, Hans Conzelmann had summarized with respect to Luke's theology of Jesus' passion ". . . that there is no trace of any Passion mysticism, nor is any direct soteriological significance drawn from Jesus' suffering or death. There is no suggestion of a connection with the forgiveness of sins." He goes on to observe that, when Luke echoes Isaiah 53, ". . . he is not thinking of atonement and substitution." "It should be noted," he avers, "that the idea of the Cross plays no part in the proclamation. Even when Luke uses the word παραδιδόναι there is no trace of the idea of atonement." According to Conzelmann, the absence of the soteriological significance of Jesus' death determines Luke's account of Jesus' passion.[1] Ulrich Wilckens similarly found no immediate witness to the saving significance of Jesus' death in the missionary sermons in the Acts of the Apostles — thus echoing the earlier view of C. H. Dodd, based on the early chapters of Acts, that "the Jerusalem *kerygma* does not assert that Christ died *for our sins*."[2] Turning the clock forward, Joseph B.

---

1. Hans Conzelmann, *The Theology of St Luke* (London: SCM Press, 1960), p. 201.
2. C. H. Dodd, *The Apostolic Preaching and Its Developments: With an Appendix on Eschatology and History* (London: Hodder & Stoughton, 1936; repr. Grand Rapids: Baker,

Joel B. Green

Tyson wrote in the first major literary-critical study of Luke's presentation of Jesus' death, "The conviction of divine necessity constitutes Luke's main contribution to the theological discussion of Jesus' death. But he seems uninterested in piercing through to an understanding of the theological reason for the death or in analyzing what it was intended to accomplish. The benefits of forgiveness of sins and the Spirit are more closely connected with the resurrection than the death."[3] These testimonies could easily be multiplied, but none would speak with more authority than the ever-prescient Henry J. Cadbury. In his magisterial work, *The Making of Luke-Acts,* he observed Luke's omission of "all references to vicarious death" and claimed that Luke's dependence on Isaiah 53 does not prove that Luke interpreted Jesus' death in substitutionary terms borrowed from Isaiah; indeed, Luke's use of Isaiah 53 noticeably bypasses all of the latter's "'vicarious' phrases."[4]

Although Conzelmann's view is pervasive in Lukan scholarship, it is not universal. Indeed, it is worth reflecting on the degree to which the terms for the discussion have often been set by Mark or by Paul, with the result that, actually, scholars have sometimes affirmed little more than that Luke's theology is not like Mark's or Paul's. "It is without doubt a serious failing that Luke does not take up the Pauline theology of the cross . . . ," wrote Martin Hengel in 1979, exemplifying the problem.[5] Indeed, Werner Georg Kümmel had already warned against using Paul as the canon against which to measure Luke: "Thus from its beginnings it has been characteristic of the redaction-critical investigation of Luke's theology that the description of this theology has been accompanied by a sharp criticism based primarily on comparison with Paul."[6] (On the other hand, given his tendency to read the whole of the New Testament through a Pauline lens, at least with regard to the

---

1980), p. 25; cf. Ulrich Wilckens, *Die Missionsreden der Apostelgeschichte: Form- und traditionsgeschichtliche Untersuchungen,* 3rd ed. (Neukirchen-Vluyn: Neukirchener Verlag, 1974), p. 185.

3. Joseph B. Tyson, *The Death of Jesus in Luke-Acts* (Columbia: University of South Carolina Press, 1986), p. 170.

4. Henry J. Cadbury, *The Making of Luke-Acts,* with a new introduction by Paul N. Anderson, 2nd ed. (Peabody: Hendrickson, 1999), pp. 280-81.

5. Martin Hengel, *Acts and the History of Earliest Christianity* (London: SCM Press, 1979), p. 67.

6. Werner Georg Kümmel, "Current Theological Accusations against Luke," *ANQ* 16 (1975): 131-45, at p. 132.

atonement, it is not surprising that a scholar like Leon Morris would find substitutionary atonement lurking in the shadows of Luke's witness to the kerygma.)[7]

In fact, attempts to read Luke on his own terms have in some cases led scholars to identify a particularly Lukan atonement theology. Given the state of the discussion after Conzelmann, for example, the title of Richard Zehnle's study from 1969 must have seemed provocative: "The Salvific Character of Jesus' Death in Lucan Soteriology."[8] Zehnle refers to attempts to void Jesus' death of soteriological value in Luke-Acts as "serious accusations."[9] He is able to do so, however, only by adopting a more nuanced vocabulary. Agreeing with previous scholarship that Luke has no "doctrine of satisfaction," Zehnle does not regard this as a wholesale denial of the soteriological significance of Jesus' death for Luke. Instead, for Zehnle, we must understand Jesus' movement from life to death, from death to resurrection, and from resurrection to ascension and glorification as a complex of events — events that find their full meaning only in relation to the whole. This allows him to speak of the relationship between Jesus' death and human salvation in terms of formal or exemplary causality rather than in terms of efficient causality. Accordingly, Jesus' death for Luke is part of a life-death-resurrection-ascension composite that demonstrates God's favor toward humanity and motivates people to trust in him.

Whatever one makes of Zehnle's analysis, it has clearly paved the way for others to let Luke be Luke, rather than to find his theological perspective lacking when measured against a predetermined (especially Pauline) perspective on the atonement. These have been helpfully surveyed by Hermie C. van Zyl, who aptly observes that, in recent scholarship, the Lukan writings have been scrutinized more with the view of a positive valuation of the soteriological meaning of Jesus' death.[10] Taking a different route George Heider has recently reminded us to think of a plurality of atonement models not only in the Christian

---

7. E.g., Leon Morris, *The Cross in the New Testament* (Grand Rapids: Eerdmans, 1965), pp. 63-143; cf. George Eldon Ladd, *A Theology of the New Testament* (Grand Rapids: Eerdmans, 1974), p. 330.

8. Richard Zehnle, "The Salvific Character of Jesus' Death in Lucan Soteriology," *TS* 30 (1969): 420-44.

9. Zehnle, "Salvific Character," p. 220.

10. Hermie C. van Zyl, "The Soteriological Meaning of Jesus' Death in Luke-Acts: A Survey of Possibilities," *Verbum et Ecclesia* 23 (2002): 533-57.

theological tradition, not only in the New Testament, but among the Gospels themselves.[11] Following Heider, then, we might ask whether the problem of locating a theology of atonement in Luke-Acts is grounded less in the Lukan narrative itself and more in the definition of atonement one brings to the task. When "atonement" is defined in sacrificial terms, such as are prominent in the Pauline writings, then we might find that evidence for atonement theology in Luke-Acts is not altogether lacking, but it is markedly sparse. For Heider, however, each of the New Testament Gospels bears witness to a different atonement model:

- Gospel of Matthew — Objective Atonement
- Gospel of Mark — At-one-ment in Baptism
- Gospel of Luke — Subjective Atonement
- Gospel of John — Christus Victor

This is not to say that Heider reduces the witness of each Gospel to these four models, but he does regard them as characteristic of each. Heider's claims are more suggestive than exegetically documented, but it is nonetheless clear that he has helped to turn attention appropriately on a Lukan atonement theology. And it is striking that his characterization of Luke's atonement theology in terms of "subjective atonement" coheres with Zehnle's analysis.

1. Salvation and Jesus' Exaltation

One of the largely underdeveloped questions in discussions of atonement theology, whether those discussions are related to Luke or Paul or some other New Testament writer, has been the meaning of salvation itself. This is likely due to prior assumptions about the doctrine of salvation, regarding which the New Testament author is then required to speak. For example, if one were to adopt a view of salvation that coheres with modern understandings of the human self, then one might think primarily in spiritual and individualistic terms.[12] Accordingly,

---

11. George C. Heider, "Atonement and the Gospels," *JTI* 2 (2008): 259-73.
12. I base this example on the analysis of Charles Taylor, *Sources of the Self: The Making of the Modern Identity* (Cambridge, MA: Harvard University Press, 1989).

the question for us would be how best to articulate the means by which people are saved in just these terms. However, this is not a particularly Lukan approach to the soteriological question.

In the New Testament, the language of salvation congregates especially in Luke-Acts, where it pervades both the Third Gospel and the Acts of the Apostles. The hymns of Luke's infancy narrative set the terms for what will follow especially with regard to transformations in human social interaction grounded in the gracious intervention of God. Salvation would be realized in the coming of status transposition, liberation from Israel's enemies in order to worship God, and the actualization of God's promise to Abraham regarding all peoples (Jew and Gentile) — that is, in the eschatological restoration of God's people. God's saving activity is realized in the person and ministry of Jesus of Nazareth, who raises up the lowly, restores persons to full health, and calls everyone to embody God's good news. Salvation is then the work of God the almighty and compassionate one who summons and liberates his people, calling them to align themselves with his restorative purpose; Jesus' advent, then, is nothing less than the revelation of God's royal rule and, then, the exposure and fall of those powers that stand against God's kingdom. For Luke's Gospel, salvation is social and concrete — healing, exorcism, restoration, cleansing, and more — resisting dichotomies like social versus individual, material versus spiritual. This vision is not lost in the book of Acts. Instead, images of salvation and restoration swirl around two expressions of salvation, both of which are synecdoches for salvation. The first of these is *forgiveness of sins* and the second is the *reception of the Holy Spirit*. Importantly, in Second Temple Jewish literature and in Luke-Acts, both forgiveness of sins and the reception of the Spirit signify Israel's restoration. For Luke-Acts, moreover, forgiveness of sins and the outpouring of the Spirit have as their sequel the multi-ethnic community of Christ-followers known for prayer, economic *koinonia,* witness, and mission.

How does Luke develop in his narrative the means by which salvation, understood in these terms, is realized? According to three texts in the Acts of the Apostles, this salvation is poured out or given by Jesus on account of his resurrection and ascension — that is, on account of his exaltation to the right hand of God. The first is the Pentecost speech in Acts 2. Luke portrays the outpouring of the Holy Spirit, leading eventually to the question of the gathered crowds, "What does this mean?" Peter replies in terms of the expected era of salvation sketched in Joel 2:28-

32, which he interprets in relation to Psalms 16 and 110. First, he insists that what has happened on this day of Pentecost (Acts 2:1-13) is nothing less than the fresh work of the Holy Spirit, poured out in fulfillment of Joel's promise of restoration. Second, he urges that the phenomena recounted in Acts 2:1-13 testify, together with the Psalms and the followers of Jesus, that Jesus has divine prerogatives so that he is able to dispense the blessings of salvation, the gift of the Holy Spirit being chief among these. Finally, Peter claims, these events comprise the onset of "the last days," which are marked by the universal offer of salvation and threat of judgment, so that all are called to contrition and repentance. For the present discussion, the central point in Peter's logic is pivotal. Borrowing words from the prophet Joel, he proclaims that "all who call on the name of the Lord will be saved." Who is this "Lord"? For Joel, of course, the Lord is YHWH, Israel's God. For Peter, however, Jesus' exaltation to God's right hand proves that "God has made him both Lord and Christ, this Jesus whom you yourselves crucified" (2:36). Raised up, the Lord Jesus now serves as coregent with God and in this capacity administers the Father's promise, the gift of the Spirit.

In the ensuing narrative, Luke cultivates further the soteriological ramifications of this association of Jesus' acclamation as Lord with his exaltation. Thus, in Acts 3, Luke reports that Peter rehearses the theological significance of Jesus' resurrection in order to attribute the "complete health" of the man born lame to the potency of "the name" (3:13-16). A few verses later, Luke summarizes the content of Peter's speech with the phrase, "proclaiming in Jesus the resurrection of the dead" (4:2). And in Acts 4:11-12, a statement regarding God's vindication of Jesus (that is, Jesus' resurrection; see 4:10) prepares for the declaration of the universal significance of Jesus' name for salvation. This association of salvation with resurrection is not at all surprising, given the intimate association in Israel's Scriptures and Second Temple Judaism of "resurrection" with a larger complex of motifs: the restoration of Israel, including Israel's triumph over its enemies (and thus Israel's experience of conclusive and end-time salvation), God's vindication of the righteous who have suffered unjustly, and the decisive establishment of divine justice.[13] Indeed, Peter's speech in Solomon's Portico

---

13. For background, see Kevin L. Anderson, *"But God Raised Him from the Dead": The Theology of Jesus' Resurrection in Luke-Acts* (Milton Keynes: Paternoster, 2006), pp. 48-91; and the summary in Richard Bauckham, "Life, Death, and the Afterlife in Second

"Was It Not Necessary for the Messiah to Suffer These Things?"

(3:12-26) is centrally concerned to assert that, with the resurrection of Jesus, the restoration of Israel is presently underway, with the healing of the lame beggar a case exhibit.

We find a second affirmation of the soteriological significance of Jesus' exaltation in Peter's speech to the Jerusalem council in 5:30-31: "The God of our ancestors raised up Jesus.... God exalted him at his right hand as Leader and Savior, to give repentance to Israel and the forgiveness of sins." This is a straightforward assertion that Jesus' exaltation has as its consequence his confirmation as Savior and that it is as Savior that he "gives" repentance and forgiveness of sins. As the gift of the Holy Spirit represented the whole of salvation in Acts 2, so here repentance and forgiveness of sins do the same.

Finally, in the midst of his preaching at Cornelius's residence, Peter proclaims, "All the prophets testify about him that everyone who believes in him receives forgiveness of sins through his name" (10:43). Again, forgiveness of sins is a synecdoche for salvation. The logic of Peter's claim depends on our recognizing the ramifications of Jesus' resurrection and ascension. The prophets (like the Old Testament as a whole) do proclaim the forgiveness of sins but identify the Lord, Israel's God, as the one who offers pardon. How is it that prophetic testimony concerning YHWH is transferred to Jesus? The answer can only be that, according to the view that pervades the book of Acts, Jesus is Lord on account of his exaltation. And as Lord, Jesus possesses the divine prerogative to administer the benefits of salvation, here represented as forgiveness of sins.

Here, then, are three clear affirmations that Luke's soteriology is grounded in Jesus' exaltation. What, then, of Jesus' death? The sheer frequency of times that we read in Luke-Acts of the divine necessity of the suffering and death of Jesus the Messiah is warning enough that salvation has not come in spite of the crucifixion. Can more be said?

2. Salvation and Jesus' Death

Students of Luke-Acts have tended to draw attention to three points in order to support their claim that Luke does not hold to a soteriological

---

Temple Judaism," in *Life in the Face of Death: The Resurrection Message of the New Testament*, ed. Richard N. Longenecker (Grand Rapids: Eerdmans, 1998), pp. 80-95.

interpretation of the significance of Jesus' death. (1) Redaction critics have long noted that, in his use of Mark's Gospel, Luke does not replicate the ransom-saying found in Mark 10:45. Accordingly, the Third Evangelist excludes this most explicit witness to the atoning death of Jesus. (2) The sermons in Acts highlight the salvation-historical necessity of Jesus' death, but seem more interested in the *that* of Jesus' crucifixion than in the *why*. In particular, they draw no immediate connection from the cross to the offer of salvation. (3) Although Luke is heavily dependent in his Christology on Isaianic texts concerned with the Servant of YHWH (including Isa. 52:13–53:12; cf., e.g., Luke 22:37; Acts 8:32-33), no Lukan text draws on any Isaianic text concerned explicitly with the vicarious, atoning significance of the Servant's suffering.

At the same time, two Lukan texts point clearly to Luke's awareness of an interpretation of Jesus' death in soteriological terms, suggesting that Luke has placed "his stamp of approval"[14] on the sort of atonement theology we find in Mark's Gospel or in Paul. Even if it remains true that Luke has done little in his narrative to develop or expound this kind of atonement theology, the presence of these two texts nonetheless undermines scholarly hyperbole regarding Luke's alleged rejection of such references. First, the words of Jesus at the Last Supper, in Luke 22:19-20, speak to the atoning significance of Jesus' death:

> Then he took a loaf of bread, and when he had given thanks, he broke it and gave it to them, saying, "This is my body, which is given for you. Do this in remembrance of me." And he did the same with the cup after supper, saying, "This cup that is poured out for you is the new covenant in my blood."

As is well known, however, 22:19b-20 — and thus those parts of the Eucharistic tradition identifying Jesus' death "for you" and developing its significance in relation to the "new covenant in my blood" — is missing in a minority of textual witnesses; additionally, the language of 22:19b-20 is uncharacteristic of Lukan usage.[15] Consequently, some in-

---

14. This phrase is borrowed from Reginald H. Fuller, "Luke and the Theologia Crucis," in *Sin, Salvation and the Spirit: Commemorating the Fiftieth Year of The Liturgical Press*, ed. Daniel Durken (Collegeville: Liturgical Press, 1979), pp. 214-20, esp. p. 219.

15. Cf., e.g., Joachim Jeremias, *The Eucharistic Words of Jesus* (Philadelphia: Fortress Press, 1966), pp. 154-55; Joachim Jeremias, *Die Sprache des Lukasevangeliums: Redaction und Tradition im Nicht-Markusstoff des dritten Evangeliums* (Göttingen: Vandenhoeck &

terpreters have argued against their originality.[16] This is now very much a minority opinion, however, even if it remains the case that Luke has done little to draw this way of reflecting on Jesus' death into his theology more fully. Indeed, altogether missing from the narrative of Acts is any reference such as we find in 1 Corinthians 11:17-34 to the use of Jesus' Eucharistic words or reflection on the salvific import of Jesus' death in the context of community meals.

The atoning death of Jesus is also apparent in Acts 20:28. In the context of Paul's farewell speech to the Ephesian elders we find a troubled text the sense of which is not straightforward — as a quick comparison of different translations might illustrate.[17] Does Paul refer to "the church of the Lord" or "the church of God"? Is that church purchased with "his own blood" or with "the blood of his own"? If "the blood of his own," then is this a reference to Jesus? To Paul himself? The difficulty here is that a plain reading of the text would have Paul affirming that God purchased the church with his (God's!) own blood — a theological infelicity addressed by ancient scribes and contemporary translators alike. After all, stated in this way, this expression would be without precedent or analogy in any other biblical text. Not surprisingly, then, Eduard Schweizer once observed that "[Luke] quotes this phrase as if it were some foreign language."[18]

In the end, the sense of this text in Acts is most likely to be something like the rendering we find in the NRSV: "Keep watch over yourselves and over all the flock, of which the Holy Spirit has made you overseers, to shepherd the church of God that he obtained with the blood of his own Son." Although Acts 20:28 uses a term not otherwise used in this sense in the New Testament, περιποιέω, we do find references elsewhere to God's acquiring (e.g., Eph. 1:14; 1 Pet. 2:9-10) or "purchasing" (1 Cor. 6:20; 7:23; cf. 2 Pet. 2:1) a people. These few words in Acts

---

Ruprecht, 1980), pp. 287-88 (the text "ist völlig frei von Lukanismen" [p. 287]); G. D. Kilpatrick, *The Eucharist in Bible and Liturgy* (Cambridge: Cambridge University Press, 1983), pp. 31-32.

16. See, e.g., Kilpatrick, *Eucharist*, pp. 28-42.

17. I say "troubling" because of variant renderings and stylistic/theological ambiguity. See the helpful discussion in Steve Walton, *Leadership and Lifestyle: The Portrait of Paul in the Miletus Speech and 1 Thessalonians* (Cambridge: Cambridge University Press, 2000), pp. 94-98.

18. Eduard Schweizer, *Luke: A Challenge to Present Theology* (London: SPCK, 1982), p. 45.

Joel B. Green

20:28 provide little sure ground on which to construct a full-blown atonement theology, but the metaphor Paul uses seems to turn on an economic exchange rooted in Jesus' sacrificial death.

3. Jesus and Isaiah's Servant

More promising for making sense of the salvation-historical necessity of Jesus' death is Luke's dependence on material in Isaiah related to the Servant of Yhwh. In fact, some have urged that, given the importance of the portrait of Isaiah's suffering servant for Luke's Christology, room must be made within his soteriology for the substitutionary suffering of Yhwh's Servant.[19] In spite of claims about what "must" have been in Luke's mind as he drew on Isaiah 53 in such Christological statements as we find in Luke 22:37 and Acts 8:32-33, however, it is hard to escape the reality that the material from Isaiah that makes explicit the servant's substitutionary death (see Isa. 53:4, 5, 6b, 10b, 11b, 12) is altogether missing in Luke.[20] Cadbury was right to observe, as we saw earlier, that Luke noticeably circumvents all of the "'vicarious' phrases" in Isaiah 53.

It may be that the theological utility of Luke's dependence on Isaiah's portrait of the Servant of the Lord lies elsewhere. Rather than turning our focus on substitutionary models of the atonement, Luke's

---

19. Recently, e.g., David Peterson, "Atonement Theology in Luke-Acts: Some Methodological Reflections," in *The New Testament in Its First Century Setting: Essays on Context and Background in Honour of B. W. Winter on His 65th Birthday*, ed. P. J. Williams et al. (Grand Rapids: Eerdmans, 2004), pp. 56-71; Hermie C. van Zyl, "The Soteriology of Acts: Restoration to Life," in *Salvation in the New Testament: Perspectives on Soteriology*, ed. Jan G. van der Watt (Leiden: Brill, 2005), pp. 133-60; Ulrike Mittmann-Richert, *Der Sühnetod des Gottesknechts: Jesaja 53 im Lukasevangelium* (Tübingen: Mohr Siebeck, 2008).

20. On the one hand, then, one might wish to argue that Luke's ample dependence on Isa. 52:13–53:12 draws into Luke's narrative theology this emphasis on substitutionary atonement. On the other hand, though, it is hard to understand (1) why Luke can draw on Isa. 52:13–53:12 repeatedly and explicitly without using Isaiah's substitutionary phraseology, (2) why Luke can emphasize the necessity of Jesus' passion repeatedly and explicitly without drawing on Isaiah's wording, and (3) why, when Luke does identify in unmistakable terms a salvific event, he does so with reference to Jesus' exaltation rather than to Jesus' substitutionary death. As I have already argued, it is not that Luke voids his narrative of all references to the substitutionary death of Jesus, but rather that we have no firm basis to argue that we find further evidence for the substitutionary death of Jesus in Luke's references to the Isaianic Servant.

use of Isaiah's Servant helps us to hold together what, for Luke, must not be pulled apart. It is precisely the collocation of Jesus' life, death, and exaltation that funds for Luke a robust soteriology — and Luke interprets Jesus' career thus imagined in Isaianic terms.

It is easy enough to urge that, for Luke, the character of Jesus' death must be grasped in relation to the character of his life.[21] That is, the crucifixion of Jesus on a Roman cross cannot for Luke be understood apart from the wider context of the narrative of Luke-Acts. Jesus is brought before Pilate as one whose life and ministry stood in opposition to the Roman empire. Jesus came to save, it is true, but this is worked out in purpose statements like these: "to bring good news to the poor" (Luke 4:18), "to proclaim the good news of the kingdom of God in the other cities" (4:43), "to call . . . sinners to repentance" (5:32), and "to seek and to save the lost" (19:10). Jesus' life thus oriented leads eventually to a series of charges brought against him: "We found this man perverting our nation, forbidding us to pay taxes to the emperor, and saying that he himself is the Messiah, a king" (23:2); "He stirs up the people by teaching throughout all Judea, from Galilee where he began even to this place" (23:5); and "You brought me this man as one who was perverting the people" (23:14). And these allegations, especially the claim that Jesus "perverts our nation/the people" (vv. 2, 14), dovetail well with the case put forward by Graham Stanton and August Strobel, that Jesus had to be eliminated as a religious deceiver and false prophet.[22] That is, reference to "perverting" would not only draw the attention of a Roman proconsul concerned with keeping the peace, but would also constitute a formal allegation against Jesus as a false prophet, rooted in Deuteronomy 13 and 18.[23] In other words, the cruci-

---

21. Cf. Stephen J. Patterson, *Beyond the Passion: Rethinking the Death and Life of Jesus* (Minneapolis: Fortress Press, 2004). Patterson's basic concern with interpreting Jesus' death "as an inevitable part of his life, and end fitting of the kind of life Jesus lived" (p. 123) stands in spite of his skepticism regarding the historical veracity of the Gospels and his too-easy rejection of the potential of some atonement theologies to aid our understanding of Jesus' passion.

22. Graham N. Stanton, "Jesus of Nazareth: A Magician and a False Prophet Who Deceived God's People?" in *Jesus of Nazareth: Lord and Christ: Essays on the Historical Jesus and New Testament Christology*, ed. Joel B. Green and Max Turner (Grand Rapids: Eerdmans, 1995), pp. 164-80; August Strobel, *Die Stunde der Wahrheit: Untersuchungen zum Strafverfahren gegen Jesus* (Tübingen: Mohr Siebeck, 1980).

23. In fact, using the same verb (διαστρέφω), Luke recounts in Acts 13:6-8 that "a Jewish false prophet . . . tried to turn the proconsul away from the faith."

fixion of Jesus points in Luke's Gospel to the nature of Jesus' life as a life of faithfulness to his mission in the service of God's kingdom and, thus, as a life of resistance to alternative kingdoms.

Similarly, one of the key features of Luke's presentation of Jesus' life and death in the missionary speeches of Acts is the contrast between the character of God's affirmation of Jesus and the rejection of Jesus by those responsible for his crucifixion. The first of several examples appears in Peter's address at Pentecost: "Jesus of Nazareth, a man attested to you by God with deeds of power, wonders, and signs that God did through him among you, as you yourselves know — this man, handed over to you according to the definite plan and foreknowledge of God, you crucified and killed by the hands of those outside the law" (Acts 2:22-23; cf., e.g., 3:13-15; 4:10-12; 13:23-29). That is, the character of Jesus' death for Luke is inseparable from the character of his fidelity to God. Even if we might put the emphasis somewhat differently, then, there is some truth to what must be one of the most-quoted footnotes in the history of scholarly study of Jesus' death: "To state the matter somewhat provocatively, one could call the Gospels passion narratives with extended introductions."[24] Martin Kähler penned these words more than a century ago (1896) in order to emphasize the concern of the Gospels with the nature of Jesus' ministry rather than his self-consciousness. Luke 1–21 is hardly an "introduction," of course, but it remains that the chapters set the stage and the conditions for understanding the significance of Jesus' death in chapters 22–23.

The claim that the resurrection and ascension — that is, the exaltation — of Jesus is well-integrated theologically into Luke's portrayal of the significance of Jesus' death is also easily observed. Jesus' own words on the road to Emmaus locate the Messiah's suffering and death together with the Messiah's entering into his glory under a singular heading of divine necessity: "Was it not necessary that the Messiah should suffer these things and then enter into his glory?" (Luke 24:26). The correlation of messianic suffering and messianic glory, we are then informed, is what Israel's Scriptures teach (24:27; cf. 24:46). The same can be said of Jesus' prediction of his passion and resurrection toward the end of Luke's journey narrative in Luke 19:31-33. Moreover, the contrast-formula to which I pointed earlier — God's affirmation of Je-

---

24. Martin Kähler, *The So-Called Historical Jesus and the Historic Biblical Christ* (Philadelphia: Fortress Press, 1964), p. 80 n. 11.

sus' ministry versus the rejection of Jesus by those responsible for his death — continues with God's validation of Jesus: God affirmed Jesus' credentials, the Jerusalem leadership rejected Jesus and had him killed, and God raised him up (e.g. Acts 2:22-24; 3:13-15).

What is critical to observe at this juncture is the correlation of Luke's soteriology, understood in terms of status transposition, with the path of Jesus' career, from humiliation to exaltation, and the correlation of both of these with Luke's interest in Isaiah's Servant of YHWH. Let me document briefly this last interest.[25] First, Luke draws on Isaiah's Servant as he sketches the universal ramifications of Jesus' salvific mission. Jesus, according to Simeon, was to be "a light for revelation to the Gentiles" (Luke 2:32; Isa. 49:6). Moreover, at Jesus' passing he is declared the Righteous One (Luke 23:47) by a Gentile — an allusion to Isaiah 53:11.[26] Note the related collocation of "righteous" with Jesus' passion in Acts 3:13-14, where Jesus' death and exaltation are developed in relation to Isaiah 52:13–53:12:

Acts 3	Isaiah 52:13–53:12
v. 13	52:13
ὁ θεὸς . . . ἐδόξασεν τὸν παῖδα αὐτοῦ ("God . . . has glorified his servant")	ὁ παῖς μου . . . δοξασθήσεται ("my servant will be glorified")
v. 13	53:6
ὃν ὑμεῖς μὲν παρεδώκατε ("whom you handed over")	παρέδωκεν αὐτόν ("he handed him over")
	53:12
	παρεδόθη [2x] ("he was handed over")
v. 14	53:11
τὸν . . . δίκαιον ("the righteous one")	δίκαιον ("righteous one")

Second, Luke identifies Jesus in his passion with the Suffering Servant. Thus, Jesus cites Isaiah 53:12 as a general allusion to his suffering and

---

25. More fully, cf. Joel B. Green, "The Death of Jesus, God's Servant," in *Reimaging the Death of the Lukan Jesus,* ed. Dennis D. Sylva (Frankfurt: Anton Hain, 1990), pp. 1-28 and 170-73.

26. Cf. Robert J. Karris, "Luke 23:47 and the Lucan View of Jesus' Death," *JBL* 105 (1986): 65-74.

death (Luke 22:37). As we have just seen, Jesus is declared "righteous" in relation to his suffering and death in Luke 23:47, a note sounded even more clearly in Acts 3. Moreover, Jesus refuses to speak in his own defense (Luke 23:9; cf. Isa 53:7) and is mocked in the language of Isaiah 42:1: "the Chosen One" (Luke 23:35). Third, outside Luke's passion account we find other references to the Servant, not least in the citation of Isaiah 53:7-8 in Acts 8:32-33.

If, as has been repeatedly observed, Luke's use of Isaiah 52:13–53:12 not only fails to draw out the substitutionary nature of the Servant's demise in relation to Jesus but actually bypasses every indication of such an interpretation we might draw from the Isaianic text, then the question remains what soteriological significance Luke's use of Isaiah's Servant might have. At last we have in place the elements that allow us to speak of Luke's emphasis on the salvation-historical necessity of the cross at the same time that we highlight Jesus' exaltation as the grounds of the offer of salvation. The Isaianic portrait of the Suffering Servant holds in tandem these two motifs, suffering and vindication. We read this particularly in Isaiah 53:11 where, following his death, "my righteous servant will justify many." Taking this interpretive path, Luke shows the necessity of Jesus' death as the Servant of the Lord who, through his being raised up, brings salvation — and he demonstrates this without depending on an interpretation of the Servant's or Jesus' suffering as a substitutionary sacrifice. In his fidelity to his mission, Jesus, by embracing the career of the Servant, both exemplifies the way of salvation for those who would come after him and opens the way of repentance, forgiveness, and Spirit-endowed life and mission. In his suffering and exaltation, Jesus embodied the fullness of salvation interpreted as status reversal; rejecting self-glorification, he embraced humiliation and was exalted by God. Though anointed by God, though righteous before God, he is rejected by people. Rejected by people, he is raised up by God — and with him those who occupy society's margins are also raised up. Accordingly, Jesus' death and resurrection, read together, are exemplary and effective.

4. Conclusion

In the end, two scholarly impulses related to Luke's soteriology are problematic. The first denies any interest in the substitutionary death of Jesus on the part of Luke. To the contrary, in Luke 22:19-20 and Acts 20:28, the third evangelist has at the very least allowed to stand in his narrative two references to Jesus' substitutionary death. These data cannot be overlooked even when it is admitted that Luke has not also recounted the ransom-saying we find in Mark 10:45/Matthew 20:28 nor developed this model of the atonement in the sermons and addresses recounted in Acts. The second scholarly impulse attempts to find evidence for the substitutionary death of Jesus in Luke's dependence on the Isaianic Servant. To the contrary, in spite of the ample number of possible phrases in Isaiah 53 from which Luke might have borrowed, he has failed to signal in any way that he was drawn theologically to Isaiah 53 for its understanding of vicarious suffering as the grounds of salvation.

The way forward for those interested in exploring the nature of the soteriological significance of Jesus' death in Luke-Acts is not thereby barricaded, however. To the contrary, I have drawn from a number of Lukan emphases to paint with broad strokes an understanding of Jesus' death, correlated with his exaltation, that does draw on Isaiah's Servant. In doing so, I have tried to take seriously some of the indications the evangelist himself has provided in understanding the career of Jesus in messianic terms shaped by the humiliation and exaltation of the servant. No doubt, Luke's narrative invites discussion of other models of the atonement as well.[27] The important question is what we find as we teach ourselves to explore in Luke's narrative models of the atonement that are not predetermined by Markan or Pauline categories.

---

27. E.g., I have briefly sketched a Lukan understanding of atonement as revelation in Joel B. Green, "A Kaleidoscopic View," in *The Nature of the Atonement: Four Views*, ed. James K. Beilby and Paul R. Eddy (Downers Grove: IVP, 2006), pp. 157-85. See further, e.g., Zehnle, "Salvific Character"; Heider, "Atonement and the Gospels."

The Giving of the Spirit in John 19–20: Another Round

Cornelis Bennema

1. Introduction

John 20:22 is a notorious conundrum in Johannine scholarship. Although it is undisputed that 20:22 records a giving of the Spirit, the precise nature of the gift remains debated. The relation, if any, between the Johannine account of the giving of the Spirit and Luke's record of it at Pentecost in Acts 2 is also unclear. I present the thesis that the giving of the Spirit is a three-stage *process* in step with the process of Jesus' glorification, whereby the two conditions for the reception of the Spirit are fulfilled on different occasions.[1] My argument unfolds as follows. I shall first show that the two conditions for the giving of the Spirit represent different requirements, creating the possibility that the giving of the Spirit is a process rather than a singular event (section 2). Pursuing this possibility, I identify two occasions that refer to a possible giving of the Spirit apart from 20:22, namely 19:30 and 19:34 (section 3). I then examine the nature of the giving of the Spirit in 20:22 (section 4), and conclude by relating the Johannine and Lukan accounts, arguing that John envisaged a three-stage process of the giving of the Spirit (section 5).

Before embarking on this task, I must explain why this is "another round." In the mid-90s, I was keen to research the topic of the

---

[1]. I use the term "conditions" in relation to the reception or giving of the Spirit to speak of the order of events that God has determined (as John perceives it) rather than the things that human beings must do or be.

Spirit under Professor Max Turner. Initially, I meant to examine the Spirit in Luke-Acts. Max responded by giving me a stack of papers that would be his monumental write-up on the Lukan Spirit.[2] While reading this fascinating work, I realized that I would be unable to contribute any further thoughts on the subject. At Max's suggestion, I then began studying the salvific role of the Spirit in John's Gospel.[3] One of the by-products of my doctoral research was an article, published in 2002, on the giving of the Spirit in John 20:22.[4] I presented the following argument:

1. The giving of the Spirit is a process related to the process of Jesus' glorification. The Spirit is given symbolically at the cross (19:30), as the Spirit of salvation in 20:22, and as Paraclete at a later time (e.g. Pentecost).
2. The nature of the gift in 20:22 is that the disciples receive a new relationship with the Spirit that secures and sustains their salvation.
3. The two eschatological conditions for the giving of the Spirit, mentioned in 7:39 and 16:7, are fulfilled on two different occasions in this process.
4. This process of the giving of the Spirit was unique for the disciples and is not paradigmatic for Spirit-reception today.

For this view, I was indebted mainly to two scholars. In 1974, Felix Porsch provided the insight that, in step with the process of Jesus' glorification, the giving of the Spirit already started at the cross (19:30) and culminated in 20:22.[5] Then, in 1996, Max Turner produced his influential work on the Spirit in the New Testament, with an entire chap-

---

2. Max Turner, *Power from on High: The Spirit in Israel's Restoration and Witness in Luke-Acts* (Sheffield: Sheffield Academic Press, 1996).

3. Cornelis Bennema, *The Power of Saving Wisdom: An Investigation of Spirit and Wisdom in Relation to the Soteriology of the Fourth Gospel* (Tübingen: Mohr Siebeck, 2002; repr., Eugene: Wipf & Stock, 2007).

4. Cornelis Bennema, "The Giving of the Spirit in John's Gospel — A New Proposal?," *EvQ* 74 (2002): 195-213.

5. Felix Porsch, *Pneuma und Wort: Ein exegetischer Beitrag zur Pneumatologie des Johannesevangeliums* (Frankfurt: Knecht, 1974), pp. 72-81, 330-40, 374-78. Porsch's own solution that 19:30 and 20:22 essentially present the same gift of the Spirit, and that 20:22 depicts the Spirit that would *become* the Paraclete in the future, has its own problems (see Bennema, "Giving," pp. 204-5).

ter devoted to the Johannine gift of the Spirit.[6] While I qualified his views, I also incorporated a suggestion he had made earlier, in a 1977 article, which he had not pursued in his 1996 work.[7]

Since 2002, many scholars have written on the subject but to my knowledge no compelling responses or rebuttals have yet been made to my proposal.[8] The aim of this study, therefore, is to engage those who have written after me in order to (re-)test my theory. Given that my 2002 article interacts with scholarship up to 2000, my conversation partners for this study will be those who have substantially written on the subject since. I shall also argue my case afresh, sharpening and further substantiating it.[9]

---

6. Max Turner, *The Holy Spirit and Spiritual Gifts — Then and Now*, rev. ed. (Carlisle: Paternoster, 1999), ch. 6.

7. Bennema, "Giving," pp. 207-11. The relevant article is M. M. B. Turner, "The Concept of Receiving the Spirit in John's Gospel," *VE* 10 (1977): 24-42.

8. Scholars marked with an asterisk (*) have mentioned or interacted with my article. Craig S. Keener, *The Gospel of John: A Commentary*, 2 vols. (Peabody: Hendrickson, 2003), esp. pp. 1148-49, 1196-1208; Tricia G. Brown, *Spirit in the Writings of John: Johannine Pneumatology in Social-scientific Perspective* (London: T&T Clark, 2003), pp. 97-113; Robert P. Menzies, "John's Place in the Development of Early Christian Pneumatology," in *Spirit and Spirituality: Essays in Honour of Russell P. Spittler*, ed. W. Ma and R. P. Menzies (London: T&T Clark, 2004), pp. 41-52; Marianne M. Thompson, "The Breath of Life: John 20:22-23 Once More," in *The Holy Spirit and Christian Origins: Essays in Honor of James D. G. Dunn*, ed. Graham N. Stanton, Bruce W. Longenecker, Stephen C. Barton (Grand Rapids: Eerdmans, 2004), pp. 69-78; John Pretlove, "John 20:22 — Help from Dry Bones?," *CTR* 3 (2005): 93-101; Robert Kysar, "'He Gave Up the Spirit.' A Reader's Reflection on John 19:30b," in *Transcending Boundaries: Contemporary Readings of the New Testament. Essays in Honor of Francis J. Moloney*, ed. R. M. Chennattu and M. L. Coloe (Rome: Liberia Ateneo Salesiano, 2005), pp. 161-72; James M. Hamilton*, *God's Indwelling Presence: The Holy Spirit in the Old & New Testaments* (Nashville: B&H Academic, 2006), esp. chs. 4-6; Sandra M. Schneiders*, "The Raising of the New Temple: John 20.19-23 and Johannine Ecclesiology," *NTS* 52 (2006): 337-55; M. A. Makambu, *L'esprit-pneuma dans l'evangile de Jean* (Würzburg: Echter, 2007), ch. 8; Mary L. Coloe, *Dwelling in the Household of God: Johannine Ecclesiology and Spirituality* (Collegeville: Liturgical Press, 2007), pp. 167-91; Tobias Hägerland*, "The Power of Prophecy: A Septuagintal Echo in John 20:19-23," *CBQ* 71 (2009): 84-103; David Crump, "Who Gets What? God or Disciples, Human Spirit or Holy Spirit in John 19:30," *NovT* 51 (2009): 78-89; John R. Levison, *Filled with the Spirit* (Grand Rapids: Eerdmans, 2009), pp. 366-80; Gitte Buch-Hansen, *"It Is the Spirit That Gives Life": A Stoic Understanding of Pneuma in John's Gospel* (Berlin: W. de Gruyter, 2010).

9. The present study supplements rather than replaces my 2002 article, where I offer my understanding of 20:22 over against six major views and in interaction with scholarship up to 2000. From this set of older scholarship, I shall only interact with Turner, due to the special occasion of this *Festschrift*.

2. The Conditions for the Giving of the Spirit

In this section, I will examine the two prerequisites for the giving of the Spirit that John specifies in 7:39 and 16:7. I will argue that these conditions indicate different requirements and may be fulfilled on different occasions, thereby creating the possibility that the giving of the Spirit is not a singular event but a process.

In 7:39, John explains that believers were soon to receive the Spirit and hence experience the salvific reality that 7:37-38 speaks about.[10] However, this Spirit-reception could not yet happen because Jesus had not yet been glorified (οὔπω γὰρ ἦν πνεῦμα, ὅτι Ἰησοῦς οὐδέπω ἐδοξάσθη [7:39b]). It is widely recognized that Jesus' glorification is a process comprising his death, resurrection, and ascension. Porsch's suggestion that the giving of the Spirit may start simultaneously with the start of Jesus' glorification (at the cross) must be considered seriously. Neither the text nor John's theology demands that the Spirit can be given only after the *completion* of Jesus' glorification. John 7:39 only states that the giving of the Spirit is dependent on Jesus' glorification, without specifying whether the former can occur at the latter's start, end, or otherwise. Thus, 7:39 allows that the Spirit be given at any time *during* Jesus' glorification. In principle, once the "not yet" of Jesus' glorification is lifted, the "not yet" of the giving of the Spirit is also removed.

The phrase "the Spirit was not yet" (οὔπω γὰρ ἦν πνεῦμα) in 7:39b is somewhat puzzling. I suggest that this phrase does not refer to the Spirit's prior non-existence or inactivity, but to the degree that people could experience the Spirit up to that time. Jesus' endowment with the Spirit in 1:32 shows that the Spirit was at least in existence. Besides, John also indicates that the Spirit was already active during Jesus' ministry. First, the Spirit enables Jesus to speak God's words, the acceptance of which provides divine life (ζωή) (3:34-36). Hence, Jesus can tell his audience that his words are "Spirit and life," that is, the Spirit mediates Jesus' life-giving words to people (6:63). Second, Jesus indicates in 4:23 that the worship in "Spirit and truth" is already a present reality (ἔρχεται ὥρα καὶ νῦν ἐστιν). Thus, the Spirit did not merely empower Je-

---

10. Contra the majority view that 7:38b depicts Jesus as the source of life-giving water, this verse most likely has the believer in view, so that *in addition to* Jesus being the source of life-giving water for the believer (7:37-38a), this water will also flow from within the believer (cf. 4:13-14) (Bennema, *Power*, pp. 192-94).

sus for his salvific mission but also affected people during Jesus' ministry. We can then understand why Jesus tells his disciples in 14:17 that they already know the Spirit that is to come — they had already experienced the Spirit through Jesus and his teaching. Nevertheless, the disciples had not yet experienced the Spirit to the extent that is possible only after the cross (cf. 13:10; 20:22). Thus, "the Spirit was not yet" probably means that the Spirit was not yet active or available in the way that was only possible later.

The second prerequisite for the coming of the Spirit is mentioned in 16:7. In view of his imminent departure from this world, Jesus informs his disciples that it is to their advantage that he leaves because otherwise the Spirit-Paraclete cannot come.[11] The coming of the Spirit as Paraclete is thus dependent on Jesus' departure from this world. It is clear that 16:7 indicates Jesus' *permanent* departure from this world as the condition for the coming of the Spirit-Paraclete (cf. "you will no longer see me" in 16:10). First, the overall purpose of the farewell discourses is that Jesus prepares the disciples for his permanent return to the Father (cf. the summary in 16:28). Second, the Spirit-Paraclete will take over Jesus' functions and mediate Jesus' presence to the disciples precisely because Jesus will be absent (14:16-26; 15:26; 16:12-15). Third, according to 15:26, Jesus will send the Paraclete *from* the Father. This implies that the giving of the Spirit-Paraclete can only occur after Jesus' permanent return to the Father, via the cross and ascension.

To summarize, John specifies two conditions for the giving of the Spirit: (i) 7:39 indicates that the giving of the Spirit can happen *after the start* of Jesus' glorification; and (ii) 16:7 indicates that the giving of the Spirit as Paraclete can occur only *after the completion* of Jesus' glorification. It appears that these two conditions are at odds or that the Spirit has to be distinguished from the Spirit-Paraclete. Neither option is very appealing. There is an alternative solution, however. The giving of the Spirit may be a *process* in step with the process of Jesus' glorification. I infer that the two conditions could specify *two different points* in the process of the giving of the Spirit. While many scholars expect these conditions to be fulfilled at a singular event, which is certainly possible, I suggest that it is equally possible that they could be fulfilled on two

---

11. I explained elsewhere that ὁ παράκλητος is a functional label for all the Spirit's activities after Jesus' departure. Hence "(Spirit-)Paraclete" denotes the Spirit as, or in the role of, Paraclete (Bennema, *Power*, ch. 5).

different occasions. If the giving of the Sprit is a process, and assuming for the moment that at least 20:22 records a giving of the Spirit, we then need to check whether John indicates other releases of the Spirit.

3. The Giving of the Spirit at the Cross

Pursuing the possibility that the giving of the Spirit is a process, I will now consider occasions in John's Gospel where the Spirit was possibly given apart from 20:22, since 20:22 certainly records a giving of the Spirit, whether symbolic, partial, or otherwise. Two such occasions present themselves — in 19:30 and 19:34. Regarding 19:34, although some scholars consider the flow of water from Jesus' side, in view of 7:38-39, as a symbolic release of the Spirit, I argued in 2002 that this view is fraught with difficulties.[12] Since no new arguments have been advanced, I shall now turn to 19:30.

John 19:28-30 swiftly narrates Jesus' death on the cross. Knowing that he has completed "everything," that is, the work the Father had entrusted to him (cf. 4:34; 5:36; 17:4), Jesus quotes Psalm 22:15, conveying his thirst (19:28). Once Jesus receives the sour wine, he exclaims that his Father's work is finished and dies (19:30). In this, Jesus follows the sequence of Psalm 22:15, where David first expresses his thirst and then requests God "to lay him in the dust of death." John describes Jesus' death in an unusual way: "And bowing his head, he handed over the Spirit" (καὶ κλίνας τὴν κεφαλὴν παρέδωκεν τὸ πνεῦμα [19:30b]).[13] While many English translations have "his spirit," referring presumably to Jesus' human spirit, the Greek does not have the possessive pronoun. Instead, the reference here is most probably to the divine Spirit as Jesus' life-force. John's somewhat peculiar expression παραδιδόναι τὸ πνεῦμα to denote Jesus' death may be reminiscent of the understanding of the Spirit in the Old Testament. In the Old Testament, the Spirit is de-

---

12. Bennema, "Giving," pp. 199-200. Others argue that the Spirit is in view in both 19:30 and 19:34 (Keener, *Gospel*, pp. 1149, 1153; Brown, *Spirit*, pp. 101-2). However, if Jesus hands over the Spirit to God in 19:30, how can the Spirit flow from Jesus in 19:34?

13. Cf. Luke 23:46, where Jesus entrusted "his" Spirit (παρατίθεμαι τὸ πνεῦμά μου) to God and died (ἐξέπνευσεν); Matthew 27:50b, where Jesus surrendered the Spirit (ἀφῆκεν τὸ πνεῦμα); *Apoc. Moses* 42.8 (possibly as early as the late first century CE), where Eve's death is described as her handing over "her" Spirit to God (παρέδωκε τῷ θεῷ τὸ πνεῦμα αὐτῆς).

picted as God's power which creates and maintains the life of all creatures, and a withdrawal of the Spirit meant death (Gen. 6:3, 17; 7:15; Job 7:7; 12:10; 27:3; 32:8; 33:4; 34:14-15; Pss. 33:6; 104:29-30; Isa. 42:5). Wisdom of Solomon 15, which will gain further significance when I discuss 20:22, expresses this concept of the Spirit perhaps most clearly: the author reminds the people that they are mortal and have God's life-giving Spirit *on loan* (Wis. 15:11, 16-17).[14] Thus, John describes Jesus' death as his giving back to the Father the Spirit that had not only empowered his ministry but also sustained his physical life.[15]

This idea can be substantiated further when we consider John's consistent use of two words for "life": (i) ζωή denotes the divine, everlasting life that the Father and Son share, and that defines them (1:4; 5:21, 26; 6:57; 14:6); (ii) ψυχή is the transient, destructible life. While ζωή cannot be laid down or destroyed, lest God ceases to be who he is, ψυχή can be laid down. In fact, Jesus frequently talks about his intention and ability "to lay down his life" (τιθέναι τὴν ψυχὴν αὐτοῦ) (10:11, 15, 17-18; 15:13), which, of course, he does at the cross. Hence, when Jesus voluntarily hands over the Spirit as his life-force — and dies — he fulfills his earlier claim to lay down his ψυχή. This implies that the Spirit provided (perhaps even was) Jesus' ψυχή in the sense of physical life (cf. Wis. 15:8, 11, 16 where ψυχή and πνεῦμα are used synonymously). Thus, Jesus' handing over the Spirit (παραδιδόναι τὸ πνεῦμα) voluntarily in 19:30 as a reference to or interpretation of τιθέναι τὴν ψυχὴν αὐτοῦ of his own accord in 10:18, strongly suggests a link between πνεῦμα and ψυχή: Jesus lays down his life (ψυχή) by handing over his life-force — the divine πνεῦμα.[16]

---

14. Hence, the "human spirit" may merely be a linguistic expression to denote the life-giving divine Spirit that is "given" to people on loan, as it were, until they die (cf. Bennema, *Power*, pp. 97-98, and Desta Heliso's essay in this volume).

15. Contra Kysar, who argues that πνεῦμα in 19:30 has a double meaning, referring to both Jesus' human spirit and the bestowal of the divine Spirit. Kysar then suggests that 19:30 and 20:22 both record a bestowal of the Spirit on the disciples ("Spirit," pp. 161-72). However, the double meaning lies not in the referent of πνεῦμα but in the expression παραδιδόναι τὸ πνεῦμα — in handing over the Spirit, Jesus dies and proleptically releases the Spirit. Crump, who claims a "new" interpretation of 19:30 ("Who Gets What?," pp. 78-89), presents essentially the same case that I did in 2002. Differently, Brown views 19:30 as Jesus' releasing the spirit, but contends that Jesus does not give the spirit to anyone — whether the disciples or God (*Spirit*, pp. 102-3).

16. Contra Crump, who contends that πνεῦμα in 19:30 does not refer to Jesus' human life-spirit or ψυχή, and hence 19:30 does not describe Jesus' death ("Who Gets What?," pp. 86, 89).

The significance of describing Jesus' death by the phrase παραδιδόναι τὸ πνεῦμα is that it constitutes a giving of the Spirit. In returning to his Father the Spirit that sustained his physical life, Jesus releases the Spirit and this act foreshadows the future release of the Spirit to the disciples in 20:22.[17] Although scholars have noted that παραδιδόναι τὸ πνεῦμα is an unusual phrase to express someone's death, I suggest that John chose this expression over, for example, more usual terms such as (ἀπο)θνῄσκειν because he wanted to emphasize the Spirit. With this particular expression, John achieved two things: he articulated Jesus' death on the cross *and* he communicated the release of the Spirit, proleptic of the giving of the Spirit to the disciples in 20:22. Since Jesus had received the Spirit to empower his mission, he could also let go of the Spirit after having accomplished it. This de-linking of Jesus and the Spirit provides the opportunity for the Spirit to be "given" or experienced more fully and widely than was possible during Jesus' ministry. In relation to 7:39, since Jesus' death heralds the start of the process of his glorification, the "not yet" of the giving of the Spirit is also removed. However, 19:30 does not fulfill 7:39 in its entirety because the disciples are not yet the beneficiaries of this giving of the Spirit.

4. The Giving of the Spirit on Resurrection Sunday

It is without dispute that 20:22 records a giving of the Spirit, but there is disagreement about the nature of the bestowal, and whether this is the final giving or whether there is more to come. On the evening of resurrection Sunday, Jesus miraculously appears to his frightened disciples (20:19). After Jesus establishes his identity before the disciples, he extends again his peace and reiterates the disciples' commission (20:20-21; cf. 14:27; 16:33; 17:18). Then, Jesus breathes on (ἐνεφύσησεν) his disciples and says, "Receive Holy Spirit" (20:22).[18] Jesus concludes

---

17. Cf. Keener, *Gospel*, p. 1149. Contra Coloe, who understands 19:25b-30 as the creation of the divine household, where disciples become children of God through a new birth and where the Spirit is breathed onto this new creation (*Dwelling*, pp. 55-56, 112-13, 145, 167). I will argue that 20:22 is the defining moment of the new creation of the disciples and the giving of the Spirit.

18. Although πνεῦμα in 20:22 is anarthrous, the reference is undoubtedly to the divine Spirit. John regularly uses πνεῦμα without the definite article — mostly in a preposi-

Cornelis Bennema

with a statement about the disciples' authority to release and retain sins (20:23).[19]

The verb ἐμφυσᾶν "to breathe upon/into," "to insufflate" is a *hapax legomenon* in the New Testament. In Jewish literature, except for Philo, the verb is uncommon and relates mostly to the concept of "life." Barring Philo, there are three other accounts that narrate the divine creation or re-creation of human beings through the act of ἐμφυσᾶν:[20]

John 20:22	Genesis 2:7 (LXX)	Ezekiel 37:9 (LXX)	Wisdom of Solomon 15:11
When he [Jesus] had said this, *he breathed on them* (ἐνεφύσησεν) and said to them, "*Receive the Holy Spirit* (Λάβετε πνεῦμα ἅγιον).*"	[T]he LORD God formed man from the dust of the ground, and *breathed into his nostrils the breath of life* (ἐνεφύσησεν εἰς τὸ πρόσωπον αὐτοῦ πνοὴν ζωῆς); and the man became a living being.	Then he [the Lord God] said to me, "Prophesy to the breath/Spirit (πνεῦμα), prophesy, mortal, and say to the breath/Spirit (πνεῦμα): Thus says the Lord GOD: Come from the four winds, O breath, and *breathe upon these slain, that they may live* (ἐμφύσησον εἰς τοὺς νεκροὺς τούτους καὶ ζησάτωσαν)."	[T]hey failed to know the one who formed them and inspired them with active souls and *breathed a living spirit into them* (ἐμφυσήσαντα πνεῦμα ζωτικόν).

Although Genesis 2:7 mentions God's "breath of life" (πνοὴ ζωῆς) as the human life-principle, elsewhere Spirit (πνεῦμα) is synonymous with breath (πνοή) in this sense of "life" (cf. Gen. 7:15 and 7:22; see also Job

---

tional phrase (1:33; 3:5; 4:23-24), but not always (6:63; 7:39) — and undoubtedly the divine Spirit is in view. For example, 1:33 mentions πνεῦμα both with and without the article.

19. For an explanation of the "missional" context of 20:21, 23, see Bennema, "Giving," pp. 210-11. Cf. Thompson, "Breath," pp. 75-76; Schneiders, "Raising," pp. 349-55; Hägerland, "Power," pp. 96-102; Johannes Beutler, "Resurrection and the Forgiveness of Sins: John 20:23 against Its Traditional Background," in *The Resurrection of Jesus in the Gospel of John*, ed. C. R. Koester and R. Bieringer (Tübingen: Mohr Siebeck, 2008), pp. 237-51.

20. Note also other passages with similar activities. In 1 Kings 17:21 (LXX), Elijah breathed thrice upon (ἐνεφύσησεν) the widow's dead son (in whom there was no longer πνεῦμα [1 Kgs. 17:17]) as a symbolic act to undergird his plea to God to return the boy's life. In Tobit 6:9 and 11:11 (LXX), at an angel's instruction, Tobias breathed upon (ἐνεφύσησεν) the eyes of his blind father Tobit to facilitate healing (Tob. 11:13-15 clarifies that the healing was an act of God).

27:3; 33:4; Isa. 42:5; Wis. 2:2-3). Thus, the insufflation of divine Spirit in 20:22 evokes the creation story in Genesis 2:7 (cf. Wis. 15:11) and the re-creation envisaged in Ezekiel 37:9.[21] These verbal allusions virtually assure that 20:22 depicts *Jesus re-creating the disciples by imparting the life-giving Spirit*.[22] This interpretation fits in well with John's presentation of the Spirit in relation to life thus far (3:34; 4:10-14; 6:63; 7:38-39).[23]

Philo's multiple references to the creation of humanity in Genesis 2:7 also provide important conceptual parallels to 20:22.[24] According to *Legum allegoriae* 1.31-42, God breathed the divine πνεῦμα into the rational soul or mind of the earthly man, Adam, and it is this divine πνεῦμα in the human mind that constitutes a *union* between the earthly man and God, whereby he can know God and relate to him. Elsewhere Philo also refers to the nexus ἐμφυσᾶν-πνεῦμα-ζωή to describe God's creation of humankind:

---

21. Although πνεῦμα can mean "wind," "breath," or "spirit," with the exception of the phrase "Come from the four winds," the other eight occurrences of the term in Ezekiel 37:1-14 refer arguably to the divine Spirit.

22. Cf. Levison, *Filled with the Spirit*, pp. 368-71. Although Levison does not explain how 20:22 relates to the Paraclete promises or when the Spirit will start as Paraclete, it seems that he views 20:22 as the full and definitive giving of the Spirit.

23. The allusions of the verb ἐμφυσᾶν to (re-)creation virtually guarantee that 20:22 cannot be merely symbolic. Contra Andreas J. Köstenberger, who supports Carson's symbolic interpretation (*John*, Baker Exegetical Commentary on the New Testament [Grand Rapids: Baker Academic, 2004], p. 574). Similarly, Pretlove contends that one of John's allegedly two audiences could have understood Jesus' command "receive the Holy Spirit" as symbolic for the giving of the Spirit at Pentecost ("John 20:22," pp. 100-101). However, instead of interpreting Jesus' command as symbolic, it is Jesus' act of insufflation that is symbolic, namely for the reality of the disciples' reception of the Spirit and their re-creation. Besides, although Pretlove sets 20:22 in the context of Ezekiel 37, he argues that 20:22 is not about the new birth of the disciples but about the comprehensive restoration of Israel ("John 20:22," p. 99). However, these views need not be mutually exclusive (Bennema, "Giving," p. 213 n. 80). At the other extreme, Hägerland entirely misses the symbolism, identifying Jesus' own breath as holy Spirit ("Power," p. 95). Besides, Hägerland rejects an interpretation of 20:22 in terms of the disciples' new creation, and opts instead for the view that the disciples receive the "Spirit of prophecy" (i.e., the Spirit that enables prophetic speech) as part of their commission as prophets to the world ("Power," pp. 94-96). However, it is problematic to reduce all the functions of the Johannine Spirit-Paraclete to one function of a narrowly-defined "Spirit of prophecy." Hägerland's position is not entirely new; Wojciechowski also interpreted 20:22 as the gift of inspired speech (see Turner, *Holy Spirit*, p. 96 n. 22).

24. Cf. Turner, *Holy Spirit*, p. 90. Contra Keener, who does not think that the Philonic parallels are helpful (*Gospel*, p. 1205).

Opif. 134-135	*Det.* 80	*Spec.* 4.123	*Quaest. Gen.* 2.59
Moses says that "God made man, having taken clay from the earth, and *he breathed into his face the breath of life* (ἐνεφύσησεν εἰς τὸ πρόσωπον αὐτοῦ πνοὴν ζωῆς)." . . . [W]hen he uses the expression, "he breathed into," he means nothing else than *the divine spirit* (πνεῦμα θεῖον).	Moses says, "And *he breathed into his face the breath of life* (ἐνεφύσησεν εἰς τὸ πρόσωπον αὐτοῦ πνεῦμα ζωῆς), and man became a living soul (ψυχὴν ζῶσαν)" [Cf. *Leg.* 3.161. Although *Her.* 56 and *Somn.* 1.34 also quote Gen. 2:7 but have πνοὴν ζωῆς instead of πνεῦμα ζωῆς, the context indicates that what is breathed into the soul is the divine πνεῦμα (*Her.* 55, 57; *Somn.* 1.30).]	For the essence of the *soul of man is the breath of God* (πνεῦμα θεῖον), especially if we follow the account of Moses, who . . . says that *God breathed into the first man . . . the breath of life* (τῷ πρώτῳ . . . ἐμφυσῆσαι πνοὴν ζωῆς τὸν θεόν); . . . And that which was thus breathed into his face was manifestly *the breath of the air* (τὸ δ' ἐμφυσώμενον δῆλον ὡς αἰθέριον ἦν πνεῦμα).	[F]or there are three parts of the human soul . . . the third that which exists in reason. Therefore the rational part is the substance of the divine spirit . . . he [Moses] says, "*God breathed into his face the breath of life* (ἐνεφύσησεν εἰς τὸ πρόσωπον αὐτοῦ πνοὴν ζωῆς)," as being what was to constitute his life . . . *the essence of the soul is* truly and beyond all possible question *spirit* (ὡς εἶναι ψυχῆς μὲν ἀψευδῶς οὐσίαν πνεῦμα).

After the Fall, the earthly man experiences a decrease or degeneration in quantity and quality of endowment with divine πνεῦμα. Nevertheless, according to Philo, he still partakes in the divine πνεῦμα and hence still has a relationship with God (cf. *Opif.* 140-146). For Philo, "salvation" then is a restoration of one's relationship with God through an *additional* endowment of divine πνεῦμα.[25]

If John had something similar in mind, 20:22 can then be explained as an endowment of the divine Spirit in order to restore the disciples' relationship with Jesus/God. Although Philo's interpretation of Genesis 2:7 is at the most suggestive for 20:22, there are indications in the gospel itself that John had such thoughts. For John, "salvation" is envisaged as ζωή experienced in relationship with Jesus and God. Ζωή refers to the divine life that the Father and Son share, and believers are drawn into this life-giving relationship if they believe in Jesus, that is, if they accept Jesus and his teaching and commit themselves to him in discipleship. This ζωή was already available *during* Jesus' ministry.

25. See further Bennema, *Power*, pp. 71-74.

For example, the disciples had sided with Jesus and begun to experience the life that was available in him (2:11; 6:68-69; 13:10; 15:3; 17:6-8, 12). The Samaritans' proclamation that Jesus is the Savior of the world implies their experience of the life-giving water that was on offer (4:10-14, 42). The former blind man's act of worship implies his experience of Jesus as the life-giving light of the world (9:5, 38). Nevertheless, Jesus clarifies to his disciples that he still needs to go to the cross, to complete and secure this salvation (13:8-10; cf. 6:51). Only after the cross and resurrection could this life/salvation be fully available. In step with this partially realized dimension of salvation, people could also experience the Spirit already during Jesus' ministry, even though the Spirit would become fully available only after the cross and resurrection. In fact, Spirit and life are inextricably linked, in that the Spirit mediates and facilitates the life that is available in and through Jesus (cf. 6:63). Before the cross, the availability of life and the activity of the Spirit were tied or limited to the human Jesus and what was available at that stage. Thus, the Spirit upon Jesus affected people already during Jesus' ministry, mediating to them the divine life available in and through Jesus.[26]

The implication for 20:22 is thus clear. Although 20:22 must be explained in salvific terms, it does not denote the disciples' first "salvation" experience. Instead, 20:22 is *climactic* of the life or "salvation" that they had already experienced during Jesus' ministry. The fuller giving of the Spirit in 20:22 *completes* or *secures* the disciples' salvation or life-giving relationship with Jesus/God.[27] In view of Jesus' imminent departure, the Spirit will naturally also *sustain* the disciples' saving relationship with Jesus/God (cf. 14:23). I thus suggest that "to receive the Holy

---

26. Contra many scholars who do not recognize the (partial) availability of divine life and the Spirit's experience during Jesus' ministry (see Bennema, *Power*, pp. 12-15, 191-92, 210-12, 242-43). Levison also appears to overlook the realized dimension of life and Spirit before the cross (*Filled with the Spirit*, pp. 366, 382). See also the recent discussion in Nicolas Farelly, *The Disciples in the Fourth Gospel: A Narrative Analysis of Their Faith and Understanding* (Tübingen: Mohr Siebeck, 2010), pp. 195-218. I contend that John obviously wrote from a post-Easter perspective but did not read a post-Easter reality back into the pre-Easter situation; rather, John draws out the reality of the pre-Easter events from a post-Easter Spirit-informed perspective (Bennema, *Power*, pp. 15-17).

27. While Turner contends that the disciples merely experienced *foretastes* of authentic faith that would be available only after the cross (*Spirit*, pp. 69, 75, 97-99), I argued that the disciples already had "adequate" (i.e., authentic and sufficiently salvific) faith before the cross, without denying the significance of the cross (Bennema, *Power*, pp. 211-12).

Spirit" signifies the start of a new relationship with the Spirit or the start of a new nexus of activities by the Spirit in relation to a person.[28] To interpret "to receive the Holy Spirit" *relationally*, then, may mean something like "to experience (the activity of) the Holy Spirit in a new way" or "to receive a new relationship with the Holy Spirit." In this case, 20:22 depicts *the gift of a new relationship with the Spirit*, or a new relationship with Jesus through the Spirit, which seals and sustains the disciples' "salvation" or life-giving relationship with Jesus. John 20:22 can be understood as the disciples' birth of the Spirit (3:5), as long as we bear in mind that they had already experienced the Spirit and life prior to this.[29]

An issue I must attend to is whether we should take the phrase "receive the Holy Spirit" literally or metaphorically (i.e., nonliterally). Although the disciples did not receive the Spirit in the sense of possessing an object, the phrase is probably not so ethereal or intangible as to reject a literal sense entirely. Noting the problems with the literal/metaphorical binary that scholars typically use, David Aaron suggests a "continuum of meaning" with *degrees* of figurative language or metaphoricalness — ranging from literal meaning to ascription to weakly figurative to strongly figurative to nonsense.[30] In contrast to a strong metaphor such as "Jesus is the bread of life," the phrase "to receive the Holy Spirit" is not so ambiguous or absurd as to reject a literal sense entirely and demand a metaphorical sense. Using Aaron's meaning continuum, I put the metaphorical strength of "receive the Holy Spirit" somewhere between "literal" and "ascriptive" (i.e., I understand the phrase as quasi-literal). While the believer may not receive the Spirit ontologically (i.e., as substance), a reception of the Spirit in functional terms of a new relationship with the Spirit can still be viewed in the lit-

---

28. Cf. Turner, "Concept," pp. 25-26, 33-34. Unfortunately, Turner did not follow through on this in his later work (cf. n. 6), with the result that he virtually interprets 20:22 as a gift given by the Spirit rather than the gift being the Spirit (Bennema, "Giving," p. 209).

29. John 20:22 may also record *an* experience of Spirit-baptism (1:33), if my case is sustainable that Jesus baptizing people with the Holy Spirit is a programmatic statement for Jesus' entire ministry of cleansing and saving people through his revelatory word *by means of* the Spirit (Cornelis Bennema, "Spirit-Baptism in the Fourth Gospel: A Messianic Reading of John 1,33," *Bib* 84 [2003]: 35-60).

30. David H. Aaron, *Biblical Ambiguities: Metaphor, Semantics and Divine Imagery* (Leiden: Brill, 2001), chs. 2-6 (esp. the diagram on p. 112).

eral sphere.[31] To say "I have (received) the Spirit" would not be very different from saying, "I have a wife" or "I have colleagues." Although I do not have the Spirit, my wife, or colleagues as I possess a non-living object, there is nonetheless a literal sense to my relationship with them.[32]

Looking at the two conditions for the giving of the Spirit, 20:22 is the fulfillment of 7:39.[33] The "not yet" of 7:39 had already been removed in 19:30, but only in 20:22 was the Spirit actually "given," in the sense that the Spirit became active in a new way, that is as life-giving water, so that the disciples could become sources of living water later in their mission. Thus, whereas 19:30 describes the symbolic giving of the Spirit, 20:22 depicts its actualization. Nevertheless, 20:22 cannot be the giving of the Spirit-Paraclete because the condition of 16:7 has not been fulfilled. According to 15:26 and 16:7, Jesus will send the Spirit-Paraclete when he has (permanently) returned to the Father in the ascension. This has obviously not yet happened in 20:22 where Jesus is still present with the disciples. Thus, in 20:22, the disciples received the Spirit as life or "salvation" but not yet as Paraclete.[34]

---

31. Cf. Volker Rabens, *The Holy Spirit and Ethics in Paul: Transformation and Empowering for Religious-Ethical Life* (Tübingen: Mohr Siebeck, 2010), p. 85. See his ch. 2 for a systematic refutation that Judaism perceived Spirit-reception in categories of substance.

32. In a similar vein, although the "indwelling" of the Spirit, Son, and Father (14:17, 23) should probably be interpreted in relational rather than ontological categories, we cannot equate relational with metaphorical and ontology with literal. It is not entirely absurd to perceive the Spirit indwelling the believer at a literal level; it probably has a literal sense of an intimate relationship without demanding the same literalness as possessing a physical object. While in my 2002 article I labelled "to receive the Holy Spirit" as a donation metaphor, I now understand it in a more literal sense.

33. Contra Turner, *Holy Spirit*, p. 94. Levison incorrectly claims that I do not see 20:22 as the fulfilment of 7:38-39 (*Filled with the Spirit*, p. 379 n. 26).

34. Although Thompson recognizes 20:22 as the re-creation of the disciples through the life-giving Spirit, she makes no attempt to solve the promise of the Spirit as Paraclete ("Breath," pp. 69-78). Similarly, Brown does not connect spirit (given in 20:22 as an impersonal force that re-creates the disciples) and the Paraclete (the personified Spirit given after Jesus' glorification but without further specification) (*Spirit*, pp. 111, 201-21; cf. Makambu, *L'esprit*, pp. 298-99, 312-13, 315). Given that Jesus' going away is a process that starts with the cross and culminates in the ascension, it could be argued that since this process has been set in motion in John 19, the condition of 16:7 is fulfilled and the giving of the Spirit as Paraclete can occur when we come to 20:22. However, as I explained in section 2, the condition of 16:7 refers to Jesus' entire departure from the earthly scene and therefore the coming of the Spirit as Paraclete is dependent on the completion of the process of Jesus' going away or glorification.

I will now consider the main alternative views. Robert Menzies presents the classical Pentecostal position, arguing that the gift of the life-giving Spirit in 20:22 and the gift of the Paraclete at Pentecost are two theologically distinct bestowals.[35] The major problem is that Menzies' case rests entirely on his argument that the functions and character of the Spirit in John 3–7 are different from those of the Paraclete in John 14–16. For Menzies, the Spirit in John 3–7 is soteriological in that the Spirit grants the disciples life-giving wisdom, but the Paraclete is missiological in that the Paraclete grants the disciples charismatic wisdom to assist their testimony in the world.[36] However, the wisdom that the Paraclete provides to the disciples to inform their testimony *also* enables continuous belief and discipleship, thus sustaining their salvation.[37] Although the Spirit's activities are unfolded in various stages, these do not constitute theologically distinct experiences — the activities of the Paraclete *include* those of the Spirit in John 3–7.

Other scholars view 20:22 as the one and final giving of the Spirit — the disciples' re-creation *and* the full giving of the Spirit-Paraclete — sometimes referred to as the "Johannine Pentecost" where John (allegedly) narrates his version of the Lukan coming of the Spirit.[38] This requires them to argue either that the ascension has occurred somewhere between 20:17 and 20:19,[39] or that Jesus had already "gone away" in a

---

35. Menzies, "John's Place," pp. 41-52.
36. Menzies, "John's Place," pp. 44-48.
37. Bennema, *Power*, ch. 5 (esp. pp. 244-46).
38. Keener, *Gospel*, pp. 1196-1206; Schneiders, "Raising," p. 351; Buch-Hansen, *Spirit*, pp. 30, 215, 405. For other scholars, see Bennema, "Giving," p. 202 n. 36. In my view, Keener's response to Turner's critique of this view is unconvincing and does not contain new arguments. Hamilton's position is difficult to classify, due to his creating an unnatural dichotomy between regeneration and indwelling. He argues that, before the cross, believers were regenerated by the Spirit (3:3-6; 6:63), but not indwelt by the Spirit — the latter occurred at 20:22, fulfilling 7:37-39 and 14:17 (*Presence*, pp. 127-43). Then, while 20:22 is the gift of the Spirit-Paraclete, Acts 2 records the baptism with the Holy Spirit as an empowerment (*Presence*, pp. 95-99). For Hamilton, the Spirit-Paraclete represents God's indwelling presence but not an empowerment for mission. He thus is a "Johannine Pentecost" proponent *in words*, but close to Turner's position *in concept*. I agree with Hamilton that "adequate belief" was possible before the cross, but the allusions of 20:22 to the (new) creation motif compel me to conclude that only at 20:22 can we speak of the disciples' regeneration. Besides, Hamilton mistakenly takes Turner's position to be mine (*Presence*, pp. 138-39).
39. So Buch-Hansen, *Spirit*, pp. 30, 215, and ch. 7.

different sense.[40] This is unlikely because the condition of 16:7, in terms of Jesus' permanent departure, has not been fulfilled by 20:22. Besides, if we can accept that 21:24 identifies the Beloved Disciple as the real author, then John 21 (at least till 21:23) is an integral part of this gospel.[41] Subsequently, if the events in John 21 at the Sea of Galilee have some correlation to those in Mark 16:7 and Matthew 28:10, 16-20, where Jesus had commanded his disciples to go to Galilee before his departure, then the events in John 21 occurred just before the ascension.

The most recent work on the Johannine Spirit comes from Gitte Buch-Hansen. Although she is a proponent of the "Johannine Pentecost" position, her approach is unique. Arguing for a Stoic understanding of the Johannine πνεῦμα, she proposes a fourfold meta-story of pneumatic transformations. First, the descent of the πνεῦμα on Jesus is his divine generation (1:32). Second, the πνεῦμα is active in and through Jesus. Third, since God is πνεῦμα (4:24), Jesus can only successfully be united with the Father, in the ascension, if Jesus *becomes* πνεῦμα (13:1; 20:17). Fourth, believers are regenerated through the infusion of πνεῦμα — a pneumatic κρᾶσις ("fusion") (3:5; 20:22).[42] Buch-Hansen's view is problematic. First, even if the Johannine πνεῦμα could be understood in Stoic categories, the question is why we should do so. Buch-Hansen's account fails to convince that the Johannine πνεῦμα can be understood better against the backdrop of Stoic cosmology than, for example, Jew-

---

40. Keener, for example, interprets Jesus' going away and return in 14:18-20 and 16:16-22 in terms of his death and resurrection (*Gospel*, p. 1198 n. 275). However, this violates the condition of Jesus' *permanent* departure in 16:7. Instead, 14:18-20 speaks of Jesus' return through the Paraclete (Bennema, *Power*, pp. 222-23 n. 45). Schneiders even argues that ascension is not a Johannine category (the risen Jesus is the ascended Jesus) and implies that Jesus' exaltation on the cross is his departure ("Raising," p. 348). However, her implication is only partially correct; although Jesus' departure starts at the cross, it ends with his permanent return to the Father (in the ascension). Besides, even though John does not use the literal term "ascension" (neither does Luke), the concept is evident through verbs such as ἀναβαίνειν, ὑψοῦν, ὑπάγειν, and ἀπέρχεσθαι. There is no reason to assume that John was ignorant about the ascension and Pentecost simply because he did not record them.

41. See especially Richard Bauckham, *Jesus and the Eyewitnesses: The Gospels as Eyewitness Testimony* (Grand Rapids: Eerdmans, 2006), ch. 14. Cf. Cornelis Bennema, *Encountering Jesus: Character Studies in the Gospel of John* (Milton Keynes: Paternoster, 2009), pp. 175-76. Contra the proponents of the "Johannine Pentecost," who claim that John 21 is an editorial appendix.

42. Buch-Hansen, *Spirit*, pp. 30-31, 59 (in brief), chs. 4-7 (in full). She views 20:22 as the full giving of the Spirit-Paraclete (cf. nn. 38-39 above).

ish wisdom. Second, Volker Rabens has painstakingly deconstructed precisely the kind of model Buch-Hansen is proposing — an infusion-transformation of a material πνεῦμα — in Greek, Jewish, and Pauline thought (including 1 Cor. 15:44-45, to which Buch-Hansen frequently refers).[43] Third, there is, of course, no hint in 20:17 (or elsewhere) of Jesus' transformation or translation into πνεῦμα; rather, he is the bearer and giver of the πνεῦμα. Similarly, instead of viewing 4:24 and 20:22 in metaphysical terms (κρᾶσις does not even occur in the NT or LXX), we should understand these verses relationally — God is present through the Spirit, and the disciples receive a new relationship with the Spirit. Instead of viewing the πνεῦμα as a hypostatic union between God, Jesus, and believers, the πνεῦμα is the relational bond or mode of communication between them, that is, they relate to each other by means of the πνεῦμα.[44]

In sum, 20:22 is the disciples' climactic experience of life or "salvation" in that the giving of the Spirit seals and sustains their life-giving relationship with Jesus that had already begun earlier. Thus, the emphasis of 20:22 is on the life-giving efficacy of the Spirit, where the disciples receive the Spirit as life or "salvation." While 20:22 records the giving of the Spirit of life/salvation, the giving of the Spirit as Paraclete will occur at a later event beyond the chronological horizon of John's Gospel, for which Pentecost in Acts 2 seems the most natural candidate.

5. Conclusion

While most scholars assume or argue that the giving of the Spirit refers to a singular event (e.g. the one recorded in 20:22), whereby the two conditions mentioned in 7:39 and 16:7 have been fulfilled, I have argued for an alternative solution that fits the data better. I have suggested that the giving of the Spirit is a process that runs parallel to, and in step with, the process of Jesus' glorification. This process of the giving of the Spirit comprises three stages or events where the Spirit gradually unfolds his activities in relation to people. First, at the cross, Jesus' re-

43. Rabens, *Spirit*, pp. 25-120. See also his "Johannine Perspectives on Ethical Enabling in the Context of Stoic and Philonic Ethics," in *Rethinking the Ethics of John: "Implicit Ethics" in the Johannine Writings*, ed. Jan van der Watt and Ruben Zimmermann (Tübingen: Mohr Siebeck, forthcoming 2012).

44. Cf. Bennema, *Power*, pp. 166, 188-89, 221-25.

turn of the life-giving Spirit to his Father indicates the symbolic and proleptic release of the Spirit that is about to be given to the disciples. Second, on resurrection Sunday, the risen Jesus gives the Spirit to the disciples in that they receive (i.e., experience) the Spirit as life/salvation. Third, after the completion of Jesus' glorification, the disciples will receive the Spirit as Paraclete for the empowerment of their mission. While John records the first two stages of the giving of the Spirit, he only indicates the third stage. In fact, John could not have recorded the third stage, the coming of the Spirit as Paraclete, because he chose not to record the ascension and hence the completion of Jesus' glorification. It would not be too wide of the mark to say that John's third stage dovetails well with Luke's record of the Spirit's coming at Pentecost. Thus, regarding the relation between John's and Luke's accounts of the giving of the Spirit, John 20:22 does not parallel Acts 2 (contra the proponents of the "Johannine Pentecost") but anticipates it.

The process of the giving of the Spirit, in relation to Jesus' glorification, can be best visualized in the following diagram:

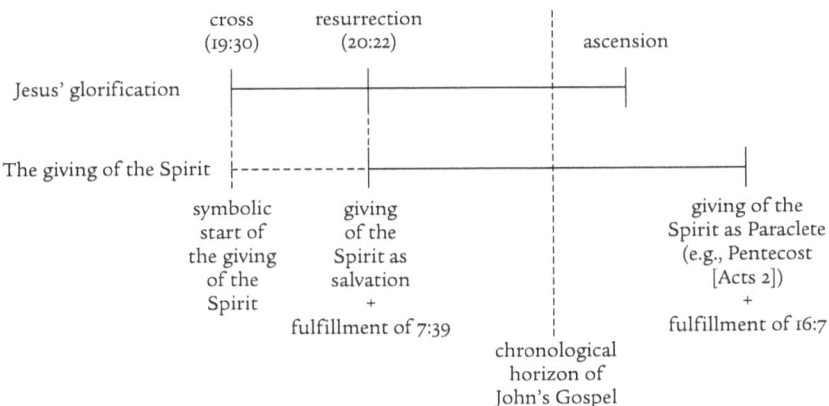

This process of the giving of the Spirit was unique for the disciples and is not paradigmatic for Spirit-reception today. Since the unique process of Jesus' glorification has been completed and can no longer be repeated, so also the process of the giving of the Spirit that was inherently embedded in the process of Jesus' glorification. The giving of the Spirit-Paraclete today has both soteriological and missiological significance, in that the Spirit who gives/mediates divine life is also the one who empowers for mission, and vice versa. The only way to experience the Spirit today is as Paraclete, that is, the reception of the Spirit as Paraclete represents the totality of the Spirit. However, this does not exclude any further experiences or "receptions" of the Spirit, in the sense of the Spirit starting new activities in relation to people.

I observe that the major interpretations of 20:22 up to 2002 continue to find support and that no substantially new views have been developed:

Major Views on the Johannine Giving of the Spirit	Scholarship up to 2002	Scholarship since 2002
20:22 is the full giving of the Spirit-Paraclete (sometimes called the "Johannine Pentecost")	Burge, majority of scholars	Keener, Schneiders, Hamilton (differently; see n. 38), Levison (perhaps), Buch-Hansen (differently)
20:22 is symbolic for Acts 2	Carson	Pretlove (partly), Köstenberger
20:22 is the gift of inspired/prophetic speech	Wojciechowski	Hägerland
20:22 and Acts 2 record two theologically distinct gifts, normative for today (classical Pentecostal position)	Ervin	Menzies
two stages (19:30 and 20:22)	Porsch	Kysar (differently; see n. 15)
two stages/bestowals (20:22 and Acts 2), but not normative for today	Dunn, Turner	Hamilton (differently; see n. 38)
three-stage process (19:30; 20:22; Acts 2), but not normative for today	Bennema	Bennema

Is Faith in Christ Without Evidence Superior Faith? A Re-examination of John 20:29

D. A. Carson

Many Johannine themes gather around John 20:29. The result is that the diverse interpretations of this verse usually reflect numerous antecedent exegetical and theological judgments about a variety of Johannine passages and trajectories. We can isolate some of the interpretive options by canvassing opinions as to how the two parts of the verse relate to each other:

> Because you have seen me, you have believed; (a)
> blessed are those who have not seen and yet have believed. (b)

Because he holds to a powerful antithesis between seeing and believing, Bultmann holds that (a) is inadequate and not praiseworthy, even though it gave rise to the great Christological confession of verse 28.[1] Only (b) reflects genuine and praiseworthy faith. Today, however, most commentators reject the thesis that this verse upholds a contrast between seeing and believing. Instead, they detect some kind of contrast between faith based on sight and faith not based on sight. Admittedly this contrast is nuanced in diverse ways. Barrett and Brown suggest that the contrast between, on the one hand, seeing and believing and, on the other, believing without seeing, is in fact the contrast between Thomas who saw and later believers who did not (and could not).[2] In other words, the contrast turns on which

---

1. Rudolf Bultmann, *The Gospel of John* (Oxford: Blackwell, 1971), p. 539.
2. C. K. Barrett, *The Gospel According to St. John* (London: SPCK, 1978), p. 573; Ray-

party is doing the believing. Cornelis Bennema argues that the contrast is not so much between different parties doing the believing as between kinds of faith: "Jesus encourages people to adopt a different approach [from that of Thomas] — one of belief without sight. In other words, a belief that is less dependent on sight of the tangible, and more on Jesus' word or a truthful eyewitness testimony, is more reliable and stable."[3]

Two other points of disharmony among scholars should be mentioned. First, although many think that there is at least a mild rebuke of Thomas in verse 29a[4] (the mildness stems from the common observation that the purpose of the narrative is not to comment on Thomas's faith but to present Christ),[5] some deny that there is any rebuke at all.[6] Second, intertwined with these discussions are the contributions of scholars who think verse 29 displays a contrast between an earthly and a spiritual perspective. For example, Culpepper thinks Thomas is a realist who embraces the earthly Jesus but does not really understand the risen Christ[7] — though in the light of 20:28 this seems less than convincing. On occasion this failure of Thomas to grasp the significance of the risen Christ is tied to the way one understands John's pneumatology. How is a believer's experience of the promised Paraclete tied to one's experience of the resurrected Jesus? Does the former merely succeed the latter? Or is it a higher form of the latter? In terms of the exegesis of this chapter, how does verse 29 relate to

---

mond E. Brown, *The Gospel according to John (xiii–xxi)*, Anchor Bible 29 (London: Geoffrey Chapman, 1970), pp. 1050-51.

3. Cornelis Bennema, *Encountering Jesus: Character Studies in the Gospel of John* (Milton Keynes: Paternoster, 2009), p. 167; Cornelis Bennema, *The Power of Saving Wisdom: An Investigation of Spirit and Wisdom in Relation to the Soteriology of the Fourth Gospel* (Tübingen: Mohr Siebeck, 2002), pp. 145-47. Somewhat similarly but with a more acute contrast, see W. Bonney, *Caused to Believe: The Doubting Thomas Story at the Climax of John's Christological Narrative* (Leiden: Brill, 2002), pp. 137-41.

4. E.g., Herman Ridderbos, *The Gospel of John: A Theological Commentary* (Grand Rapids: Eerdmans, 1997), p. 649; George R. Beasley-Murray, *John*, Word Biblical Commentary 36 (Waco: Word, 1999), p. 386; Rudolf Schnackenburg, *The Gospel According to St John*, 3 vols. (London: Burns & Oates, 1968-82), vol. 3, p. 334.

5. E.g. S. Harstine, "Un-Doubting Thomas: Recognition Scenes in the Ancient World," *PRSt* 33 (2006): 435-47.

6. E.g., Barrett, *Gospel*, p. 573.

7. R. Alan Culpepper, *Anatomy of the Fourth Gospel: A Study in Literary Design* (Philadelphia: Fortress Press, 1983), pp. 123-24.

20:22-23, Jesus breathing and telling his disciples to receive the Holy Spirit?

What follows is a series of exegetical and thematic evaluations so as to stake out a defensible reading of John 20:29. Insofar as the argument bears on one's understanding of the role of the Spirit in the Fourth Gospel, it is appropriately offered to Max Turner, a friend and colleague for four decades, whose studies of the Spirit, especially in Luke-Acts, have largely set the standard for contemporary discussion of such themes.

1. On Signs and Believing in the Fourth Gospel

If one holds that the contrast between (a) and (b) in verse 29 turns on whether or not a sign supports the believing, one should pause and reflect on the relations between signs and believing across the Gospel of John. Is it the case that faith[8] is invariably weaker or in some other way inferior if it is tied to signs?

The issues are complex. The disciples may see a sign and in consequence believe (2:11). Certainly one of the purposes of the signs is to elicit faith, not least by "*sign*ifying" something beyond the mere miracle. There are two instances in John where some who do not believe demand a sign (2:18; 6:30), but the inference to be drawn from the context is that if Jesus had then performed a sign the "faith" that would have ensued would have been faulty: the miracle would have been mere spectacle and the faith unreal. Moreover, there are passages where people come to believe because of signs, yet their faith is clearly unsatisfactory (2:23-25; 4:48; 6:26), apparently because they are drawn to the display of power but grasp little of what this attests about Jesus, and still others where people see signs in some sense and yet the signs do not evoke faith (3:19-21; 11:46; 12:37-41). On the other hand, sometimes unbelief in John's Gospel is the result, not of Jesus' signs, but of what he *said* (6:60-61); indeed, precisely *because* Jesus tells them the truth, some do not believe in him (8:45). Not infrequently in John, people come to faith partly as a result of Jesus' words and partly as a result of signs: consider,

---

8. As is well known, the noun πίστις does not occur in John. Owing to the awkwardness of an English usage that invariably deploys "believing" instead of "faith," however, I shall happily resort on occasion to the English noun.

for instance, the combination of 1:49 and 2:11.⁹ Moreover, when people do not believe in him, Jesus can exhort them to consider afresh his "works," and to believe on that basis (10:38).

In other words, there is little evidence in the rest of this Gospel to support the view that faith based on word is always strong, good, and praiseworthy, while faith based on signs is always weak, bad, and inferior. That does not necessarily mean that 20:29 should not be taken that way, but it does mean that there is precious little support for such an antithesis outside this chapter.

More importantly, as many have observed, even the context of 20:29 is careful not to relegate faith based on signs to some secondary tier. After all, the final two verses of the chapter find the evangelist declaring that the purpose of his writing is to record this selection of signs with the intention that the readers might believe "that Jesus is the Messiah, the Son of God, and that by believing you may have life in his name" (20:30-31). Whatever the complexities of this pair of verses (some of which are mentioned below), signs as a basis for faith are in no way depreciated.

2. On Tangibility

Is there, then, a more subtle contrast between (a) and (b) in verse 29 — not tied to signs or their absence, but to the tangible over against the intangible, to the contrast between faith grounded in the tangibility of an immediate experience of the sign of Jesus' resurrection over against the intangibility of a mediated experience of the sign of Jesus' resurrection through the words of witnesses? To put the question more acutely, does verse 29 suggest that the faith of the former is intrinsically weaker than or inferior to the faith of the latter?

One of the ablest supporters of this view is Cornelis Bennema in the works already cited.¹⁰ He argues that in all three earlier encounters

---

9. W. Hulitt Gloer, "'Come and See': Disciples and Discipleship in the Fourth Gospel," in *Perspectives on John: Method and Interpretation in the Fourth Gospel*, ed. Robert B. Sloan and Mikeal A. Parsons (Lewiston: Edwin Mellen Press, 1993), pp. 269-301, overstates the argument, but he rightly observes how many people enter into some kind of believing with minimal help from signs. Cf. Craig S. Keener, *The Gospel of John: A Commentary*, 2 vols. (Peabody: Hendrickson, 2003), p. 1212.

10. Cf. n. 3 above.

Is Faith in Christ Without Evidence Superior Faith?

with the risen Jesus in John 20 (viz. 20:1-10; 20:11-18; 20:19-23), "The common element . . . is that a tangible experience of the risen Jesus leads to greater faith."[11] I am not certain that "tangible" is the most helpful word. In its most common sense, it refers to what is actually touched, but there is no touching of Jesus, or even of his grave garments, in 20:1-10. In the account of Mary Magdalene, the account reads as if it is her hearing of Jesus' use of her name (20:16) that brings her to recognize Jesus' resurrection existence, rather than her grasping him — and this observation lends credence to the interpretation of 20:17 that suggests Jesus tells her to stop hanging on to him because his final departure is not yet imminent. As for Jesus' appearance to the ten disciples, although we are told that he showed them his hands and his side (20:20), there is no specification that they touched him, as Thomas was invited to do a week later — and even there we are not told that Thomas took Jesus up on his offer. Tangibility, in the strong sense of that word, is not in focus.

If we understand "tangible" in its weaker sense of what is intelligible or directly perceived, over against what is visionary, then doubtless the word can apply to all four resurrection-appearance scenes in this chapter (though the last one, Thomas, *may* involve actual touching). In that case, however, we must question the assertion "that a tangible experience of the risen Jesus leads to greater faith."[12] In each case it leads to *faith* — but where is the evidence that it leads to *greater faith,* presumably on the order of faith that does not need the tangible? The point of the episode in which Peter and the other disciple (I will assume it was John) race to the tomb is not to present varieties of faith, but to show how the appearances of Christ unfolded so as to bring two prominent disciples to believe that Jesus really had risen from the dead. Thus it makes little sense to say, "Even the Beloved Disciple is portrayed ambiguously: the nature of his 'belief' in 20:8 is unclear, and even if it is resurrection faith, he does not testify and has no narrative impact."[13] No narrative impact? If we assume, entirely reasonably, that the Beloved Disciple is responsible for writing this Gospel, then his own coming-to-believe that Jesus has risen from the dead constitutes part of the witness of the entire book itself (20:30-31). The narrative impact is massive. When Mary Magdalene comes to believe that Jesus has risen from the

---

11. Bennema, *Encountering,* p. 165.
12. Bennema, *Encountering,* p. 165.
13. Bennema, *Encountering,* p. 167 n. 12.

dead (again: based first of all on Jesus' self-disclosure in word, not on touch), she becomes part of the chain of witnesses — but it is difficult to see how she then moves to a new and superior gradation of faith based on something other than the "tangible." Something similar must be said for the coming-to-faith of the ten disciples. So when we arrive at the Thomas pericope, there is nothing in the earlier parts of the chapter to drive us to the expectation that Thomas' coming-to-faith will be in two parts: based on the tangible, and then on the intangible. Even on the broadest understanding of "tangible" (i.e., if Thomas did not actually *touch* Jesus despite his invitation to do so), Thomas's glorious confession (20:28) is a result of this encounter, *not* the result of some later and superior gradation of faith. Of course, on a certain reading of verse 29 one might still argue that the evangelist is passing judgment on two gradations of faith, declaring one of them to be superior. Yet if there is a more plausible reading of verse 29, as I shall argue, one must conclude that there is nothing in the chapter before verse 29 to support that particular contrast.

3. On Thomas and Doubt

Many have pointed out that the label "Thomas the Doubter" is not quite fair. In his earlier appearances in this book Thomas shows little understanding, but considerable resolution and even courage (11:7-16; 14:5). Yet the "doubter" label will never be detached from him because of Jesus' words: "Stop doubting and believe" (20:27).

What kind of doubt was Thomas displaying? There is no evidence that he was *more* of a doubter than the Ten. Had he been with them the previous Sunday (20:19-24) and persisted in doubt while they believed, he could be so charged. The reality, however, was that he was not present. Moreover, what Thomas asks for, if he is to believe — viz, "Unless I see the nail marks in his hands and put my finger where the nails were, and put my hand into his side, I will not believe" (20:25) — is no more than what Jesus had already voluntarily shown to the Ten (20:20). He was asking for unambiguous evidence that the pre-death Jesus who was killed and placed in the tomb, complete with telltale *stigmata*, was to be identified with the person who came out of the tomb. It is possible to imagine that Jesus' words, "Stop doubting and believe," mean something like "Stop doubting the testimony of the Ten who *have* seen me,"

Is Faith in Christ Without Evidence Superior Faith?

but that is not what Jesus actually says. As it is not clear that Thomas's doubt is any more morally culpable than the doubt of the Ten before *they* saw the resurrected Christ, so it is not clear that Jesus' command to Thomas to stop doubting ascribes any more guilt to him than to the others who had earlier found it difficult to believe, for whom the resurrection was a shattering surprise. What Jesus does *not* say to Thomas is that what he needs is a steadier faith: he simply provides exactly the same evidence he had one week earlier provided to the Ten.[14]

4. On Misunderstandings, the Paraclete, and History

Ever since the seminal works of Oscar Cullmann and H. Leroy,[15] scholars have expressed considerable interest in the "misunderstanding" theme in John's Gospel.[16] The literature is too lengthy and complex to summarize here. The discussion of the misunderstanding theme nevertheless bears on our subject in at least two ways.

First, several scholars hold that one of the interpretive keys to what is going on in this passage is a misunderstanding that Thomas displays. For instance, Bennema argues that in each of the three passages in John's Gospel where Thomas puts in an appearance he shows a misunderstanding (11:7-16; 14:5; 20:25). The only instance of interest to us is the third and final one: when Thomas says, "Unless I see the nail marks in his hands and put my finger where the nails were, and put my hand into his side, I will not believe" (20:25), Bennema concludes, "[L]ike Mary Magdalene, Thomas's desire for a tangible presence of Je-

---

14. Bonney, *Caused to Believe*, pp. 165-66, asserts that what causes Thomas to believe is Jesus' knowledge of Thomas's thoughts. Transparently Jesus *does* know Thomas's thoughts (cf. vv. 25b, 27a), but that it is this fact that evokes Thomas's faith is merest assertion without textual warrant. The supernatural knowledge is saying something about Jesus, not something about Thomas; indeed, Bonney's interpretation would mean that Jesus' resurrection appearance to Thomas is out of character with the three other resurrection appearances in this chapter, where the writer makes clear how the various parties came to believe *the truth of the resurrection, and trust the resurrected Jesus.*

15. Oscar Cullmann, "Der johanneische Gebrauch doppeldeutiger Ausdrücke als Schlüssel zum Verständnis des vierten Evangeliums," *TZ* 4 (1948): 360-72; H. Leroy, *Rätsel und Missverständnis: Ein Beitrag zur Formgeschichte des Johannesevangeliums* (Bonn: Peter Hanstein, 1968).

16. E.g., J. Rahner, "Missverstehen um zu Verstehen: Zur Funktion der Missverständnisse im Johannevangelium," *BZ* 43 (1999): 212-19.

sus indicates that he has not understood that Jesus' ongoing presence with his disciples will be *by means of the Spirit* — as Jesus had mentioned to his disciples in 14:17-23."[17]

Two comments are in order. (1) It is possible to read the account of the resurrection appearance to Mary Magdalene as a reflection of her wanting something tangible, but interestingly enough Jesus does *not* tell her, "My dear Mary. Don't you understand? Henceforth you will know me only by the Paraclete — so unhand me!" Quite the contrary: he tells her to stop holding on to him because *he himself* has not yet gone away. In other words, his successor, the Paraclete, is not in view; the focus at this juncture in the narrative sequence remains the resurrected Jesus, not the promised Holy Spirit. In short, it is not clear to me that Mary is displaying a misunderstanding grounded in a failure to grasp the role of the Paraclete. (2) In much the same way, it is difficult to see why Thomas should be charged with misunderstanding the way Jesus will manifest himself by means of the Paraclete *in the future,* when the focus of Thomas's concern is the reality or otherwise of the claimed resurrection *in his own time.* As we have seen, by stipulating the stigmata, Thomas is not only ensuring that the body which has ostensibly risen and escaped the tomb is in continuity with the body that was laid in that tomb; more importantly, Thomas is asking for no more than the evidences with which the Ten had already been provided (20:20). More striking yet, Jesus does not respond to Thomas by saying, "Thomas, I know what you are asking for, but frankly you are asking for the wrong thing. Henceforth I shall be known only by means of the Paraclete." Far from it: Jesus provides him with exactly the physical demonstration Thomas asked for, exactly the physical demonstration he had given to the Ten one week earlier.

This is not to deny that once Jesus has finally returned to his Father, he will send the Holy Spirit who will in many ways succeed him here on earth. It is merely saying that that lies in the future. The entire focus at this juncture is on the reality of Jesus' resurrection. That is also one of the reasons why 20:22-23, difficult as they are, are best *not* taken as the Johannine Pentecost, *for nothing dramatically changes in their wake* — not in the remaining verses of chapter 20, and certainly not in chapter 21. It seems much wiser to take 20:22-23 as a symbol-laden anticipation of what is still to come in the gift of the Spirit, rather than as the

---

17. Bennema, *Encountering,* p. 166.

actual outpouring of the Spirit. If that is the case, then there is even less reason for thinking that in 20:25 Thomas is displaying a formidable misunderstanding.

Second, in an article I wrote some years ago on misunderstandings in John,[18] I tried to show, among other things, that there are not fewer than sixteen episodes in John where the misunderstanding displayed by this party or that *would only be removed by the resurrection of Jesus Christ.* For instance, one of the early ones occurs in John 2:19-22, where Jesus says, "Destroy this temple, and I will raise it again in three days" (2:19). The context shows that even the disciples have no idea what Jesus is talking about. The evangelist comments, "After he was raised from the dead, his disciples recalled what he had said. Then they believed the scripture and the words that Jesus had spoken" (2:22). One dramatic instance of this kind is interesting; sixteen of them provide compelling evidence that the evangelist was willing and able to distinguish between what the disciples understood *back then, in the time of Jesus' earthly ministry,* and *what they came to understand only after they were convinced that Jesus had risen from the dead.* If many of the Johannine misunderstandings turn on the evangelist's willingness and capacity to make this distinction between *back then* (Jesus' earthly ministry) and *now* (the time of his writing), we ought to be especially suspicious of theories of two-level narratives in which John ostensibly obscures the distinction or may not even be able to distinguish the two.[19]

Applying this insight to the passage at hand, we must conclude that John is capable of, and interested in, exploring what took place *back then* when Jesus rose from the dead, *before* he returned to the glory he had with the Father before the world began and then bequeathed his Spirit. If that is the case, the distinction between (a) and (b) in verse 29 is not between inferior faith that clings to the tangible, and superior faith that accepts the witness of the disciples, nor between the faith of those who look for a touchable Jesus, and those who are satisfied with the presence of God mediated by the Paraclete, but between a faith grounded on "a first-hand experience of the risen Jesus"[20] which was en-

---

18. D. A. Carson, "Understanding Misunderstandings in the Fourth Gospel," *TynBul* 33 (1982): 59-89.

19. See esp. J. Louis Martyn, *History and Theology in the Fourth Gospel,* 3rd ed. (Louisville: Westminster John Knox Press, 2003 [orig. 1968]).

20. In Bennema's apposite words (*Encountering,* p. 167) — much better than the ambiguous "tangible."

tirely appropriate and even necessary at that point in history, and the faith grounded *in the witness* of the first-hand experiences of the earliest disciples, a faith that could not be secured any other way precisely because Jesus by that point had returned to his Father and was not physically available for inspection. In other words, the accumulating evidence suggests that the contrast between (a) and (b) in verse 29 is not so much between inferior and superior faith (along whatever axes), as between the grounds of faith that were possible for the first generation of believers and the grounds of faith needed by subsequent generations.

5. On the Connection Between 20:29 and 20:30-31

If this reasoning is accepted, then the connection between verse 29 and verses 30-31 becomes clearer. The evangelist is interested in demonstrating how we moved from the first generation of believers to later generations — his readers — in line with his constantly demonstrated ability to distinguish what happened *back then* and what is needed *now*. The appearance of Jesus not only to the Ten but to Thomas becomes part of the list of signs that *are* recorded in this book in order to call men and women to faith as those first-hand experiences are reported in preaching and in the pages of this book. To insert an editorial heading before verses 30-31 — e.g., "The Purpose of John's Gospel" or the like — obscures the tight logical connection between verse 29 and verses 30-31. As Brown puts it:

> As long as Jesus stood among men, one had to come to faith through the visible. Now, at the end of the Gospel, another attitude becomes possible and necessary. This is the era of the Spirit or the invisible presence of Jesus (xiv 17), and the era of signs or appearances is passing away. The transition from 29a to 29b is not merely that one era precedes the other, but that one leads to the other. "But for the fact that Thomas and the other apostles saw the incarnate Christ there would have been no Christian faith at all" (Barrett, p. 477). Or as the evangelist himself phrases it in xx 30-31, he has narrated signs so that people may believe — certainly not a rejection of the value of signs for faith.[21]

21. Brown, *John*, pp. 1050-51.

I am still inclined to the view that this Gospel was written to evangelize Jews, proselytes and God-fearers in the Diaspora.[22] Most commentators today assume the opposite, viz. that this Gospel was written to strengthen the faith of believers, without really arguing the case in any detail.[23] But none of my arguments regarding the logic of the relationship between (a) and (b) in 20:29 depends on a firm decision as to whether 20:30-31 is focusing on coming to faith or confirming people in their faith, but rather on the distinction between how the faith of the first disciples was established and how the faith of later believers was established (i.e., after Jesus had returned to his Father and bequeathed the Spirit), so we need not dwell on the problem here.

6. On οἱ μὴ ἰδόντες καὶ πιστεύσαντες (v. 29)

The logic of the exegesis of verse 29 to this point requires that the people referred to in (b) are future to the time of Jesus' exchange with Thomas, though doubtless contemporary with the time of the evangelist's writing. How, then, shall we understand these two aorist participles? Rather surprisingly, Michaels detects a problem that must be resolved:

> To whom is Jesus referring? Quite clearly to the readers of the Gospel, and others of their generation, whether Jews or Gentiles, who now believe in Jesus without having lived through the events of his ministry. Yet the aorist participles are surprising: "Blessed are those who *did not* see, and *believed.*" We might have expected, "Blessed are those who *will* believe — or even just 'believe,' as in 17:20 — without having seen." How seriously are we to take the past tenses?[24]

---

22. D. A. Carson, "The Purpose of the Fourth Gospel: John 20:30-31 Reconsidered," *JBL* 108 (1987): 639-51; D. A. Carson, "Syntactical and Text-Critical Observations on John 20:30-31: One More Round on the Purpose of the Fourth Gospel," *JBL* 124 (2005): 693-714.

23. Alternatively, outsize conclusions are drawn from the textual variant, aorist or present, behind "that you may believe." It has long been noted, however, that in the Fourth Gospel *both* the present tense and the aorist tense are used *both* in instances where people are coming to faith and in instances where they are persevering in or deepening faith, so that the textual variant is of minimal importance to the purpose of John's Gospel.

24. J. Ramsey Michaels, *The Gospel of John,* New International Commentary on the New Testament (Grand Rapids: Eerdmans, 2010), p. 1019.

Michaels proposes two possible solutions: (1) Jesus is speaking anachronistically for the sake of the readers of John's day. (2) Alternatively, this is in line with Jesus' utterances that he has "other sheep" (10:16), that he is going to gather into one "the children of God who are scattered" (11:52). On this view, Jesus speaks of these other sheep "as if they have *already* believed, knowing that when they do believe, it will in fact be without seeing, at least in the way Thomas and his fellow disciples have seen."[25]

But this is to create problems where there are none. Ever since the rise of *Aktionsart* theory, in the second half of the nineteenth century, almost all grammarians have recognized that Greek tenses do not grammaticalize time in the oblique moods. Some scholars still argue that *adverbial* participles grammaticalize *relative* time (relative, that is, to the time of the main verb in the clause), though in reality the statistics are so mixed that there is no reliable alignment with this conclusion. But the point is that these participles in 20:29 are *not* adverbial, so even that argument must be set aside. Moreover, the last seventy years have witnessed a dramatic increase in the application of aspect theory to the Greek verb.[26] Clearly not all the scholars who promote aspect theory agree in every detail, and inevitably there are some grammarians who reject aspect theory root and branch.[27] Yet aspect theory has made enough strides that it cannot be rightly overlooked. However defenders of aspect theory disagree on this or that detail, they all recognize that the primary semantic function of the various morphological tenses in Greek is not to convey time ("past tense," "present tense"), *even in the indicative*, but the writer's or speaker's (usually unwitting) subjective choice as to how an action or state is to be conceived.

In other words, both under *Aktionsart* theory and under verbal as-

---

25. Michaels, *Gospel*, p. 1019.
26. Among the seminal works are Stanley E. Porter, *Verbal Aspect in the Greek of the New Testament, with Reference to Tense and Mood* (New York: Peter Lang, 1989); Buist M. Fanning, *Verbal Aspect in New Testament Greek* (Oxford: Clarendon, 1990); K. L. McKay, *A New Syntax of the Verb in New Testament Greek: An Aspectual Approach* (New York: Peter Lang, 1994); Constantine R. Campbell, *Verbal Aspect and Non-Indicative Verbs: Further Soundings in the Greek of the New Testament* (New York: Peter Lang, 2008). For a brief introduction to the voluminous literature, see Andrew David Naselli, "A Brief Introduction to Verbal Aspect in New Testament Greek," *DBSJ* 12 (2007): 17-28.
27. See esp. Chrys C. Caragounis, *The Development of Greek and the New Testament: Morphology, Syntax, Phonology, and Textual Transmission* (Tübingen: Mohr Siebeck, 2004).

pect theory, there is no reason here for supposing that the pair of aorist participles are past-referring. Time in Greek is much more commonly conveyed by other devices. There is no *grammatical* reason, then, for not translating verse 29:

> Because you have seen me you have believed;[28]   (a)
> blessed are those who will believe without seeing.   (b)

7. On the Blessing in Verse 29

The one detail in verse 29 that might overturn the balance of judgments in everything that has been argued in this paper so far is the word "Blessed." It is of course attached only to those who do not see and believe; there is no accompanying blessing articulated for Thomas who has seen and believed. Of course, the absence of a "Blessed" in (a) is, formally speaking, an argument from silence, but on first glance it is a telling argument from silence because the parallelism is so obvious. If Thomas is somehow *not* blessed, then is there not at least a hint that his faith is in some sense inferior to that of those mentioned in (b) after all?

The only other place in John's Gospel where certain people are declared to be "blessed" is 13:17. There, however, there is no contrasting statement without the word "blessed," so interpretatively speaking it sheds no light on this passage.

There is one instance of paired statements in John, however, that may shed some light on 20:29, even though the word "blessed" is absent from both elements of the pair. It is found in 1:17:

> For the law was given through Moses;
> grace and truth came through Jesus Christ.

What is striking is that there is no adversative ἀλλά or equivalent conjunction at the beginning of the second line, even though *some* kind of contrast is clearly implicit.

---

28. Some translations render (a) as a question, viz. "Because you have seen me, have you believed?" (so RSV, NRSV, NASB, NAB, ESV). That probably conveys a hint of rebuke. Nevertheless, in the light of the arguments of this paper it is difficult to see why we *should* read a rebuke here, and most translators and commentators opt for the assertion. In fact, the logical relation between (a) and (b), along a historical axis, remains the same.

Observing the flow of the argument helps. At the end of verse 16 we are told that from the fullness of the Word/Christ, we have all received καὶ χάριν ἀντὶ χάριτος. Despite the best efforts to read this as "grace upon grace" or the like, it more plausibly reads as "even grace instead of grace," or, more paraphrastically, "grace in place of grace already given." The explanation is provided in the next verse: note the explanatory "For" (ὅτι). The first "grace" was the good gift of the law given through Moses; the second grace was the fullness of "grace and truth" given through Christ. This way of wording it, without an adversative at the head of the second line, means that *all* of verse 17 is the explanation (ὅτι) of verse 16, *without in any sense depreciating or deprecating the great gift of the law itself,* once that law is rightly understood, from the evangelist's perspective, in its relation to Christ. *And the advance from the first part of verse 17 to the second part is along a salvation-historical axis.*

Formally speaking, of course, 20:29 is not structured exactly the same way. Yet the conceptual parallelism is striking. The great Christological confession of 20:28 is not for Thomas only, but for believers everywhere. The first part of verse 29 affirms that Thomas came to this theological conclusion, this theological believing, on the basis of his own personal experience of the risen Jesus. But Jesus already has his eyes on the many who will believe without ever enjoying the immediacy of evidence that Peter, the Ten, and others did. They are blessed because they believe, even without seeing, not because their faith is intrinsically superior (for no other grounding of their faith was open to them), but simply because they believe. After all, we have already reminded ourselves how earlier in this book Jesus spoke of other sheep he must gather, other scattered children he would draw to himself. Even the promised Paraclete would help the disciples in bearing witness to such folk who at the time of Jesus' interchange with Thomas are still outsiders (15:26-27); indeed, he himself would convict the word (16:7-11). So the gradation from (a) to (b) in verse 29 is, like 1:17, along a salvation-historical axis, and the very means by which this vision of the future would be fulfilled is stipulated in verses 30-31.

Apollos and the Ephesian Disciples: Befores and Afters (Acts 18:24–19:7)

Conrad Gempf

1. Introduction

1.1. The Curiosities of These Stories (Particularly the Problem with Apollos)

The paired stories of the Ephesian "disciples" and the teacher Apollos have baffled readers and commentators for centuries. Who are these disciples and this teacher? They have connections with the Christians and their story, but what unites the two groups of antagonists is that their main connection is with John the Baptist.

Studies throughout the twentieth and into the twenty-first centuries have attempted to enlist these stories into larger views involving an alleged *early catholicism*[1] or the social struggle between a Pauline and a Judean Christianity,[2] or again pneumatics and Paul,[3] filling in from a rich background understanding rather than from the text itself. By such means they have tried to explain unusual details and supply answers to the many difficult questions the text throws up.

Among these many questions about the meaning of μαθηταί and what deficiencies in Apollos's teaching Priscilla and Aquila felt they

---

1. See, e.g., Ernst Käsemann, "The Disciples of John the Baptist in Ephesus," in *Essays on New Testament Themes*, ed. Ernst Käsemann (London: SCM Press, 1964), p. 145, although the term itself is not used.

2. Randall J. Hedlun, "A New Reading of Acts 18:24–19:7: Understanding the Ephesian Disciples Encounter as Social Conflict," *R&T* 17 (2010): 40-60.

3. Michael Wolter, "Apollos und die ephesischen Johannesjünger (Act 18,24–19,7)," *ZNW* 78 (1987): 49-73.

had to address, the primary one must surely be: What does Luke intend his readers to understand from these stories — what is Luke doing?

For this we may be helped by understanding not just *what* Luke says — what words he uses — but *how* he says it — what forms and devices he puts the words into; the *shape* of the narrative as well as the content.

Two major features come to mind. The first is that the two stories form a contrasting pair, which is widely noticed and not atypical of Luke's composition elsewhere. By noting what appear to be deliberate points of contrast, we come closer to understanding Luke's purposes. The second, however, has not been widely employed, at least consciously. It is the observation that these stories might be seen in the context of the old form-critical category of "healing story" or, more precisely for our purposes, what we might call a "before and after" story.

1.2. Form and Narrative Function

Form criticism, fairly early in its history, was hijacked. Form criticism began with the useful observation that stories are told with certain purposes in mind, unlike the events on which they are based, which just happen. Thus when telling a story for a particular purpose, details of an event perceived as irrelevant to the purpose are allowed to drop away in the telling and retelling, while facets of the event perceived to be relevant to the purpose of the telling are preserved and emphasized and perhaps even put in particular formulaic order. As useful as this task may have been, however, what truly fired the imagination of scholars in the middle of the twentieth century was not the text itself but using all methods of analysis as tools for digging behind the text, to the oral period of telling and retelling at least, if not back to the events themselves (if there were such events).[4] The success or otherwise of the digging aspect, however, cannot invalidate the more prosaic findings in terms of there in fact being forms that can help us to understand the message and intention of the story by seeing the characteristic facets for what they are.

One of the most formulaic of all the forms is the healing story;

4. See Graham Twelftree, *Jesus the Miracle Worker* (Downers Grove: IVP, 1999), p. 35.

Bultmann found the pattern of the Gospels was also shared with other stories of Hellenistic origin.[5] It is still true today that when an advertiser wishes to demonstrate the value of a remedy or of any product, the obvious and most powerful way to tell the story is similar to the basic pattern found in the Gospel stories: there is (1) a "Before" portrait, with details chosen to clearly portray the severity of the symptoms of the defect; (2) the encounter in which the healing person or product is applied to the problem; and (3) the "After" portrait, with details again chosen carefully, this time to show just how well the defective features have been restored to as good as new or beyond. Thus, for instance, the lame do not just stand, but leap and jump.

Although the stories in Acts 18:24–19:7 in no way display miraculous healings, they are still stories told with a similar purpose and seem to fall into a similar literary pattern. We are introduced to antagonists who have something not right with them. These characters have encounters with trusted protagonists. The narrator then follows the antagonists after this encounter and demonstrates that they are now functioning well. What a deliberate investigation of these stories within this pattern adds, however, is the possibility that we can gain a better understanding of one facet of the pattern through understanding other parts of the pattern. Thus when Shauf writes of our stories "The initial state . . . may be in question, but their final status is not"[6] we can perhaps use the one to help us understand the other. Specifically, to take one major example, we may well shed light on the vexing question of what Apollos was like before the encounter with Priscilla and Aquila by understanding it as a "Before" portrait that Luke will have intended to relate directly to the "Healing" encounter and to strengths emphasized in the "After" portrait. To exaggerate for purposes of making the point, if we did not know the meaning of the phrase for "withered arm," the nature of the healing story pattern means that we can safely conclude from the "After" portrait of a person stretching their arm all the way out, that the unknown quantity in the "Before" portrait was an arm that could not do that.

We will therefore first look at the rather clearer story of the

---

5. Rudolf Bultmann, *The History of the Synoptic Tradition*, trans. John Marsh (Oxford: Blackwell, 1963), pp. 214-15.

6. Scott Shauf, *Theology as History, History as Theology: Paul in Ephesus in Acts 19* (New York: W. de Gruyter, 2005), pp. 148-49. He is here writing of the story in chapter 19 in particular, but the question rings even more true for the story in chapter 18.

Ephesian disciples with this dynamic in mind before turning to the more difficult case of Apollos in the hopes that his "Healing" and his "After" can help us discern the problem with his "Before."

2. The Story of the Ephesian Disciples (Acts 19:1-7)

2.1. The Ephesian Disciples' "Before"

A healing story will often go directly to the symptoms of the problem, though not usually by means of dialogue, as this one does. The streamlining of the conversation down to the nub question "Did you receive the Holy Spirit . . . ?" should be seen as a function of the type of story this is. With physical healings, the condition of the person is clearly apparent, and often the circumstances of the healing encounter have to do with the problem; thus, for instance, in Acts 3:2, the very reason that Peter and James came upon the lame man at the Gate Called Beautiful is that he was brought there daily to beg. There are cases, however, where the condition is more subtle and, as here, discovered later through words said. Jesus' asking of the blind man "What would you have me do for you?" is not, of course, a good analogy, for the reader has been told in advance that the man is blind. A better analogy is found closer to hand, however. Acts 16:16-19 involves an exorcism and has two unusual features that make it like our own passages: first, the person to be "healed" is initially a somewhat ambiguous character. Although the readers are informed clearly enough that she has a "spirit,"[7] the effects on her were at first surprisingly ambiguous, and it was only after a few days of her following the Christians, calling out that they were messengers of salvation, that Paul performed the exorcism (16:18).[8]

In 19:1 the ambiguity surrounds the words τινες μαθηταί with some commentators holding to the universal use of the word *disciples* as exclusively Christian,[9] while others find the lack of definite article and

---

7. On the "pythonic spirit," see F. F. Bruce, *The Book of the Acts*, New International Commentary on the New Testament (Grand Rapids: Eerdmans, 1988), p. 312.

8. Witherington's treatment of vv. 17-18 tries to make the girl's utterances unambiguously pagan, but does not really explain why it then would take days for Paul to become annoyed. Ben Witherington III, *The Acts of the Apostles: A Socio-Rhetorical Commentary* (Grand Rapids: Eerdmans, 1998), pp. 494-95.

9. So for instance, Fitzmyer calls them "fringe Christians"; see Joseph A. Fitzmyer,

employment of τινες to be a clear marker that these are *not* Christian disciples.[10] But, of course, most recognize that it is what happened later in the story that most supports the conclusion that these people are non-Christians,[11] although none of the commentators surveyed explicitly compares this to the "Before" and "After" of a typical healing story.[12]

It may at first seem surprising that there are followers of John so far away temporally and geographically from his days preaching on the banks of the Jordan River. But the oddness may be an optical illusion caused by the dominance of Christian records of the period, as the writings of Josephus suggest.[13] For without the third chapter of Luke's Gospel, one might be forgiven for thinking that the whole of John's message revolved around Jesus. Luke shows us that he had substantial teaching and preaching of his own to do. That the Christians remembered and preserved primarily the sayings of John that related to the Jesus whom they followed could easily be read against a backdrop where John the Baptist was the more well-known figure,[14] and his recommendations of Jesus could have read like the quotation from a best-selling author on the cover of a new author's first work and been included for very much the same reason.

Since for Luke's readers this story falls directly *after* the Apollos story, the contrast between Apollos who does the things he does with the fervor of the Spirit (ζέων τῷ πνεύματι ἐλάλει; 18:25) on the one hand and the disciples who claim they have not even heard of the Spirit on

---

The Acts of the Apostles, Anchor Bible 31 (New York: Doubleday, 1998), pp. 641-42 and the literature there cited, along with Beverly Roberts Gaventa, *The Acts of the Apostles,* Abingdon New Testament Commentaries (Nashville: Abingdon, 2003), p. 265.

10. Dunn speaks of them being treated as "first time converts"; see James D. G. Dunn, *The Acts of the Apostles* (Peterborough: Epworth, 1996), pp. 255-56, citing 256; see also Mikael C. Parsons, *Acts,* Paideia Commentaries (Grand Rapids: Baker, 2008), pp. 264-65.

11. Shauf, *Theology,* p. 148, usefully reminds us that we use the category of "Christian" of characters in Acts only as an anachronistic convenience.

12. Although Parson's recent commentary openly uses terms like "deficiency" and "remedy." See, e.g., Parsons, *Acts,* pp. 266-67.

13. Although we are not certain of Josephus's exact words about Jesus, arguably John seemed more important to him than Jesus; compare *Ant.* 18.3.3 §63-64 with *Ant.* 18.5.2 §116-19.

14. See Charles H. Scobie, *John the Baptist* (London: SCM Press, 1964), pp. 190-202, for extra-biblical evidence pointing to a John the Baptist sect independent of the Christians.

the other is emphasized very nearly to the point of humor ("Spirit? What spirit?" 19:2).[15] This, clearly, is the manifestation of what is "wrong" with them, the "symptom" that defines their "Before" phase and shows them in need of "healing."

2.2. The Ephesian Disciples' "Healing"

The disciples' transformation began with education, as was also the case with Apollos. The revelation that they did not know the Spirit leads directly to a question about their baptism. Once the disciples had confessed both their lack and their connection with John the Baptist, Paul connects John's repentance-baptism with John's preaching of the One who was to come after him, namely Jesus.

Pesch's view that the twelve did not know that John looked for a Coming One[16] is not universally held. Turner thinks that Paul's confusion about them could not have occurred without their having messianic hopes from John.[17] When Paul informs them that John looked forward to a Coming One who was Jesus, Turner writes: "This much they must have known to be John's disciples at all."[18] It is Luke's writing in particular, however, that gives us a broader view of John's ministry that makes the Pesch view more credible.[19] The additional perspective of Luke's Gospel, aligned with the characterization in Josephus,[20] shows that John's preaching could be characterized as practical ethical material that was prophetic in terms of forth-telling as well as fore-telling.

And, of course, John's teaching and that of Jesus are very similar. These disciples could have a very similar attitude to traditional Juda-

---

15. This, in itself, is good reason for doubting that the Ephesian disciples learned from Apollos. See Max Turner, *Power from on High: The Spirit in Israel's Restoration and Witness in Luke-Acts* (Sheffield: Sheffield Academic Press, 1996), p. 389.

16. See Rudolf Pesch, *Die Apostelgeschichte (Apg 13–28)*, Evangelisch-Katholischer Kommentar zum Neuen Testament V/2 (Zürich: Benziger Verlag, 1986), pp. 165-66.

17. Turner, *Power*, pp. 390-91. See also C. K. Barrett, *The Acts of the Apostles*, International Critical Commentary (Edinburgh; T&T Clark, 1998), vol. 2, p. 894.

18. Turner, *Power*, p. 390. This is thus, for him, merely "reminder."

19. See Pesch, *Apostelgeschichte*, p. 166.

20. Josephus, *Ant.* 18.5.2, is able to report on John without including prophecies of a Coming One.

ism, could talk about the Kingdom of God in near-Christian terms, and perhaps even share an eschatological motivation and outlook.[21]

In light of Jesus' ministry, death, and resurrection, the Christians would come to see John's words about the Coming One as the important bit. But people like these disciples, operating without the benefit of hindsight, could well have understood (or misunderstood) John; practically-minded people would think that the ethical teaching was the important thing for human beings to get on with . . . whatever Spirit-and-fire-baptism judgment was coming was for God to worry about, not them, so long as they did not mistake John himself for the bringer of it (cf. Luke 3:15-17).[22] As Tannehill wrote: "They represent a degenerate form of John's heritage, from the viewpoint of Paul and the narrator. Even so, John's heritage helped lead them to recognize what they had missed."[23]

Unlike the case of Apollos, as we shall see, the "Healing" of the disciples goes past education to their re-baptism, this time in the name of the Lord Jesus (19:5). And this is the *novum* that unlocks the door to what was missing.[24] The "Healing" thus sheds light on the "Before." The "Before" portrays them as lacking the Spirit, the "Healing" displays that lack as being caused by their not being disciples of Jesus. It seems odd to us, perhaps, that their problem was detected by talk about the Spirit rather than talk about Jesus, but there are good rhetorical reasons for this within the flow of Acts and within this story itself, particularly because of the "After."

2.3. The Ephesian Disciples' "After"

They lacked the Spirit, they were informed about the Christ who was to come. They accepted him in baptism, and as a result received the Spirit

---

21. This, I think, answers the question about how it was possible for Paul to mistake these people for μαθηταί even for a moment.

22. Thus Parratt writes that although these people had "undergone 'the baptism of John' they had not fully understood its significance" (J. K. Parratt, "The Rebaptism of the Ephesian Disciples," *ExpT* 79 [1967/1968]: 182). Turner, *Power*, p. 175 n. 18, does not allow for the possibility that these people had misunderstood John's message or de-emphasized part of it.

23. Robert C. Tannehill, *The Narrative Unity of Luke-Acts: A Literary Interpretation* (Minneapolis: Fortress Press, 1990), vol. 2, p. 234.

24. *Pace* Turner, *Power*, pp. 390-91.

they lacked. This provides nice balance in the story, and throughout Acts, what Turner calls *invasive charismatic praise*[25] is a mark of a category of people, a people-group, becoming Christians. Given that that is the sign, it makes sense to show the deficiency as a lack of that sign. We see this used similarly in the story of the Samaritans (Acts 8:14-17).

Paul placed his hands on them and they spoke in tongues and prophesied, much as we have seen happen to other groups. Just as the "After" picture of a person leaping and dancing and praising God speaks to a "Before" of being paralyzed, so an "After" of unambiguously demonstrating belonging speaks to us of a "Before" in which that was not the case. And that the healing took place by reminding them that John looked forward and looked forward specifically to Jesus, reinforces this. Those who understand the ethics of the Kingdom are not far from the Kingdom but are not yet in the fold.

The peculiar addition of verse 7, "and there were about 12 men in all," becomes less unusual if we think that perhaps by this, Luke is making clear that we are talking about a people-group, John's disciples, rather than about some individuals. An obvious parallel is the healing of the 10 lepers, although there the number arguably serves a different purpose: that of contrasting the one grateful one with the others (Luke 17:11-19). And in any case, it looks less out of place when the story is seen as being retold in the form of a "Before and After" healing story, where such details do pop up as they are thought interesting; see most strikingly, Mark 5:42, "Immediately, the girl stood up and walked around (she was twelve years old)."[26]

2.4. The Ephesian Disciples: Summary

So we see that the story appears to function well as a healing "Before and After" story, and that the "Healing" itself as well as the "After" picture aids us in understanding the "Before" condition that is in need of rectification. The marker that there were 12 and the use of the typical people-group result of speaking in tongues and prophesying suggest

25. Turner, *Power*, p. 350.
26. That Luke goes out of his way to say that there were 12 in the "After" rather than the "Before" surely is a disappointment to Hedlun's whole enterprise in which words like twelve are markers of belonging to the Judean strand of anti-Antiochene Christianity.

Apollos and the Ephesian Disciples

that the meaning of the story is: John's disciples are not automatically Christians, they need to be reminded that John looked forward, and to be shown that it was Jesus to whom he looked forward, and that they need to rededicate their lives to *him,* at which point they are very welcome by God, and therefore should be by the church.[27]

3. The Story of Apollos (Acts 18:24-28)

The meaning of Apollos's "Before" is precisely the question at issue. Therefore we will look first at the "Healing" encounter and his "After" from which we might glean clues to help us come to a more adequate understanding of the "Before." The fix and the demonstration may well highlight what the problem was.

3.1. Apollos's "Healing"

Encounter, diagnosis, and healing action all take place in half of verse 26, a sentence. That there even was a diagnosis is only implicit. He spoke boldly in the synagogue. But on hearing him, Priscilla and Aquila took him aside to talk to him.

Despite the clear implication that Priscilla and Aquila detected a lack, what they actually do appears as though it is building on strengths rather than weaknesses. Apollos "had received information in the way of the Lord . . . and taught accurately . . ." (18:25). Paul's friends "more accurately for him set out the way of God" (18:26).

The main thing that happened, then, is that Apollos's knowledge went from ἀκριβῶς to ἀκριβέστερον! Luke is the only New Testament writer to use this intensification.[28] The same word is found twice in the story about the proposed ambush: "ask them to send Paul down to the council as if you were going to determine his case more exactly" (23:15, 20), and once as a description of Felix in 24:22 with wording that parallels our passage: what he has is a more accurate knowledge of the way. Revealingly, even this most excellent knowledge is not complete, as Fe-

---

27. *Pace* Turner, *Power,* p. 394, who sees this people-group as uncontroversial.
28. See, however, Barrett, *Acts,* p. 889, who finds the pairing "contrived" and suggests some alternative understandings.

lix and Drusilla come back in 24:24-25 to hear more about Christianity and seem surprised by what they hear. For this reason, perhaps, the ESV translates ἀκριβέστερον not as "more exact knowledge" but as "a rather accurate knowledge." We will revisit the ἀκριβῶς — ἀκριβέστερον pairing in the "Before" section below.

How surprising it is that the eloquent and knowledgeable Apollos receives this increase in accuracy not from apostles from Jerusalem or leaders of the Antioch church but from Priscilla and Aquila, leather-workers from Rome.[29] Much has been written, understandably, on the placement of Priscilla first in this formulation. But one cannot help wonder if the purpose was not only to elevate Priscilla, but also to make a statement about Apollos. With all his great learning and accuracy, his shortcomings are visible and mendable by non-apostolic associates of Paul — by a woman! While Luke follows Jesus and Paul in regarding women highly — this is no problem for the church — Luke will certainly have known some readers'/hearers' reaction to this.

Perhaps more tellingly, the pair do not "teach" Apollos the way of God, but explain or lay it out for him, ἐκτίθημι.[30] But, given the context, it seems more likely that the wording variation is another way of emphasizing that the eloquent teacher was able to learn not from these people who were more eloquent teachers, but ordinary people who simply explained rather than sophist/experts who gave a lecture.

What we learn, then, from Apollos's "Healing" is that there was something wrong with him — something that Christians who were not apostles could detect. What was needed, however, was having something explained, and in a way that Christians like Priscilla and Aquila could manage.

---

29. Bruce writes "They themselves had probably had the same experience when they met Paul and he supplemented the knowledge of the Way which they had acquired in Rome," without noticing that the implication of this is that Apollos is below them who are below Paul (Bruce, *Book*, p. 360).

30. Although he does not seem to notice it, this word plays right into Hedlun's hand; not only is Acts the only book of the New Testament in which it is found, but in those other passages where Luke uses it with the meaning of "explain," it is always progressive Christians explaining to those more "Jewish" than themselves: Peter explaining the Cornelius incident in 11:4 and Paul explaining his position to the Roman Jews in 28:23. See Hedlun, "Reading," p. 49.

3.2. Apollos's "After"

There are two verses in Apollos's "After." Verse 27 seems primarily "social" — about his place in the community. In fact, the beginning of the sentence is written in such a way that it is "the brothers" who are the subject of the sentence, rather than Apollos: the Christians encouraged him and wrote letters of recommendation.

He becomes more active in the second clause in the sentence. When he arrived in his new situation, he was helpful. Some commentators think that this is meant to contrast with his effect on (his) Ephesian disciples — he did not help then, but he helps now — but as Turner and others have shown, there is no compelling reason to suppose that he was in contact with those people.[31]

The force of the γάρ in verse 28 means that we should probably not think that there are two separate spheres of influence — (1) he helped the believers and (2) he refuted the Jews — but rather that he helped the believers *by* powerfully and publicly arguing with the Jews. We are also told that his method was to "show by the scriptures."

Thus all of the "After" leads up to and is climaxed by the end of verse 28 and the content to his message. People recommended him and he helped, doing so by refuting the Jews by the Scriptures. And since his "Healing" consisted of the reception of more accurate information, it would be natural to see that played out in his "After" in the substance of this helpful refutation of the Jews.

As to the content of that refutation, we are told only that he showed that Jesus is the Christ. The placement of the name of Jesus at the end of the sentence makes it slightly more emphatic: he "showed by the scriptures that it is Jesus who is the Christ" (18:28).[32]

Thus we can see five steps in Apollos's "After": (1) the new Apollos enjoyed the confidence of the Christians; (2) he was much help to the believers by (3) powerfully confuting the Jews, (4) showing from the Scriptures that (5) Jesus is the Christ. But the main thrust is the last. That Apollos could (now) show that Jesus is the Christ is how he helped the believers in Corinth and validated the trust shown in him by the brethren who encouraged him and wrote his letter of recommendation.

---

31. Turner, *Power*, p. 389.
32. See Barrett, *Acts*, p. 892, for a discussion of textual variants and the emphasis.

Conrad Gempf

3.3. Apollos's "Before"

The "Before" picture of Apollos, verses 24-25 or 24-26a, at first glance, does not appear to be the portrayal of someone in need of repair or healing. In its simplest form, it is comprised of two statements: "A certain Jew arrived at Ephesus. This person spoke and taught accurately the things about Jesus." Hanging off of these two statements are various qualifying clauses.

A Certain Jew Arrived in Ephesus The first main statement, a certain Jew arrived at Ephesus, bristles with clauses describing him, and they are things that are *not* problems (18:24).[33] That his name was Apollos, and reminiscent of the god Apollo, is probably the reason for introducing him as a Jew.[34] Luke also tells us that he was a learned and eloquent man and that he was mighty in the Scriptures. These characteristics are the same "before and after." As we will see, the phrases "powerfully confuted" and "showed using scripture" of verse 28 are their echoes.

Had Been Informed about the Way of the Lord This is the first of three clauses in verse 25 that seem to force us to conclude that Apollos was already a Christian in his "Before" phase. Although ὁδός is a common word used with a variety of meanings, that the Christian Way is meant here seems a virtually inescapable conclusion. Since we have just been told in the previous verse that Apollos is a Jew and that he was mighty in the Scriptures, the phrase cannot bear the more generic meaning about God's plans as revealed in Scripture. It is tempting to force a connection with John the Baptist's preparing the way of the Lord (Luke 1:76; 3:4), but ultimately, the special meaning Luke first

---

33. In common with the "certain" disciples in Ephesus, Apollos is introduced using the adjectival indefinite pronoun. It is suggestive but not conclusive that "defective" Christians such as Ananias in 5:1 and Simon Magus in 8:9 are introduced using this construct while major positive characters such as Barnabas in 4:36, Stephen in 6:5, and Saul/Paul in 7:58 are introduced without it, even though it would be natural enough in the construction. But as explained above, the pattern is not inviolate and we cannot be certain from the grammar that distancing or disapproval is indicated.

34. Hedlun believes that Luke introduces him as a Jew in order to connect him to Judean Christianity ("the circumcision-covenant social world"); Hedlun, "Reading," pp. 46-47. See Gaventa, *Acts*, p. 264. It is also worth noting that one of the Jew Apollos's correctors, Aquila, was also introduced to the reader as a Jew in Acts 18:2.

Apollos and the Ephesian Disciples

spells out in contrast with another educated Jew mighty in Scriptures, Saul of Tarsus, must hold here (Acts 9:2) not only because of the precedent, but because the phrase must mean Christianity in the following verse.[35]

There remains, however, a question mark over what Luke intends us to understand by κατηχέω. Since this is the word from which our English word *catechism* derives, it is not surprising that in Paul's letters, it generally means a deliberate and systematic instruction on Christian matters.[36] In Luke's writing, however, the meaning is less clear. In Acts 21:21 and 24, the author clearly wants the readers to believe that what others have been "informed about" is wrong; the word means little more than "heard reports or rumors about," regardless of their truth. The programmatic usage in the prologue of the Gospel, 1:4, is almost always translated as if it meant that Luke expects his readers to "have done their catechism" before reading his work. But the phrase there could easily be translated "so that you may know the truth behind the tales that you have heard."[37] If Luke here means only that Apollos had heard reports about Jesus rather than received a course of instruction, much that follows makes better sense. It explains the use of ἀκριβῶς later in the verse; inaccuracy was a real possibility. It also makes sense given the following verse — else we would have to believe that one aside by Priscilla and Aquila was of more help than a systematic instruction. That Apollos has heard things about Christianity may be a better translation than "he had been instructed in the way of the Lord."[38]

Fervent in Spirit Virtually all modern translations relegate the Spirit in verse 25 to the margins, seeing the phrase as referring to Apollos's own spirit within him being fervent.[39] This allows him to fit as a parallel to the Ephesian disciples who also knew only the baptism of John. It is clear that they did not have the Holy Spirit, so the rule of interpreting the ambiguous example by means of the clear one comes into play and translators play it safe.

---

35. The variation of "way of the Lord" and "way of God" is certainly not significant.
36. See especially Galatians 6:6, but also Romans 2:18 and 1 Corinthians 14:19.
37. See John Nolland, *Luke 1–9:20*, Word Biblical Commentary 35A (Dallas: Word, 1989), pp. 10-11.
38. *Pace* Witherington, *Acts*, p. 566.
39. So also, Parsons, who translates it merely "he spoke with great enthusiasm" (*Acts*, pp. 262-63).

Most commentators since Käsemann's influential essay, however, find much more pull in parallel constructions elsewhere, particularly in Romans 12:11,[40] to argue that this must mean Luke intends for us to see him as fervent in the Holy Spirit. But this parallel is not sufficient. Luke and Paul do not always use the words the same way.

There are also reasons from the immediate context. Sandwiched between clauses telling the reader that Apollos knew about the Way and that he spoke and taught accurately, that he was enthused by the Holy Spirit is the natural reading.[41] Barrett writes "it is unlikely that one as interested as Luke in phenomena due to the Spirit would use ζέων τῷ πνεύματι to mean no more than an effervescent, lively spirit."[42]

If our classification of these stories as "Before and After" stories is correct, however, this provides independent corroboration that, in contrast to the Ephesian disciples, neither Apollos's "Healing" nor his "After" state includes demonstrations that he had now received the Spirit, making it unlikely that Luke feels that he lacks the Spirit in his "Before" state.

Speaking and Teaching Accurately the Things about Jesus The information he had received enabled him to speak and teach "accurately" the things about Jesus. In this clause again, two phrases in particular warrant attention: the "accurately" and the phrase "the things about Jesus."

The ἀκριβῶς of verse 25 will be, as we have seen above, intensified in the "Healing" section, verse 26. The impression we take from there is that while ἀκριβέστερον is an improvement, it is not intended to mean that Apollos even afterward had exhaustive expert knowledge. It is a comparative rather than a superlative. The other usages in Acts, where it conveys a fairly basic level of knowledge, confirm that Apollos's starting "accurate" knowledge was not very extensive.[43] Perhaps all it means is that he was not repeating false tales about Jesus, very much to the point if our interpretation of κατηχέω is correct.

But, at first, it seems difficult to reconcile the ἀκριβῶς here as

---

40. Käsemann, "Disciples," p. 143.

41. See also Turner, *Power*, p. 389 n. 124, on this and further evidence for this interpretation.

42. Barrett, *Acts*, p. 888.

43. "Apollos accurately taught everything he knew about Jesus although his knowledge was limited" (Parsons, *Acts*, p. 263).

something less than "a rather accurate knowledge" on the one hand with the author's willingness to use the word of himself in the Gospel's preface on the other hand: "having traced the course of all things accurately from the first" (Luke 1:3). This is a problem under any interpretation and wider than our passage. Luke presents himself as having traced things accurately and presents Apollos with similar words, yet Apollos's ἀκριβῶς is clearly defective.

One possibility is to see this "accurate knowledge" as something like objective, factual knowledge apart from involvement — what people today might call "head" rather than "heart" knowledge (and the ancients might have called "heart" rather than "gut" knowledge). Were this the implication of the word choice, it could fit both settings admirably in creating a distance between the facts and the belief system they imply, which would create a lack as far as Apollos was concerned but could be seen as rhetorical understatement for the historian of the preface.[44] It also would make a clear distinction with Luke's hero, Paul, who is portrayed as fulfilling his duty in the final verse of Acts with many of the same words, omitting the word ἀκριβῶς. In contemporary English we sometimes use the adjective "technically" to denote the difference: "Paul was teaching people the things about Jesus, and Apollos was technically doing the same."

The phrase "the things about Jesus" is amply paralleled elsewhere in Luke-Acts, perhaps most famously at the ending of the book, Acts 28:31, in which context Paul is clearly being portrayed as a champion of the faith. Less frequently cited is Luke 24:19, where the Emmaus disciples are clearly speaking about things they do not fully understand.

Further, in Acts 24 Luke speaks of Felix as having "a more exact knowledge concerning the Way" (24:22) and then listening to Paul "concerning the faith in Christ Jesus" (24:24). In these two passages, however, only περί is used, rather than the construct τὰ περί + genitive.

Another difference worth noticing is that, in 28:31, Paul teaches the things concerning the Lord Jesus Christ, whereas in Apollos's "Before" it is simply "the things concerning Jesus." It is not until the "After" that he is said to explicitly show (through the Scriptures) that Je-

---

44. For a useful discussion about the extent of Theophilus's instruction and need of more accuracy, relating it to our passages, see Joel B. Green, *The Gospel of Luke*, New International Commentary on the New Testament (Grand Rapids: Eerdmans, 1997), pp. 45-46.

sus is the Christ. Similarly in Luke 24:19, the Emmaus disciples, their hopes still dashed when they encounter the stranger on the road, speak about "the things concerning Jesus of Nazareth."

Having Known Only the Baptism of John As with the Ephesian disciples, this is an obvious limiter and the first explicit clue of defect: "he was only acquainted with the baptism of John." That this is a limiter could take the reader by surprise, given the significance it plays in Acts 1:22 as a necessary qualification for the replacement twelfth apostle. But the use of μόνον as well as the clear implications of context make the nature of the matter clear: the thrust appears not to be "he spoke and taught accurately with this one defect," as much as, "is it not amazing that he spoke and taught so well given that he knew only this much?"

"After" and "Before": Summary Many of our five "After" facets rehearse themes already in Apollos's "Before" image. The first two, that the "After" Apollos enjoyed the confidence and recommendations of the Christians and helped them, are the most obvious contrast. The "Before" Apollos's presentation, for all its eloquence and "accuracy" and mighty use of Scripture, was such that Christians who heard it made the decision to pull him aside to give him further instruction. The "Before" Apollos required aid; the "After" Apollos inspired recommendations.

The third "After" facet, his powerful confutation of the Jews (18:28), seems to reflect his eloquence (18:24) and his speaking boldly in the synagogue (18:26). There is no contrast in terms of successfulness before and after. It would be going too far to argue that we have no indication of success in the "Before" since the "After" contains no bragging about the results either; neither formulation demands nor rules out the possibility that no Jews were convinced by his work.

The fourth facet of the "After" — that he argued in Corinth using the Scriptures — clearly relates directly to the "Before" notice that he was mighty in the Scriptures (18:24).

The fifth facet is debatable. He taught that it was Jesus who was the Christ. We might ordinarily believe that this correlates with the "Before" clause that he spoke and taught accurately the things about Jesus. But this easy correlation is brought into question by the nature of the "Healing" which completely undermines the word "accurately" in the "Before," and also by the emphasis put upon the content in the "After" by the author.

3.4. Apollos: Summary

If this story follows the Healing Story pattern and we are correct that both the "Healing" section and the "After" section are pointing to insufficient information, specifically about the connection between Jesus and Messiah, then two possibilities present themselves.

The first possibility is that Apollos, unlike the Ephesian disciples, understood the whole of John's message and centered his theology not on ethical teaching but on the hope of the One whom John announced was coming. On this hypothesis, we might paraphrase verse 25: "his teaching about the coming one fitted Jesus accurately, even though his knowledge went no further than the baptism of John."

This interpretation has two major points against it: were this Luke's intention, he would have done much better to tell us that Apollos taught about *the Christ* accurately, even though he knew only the baptism of John. We would also be required to adopt an unnatural interpretation of the beginning of verse 25: that "the way of the Lord" he was taught should be linked to John's "preparing the way of the Lord" rather than to "the Way" as it is usually used in Acts. These two things together make this interpretation, as attractive as it is narratively, unlikely.

The second possibility is that Apollos had been informed or told of the information about Jesus, but that he interpreted it incompletely, regarding Jesus as the successor to John's mission rather than its fulfillment, an Elisha to John's Elijah. He knew about the way accurately, but not necessarily more accurately than Felix or others knew the way accurately; Priscilla and Aquila helped him to see the connections and conclusions he should draw from it.

The points that go against this interpretation are not in the text, but largely come from what is *not* said or done and the implications. Apollos appears not to need rebaptism or to receive the Spirit; he is adjusted rather than converted. But if his situation *is* like that of Felix, we would expect more than that, and this is even more acutely felt when we contemplate what it is Luke intends to teach his readers from the pair of stories. Whatever the state of his knowledge, of course, he appears to be acting in line with the Spirit, in a way that Felix or others were not.

4. Conclusion: Luke's Message

Throughout the book of Acts, we must remind ourselves that although we learn much about Luke's pneumatology through what he writes, it still remains the case that he is not, primarily, writing to teach pneumatology. Much closer to his aims is the demonstration that all people-groups can be accepted into the church. It seems most likely that this pair of stories is intended to demonstrate that that is true about followers of John the Baptist.

Barrett cautiously wrote "You could not treat the disciples of . . . John . . . as if they were the enemy; yet they were not in any full sense Christians. If they decided to become Christians, what was to be done with them?"[45] Because these two stories are intended as contrast, the message about John's followers must be seen as: It depends. There are those who, like the Ephesian Disciples, were impressed by John's prophetic preaching of the need for repentance and radical eschatologically-conscious living, but who have not followed this through with knowledge or understanding of Jesus. These need to be taught the teaching of *John himself* more adequately and brought to Jesus with (re)baptism and given the Spirit. Then there are those who, like Apollos, already have knowledge of Jesus and are already working in line with the Spirit. These are already on the right track, but need to be taught about the connections more adequately before they can be whole-heartedly recommended and accepted.

Thus, a close look at Apollos's "After" state suggests a social change and a doctrinal change from the "Before." The ending of the story emphasizes the confidence that the Christians came to have in him and the help that he was to the community, in contrast to the "Before" state where we hear of his scholarship and Priscilla and Aquila's apparent lack of confidence. But this social aspect leads up the main demonstration of his "healing," which concerns Scriptural proof that

---

45. C. K. Barrett, "Apollos and the Twelve Disciples of Ephesus," in *The New Testament Age: Essays in Honor of Bo Reicke*, ed. William C. Weinrich (Macon: Mercer University Press, 1984), vol. 1, p. 37.

Jesus is the Christ, strongly suggesting a doctrinal change or adjustment concerning his Christology.

There is a connection between Apollos's accurate, though improvable, knowledge of Jesus and the presence of the Spirit. That this connection is no accident is demonstrated by the fact that the Ephesian disciples' healing encounter is portrayed as including learning about Jesus to deal with symptoms of a lack of Spirit. What this connection is, exactly, is a more subtle question and requires further work. Teaching this is not Luke's primary goal. In the meanwhile, seeing the stories broadly within the pattern of "Healing" stories supplies a tool to understanding the "Before" state given the details of the "Healing" and the "After." Doing so has provided some independent corroboration for positions arrived at on other grounds.

Power from In Between:
The Relational Experience of the Holy Spirit and Spiritual Gifts in Paul's Churches

Volker Rabens

Max Turner concludes his *magnus opum* on Lukan Pneumatology, *Power from on High,* with the words: "Both restoration and mission ... lie at the heart of Lukan pneumatology: the 'Power from on High' may not be truly felt unless we are willing to be committed to both."[1] Turner is hence convinced that, according to Luke, the work of the Spirit encompasses and empowers the entire breadth of Christian life, from its inception to its multiplication. And he believes that this power may be "truly felt." In this essay I want to ask whether this conclusion could also apply to Paul. How are we to envision the work of the Holy Spirit and the practice of spiritual gifts in Paul's churches, and, moreover, is it appropriate to speak in this regard of spiritual *experiences* or perhaps even "true feelings"? One of the results of this inquiry into the experiential side of New Testament pneumatology will be that, as in Luke-Acts, the Spirit in Paul is "Power from on High." However, it seems that the way in which this empowering is experienced can be best understood by employing the notion of *power from in between*. That is, the actual endowment with power from *on high* is experienced in Paul's churches as the Spirit's drawing people *nearby* — to God and to one another.

One of the most outstanding proponents of the experiential dimension of early Christian pneumatology emphasized by Turner was Hermann Gunkel. Writing more than a hundred years before Turner, Gunkel in his groundbreaking dissertation *The Influence of the Holy*

---

1. Max Turner, *Power from on High: The Spirit in Israel's Restoration and Witness in Luke-Acts* (Sheffield: Sheffield Academic Press, 1996), p. 455.

Spirit places the experiences of the Spirit at the center of early Christian spirituality. In addition to this emphasis on experience, Gunkel is of the opinion that all later readers of the ancient reports of these experiences need to put themselves in a position of "feeling" or "living" the early Christian pneumatics' inner states after them. Only then can the readers understand that these reports are based on the immediate experiences of the enthusiasts themselves who have sensed a foreign being inside themselves.[2]

However, within New Testament scholarship this emphasis on the possibility or even necessity of emotionally experiencing the indwelling Spirit is a matter of debate. For instance, in his *Identity and Experience in the New Testament*,[3] Klaus Berger rejects the view that early Christians had an emotional spirituality as a historical anachronism. According to Berger, the "new creation" (dying in baptism and newness of life, cf. Rom. 6:4; 12:2) is for Paul not a matter of emotions and inner experiences. For Paul, spirituality has nothing to do with this kind of psychology. Rather, he considers feelings, emotionality, and particularly the human ability for striving, to be inherently suspicious. In this way, Paul is a real opponent of the "modern union between pietism and psychology."[4]

Friedrich Wilhelm Horn's criticism of Gunkel is even more intimately related to the question of how to interpret the early Christian reflections on pneumatic experiences. Horn is opposed to Gunkel giving spiritual experiences precedence over the doctrine of the Spirit. He claims the opposite: the early Christian statements regarding the Spirit are primarily dogmas and not reflections of experiences.[5] Gunkel had justified this division in the following way: "In order to evaluate pneumatic experiences we must first of all sharply distinguish the *experience*

---

2. Hermann Gunkel, *Die Wirkungen des heiligen Geistes nach der populären Anschauung der apostolischen Zeit und der Lehre des Apostels Paulus*, 3rd ed. (Göttingen: Vandenhoeck & Ruprecht, 1909), pp. IV, 80-81; Hermann Gunkel, *The Influence of the Holy Spirit: The Popular View of the Apostolic Age and the Teaching of the Apostle Paul* (Philadelphia: Fortress Press, 1979), pp. 1-8.

3. Klaus Berger, *Identity and Experience in the New Testament* (Minneapolis: Fortress Press, 2003), translation of Klaus Berger, *Historische Psychologie des Neuen Testaments* (Stuttgart: Katholisches Bibelwerk, 1991).

4. Berger, *Identity*, p. 128; cf. pp. 129-33.

5. Friedrich Wilhelm Horn, *Das Angeld des Geistes: Studien zur paulinischen Pneumatologie* (Göttingen: Vandenhoeck & Ruprecht, 1992), p. 15.

Volker Rabens

of the pneumatic himself from the *interpretation* given it by him or his observers. Such interpretation varies according to the cultural epoch and religion of the evaluator."[6] Horn fundamentally disagrees with this position and rightly points to the interdependence between observance and interpretation of an experience.[7] This interdependence, which is central for understanding pneumatic experiences, will be the object of close scrutiny in the next section. On the basis of our findings we will then turn to the religious-historical context of Pauline pneumatology and, finally, to Paul and his churches themselves.

1. Experience and Interpretation

Gunkel speaks of pneumatic experiences, of events and their interpretations. How do these concepts relate to each other? One possibility of differentiating is provided by the following definition by Gerd Theissen: An event *(Erlebnis)* is an individual experience *(Erfahrung)*, and an experience is the processing of recurring events. Both are subject-related, dependent on perception and dependent on interpretation. They are subject-related because they are accessible to an individual person (or inter-subjective if others share the same experience). They are dependent on perception because they are a matter of sensory perceptions which are received by human beings.[8] Most important for our discussion, however, is the fact that experiences are dependent on interpretation, because, alongside the sensory perceptions, a pre-structuring cognitive interpretation is part of the experience. "Perception is always perception of an object 'as' something, of a table as a ta-

---

6. Gunkel, *Influence*, p. 5, his italics (see Gunkel, *Wirkungen*, p. VI); cf. pp. 13-14, et al.
7. Horn, *Angeld*, p. 14.
8. Gerd Theissen, *Erleben und Verhalten der ersten Christen: Eine Psychologie des Urchristentums* (Gütersloh: Gütersloher Verlagshaus, 2007), p. 111. Theissen defines *religious* experience as "(1) contact with a reality that transcends the everyday world, which (2) is spontaneously interpreted as valid and intentional, which (3) has the power to build community and (4) motivates for action" (p. 114). However, see Werner H. Ritter, "Was meint Erfahrung? Versuch einer Verständnisbestimmung im christlichen Kontext," *MTZ* 61 (2010): 34, who points out that experiences of self-transcendence *(Selbsttranszendenz)* can in principle happen to everyone and need not be religious experiences as such. Experiences of self-transcendence usually become religious experiences in the context of a particular framework of interpretation and a concrete community that shares these experiences *(Erfahrungsgemeinschaft)*.

ble, of a human being as a human being. We match the inflowing data of the senses spontaneously with patterns and cognitive schemes which are coded in our brain so that every perception contains interpretations: We assimilate the data of the senses into the world as it is interpreted by us."[9] Since religious experiences are feelings and events in which religious patterns of interpretation are effective, it is necessary to examine these religious patterns of interpretation more closely. In this way a positivistic epistemology of starting with "facts" and "events" can be avoided, against which Horn justifiably warns.[10]

Focusing on doctrine to the exclusion of the dimension of experience, on the other hand, may lead to being in danger of projecting one's own (modern) horizon of interpretation in a positivistic way onto the ancient world.[11] In the next section we will see that the theological and religious-historical framework of interpretation of the early Christian discourse on the Holy Spirit suggests that the Spirit-texts which relate an experiential dimension should by and large indeed be understood to be a reflection of tangible experiences. For a "Spirit-reception" without the dimension of experience would, considering this religious-historical background, not have been comprehended as such. However, we will first of all show from the example of two Pauline texts and some further considerations that even Paul's argumentation on its own presupposes an experience of the Spirit and that it is thus not merely a theoretical reflection of early Christian theology produced by the eschatological awareness of the early church.[12]

---

9. Theissen, *Erleben*, p. 112 ("Wir assimilieren die Sinnesdaten an eine von uns gedeutete Welt"); cf. pp. 113-18; Peter L. Berger and Thomas Luckmann, *Die gesellschaftliche Konstruktion der Wirklichkeit: Eine Theorie der Wissenssoziologie* (Frankfurt: Fischer, 1969), pp. 98-124. See further Ulrich Barth, "Was heißt 'Vernunft der Religion'? Subjektphilosophische, kulturtheoretische und religionswissenschaftliche Erwägungen im Anschluss an Schleiermacher," in *Der Gott der Vernunft: Protestantismus und vernünftiger Gottesgedanke*, ed. Jörg Lauster and Bernd Oberdorfer (Tübingen: Mohr Siebeck, 2009), pp. 200-203, and the discussion in part 3 of André Munzinger's essay, pp. 347-53 in the present volume.

10. Horn, *Angeld*, p. 21.

11. Apart from that, one also needs to note that experiences can transcend the boundaries of one's interpretative horizon. So, e.g., the so-called Damascus Road experience in Acts 9. While we interpret everything new that we encounter according to existing cognitive structures ("assimilation"), these cognitive structures continue to be modified through such encounters ("accommodation").

12. Thus, however, Horn, *Angeld*, pp. 15, 109, 172, who even disputes the experiential character of the reception of the Spirit in Gal. 3:1-5.

Volker Rabens

In the course of his argumentation in his letter to the Galatians — in which Paul tries to convince his audience that they have become part of the church of God through Christ and not through works of the law — Paul asks the Galatians if they have received the Spirit through the works of the law or through believing the gospel (Gal. 3:1-5). This argumentation can only be persuasive if the Galatians can indeed recall receiving the Spirit. However, that this memory is tied to a tangible experience comes explicitly to the fore through the way in which Paul connects in parallel "receiving the Spirit" (ἐξ ἔργων νόμου τὸ πνεῦμα ἐλάβετε ἢ ἐξ ἀκοῆς πίστεως; [v. 2]) and "experiencing so much" (τοσαῦτα ἐπάθετε εἰκῇ; [v. 4]). The Spirit-reception was, therefore, a "great experience." In the subsequent sentence it is listed together with powerful deeds brought about by God ("does God supply you with the Spirit and work miracles among you . . . ?" [v. 5]).[13] Paul advances a similar argument in 1 Thessalonians 1:4-6, where he refers back to the experience of the Spirit in the same foundational way: "For *we know*, brothers and sisters beloved by God, that he has chosen you, *because* our message of the gospel came to you not in word only, but also *in power and in the Holy Spirit and with full conviction;* . . . And *you became imitators* of us and of the Lord, *for* in spite of persecution you received the word with *joy inspired by the Holy Spirit.*"

Also Berger affirms the possibility of experiencing the Spirit — and this reveals a certain tension to his earlier statements regarding Christian spirituality and the new creation. However, he emphasizes that the power which Christians receive from God does not usually become perceptible as emotion or sentiment but manifests itself in concrete deeds. These deeds reveal themselves particularly in the realization of genuine fellowship among Christians. "Here, above all, is where the empirical dimension of Christianity is to be found. This is also why Paul gives such great attention to the works of Christians. The reality of faith for Paul is not primarily to be found in a subjective state of feelings but quite decisively in an experience that is distinct and verifiable."[14] According to Berger, Spirit-wrought works thus lead to Christian fellowship, and this fellowship is a truly verifiable experience. I endorse this view. However, it seems to be unnecessary to reject the no-

---

13. Cf. Rudolf Schnackenburg, "Geisterfahrung im Leben des Christen," in R. Schnackenburg, *Maßstab des Glaubens: Fragen heutiger Christen im Licht des Neuen Testaments* (Freiburg: Herder, 1978), p. 180.

14. Berger, *Identity*, p. 204.

tion of a "subjective state of feelings" because actions usually trigger emotions. If these actions are Spirit-wrought, then the emotions are at least secondarily Spirit-wrought or provoked by the Spirit. This applies particularly to fellowship since fellowship does not exist without (fellowship-)feelings *(Gemeinschaftsgefühl)*. In these interpersonal interactions human beings are involved in their entirety, including their emotions. Moreover, Berger lists a multitude of early Christian experiences of the Spirit, of which the majority clearly have emotional components: peace, praise and singing songs (including glossolalia), scriptural interpretation, joy ("the emotional counterpart to all kinds of desire [cf. Rom. 14:17; Gal. 5:19-23]"[15]), the power to resist (e.g. adverse political powers), abolition of differences between human beings, the groaning of the Spirit, the experience of charisms, etc.[16]

We can thus establish a "both and" with regard to the contrasting pairs discussed above (i.e. "primarily experience or primarily doctrine" and "primarily deeds or primarily emotions") — experience and interpretation are interdependent and belong together in the same way as actions and emotions. Such a balanced approach should also be applied to yet another alleged opposition: According to Bultmann, who is building on Gunkel, Paul knows two different concepts of (the work of) the Spirit. Namely, on the one hand the Spirit is seen as a *disposition* which all Christians have received in baptism, and on the other hand it is seen as an *actual power* given now and again, seizing a human being for the occasion and enabling her to accomplish extraordinary things. According to the first understanding of the Spirit, all Christians are pneumatics. According to the second understanding, only those who possess the Spirit in a special way are pneumatics (thus contradicting what Paul says elsewhere, i.e., that all gifts of the Spirit are of equal value [1 Cor. 12-14]).[17]

However, as we shall see in more detail in Part 3 of this article, the spectrum of the work of the Spirit in Paul is not divided into two different concepts of the Spirit or two types of bearers of the Spirit. Every Christian is entitled to the diverse spectrum of spiritual manifestations for every Christian is a pneumatic, even if there are different gifts (cf. 1 Cor. 12-14; Rom. 8; etc.). However, it is crucial for Paul that all dimen-

---

15. Berger, *Identity*, p. 200.
16. Berger, *Identity*, pp. 199-201.
17. Rudolf Bultmann, *Theology of the New Testament* (London: SCM Press, 1952), vol. 1, pp. 157-63. Cf. the critique by Theissen, *Erleben*, pp. 119-20.

sions of the work of the Spirit manifest themselves primarily in the community and, moreover, serve the formation and deepening of this very community. According to Paul, the empowering work of the Spirit is, therefore, deeply relational ("power from in between"): The Spirit is experienced as bringing about relationships, because the Spirit facilitates a vivid connection to God (cf., e.g., 1 Cor. 2:9-11) and places the individual into a loving fellowship with fellow believers (cf., e.g., Gal. 4:4-7; 1 Cor. 12:7-27). At the same time, the quality of these experiences is both the empowerment for and the measure of loving togetherness in the community. Through the Spirit-wrought experience of loving relationships Christian life is thus determined by the Spirit with regard to both empowerment and ethos.[18]

The realization that the experience of love and fellowship is a life-transforming event is also certified by modern psychological research.[19] More important for our study, however, is the fact that this insight has a broad foundation in biblical literature.[20] Paul too stands firmly within this tradition.[21] For example, in Philippians 2:1 we find a list of sources of strength for the life of the church: encouragement in Christ, consola-

---

18. For more details, see Volker Rabens, *The Holy Spirit and Ethics in Paul: Transformation and Empowering for Religious-Ethical Life* (Tübingen: Mohr Siebeck, 2010), chs. 4 and 6. This relational approach to the empowering of religious-ethical life can be differentiated from that of "infusion-transformation" as represented by the work of Horn and Engberg-Pedersen which is based on a Stoic concept of πνεῦμα as a physical substance (see the discussion in Rabens, *Spirit*, chs. 1-3). For a brief comparison of these two approaches, see the comparative review by Peter Orr of Troels Engberg-Pedersen, *Cosmology and Self in the Apostle Paul: The Material Spirit* (Oxford: Oxford University Press, 2010) and my *The Holy Spirit and Ethics in Paul*, in *Themelios* 35 (2010): 452-55.

19. See, e.g., Robert A. Hinde, *Towards Understanding Relationships* (London: Academic Press, 1979), pp. 4, 14, 273, 326; John Bowlby, *A Secure Base: Parent-Child Attachment and Healthy Human Development* (New York: Basic Books, 1988), pp. 119-36; Hugh LaFollette, *Personal Relationships: Love, Identity, and Morality* (Oxford: Blackwell, 1996), pp. 89-90, 197-99, 207-9; Ludwig Stecher, *Die Wirkung sozialer Beziehungen: Empirische Ergebnisse zur Bedeutung sozialen Kapitals für die Entwicklung von Kindern und Jugendlichen* (Munich: Juventa, 2001), pp. 249-50; Phillip R. Shaver and Mario Mikulincer, "Attachment Theory, Individual Psychodynamics, and Relationship Functioning," in *The Cambridge Handbook of Personal Relationships*, ed. A. L. Vangelisti and D. Perlman (Cambridge: Cambridge University Press, 2006), pp. 251-71.

20. Cf. the overview in Reinhold Boschki, *"Beziehung" als Leitbegriff der Religionspädagogik: Grundlegung einer dialogisch-kreativen Religionsdidaktik* (Ostfildern: Schwabenverlag, 2003), pp. 239-60.

21. Cf. Rabens, *Spirit*, pp. 135-38.

tion from love, fellowship in the Spirit, and affection and sympathy. "Love builds up" (1 Cor. 8:1) — this is the experience of those who are loved by God and who share this love (8:3; cf. 2 Cor. 1:3-5; 1 Thess. 3:12-13). Even in the face of persecution the church is empowered by the love of Christ from which no-one can separate her (Rom. 8:35, 39). The church can conquer these adversities through him who has *loved* her (8:37; cf. Phil. 4:13). This transforming power of love works not only on the "vertical" but also on the "horizontal" level of relationships: Paul builds on this "power from in between" when he, for instance, writes to the Romans that he longs to meet with them personally, "so that I may share with you some spiritual gift to strengthen you — or rather so that we may be mutually encouraged by each other's faith, both yours and mine" (Rom. 1:11-12; cf. 2 Cor. 2:2-4; 3:2-3; Phlm. 20).

The spirituality that Paul conveys to his churches builds firmly on these relational experiences. And the Spirit plays a central role in this. The Spirit draws believers closer to God and fellow human beings as we will see in the exegesis below. Textual analysis will show, further, that the dualism of pneumatic experiences in Paul postulated by Bultmann cannot be upheld. Rather, also in the continuous disposition of having received the Spirit, people are "seized" and transformed by the Spirit (as Bultmann had put it with regard to the special moments of the work of the Spirit). In order to "trace" *(nachspüren)* this dimension of spiritual life in Paul's churches, we will, in contrast to Gunkel, at first endeavor a religious-historical contextualization of Paul's pneumatology. In the next section we will therefore examine whether the pneumatological reflections and expectations in the religious context of Paul's churches are not only dogmatic assertions but are based on or imply an experiential dimension. It will be shown that the relational model of the work of the Spirit presented above was clearly anchored in these religious traditions which could be accessed by Paul and his churches. They have thus provided a potent horizon of reception and interpretation for the early Christian experience of the Spirit.

2. The Horizon of Interpretation of the Early Christian Experience of the Spirit

Against which religious-historical background should we interpret the early Christian formulations which mention experiences of the Spirit?

Volker Rabens

This question is part of a wider complex of questions which has occupied New Testament scholarship since its beginnings. Namely, should one comprehend Pauline Christianity against a Jewish or rather against a Hellenistic background? After decades of spirited disputes it has become increasingly clear that Judaism and Hellenism were not two hermetically sealed spheres, and that Paul was a man of both worlds.[22] Paul's churches were part of this hybrid world too, but they were potentially more at home in Greco-Roman culture because, unlike Paul, they were not trained as Pharisees in the study of the Hebrew Bible and thus not as firmly rooted in the Jewish faith. Hence, one could assume that they would draw on Hellenistic concepts of πνεῦμα when attempting to describe spiritual experiences.

However, an extensive examination of Greco-Roman literature reveals that these writings provide only very few direct links for the early Christian statement "God has given us the Spirit."[23] According to the teaching of the philosophical school in which πνεῦμα plays a special role, namely the Stoa, everything and everyone "possesses" πνεῦμα. This is due to the fact that, in Stoic philosophy, πνεῦμα was understood as a physical principle that permeates the entire cosmos and holds it together. No comparable distinction was made between divine and human S/spirit[24] as this seems to be presupposed in Pauline texts like Romans 8:16 ("it is that very Spirit bearing witness with our spirit") and 1 Corinthians 2:10-12 (πνεῦμα τοῦ ἀνθρώπου/πνεῦμα τοῦ θεοῦ).[25] In

---

22. On the former, see especially Martin Hengel, *Judaism and Hellenism: Studies in Their Encounter in Palestine during the Early Hellenistic Period* (London: SCM Press, 1974), and on the latter Troels Engberg-Pedersen, ed., *Paul Beyond the Judaism/Hellenism Divide* (Louisville: Westminster John Knox Press, 2001).

23. See the more detailed treatment in Volker Rabens, "Geistes-Geschichte: Die Rede vom Geist im Horizont der griechisch-römischen und jüdisch-hellenistischen Literatur," *ZNT* 25 (2010): 46-55.

24. Seneca's "holy spirit that indwells within us" (*Ep.* 41.1) is no exception to this rule, for he explains a little later that this spirit is the God-given human soul that human beings should live in accord with (41.8-9).

25. John R. Levison has recently ventured to establish a stronger continuity between human and divine s/Spirit in biblical literature (*Filled with the Spirit* [Grand Rapids/Cambridge: Eerdmans, 2009]; see the critique of this point by Max Turner, "Levison's *Filled with the Spirit*: A Brief Appreciation and Response," *JPT* 20 [2011]: 193-200, and Levison's reply in the same issue). This endeavor is to be welcomed also with regard to Paul, for it is both feasible as well as theologically attractive to imagine that for the apostle there was only one metaphysical entity behind his various Spirit-

Stoicism, the human spirit is a fragment of the all-pervading world-pneuma, which can also be referred to as "divine" (e.g. Cicero, *Nat. d.* 2.19). Paul, however, uses a different concept when he speaks about "the Spirit of his Son" who is sent by God into the hearts of the believers (Gal. 4:6). As the presence of God and presence of Christ the Spirit bears personal traits and is "received."[26]

---

locutions — i.e., all of them refer to the same divine Spirit in different manifestations. However, it appears that explicit evidence which would speak for this interpretative option is missing from Paul's letters. The most straightforward reading of 1 Cor. 2:11 and Rom. 8:16 even seems to suggest the opposite: In 1 Cor. 2:11 Paul says that only the human spirit that is within the human being (πνεῦμα τοῦ ἀνθρώπου τὸ ἐν αὐτῷ; cf. 1 Cor. 14:14: πνεῦμα μοῦ) knows what is truly human, and that only the divine Spirit (πνεῦμα τοῦ θεοῦ) comprehends what is truly God's. So, *at least* on a linguistic level Paul clearly distinguishes both entities. However, the more interesting question in our context is what happens to the πνεῦμα τοῦ ἀνθρώπου when a person "receives" the πνεῦμα τοῦ θεοῦ. Neither 1 Cor. 2:11 nor Paul's other πνεῦμα-texts provide a systematic answer to this question. Nonetheless, what he says in Rom. 8:15-16 certainly contradicts the Stoic concept of *toning up* the soul through philosophy — developing its muscles, assisting its use of its own capabilities more effectively, etc. (Seneca, *Ep.* 15; cf. 6.1 where Seneca uses *anima*, not *spiritus*). Rom. 8:15-16 does not depict the human spirit as being "topped up" or "increased." Rather, Paul speaks about *receiving* the Spirit (ἐλάβετε πνεῦμα υἱοθεσίας, v. 15). More importantly, if the referent of τῷ πνεύματι ἡμῶν in verse 16 were the same as that of αὐτὸ τὸ πνεῦμα, one wonders for what reason Paul uses these *two separate* expressions (which are not equated with ἐστιν, as κύριος and πνεῦμα in 2 Cor. 3:17) when he says αὐτὸ τὸ πνεῦμα συμμαρτυρεῖ τῷ πνεύματι ἡμῶν ὅτι ἐσμὲν τέκνα θεοῦ (Rom. 8:16; cf. v. 26). It is clear from the preceding verses that αὐτὸ τὸ πνεῦμα refers to πνεῦμα θεοῦ/πνεῦμα υἱοθεσίας (vv. 14-15). However, if τῷ πνεύματι ἡμῶν would refer to the same (divine) Spirit too, the meaning of "testifying *with/to*" of συμμαρτυρέω is lost. This would become even more problematic if Deut. 19:15 was in the background of Paul's use of συμμαρτυρέω ("Only on the evidence of two or three witnesses [δύο/τριῶν μαρτύρων] shall a charge be sustained").

The distinction between human and divine s/Spirit conveyed in these two verses should certainly not be overdrawn, but it should preserve us from speaking about the identity of the two, or even a "fusion" — a view championed 140 years ago by Pfleiderer (Otto Pfleiderer, *Paulinism: A Contribution to the History of Primitive Christian Theology* [London: Williams and Norgate, 1877], vol. 1, pp. 213-16). On the anthropological and literary presuppositions of Paul's notion of human beings being "indwelled" by the Spirit, see Rabens, *Spirit*, pp. 82-86, 138-44. For an alternative interpretation of 1 Cor. 2:11 and Rom. 8:16, see Desta Heliso's article in the present volume ("Divine Spirit and Human Spirit in Paul in the Light of Stoic and Biblical-Jewish Perspectives").

26. This is not to say that Paul had a fully developed concept of the Spirit as a "person." Cf. the discussion in Volker Rabens, "The Development of Pauline Pneumatology: A Response to F. W. Horn," *BZ* 43 (1999): 177-78; Max Turner, "'Trinitar-

However, the discontinuity between the former life and the invasive work of the Spirit expressed in Paul's letters is more in tune with the experiences and expectations regarding the Spirit reflected in early Jewish literature and the prophecies of the Hebrew Bible. While the (Hellenistic) Jewish context of interpretation of Paul's letters should not principally be played off against a Greco-Roman one, close examination shows that Paul interprets the early Christian experiences of the Spirit by and large in the tradition of the Hebrew Bible and ancient Judaism. As far as we can see from today's perspective, Paul's churches followed the apostle in adopting this horizon of interpretation.²⁷

---

ian' Pneumatology in the New Testament? — Towards an Explanation of the Worship of Jesus," *ATJ* 57/58 (2002/2003): 167-86; Jörg Frey, "Vom Windbrausen zum Geist Christi und zur trinitarischen Person: Stationen einer Geschichte des Heiligen Geistes im Neuen Testament," *JBTh* 24 (2009): 121-54.

27. As far as we can tell, only in his dialogue with the church at Corinth there appear to have been tensions between Paul and his audience regarding the interpretation of spiritual experiences. The Corinthian overrating of ecstatic experiences may have had its background in the ideas of inspiration surrounding the oracles of Delphi and Dodona (on this tradition, see Levison, *Filled with the Spirit*, pp. 154-57; more generally on the situation in Corinth, see, e.g., Anthony C. Thiselton, *The First Epistle to the Corinthians: A Commentary on the Greek Text*, New International Greek Testament Commentary [Grand Rapids: Eerdmans/Carlisle: Paternoster, 2000], pp. 40-41). Apart from that, although we do not have evidence for this, it cannot be ruled out from the perspective of the reception of Paul's letters that Paul's Spirit-language, as for instance the image of being made to drink of the Spirit (1 Cor. 12:13c), evoked associations of Stoic pneumatology in Paul's audience. Erlemann even thinks that this is what Paul deliberately intended to do. However, he does not provide detailed evidence for his view (Kurt Erlemann, "Die Rezeption des griechisch-hellenistischen πνεῦμα-Begriffs im Neuen Testament," in *Geschehen und Gedächtnis: Die hellenistische Welt und ihre Wirkung. Festschrift für Wolfgang Orth zum 65. Geburtstag*, ed. J.-F. Eckholdt, M. Sigismund, and S. Sigismund [Münster: LIT, 2009], 297; however, see the more elaborate work of Engberg-Pedersen and my critique of it, as mentioned in note 18 above). Generally speaking, however, the philosophic language and conceptual world of Stoicism fundamentally differs from that of Paul. This is also true for the ancient medical texts (on which, see Troy W. Martin, "Paul's Pneumatological Statements and Ancient Medical Texts," in *The New Testament and Early Christian Literature in Greco-Roman Context: Studies in Honor of David E. Aune*, ed. J. Fotopoulos [Leiden: Brill, 2006], pp. 105-26, and the discussion in Rabens, *Spirit*, pp. 99-101). Furthermore, the proponents of these approaches would need to provide evidence that Stoic and medical pneumatology was part of the general education of the members of Paul's churches (and not just of the educated elite), and that they would, over and above that, be able to fill the logical gaps between the role of πνεῦμα in Stoic physics and ancient medicine on the one hand and Paul's Spirit-language on the other.

In the Hebrew Bible, the Spirit — the presence of Yhwh — is characterized by *charismatic-prophetic* as well as religious-ethical expressions of life. According to the biblical narratives, prophets could show signs of ecstasy when the Spirit of Yhwh came upon them.[28] The Scriptures prophesy that in the future there will be a powerful intensification of the presence of the Spirit which will be accompanied, for one thing, by charismatic-prophetic phenomena. Against exactly this background early Christianity interpreted the events of Pentecost as *experiences of the Spirit*. For his international audience at the event, Peter explains Pentecost in the following way: "Indeed, these are not drunk, as you suppose. . . . No, this is what was spoken through the prophet Joel: 'In the last days it will be, God declares, that I will pour out my Spirit upon all flesh, and your sons and your daughters shall prophesy, and your young men shall see visions, and your old men shall dream dreams. Even upon my slaves, both men and women, in those days I will pour out my Spirit; and they shall prophesy' [Joel 3:1-2]" (Acts 2:15-18).

Moreover, also an intensification of the *ethical-religious* effects of the Spirit was foretold for the future of the people of God. A central text within this prophetic tradition is Ezekiel 36:26-28 (cf. Isa. 44:3-5): "A new heart I will give you and a new spirit I will put within you. I will put my spirit within you and make you follow my statutes and be careful to observe my ordinances. Then you shall live in the land I gave to your ancestors; and you shall be my people, and I will be your God." In this prophecy the relational work of the Spirit mentioned above is clearly suggested. It is even more dominant in the early Jewish traditions based on the promises in Ezekiel 36–37 (1QS 4.20-21; *Num. Rab.* 9.49; *Soṭah* 9.15; etc.). For instance, in the book of *Jubilees* 1.23-25 it is foretold that God will create in his people a H/holy S/spirit and that the souls of the recipients of the Spirit will hold on to God and his commandments, that he will be a father to them and they sons to him and that he will love them.[29] Similarly, the author of *Testament of Judah* 24.2-

---

28. E.g. Judg. 14:6: "The spirit of the Lord rushed on him, and he tore the lion apart barehanded as one might tear apart a kid." Cf. 15:14; etc. On the correlation of the Spirit coming upon people and prophecy, see, e.g., 1 Sam. 10:6: "Then the spirit of the Lord will possess you, and you will be in a prophetic frenzy along with them and be turned into a different person." Cf. 10:10; 19:20; Num. 11:25; 24:2-3; 2 Chron. 20:14-15; etc.

29. On the reference to S/spirit in this verse, see the discussion in Rabens, *Spirit*, pp. 164-65, and Heliso, "Spirit," pp. 163-64 in this volume.

3 notices a connection between Spirit-endowment, an intensification of both the experience of God's presence and of community as a "family of God," and ethical life in the sense of Ezekiel 36: God will pour out the Spirit of grace, the recipients of the Spirit will truly be God's children, and they will walk in his commandments. Besides numerous other early Jewish texts which deepen this connection between Spirit-wrought, vibrant spirituality and ethical life (e.g. Philo, *Leg.* 1.33-39; *Opif.* 144; *Gig.* 54-55; 1QH^a 6.12-14; 8.19-20; 20.11-14),[30] also Paul places himself and his churches within this tradition of interpretation. In the next section we will see further how closely Paul integrates the charismatic-prophetic dimension with the ethical work of the Spirit.

3. The Relational Experience of the Spirit and Spiritual Gifts in Paul's Churches

For Paul and the early Christian churches it is clear: "We have received the Spirit" (Gal. 3:2; 1 Cor. 2:12; 3:16; 2 Cor. 5:5; Rom. 8:9, 15). In accordance with the horizon of expectation and interpretation unfolded above, Paul presents charismatic-prophetic and ethical-religious expressions of life as effects of the Spirit. We have already seen that the reception of the Spirit as it is referred to in 1 Thessalonians 1:5-6 and Galatians 3:1-5 had distinctive dimensions of experientiality. Moreover, Paul explains in 1 Corinthians 12:7 that the manifestation of the Spirit (φανέρωσις τοῦ πνεύματος) is given to *everyone* in the church. The spectrum of these "charismatic phenomena," the χαρίσματα (gifts of grace), is expanded by Paul to include not only the prophetic impressions mentioned in Joel 3:1-3 but also a multitude of further gifts (see 1 Cor. 12:8-10). As these gifts are given to everyone, that is, to men and women of different social statuses alike, the work of the Spirit has a distinctively egalitarian ethos (cf. Joel 3:1-2; 1 Cor. 12:12-17).[31] Moreover, a number of the gifts of the Spirit appear to be "common human gifts" (natural abilities or *Schöpfungsgaben,* cf. Gen. 2:7) — at least they fall outside the sphere of the "ecstatic" thus labeled by Gunkel: wisdom and knowledge (1 Cor. 12:8), service, teaching,

---

30. See the textual analysis in Rabens, *Spirit,* ch. 5.
31. Cf. Michael Wolter, *Paulus: Ein Grundriss seiner Theologie* (Neukirchen: Neukirchener Verlag, 2011), pp. 179-80, 323-27; Hildegard Scherer, *Geistreiche Argumente: Das Pneuma-Konzept des Paulus im Kontext seiner Briefe* (Münster: Aschendorff, 2011), pp. 257-59.

and exhortation (Rom. 12:7-8). However, Paul nonetheless attributes these gifts to the same one Spirit (cf. 1 Cor. 12).[32]

Spiritual gifts played an important role for the experience of God and of Christian fellowship in Paul's churches. According to Paul, when spiritual gifts are exercised in a community-promoting way, visitors from outside the church will interpret this as a sign of the presence of God: "God is really among you" (1 Cor. 14:24-25). This is significant for our epistemological investigation of the early Christian statements concerning spiritual experiences, because this line of reasoning gives a foundational value to experience. From the experience of someone who enters the church and experiences how the gifts of the Spirit are exercised, a theological deduction is being made ("God is really among you"). This deduction is of course to some extent dependent on a preconceived interpretative framework. Nonetheless, also this very interpretative framework (which Paul ascribes to the visitor) is one in which the presence of God is believed to be a tangible and experiential phenomenon. In accordance with this line of argumentation, Paul likewise believes that this same Spirit (of Christ) leads people on to confess Christ as "Lord" (1 Cor. 12:3).

For Paul, the cooperation and togetherness in the church that develops through exercising spiritual gifts implies that every member of the community is "edified," that is, she is strengthened and empowered for religious-ethical life (12:7; cf. the parallel in 10:23-24). As mentioned in Part I, Spirit-inspired relationships as "power from in between" shape ethical life not only in respect to its empowerment but also in respect to its "form and content," that is, its ethos. Paul elucidates this effect of exercising spiritual gifts in 1 Corinthians 12–14. He emphasizes that a positive experience of Christian fellowship is only possible if spiritual gifts are used in love and consideration for the fellow believers. Love (ch. 13) is at the center of Paul's chapters on the Spirit and spiritual gifts (chs. 12 and 14). According to 1 Corinthians 14:28-31, the Spirit even shapes the actual structure of the individual interpersonal interactions within the community. Paul says that "if there is no one to interpret, let them [i.e. those who speak in tongues] be silent in church and speak to themselves and to God" (v. 28). The Spirit is thus able to inspire greater sensitivity to others in the community. People need to

---

32. See the detailed exposition in Max Turner, *The Holy Spirit and Spiritual Gifts — Then and Now*, rev. ed. (Carlisle: Paternoster, 1999), ch. 15.

listen to one another in order to be built up (cf. vv. 29-30). Again, the result of this Spirit-inspired dynamic is that "all may learn and all be encouraged" (v. 31).

According to the testimony of the Pauline letters, practicing the gifts of the Spirit belonged to the "daily church life" of the early Christian movement (1 Cor. 14:26; Rom. 12:5-8). However, next to the gifts of the Spirit, further spiritual experiences were characteristic for Paul's churches. The experience of spiritual gifts created identity and community — but so did also the individual as well as communal experience of being (a) child(ren) of God. This is, first of all, a soteriological dimension of the work of the Spirit, for the Spirit is the "Spirit of adoption as sons" (πνεῦμα υἱοθεσίας, Rom. 8:14-16). The Christians in Rome were pulled out of slavery and fear and were moved into the family of God through the Spirit of the Son (8:9, 15). In this way, moreover, the work of the Spirit of "sonship and daughtership"[33] not only marks the initiation into ("adoption") and the finalization of Christian life ("glorifying" and "revealing," 8:17-27) but determines all of Christian spirituality in the present. The new identity as children of God has, on the one hand, a cognitive dimension in the sense of a new self-understanding. On the other hand, however, it is shaped by the continual experience of the Spirit-wrought crying "Abba! Father!"[34] "It is that very Spirit bearing witness with our spirit that we are children of God" (8:16). These Spirit-induced experiences also include emotions. For one thing, this is revealed through the notion of "crying" (κράζομεν). Moreover, through the contrast with fear (8:15) Paul expresses that the relational experiences described here are those of love and intimacy (cf. 5:5; Eph. 3:14-19).

This interpretation of the work of the Spirit as creating relational intimacy is rooted in a tradition-historical framework of interpretation in which the father-child relationship functions as a motif for how God relates to his people. In the Hebrew Bible and in early Jewish literature God is characterized as a loving and caring father (or mother, cf. Isa. 49:15-16; 66:13). Here are two examples which represent a wealth of literary evidence:[35] In Hosea 11:1, 3-4, YHWH's attitude to Israel is described

---

33. In 8:15-16 Paul moves explicitly from υἱοθεσία (v. 15) to τέκνα θεοῦ, thus including women.

34. Cf. Gal. 4:6, where it is the Spirit himself who "calls" (κρᾶζον).

35. See, e.g., Deut. 1:31; 7:7-8; Ps. 27:10; 68:6; Jer. 31:9; 1QH^a 17.35-36; *4 Ezra* 6.58; *Jub.* 2.20; 19.29; *T. Job* 40.2; Philo, *Sobr.* 55-57; *Conf.* 145.

in the following way: "When Israel was a child, I loved him, and out of Egypt I called my son.... Yet it was I who taught Ephraim to walk, I took them up in my arms.... I led them with cords of human kindness, with bands of love...." Similarly, *Joseph and Aseneth* 12.8, 15 expresses an intimate relationship between God and believer: "For (just) as a little child who is afraid flees to his father, and the father, stretching out his hands, snatches him off the ground, and puts his arms around him by his breast, and the child clasps his hands around his father's neck, ... and rests at his father's breast, ... likewise you too, Lord, stretch out your hands upon me as a child-loving father, and snatch me off the earth.... [15] What father is as sweet as you, Lord, and who (is) as quick in mercy as you, Lord ... ?"

The interconnection of Spirit-wrought sonship of God and ethical life in Romans 8:12-17 follows the tradition of Ezekiel 36–37, *Jubilees* 1, *Testament of Judah* 24 etc. mentioned in Part 2. In fact, in the case of Paul one can even speak of an intensification of one aspect of this tradition. This intensification concerns the causal connection between the "power from in between" and ethical life: Paul grounds his implicit request in 8:13 to put to death through the Spirit the "deeds of the body" (πνεύματι τὰς πράξεις τοῦ σώματος θανατοῦτε) in the experiential reality of the Spirit leading (8:14), freeing from fear, enabling to cry "Abba" (8:15) and bearing witness to one's being a child of God. This line of reasoning is indicated through the employment of the causative conjunction "because" (γάρ) at the beginning of both verses 14 and 15. Paul can describe the Spirit in verse 13 as an instrument (πνεύματι) for fighting temptations, because the indicatives of the Spirit's relational work in the following verses enable (and require) such ethical behavior. Thus, we see once again that the quality and character of these Spirit-wrought experiences of love and fellowship function as empowerment ("power from in between") as well as criteria for living as children of God (cf. 2 Cor. 3:18).[36]

It should be noted that in spite of the wealth of his positive accounts of the experience of the Spirit as "power from in between," Paul does not fall into the trap of triumphalism as it appears to have been the case with a number of Corinthian church members (cf. 1 Cor. 2–3; 12–14).[37] Romans 8 thus unravels a further, perhaps unexpected dimen-

---

36. On the interpretation of Rom. 8, 2 Cor. 3, and further texts supporting this thesis, see Rabens, *Spirit*, pp. 171-242.

37. Cf. note 27 above.

sion of the work of the Spirit: The Spirit is also present in all the experiences of weakness, fear, and oppression to which the whole of creation is subject. However, the Spirit does not merely function as a means of rescue. Rather, the Spirit comes into all "bondage to decay" and longing for freedom (8:21; cf. 2 Cor. 4:7-15). "Likewise the Spirit helps us in our weakness; for we do not know how to pray as we ought, but that very Spirit intercedes with sighs too deep for words" (Rom. 8:26). The Spirit of God identifies and shows solidarity with creation in an almost incarnational way, because the Spirit articulates on behalf of the world the experience of incompleteness and fragility in a depth that the world itself cannot express ("sighs too deep for words"). Thus, the Spirit comes into and has an effect on the entire breadth of human experience.

4. Conclusion

The experiences of the Spirit described in Paul's letters display a broad spectrum. A division of these experiences into ordinary experiences of daily life on the one side (i.e. continuous Spirit endowment), and momentary experiences of the extraordinary on the other side (i.e. being seized by the Spirit in ecstasy), is not suggested by the Pauline writings in the way it was proposed by Bultmann and others. Rather, exercising spiritual gifts was part of the daily life of the early Christian movement. In addition to this sign of endowment with the Spirit, the statement "you have received the Spirit of adoption" (Rom. 8:15) was based on nonverbal, identity-forming experiences of the Spirit of the Son (8:15: crying "Abba! Father!"; 8:16: the Spirit, together with the human spirit, bearing witness of one's being a child of God). These individual and communal experiences of the love and closeness of God also include emotions. They are the empowerment of as well as the standard for spiritual life. The power from on high experienced in Paul's churches is thus the Spirit's drawing people close to God and to one another, and this "power from in between" can indeed "be truly felt."

It is important to take into account the interdependence of experience and (framework of) interpretation when trying to fathom early Christian pneumatology. The religious experiences of the early churches were interpreted against the backdrop of (biblical) prophecies and expectations. These were developed further into propositions and dogmas which incorporated these experiences (cf. Acts 2:15-21, 38). On the one hand, experience could inspire teaching (cf. Acts 10:44-48), and, on the other hand, teaching could correct practice (cf. 1 Thess. 5:19-20; 1 Cor. 12-14). We have seen that the declaration "God has given us his Spirit" is best interpreted in the context of the early Jewish horizon of expectation as a statement of experience. Within this tradition it was impossible to separate the Spirit from works of power, from prototypical gifts and religious-ethical effects (Joel 3; Ezek. 36–37; etc.).[38] It is hence precarious to comprehend the early Christian affirmations that they have received the Spirit as a mere postulation without experiential foundation. Paul's letters give evidence of the opposite: argumentations such as Galatians 3:1-5 and 1 Thessalonians 1:5-6 presuppose and explicate the experiential dimension of the reception and work of the Spirit.

In Paul's churches the work of the Spirit was a communal experience. However, it could not be reduced to group dynamics but also had a "private" dimension (see, e.g., 1 Cor. 14:18-19, 28). The work of the Spirit served the edification of the individual *and* the community (1 Cor. 12:7; cf. Eph. 4:11-16). While Paul's reflections on the work of the Spirit have provided many stimuli for Christian spirituality throughout the ages, this communal dimension of the experience of the Spirit in Paul's churches can be one of the lasting inspirations for spiritual life in the present times of globalization and postmodernity where many people long for the experience of community and "connectedness."[39]

---

38. Cf. Turner, *Power,* chs. 3-5.

39. For further ideas on how Paul's pneumatology can inspire spirituality today, see Marlis Gielen, "'Löscht den Geist nicht aus, verachtet prophetische Rede nicht!' (1Thess 5,19f): Zur Grundlegung einer christlichen Spiritualität bei Paulus," in M. Gielen, *Paulus im Gespräch — Themen paulinischer Theologie* (Stuttgart: Kohlhammer, 2009), pp. 131-57, and Volker Rabens, "Mein neues Leben: Predigt zu Römer 8,1-2.9," *ThGespr* 35 (2011): 36-42. On the role of experience in early Christianity as well as church history, see further the helpful overview in James D. G. Dunn, *Unity and Diversity in the New Testament: An Inquiry into the Character of Earliest Christianity,* 3rd ed. (London: SCM Press, 2006), ch. 9.

Divine Spirit and Human Spirit in Paul in the Light of Stoic and Biblical-Jewish Perspectives

Desta Heliso

1. Introduction

Paul's use of human spirit and divine spirit, particularly in Romans 8:16 and 1 Corinthians 2:11, continues to divide and baffle scholars. How do divine spirit and human spirit relate to each other? Do they represent two different entities? By way of answering these questions, "human spirit," for example, has been understood as "that dimension of the human personality by means of which the person relates most directly to God,"[1] the believer's spirit where "the human and divine interface in the believer's life,"[2] or the apportioned divine spirit given to Christians in the eschatological period at baptism.[3] Engberg-Pedersen argues that "the spirit itself" and "our spirit" in Romans 8:16 stand for God's spirit, but he does not clearly address issues relating to 1 Corinthians 2:11.[4] Levison argues that in Israelite literature the initial endowment of "spirit" or the so-called life principle (human spirit) and later charismatic endowments of spirit (the spirit of God) were understood to be the same.[5] He then attempts to show how this conception "evapo-

---

1. J. D. G. Dunn, *The Theology of Paul the Apostle* (Edinburgh: T&T Clark, 1998), p. 77.
2. G. Fee, *God's Empowering Presence: The Holy Spirit in the Letters of Paul* (Peabody: Hendrickson, 1994), p. 25.
3. R. Jewett, *Paul's Anthropological Terms: A Study of Their Use in Conflict Settings* (Leiden: Brill, 1971), p. 195.
4. T. Engberg-Pedersen, *Cosmology and Self in the Apostle Paul: The Material Spirit* (Oxford: Oxford University Press, 2010), pp. 62-67.
5. J. R. Levison, *Filled with the Spirit* (Grand Rapids: Eerdmans, 2009), p. 12; J. R. Levison, *The Spirit in First Century Judaism* (Leiden: Brill, 1997).

rates" in early Christian literature, though he confines Romans 8:16 and 1 Corinthians 2:11 to a footnote.[6]

Our task is to answer the question as to whether human spirit and divine spirit represent two different entities for Paul. We will argue that any reading of Romans 8:16 and 1 Corinthians 2:11 should take into account the influence of Genesis 2:7 on Paul's thinking and the idea of Christ as the *life-giving Spirit* residing in the Christian. We will start our discussion with a brief analysis of Stoic perspectives. We will then move on to biblical perspectives focusing on the Old Testament, and selected texts from Jewish Second Temple literature. We will then analyse Romans 8:16 and 1 Corinthians 2:11, and conclude by bringing together the core arguments from the different sections.

2. Stoic Perspectives

In this section, we will briefly explore how πνεῦμα within Stoicism is used with both divine and human associations. As Levison points out, the conception that "*pneuma* pervades a living and rational cosmos" is foundational in Stoicism.[7] In Praxagoras, for example, πνεῦμα in human beings was thought to be the main element that determined psychic movement within the human body.[8] There was also a belief that πνεῦμα was "the unifying element that permeates both cosmos and psyche" where the two correspond with each other, as human soul was believed to be a "fragment of cosmic soul."[9] In short, in Stoic thought we cannot find anything about the existence of divine spirit and human spirit as two different entities. Spirit is spoken of as a single entity. This is based on the Stoic system, which, as Rabens notes, is widely regarded as "materialistic monism."[10]

In Seneca, for example, spirit is something one possesses. He

---

6. Levison, *Filled with the Spirit*, p. 238 and n. 2.
7. Levison, *Filled with the Spirit*, pp. 138-39. See also V. Rabens, *The Holy Spirit and Ethics in Paul: Transformation and Empowering for Religious-Ethical Life* (Tübingen: Mohr Siebeck, 2010), pp. 25-35; V. Rabens, "Geistes-Geschichte: Die Rede vom Geist im Horizont der griechisch-römischen und jüdisch-hellenistischen Literatur," *ZNT* 25 (2010): 46-49.
8. Levison, *Filled with the Spirit*, p. 139.
9. Levison, *Filled with the Spirit*, p. 140.
10. Rabens, *Spirit*, p. 28.

praises Lucilius for his contest with Fortune, which is the result of Lucilius having "plenty of spirit" (*Ep.* 13.1). Seneca also says that virtue is spirit that "young men of noble breeding assume" and which is "assuredly infused in us and communicated to us by wisdom" (*Ep.* 71.19). But spirit is not only something one possesses, it is also something that can be transformed. Seneca says that his perception of being transformed is proof that "my spirit is altered into something better" (*Ep.* 6.1). In his *Epistles,* Seneca does not speak of divine spirit and human spirit as distinct entities, but he talks about God that is "with you ... within you" and a "holy spirit" that "indwells within us." He also refers to spirit and God as the same thing and talks about being "treated by the [spirit]" in terms of being good with the help of God (*Ep.* 41.2). Reason is "a portion of the divine spirit set in a human body" (*Ep.* 61.12). The presence of spirit in a person makes that person equal to the gods, from whom, as Seneca seems to believe, that person came. Indeed he argues that a person is a part of God.[11] For Seneca, spirit represents a person even beyond death, as he reports to Lucilius that he did "reverence to the spirit" of a great warrior called Scipio Africanus, whose "soul has indeed returned to the skies" (*Ep.* 86.1).

Thus, in Stoicism the use of spirit with human and divine associations seems to have the same meaning and significance, namely divine spirit in a person. In Seneca in particular, the spirit one possesses or the spirit infused in human beings is the same thing as the holy spirit that dwells within human beings or the divine spirit that is set in a human body. In short, spirit in Seneca is divine spirit that represents a human person who is a part of God.

3. Old Testament

According to Genesis 2:7, the formed אָדָם ("humanity") was directly animated by YHWH's own "breath of life" (נִשְׁמַת חַיִּים) so as to become a "living being." Although in Genesis 2:7 it is not the spirit of God which makes Adam a living being but the "breath of life," in Genesis 6:3 it is the presence or absence of the "divine spirit" (רוּחִי), rather than the

---

11. He says: "And why should you not believe that something of divinity exists in one who is a part of God? All this universe which encompasses us is one, and it is God; we are associates of God; we are his members" (*Ep.* 92.30).

"breath of life," that determines life or death. One might thus wonder if recognisable semantic distance exists between "spirit" and "breath of life." There probably does not, because numerous Old Testament texts show that there exists a semantic congruency between the two terms.[12]

In Ezekiel 37, although the reference is not to the "breath of life" but to the "spirit" (vv. 5, 9, 10, 14), the inbreathing language in verse 9 echoes the inbreathing language in Genesis 2:7. And in verse 10, the inbreathing results in life. This expression is paralleled with another expression in verse 14 where YHWH's bestowal of his spirit results in life, all of which is linked with Israel's repossession of the Land, acquisition of a fresh knowledge of YHWH, and new potential and opportunity to live as the people of YHWH (Ezek. 36:22, 27-28; 37:27-28). The point is that "spirit [of God]" and "breath of life" have the same meaning in Ezekiel as in many Old Testament passages and, therefore, the "breath of life" in Genesis 2:7 should probably be understood as the "spirit" *from/of God*. But the breath of life God breathed into the nostrils of *the formed Adam* in Genesis 2:7 is described in terms of the "human spirit" that was *formed within* in Zechariah 12:1. And Numbers 27:16 unambiguously describes God as the God of "human spirit" (cf. Num. 16:22).[13] The "breath of life" can, thus, be described as "human spirit." This brings us to issues relating to the human spirit and divine spirit.

The question here is whether the "breath of life" in Genesis 2:7 — which can now be referred to as "human spirit" — and "spirit of God" in Genesis 1:2 and 6:3 are two distinct entities. Knierim, referring to Genesis 2:7, speaks of *the spirit of life* as that which is common to all and *the spirit of God* as manifestations of YHWH's spirit.[14] But the common spirit of life, in his view, cannot be separated from charismatic intensifications of YHWH's spirit.[15] He goes on to argue that sporadic eruptions on special occasions are "specific intensifications of the common human life-endowment" as well as "life manifestations of a specific di-

---

12. See, for example, Gen. 7:22; Deut. 20:16; 2 Sam. 22:16; Job 4:9; 27:3; 32:8; 34:14; Pss. 18:15; 150:6; Isa. 2:22; 42:5; 57:16. See also C. Bennema, *The Power of Saving Wisdom: An Investigation of Spirit and Wisdom in Relation to the Soteriology of the Fourth Gospel* (Tübingen: Mohr Siebeck, 2002), p. 97.

13. יְהוָה אֱלֹהֵי הָרוּחֹת לְכָל־בָּשָׂר (ὁ θεὸς τῶν πνευμάτων καὶ πάσης σαρκός).

14. R. P. Knierim, *The Task of Old Testament Theology* (Grand Rapids: Eerdmans, 1995), pp. 272, 275-76.

15. Knierim, *Task*, p. 276.

vine identity."[16] In short, for Knierim, the "spirit *of* God is the same substance as the spirit of life *from* God."[17] Levison also argues against scholars who create a dichotomy between "the physical or anthropological spirit given at birth" and "the spirit understood as a subsequent charismatic endowment." He argues that this sort of understanding "leads to an unnecessary eclipse," for "[a]ncient Israelite literature fails to make such a distinction."[18]

One might be hesitant about sharing the sort of boldness that Levison adopts. And *contra* Knierim, it is unlikely that the Hebrews understood רוח as substance. However, Knierim and Levison's views have merit. As discussed above, the "breath of life" in Genesis 2:7 should probably be understood as the "spirit of God." And in many Old Testament passages, references to spirit with both divine and human associations are references to the spirit of/from God. For Israelites (individually and corporately), human existence in its entirety is understood as the ultimate outcome of possessing the spirit, without which — as some Old Testament texts clearly show — the state of humanity is ordinary (unexceptional), unconscious, disconcerted, flesh, dust, dead, and buried in graves.[19] Indeed, the very fact that human beings live, breathe, and have various dispositions means that they have spirit on the basis of Adam's reception of the breath of life from God. This could also mean that spirit (of God), as an extension of God's personality, is incorporated into humanity and has become its life, vitality, and identity.[20] The absence of the spirit for Israel means that Israel could no longer live and relate to YHWH (cf. Deut. 30:19-20). Conversely, the presence of the spirit in a person (an Israelite) resulted not only in life but also in wisdom, knowledge, extraordinary understanding, and performance of justice and mighty activity.[21]

---

16. Knierim, *Task*, p. 276. See, for example, Num. 11:24-25; Judg. 3:10; 15:14; 1 Sam. 10:6.

17. Knierim, *Task*, p. 273.

18. Levison, *Filled with the Spirit*, p. 33.

19. Gen. 2:7; 6:3; Judg. 14:6; 16:17; 1 Kgs. 10:5; 17:17-21; Eccl. 12:7; Ezek. 37:1-14. See also Levison, *Filled with the Spirit*, p. 18.

20. See also Ps. 139:7; Isa. 30:1; 63:9-10; M. Turner, *The Holy Spirit and Spiritual Gifts — Then and Now*, rev. ed. (Carlisle: Paternoster, 1999), p. 3.

21. See, for example, Job 32:16-20; Gen. 41:38; Exod. 31:3; Num. 27:18; Deut. 34:9; Mic. 3:8; Dan. 4:8-9, 18; 5:11-12, 14; 6:3. For an extensive discussion of these passages, see Levison, *Filled with the Spirit*, pp. 36-86.

Divine Spirit and Human Spirit in Paul

Furthermore, Ezekiel 36:26-28 shows that the presence of the spirit results in the possibility of transformation and living in the land of promise. But one might wonder if "spirit" in this passage is used with human and/or divine associations. In Ezekiel 36:26, the Lord says "a new spirit I will put within you" (πνεῦμα καινὸν δώσω ἐν ὑμῖν) and in 36:27, he says "I will put my spirit within you" (τὸ πνεῦμά μου δώσω ἐν ὑμῖν) (cf. Ps. 51:12). But do πνεῦμα καινόν (רוּחַ חֲדָשָׁה) and τὸ πνεῦμά μου (אֶת־רוּחִי) carry the same sense? Scholars such as Turner,[22] Bennema,[23] Rabens,[24] and Levison,[25] for example, discuss this passage with different concerns,[26] but only Rabens attempts to address this question as he talks about Israel's "(anthropological) renewal" with reference to 36:25-26 and the promise of the "giving of God's Spirit" with reference to 36:27-28.[27] Bennema simply assumes that רוּחַ/πνεῦμα in the passage refers to "divine Spirit."[28] Levison's silence in this respect might be based on his thesis that ancient Israelite writings do not contain such categories as anthropological spirit and divine spirit. One could equally argue from Ezekiel 36:26-27, however, that the prophet uses πνεῦμα καινόν anthropologically and τὸ πνεῦμά μου theologically. But that Genesis 2:7 plays a consistent role in Ezekiel's oracles and visions mitigates against this. As the *breath of life* in Genesis 2:7 probably refers to the *spirit of God* as in Genesis 1:2 or the *spirit of YHWH* as in Genesis 6:3, the same can be said regarding the spirit used in relation to the moving wheels (Ezek. 1:19-20), Ezekiel (Ezek. 2:2), and the exiles (Ezek. 11:19-20). If valid, πνεῦμα καινόν and τὸ πνεῦμά μου in 36:26-27 refer to the divine spirit.

In conclusion, the "breath of life" and "spirit of God" in the Old Testament probably have the same referent and רוּחַ/πνεῦμα represents *the* God-given life and identity of humanity in general and Israel in particular. So what is referred to as *breath of life* or *human spirit* in the Old Testament is the *divine spirit* expressed, by and large, in contexts where human existence, common human life-endowment, or divine-human

---

22. Turner, *Holy Spirit*, pp. 106-9, 112-14.
23. Bennema, *Power*, pp. 170-73.
24. Rabens, *Spirit*, pp. 163-67.
25. Levison, *Filled with the Spirit*, pp. 87-103.
26. See, e.g., Bennema, *Power*, p. 171; Rabens, *Spirit*, p. 167; Levison, *Filled with the Spirit*, p. 103.
27. Rabens, *Spirit*, p. 163 and n. 61.
28. Bennema, *Power*, p. 171.

Desta Heliso

(and human-human) relationship — rather than charismatic manifestation or display of mighty phenomena — is in focus.

4. Jewish Second Temple Literature

Due to various restraints, we will consider only some examples from deuterocanonical, pseudepigraphal, Qumranic, and Philonic writings that are directly relevant to our purpose.

4.1. Deuterocanonical Writings

In these writings, πνεῦμα (sometimes used interchangeably with ψυχή) is used in different but interrelated ways: (1) the Lord sent forth πνεῦμα to form humanity (Jdt. 16:14); (2) the Lord breathed it into humanity as πνεῦμα ζωτικόν (Wis. 15:11); (3) it was borrowed *from the Lord* and became "human spirit" (Wis. 15:16); (4) it is referred to as Elijah's πνεῦμα that filled Elisha and enabled the latter to perform signs (Sir. 48:12); (5) its presence or absence determines human life or death (Tob. 3:6; Wis. 2:3; Sir. 38:23; Bar. 2:17; 2 Esd. 7:78); and (6) the fear of the Lord is a criterion for the "spirit of [humanity]" to live (Sir. 34:14). The unambiguous human associations in the above references could lead us to understand the depictions of πνεῦμα as that of *human spirit*. However, since it is equally unambiguous that the source of πνεῦμα in the references is God, the distinction between πνεῦμα with divine association and human association is not clear-cut.

There are also references with clear divine association. In Wisdom of Solomon, for example, the author refers to πνεῦμα κυρίου that has filled the world (1:7) and the *holy spirit* of the Lord that is sent from on high (9:17). The sending of the "holy spirit," for the writer, is closely linked with or even the result of the coming of πνεῦμα σοφίας to Solomon upon his prayer to God (7:7). For there is in σοφία "a spirit that is intelligent, holy, unique" (7:22).[29] One could argue that the *wisdom* or

---

29. See Bennema for a thorough analysis of issues relating to πνεῦμα and σοφία in Wisdom of Solomon (*Power*, pp. 61-71). Bennema also argues that in Jewish writings such as Wisdom of Solomon, Qumran, and Philo, behind human spirit is the reality of divine spirit; hence, human spirit and divine spirit are not two distinct metaphysical entities (*Power*, pp. 68, 72, 83, 90-91, 95-98).

holy spirit that comes from the Lord to Solomon in Wisdom of Solomon 7:7 and 9:17 is the same as the "spirit of the Lord" that has filled the world in Wisdom of Solomon 1:7,[30] "the spirit of Almighty God" in 2 Esdras 16:22, the "spirit of understanding" that fills a person in Sirach 39:6 (cf. 38:34), and the *holy spirit* that inspires the scribe in 2 Esdras 14:22. But one could equally argue that the *wisdom* or *holy spirit* that comes from the Lord is the same as "a holy spirit of discipline" (ἅγιον πνεῦμα παιδείας) that flees from deceit in Wisdom of Solomon 1:5 and the *holy spirit* that God stirred up in Daniel to save Susanna from unjust death (Sus. [Th] 1:45). Thus, it is probably unnecessary to strictly categorize these depictions as "holy spirit" with divine association and "holy spirit" with human association and understand each category with differing meaning and significance.

4.2. Pseudepigraphal Writings

In *Jubilees*, one's identity is characterized either by the "spirit of Beliar" or by an "upright spirit" or "holy spirit" that God himself creates in the people of Israel (1.20-23). Whether "holy spirit" here has the same meaning as "[God's] spirit" in 5.8-9 is not clear. Nor is it clear whether the "holy spirit" here has the same meaning and significance as the "spirit of prophecy" that "came down into [Isaac's] mouth" (31.12) or the "spirit of the Lord" that was with Joseph and provided him with the quality of wisdom and discretion (40.5-6). Rabens and Bennema rightly acknowledge an ambiguity here,[31] but by speaking of uncertainty about the "holy spirit" in *Jubilees* 1.23 being divine spirit — which many would argue to be the case — they seem to imply that the term could refer to human spirit. There are also others who attach anthropological meaning to the term.[32] This means that the "holy spirit" that God created in human beings is understood as human spirit and other descriptions (God's spirit, spirit of prophecy, and the spirit of the Lord) as divine spirit. But this distinction is unwarranted.

30. So Levison, *Filled with the Spirit*, pp. 143-45. Bennema, however, views wisdom and spirit as different entities (*Power*, pp. 65-66).
31. Rabens, *Spirit*, p. 165; Bennema, *Power*, p. 92.
32. For the catalogue of references on theological and anthropological interpretations, see Rabens, *Spirit*, pp. 165-66 and n. 71, in which he concludes "that the two may not be as strongly differentiated as is often assumed."

Jubilees 1.23 comes partly from Ezekiel 36:26-27, where the Lord promises to put πνεῦμα καινόν and τὸ πνεῦμά μου within Israel. The divine promise to create a "holy spirit" in Israel in *Jubilees* could be taken as a parallel to the promise to put a "new spirit" or "my spirit" in Ezekiel. We could then understand the "holy spirit" in *Jubilees* as the divine spirit, which is also how we read a "new spirit" or "my spirit" in Ezekiel. Against this, one might argue that "holy spirit" in *Jubilees* 1.23 is to be paralleled with an "upright spirit" in verse 20 and that both references have an anthropological meaning. But an "upright spirit" here is contrasted with the "spirit of Beliar," which stands against the spirit of the Lord. This is not to suggest that the "holy spirit" does not acquire both divine and human qualities (cf. *Ass. Mos.* 11 with *Ps. Sol.* 17.42). It is to say that in *Jubilees* it may be more akin to the context to understand the "holy spirit" against the Ezekielic background and, hence, with the same meaning that we afford concerning "God's spirit," the "spirit of prophecy," and the "spirit of the Lord." The "holy spirit" that the Lord creates in his people in *Jubilees* 1.23 is, in short, divine spirit.

In *Joseph and Aseneth,* the "spirit of God" that is upon Joseph appears to be understood as a source of Joseph's "great wisdom and knowledge" (4.9). But it is also depicted as an extension of the identity of God. In 8.11, for example, the spirit of the Lord that can renew Aseneth is paralleled with the Lord's *secret hand* that can remold her and the Lord's *life* that can quicken her. The Lord's life that can quicken Aseneth is probably related to the honeycomb, the smell of which is like the "breath of life" (16.4). By virtue of eating the honey (16.8-9), which corresponds to the idea of eating the "bread of [the Lord's] life" in 8.11, Aseneth received the "breath of life" and was transferred from "darkness into light," "error into truth," "death into life" (8.10).[33] While we cannot notice any clear description of the human spirit in *Joseph and Aseneth,* the divine spirit that is upon Joseph and received by Aseneth appears to be an extension of God's identity that characterizes the new identity of Aseneth.

4.3. Qumran Writings

In the Qumran text *1QHodayot*ª, the hymnist thanks God for "the spirits (רוחות) you placed in me" (1QHª 4.17). The plurality of רוח is un-

---

33. See also Rabens, *Spirit,* pp. 54-67.

Divine Spirit and Human Spirit in Paul

clear here. But the hymnist also uses the term in the singular in 1QH^a 5.25, where he says "And I, your servant, have known thanks to the spirit you have placed in me." Here the "spirit" *within* is the source of knowledge (5.24). There is a similar idea in 1QH^a 21.14, where the hymnist says "[And I, cr]eature from dust, I have known by the spirit which you have given in me." This appears to allude to Genesis 2:7, although the "spirit" for the hymnist is the means through which knowledge, rather than human life or identity, is acquired. But the hymnist also speaks of the "spirit" as representing a human person (5.19-20). This may have a connection with his assertion that God is the fashioner of the "spirit" and originator of "its task" (7.25). The fashioned "spirit," as 9.11-12 shows, could be a reference to angelic spirits. In the same column (27-28), however, the hymnist talks about God creating רוח on the tongue. One could argue from this, as Levison does, that the fashioned "spirit" refers to the divine breath of Genesis 2:7.[34] Levison's argument probably is valid for several reasons: the context is loaded with allusions to the Genesis creation narrative; the hymnist often refers to the divinely given "spirit" in him; in 17.12 the hymnist attributes the establishment of his רוח to God; and in 18.22 he claims that God fashioned his "spirit." However, since the inbreathing language of Genesis 2:7 is not clearly employed in any of the passages discussed, certainty is not possible about the hymnist's dependence on Genesis 2:7.

But how does the hymnist present the "spirit" in relation to "holy spirit"? Three things may be said by way of answering this question. First, the hymnist thanks God for the "spirits" placed in him in 1QH^a 4.17. Then in 4.26, he says "[I give you thanks, because] you have spread [your] holy spirit upon your servant." Given that the plurality of רוח in the former should not be taken literally, the "spirit" placed within the hymnist could be seen as God's "holy spirit" that was spread upon him. Second, in 8.14-15, the hymnist says that he seeks the "spirit." His reason for doing so cannot be known from the text because much of line 14 is lost but line 15 says "to be strengthened by [your] ho[ly] spirit, to adhere to the truth of your covenant." From this, it seems that the "spirit" and God's "holy spirit" carry the same sense. Third, that the hymnist views the "spirit" and "holy spirit" as the same thing is unambiguous in 20.11-12, where he says, "And I, the Instructor, have known you, my God, through the spirit which you gave in me, and I have lis-

---

34. Levison, *Filled with the Spirit*, pp. 186-87.

tened loyally to your wonderful secret through your holy spirit." In short, for the Qumran hymnist the "spirit" within a person, which probably represents the divine breath in Genesis 2:7, and the "holy spirit" refer to the same entity that is the source of knowledge and strength.

In *1QRule of the Community* (1QS) 3.6-8, the "spirit of the true counsel of God" or the "spirit of uprightness" has the role of *atonement* and the "holy spirit of the community" the role of *cleansing*. This evokes the language of cleansing in Ezekiel 36:25. Levison, probably wrongly, argues that 1QS and Ezekiel 36-37 represent differing ideologies, whereby for 1QS "spirit" is the means through which knowledge is acquired (so 1QH^a) whereas for Ezekiel it is the means through which life is acquired.[35] For the prophet, the "spirit" is indeed the means through which Israel is restored (Ezek. 36:27-28). A similar notion appears to be evident, for example, in 1QS 4.20-23.[36] Here the "spirit of truth" and the "spirit of holiness" represent the divine spirit.[37] For the writer of 1QS (3.19; 4.2-14, 23), either the "spirit of truth" — which leads to eternal life and the glory of Adam — or the "spirit of deceit" — which leads to eternal damnation — determines the identity of humanity. These opposing entities represent opposing cosmic metaphysical forces.

Bennema argues that the influence of these conflicting forces is reflected in human existence "as a psychological or ethical dualism."[38] He further argues that "salvation" in 1QS results from the "spirit of truth" increasing in intensity in a person and overcoming the intensity of the "spirit of deceit."[39] There exists in 1QS the upgrading or demoting of one on different grounds (5.20-25). But such a process has to do with one's place and spiritual status within the community rather than a degree of intensity. The "spirit of truth" defines the life and identity

---

35. Levison, *Filled with the Spirit*, pp. 211-12. We are uncertain about Levison's sharp contrast, since for the writer of 1QS life is achieved through the "spirit of truth" (4:7). Levison's contrast appears to reflect the ideological difference between Ezekiel and 1QH^a.

36. For treatment of 1QS 3-4 from different perspectives, see Bennema, *Power*, pp. 84-89; Rabens, *Spirit*, pp. 156-63; Levison, *Filled with the Spirit*, pp. 208-12.

37. See also Bennema, *Power*, pp. 85-89.

38. Bennema, *Power*, p. 87; Levison, *Filled with the Spirit*, p. 281 and n. 27. See also Levison (*Filled with the Spirit*, pp. 386-90) for a detailed discussion of 1QS's teaching of the two spirits in relation to the Gospel of John.

39. Bennema, *Power*, pp. 88-89.

of the community as people who share in the *glory of Adam* and exist in the dominion of God as against the dominion of Belial. The role of the divine spirit in 1QS, therefore, is not *only* to impart knowledge (rather than life)[40] or to ensure the "level of total purification,"[41] or to *transform* and *empower* the community to live according to God's precepts,[42] but is largely to define the life and identity of the community in terms of the *glory of Adam*, the ideal humanity.

4.4. Philo

Philo occasionally contrasts the "heavenly man" who is νοῦς with the "earthly man" who is σῶμα (*Leg.* 1.31-32; *Gig.* 60). He also depicts ὁ νοῦς as the receiver of τὸ πνεῦμα which is breathed out by God (*Leg.* 1.32, 37). It is not easy to distinguish when Philo is employing anthropological allegory and literal interpretation, particularly in his discussion of Genesis 1:26-27 and 2:7, which, he says, speak of *empirical man* or mind and *the composite man* as the recipient of the divine πνεῦμα (*Opif.* 69, 76, 144; *Leg.* 1.33, 42, 92; *Spec.* 3.207).[43] It seems clear, however, that Philo allegorically refers to "body" for one who remains earthly and "mind" for one who receives the divine spirit (e.g. *Leg.* 1.32). For Philo, the "breath of life" God breathed into Adam is the divine spirit. It is the divine spirit (shaped within humanity according to the archetypal form of the divine image) which seems to play a decisive role in human existence by guiding the mind to the truth (*Mos.* 2.265; *Spec.* 1.171). The notion of human spirit cannot be noticed in his writings.[44]

5. Paul

We now come to the reading of Pauline texts, focusing on Romans 8:16 and 1 Corinthians 2:11. The obvious reason for this is that these are the only passages in which Paul uses the human spirit and divine spirit to-

---

40. Levison, *Filled with the Spirit*, p. 211.
41. Bennema, *Power*, p. 89.
42. Rabens, *Spirit*, p. 163.
43. See A. J. Wedderburn for an overview of some of Philo's inconsistencies ("Philo's Heavenly Man," *NovT* 15 [1973]: 301-26).
44. See also Bennema, *Power*, p. 83.

gether. Our question is whether Paul understood the divine spirit and human spirit as two different entities with differing sets of meaning.

5.1. Romans 8:16

Romans 8:16 reads αὐτὸ τὸ πνεῦμα συμμαρτυρεῖ τῷ πνεύματι ἡμῶν ὅτι ἐσμὲν τέκνα θεοῦ ("the spirit himself bears witness with our spirit that we are children of God"). Does Paul's use of αὐτὸ τὸ πνεῦμα and τῷ πνεύματι ἡμῶν indicate two different categories or entities?

In the preceding verses, Paul has talked about πνεῦμα in different ways. In verse 2, he uses the term in a context where two laws oppose each other: the law of "the spirit of life" (τοῦ πνεύματος τῆς ζωῆς) and the law of "sin and death." Paul's reference to the "spirit of life" probably depends on Genesis 2:7. In Romans 8:2, when we take τῆς ζωῆς as dependent on τοῦ πνεύματος, we understand the new law as the law of the life-giving spirit[45] or the spirit "in his ruling function in the sphere of Christ."[46] In either case, the function of πνεῦμα in the sphere of Christ is one of life-giving and liberating for the Christian. This life-giving spirit is employed subsequently in a context where Paul uses κατὰ σάρκα versus κατὰ πνεῦμα or τὸ φρόνημα τῆς σαρκός versus τὸ δὲ φρόνημα τοῦ πνεύματος (vv. 4-6). These antithetical phrases could describe metaphorically some opposing outlooks and ethical principles, but they could also refer to opposing spheres controlled by opposing forces.[47]

So far, Paul has not used πνεῦμα with either human or divine association. When we come to verse 9, however, he says to his readers that "if indeed the spirit of God dwells in [them]," they are not "in flesh" but "in spirit." The πνεῦμα that is contrasted with σάρξ, therefore, is

---

45. C. B. Cranfield, *Romans 1-8*, International Critical Commentary (Edinburgh: T&T Clark, 1975), p. 376.

46. E. Käsemann, *Commentary on Romans*, trans. and ed. Geoffrey W. Bromiley (London: SCM Press, 1980), pp. 215-16; C. K. Barrett, *The Epistle to the Romans*, Black's New Testament Commentaries, rev. ed. (London: Black, 1991), pp. 145-46.

47. For the various views, see Käsemann, *Commentary*, pp. 219-20; P. Stuhlmacher, *Paul's Letter to the Romans: A Commentary*, trans. S. C. Hafemann (Louisville: Westminster John Knox Press, 1994), p. 121; J. D. G. Dunn, *Romans 1-8*, Word Biblical Commentary 38 (Dallas: Word, 1988), p. 424; J. Fitzmyer, *Romans: A New Translation with Introduction and Commentary*, Anchor Bible 33 (London: Doubleday, 1992), p. 489; Cranfield, *Romans 1-8*, p. 386; T. Schreiner, *Romans*, Baker Exegetical Commentary on the New Testament (Grand Rapids: Baker Academic, 1998), p. 411.

the "spirit of God" that indwells the believers. Not only that, πνεῦμα enables them to put the deeds of the body to death (v. 13), leads them (v. 14), makes them known to be "sons of God" (v. 14), helps them in their weaknesses (v. 26), and intercedes for them according to the will of God (v. 27). Furthermore, being indwelt by the "spirit of God" is the same thing as believers having the "spirit of Christ" (v. 9), which is described in verse 11 in terms of the "spirit of him who raised Jesus from the dead" and "his spirit which dwells in [them]." So the indwelling spirit is the spirit that made the resurrection of Christ possible. The spirit, in other words, is the spirit of life in relation to Christ as well. So Paul can say in verse 10, if the risen Christ is in the believers, "the spirit [that is in them] is life because of righteousness" (πνεῦμα ζωὴ διὰ δικαιοσύνην).[48] Therefore, to say that "the spirit is life" is the same thing as saying "Christ is life." This takes us back to Paul's use of πνεύμα τῆς ζωῆς (v. 2), which, as we argued above, probably depends on Genesis 2:7.

We further argue that the idea of God's breathing of the *breath of life* into the *formed Adam* influenced Paul's christological as well as anthropological thinking. This can be noticed in Romans 5:12-21, where Adam is compared with Christ. In verses 17-21, for example, Christ is the one through whom grace, righteousness, and ζωή are possible for all humanity who face death through Adam. There are corresponding descriptions in 1 Corinthians 15. In verse 22, Paul says that all who die in or through Adam "shall be made alive in or through Christ" (ἐν τῷ Χριστῷ πάντες ζῳοποιηθήσονται). Then in verses 45-58, Christ, in contrast to Adam, is presented as the "life-giving spirit" (πνεῦμα ζῳοποιοῦν), the "spiritual" (τὸ πνευματικόν) and the "heavenly man" (ἄνθρωπος ἐξ οὐρανοῦ). All this supports our interpretation of the "spirit of life" in Romans 8:2 in terms not only of the "spirit of God" or the "spirit of Christ" but also in terms of *Christ who is in the believers*.

When we come to Romans 8:16, it seems obvious that αὐτὸ τὸ πνεῦμα refers to the divine spirit represented in πνεῦμα υἱοθεσίας ("spirit of sonship" — as opposed to the "spirit of slavery") in verse 15. But scholars understand the referent of τῷ πνεύματι ἡμῶν differently from this. Even Barrett, who understands πνεῦμα υἱοθεσίας as the divine spirit, interprets "our spirit" as conscience that leads to conscious

---

48. And in verse 6, he had already said "to set the mind on the spirit is life and peace."

faith.[49] So, as in Deuteronomy 19:15, there are two witnesses about one being a child of God: a person's conscience and the direct action of the spirit.[50] But others understand "our spirit" as human spirit. For example, Cranfield, while accepting πνεῦμα υἱοθεσίας as the divine spirit,[51] argues that "our spirit" should be understood in its natural sense. He sees a problem with this, however, because the natural meaning maintains the Deuteronomistic idea of two witnesses, human spirit and the spirit of God. This gives the human spirit the same right as the divine spirit to testify to our being children of God, which is almost like giving a human being the same status as God in the divine court. And yet, Cranfield declines to go along with Barrett's view or the idea of "our spirit" as the χάρισμα given to us, or as our new nature, or as the self that is regenerated by Christ. He instead maintains the natural meaning for "our spirit" and translates συμμαρτυρεῖν as "testify to," "assure." The result of this is that the spirit of God testifies to or assures our human spirit that we are children of God.[52] Hence the human spirit and the divine spirit are independent entities.

However, while this interpretation has some validity, particularly as συμ in συμμαρτυρεῖν seems to suggest that Paul is referring to two independent entities, it does not take into account the context of Romans 8, where πνεῦμα, by and large, represents the human person as a new being, a child of God. This has become possible because Christ, as the *life-giving Spirit*, is *in the believers*. Paul understands Christ in this way probably on the basis of Genesis 2:7. For him, it seems, the divine *breath of life* that turned the *formed Adam* into a living being is now Christ, who — as the *life-giving Spirit* — defines the life and identity of Christians. So, in Romans 8:16, the referent of τῷ πνεύματι ἡμῶν should not be different from the referent of αὐτὸ τὸ πνεῦμα — the spirit of sonship, the spirit set against flesh, the spirit that indwells Christians, the spirit that serves as a liberating force and ethical weapon, the spirit that helps and intercedes for Christians, and the spirit described as the spirit of life, the spirit of God, the spirit of Christ.[53] Paul's talk about "the spirit himself"

49. Barrett, *Romans*, pp. 153-54.
50. Here συμμαρτυρεῖν is understood as "witness together with" — so Romans 2:15 and 9:1. Thus Barrett translates Romans 8:16: "the Spirit himself in this way bears witness with our spirit that we are children of God" (*Romans*, pp. 153-54).
51. Cranfield, *Romans 1–8*, pp. 399, 403.
52. Cranfield, *Romans 1–8*, p. 403.
53. Cf. Engberg-Pedersen, *Cosmology*, p. 66.

Divine Spirit and Human Spirit in Paul

bearing witness with "our spirit" is then a linguistic expression, which is based on his theological conviction that the new life and identity of the Christian resulted from the indwelling of the divine spirit. This theological conviction is probably informed and shaped by Genesis 2:7.

5.2. *1 Corinthians 2:11*

In 1 Corinthians 2:11, Paul says τίς γὰρ οἶδεν ἀνθρώπων τὰ τοῦ ἀνθρώπου εἰ μὴ τὸ πνεῦμα τοῦ ἀνθρώπου τὸ ἐν αὐτῷ; οὕτως καὶ τὰ τοῦ θεοῦ οὐδεὶς ἔγνωκεν εἰ μὴ τὸ πνεῦμα τοῦ θεοῦ. According to this passage, there are two different spheres (divine and human) within which knowledge is acquired through πνεῦμα. One could argue that Paul is subscribing to a dualist-Platonic standpoint where πνεῦμα is within the human body.[54] But one could also read the passage on the basis that πνεῦμα embodies a natural correspondence between the human person (τὸ πνεῦμα τοῦ ἀνθρώπου) and God (τὸ πνεῦμα τοῦ θεοῦ). Thiselton treats these views as "superficial."[55] Following Jewett, he rejects the earlier understanding that the human spirit is a central anthropological category for Paul.[56] For Thiselton, by using spatial language to indicate *"modes or aspects of being"* (italics his) rather than location, Paul is saying that as "one person cannot know the least accessible aspects of another human being unless that person is willing to place them in the public domain. . . . God's own self could [not] be open to scrutiny unless his spirit makes them accessible by an act of unveiling them."[57]

This interpretation depends on how τὰ τοῦ θεοῦ and the corresponding τὰ τοῦ ἀνθρώπου are understood. Thiselton understands τὰ τοῦ θεοῦ as *"what pertains to God."* Hence, the phrase represents a meaning of "that which makes God what he is, that is, his character or Godhood, but also leaving open room for purposes, thoughts, and depths."[58] Although

---

54. E. Käsemann, *Perspectives on Paul*, trans. M. Kohl (London: SCM Press, 1974), p. 14. See also D. W. Stacey, *The Pauline View of Man in Relation to Its Judaic and Hellenistic Background* (London: Macmillan, 1956), pp. 36-38, 143-145.

55. A. Thiselton, *The First Epistle to the Corinthians: A Commentary on the Greek Text*, New International Greek Testament Commentary (Grand Rapids: Eerdmans, 2000), p. 257.

56. Thiselton, *Corinthians*, p. 258. See also Jewett, *Terms*, p. 167.

57. Thiselton, *Corinthians*, p. 259.

58. Thiselton, *Corinthians*, p. 259.

Thiselton understands τὰ τοῦ ἀνθρώπου as "what pertains to the human person in view," the phrase does not seem to represent a corresponding meaning, that is, that which makes the human person what she is — her character or personhood. This means that the term τά in the passage represents two different denotations: in relation to God, his being, whereas in relation to the human person, her stance, thoughts, and intentions. This is further confirmed by Thiselton's depiction of πνεῦμα in relation to the human person as one's "initiative to reveal one's thoughts," whereas in relation to God as God's spirit that, in Athanasius's words, is ἐκ τοῦ θεοῦ or God himself.[59] One might allege from this that Thiselton's approach replaces the existing anthropological interpretative category with a psychological interpretative category. Thiselton, of course, denies that his interpretation seeks to "impose modern psychology onto Paul."[60] This, however, can be challenged on the basis of his appreciation of and, to a degree, dependence on Theissen's *Psychological Aspects of Pauline Theology*.[61] This probably leads him to understand τὸ πνεῦμα τοῦ ἀνθρώπου and τὸ πνεῦμα τοῦ θεοῦ from two different perspectives, psychological and metaphysical respectively.

Both phrases must probably be understood on the basis of the premise that Paul depended on the Scripture while formulating this analogy. So, for example, in Numbers 27:16, God is depicted as the God of human spirit (ὁ θεὸς τῶν πνευμάτων καὶ πάσης σαρκός). In Zechariah 12:1, YHWH is presented as the *creator* (MT) or *former* (LXX) of the human spirit in a person (πλάσσων πνεῦμα ἀνθρώπου ἐν αὐτῷ). These assertions are clearly based on Genesis 2:7, where God breathed into Adam the breath of life (πνοὴν ζωῆς), which is later described as the spirit of the Lord (Gen. 6:3). The Genesis, Numbers, and Zechariah backgrounds show that the πνεῦμα *within a person* (τοῦ ἀνθρώπου τὸ ἐν αὐτῷ) that Paul is talking about is the same thing as the πνεῦμα that was divinely *breathed out* and received by Adam in creation. It seems to us to be the case that these and similar scriptural expressions gave rise to a conventional linguistic reference to πνεῦμα as divine and human. So any consideration of πνεῦμα in 1 Corinthians 2:11 should take into account scriptural backgrounds.

---

59. Thiselton, *Corinthians*, pp. 258-59.
60. Thiselton, *Corinthians*, p. 258.
61. See, for example, G. Theissen, *Psychological Aspects of Pauline Theology*, trans. J. P. Galvin (Edinburgh: T&T Clark, 1987), p. 385.

Divine Spirit and Human Spirit in Paul

The meaning of πνεῦμα here should also be informed by the immediate context. In 2:6, the wisdom Paul and his colleagues speak among those who are mature (τοῖς τελείοις) is not the "wisdom of this age" but the wisdom of God or the hidden mystery, which οἱ ἄρχοντες failed to recognize and, as a result, crucified the Lord of glory (2:7-8). Although the source of the citation in verse 9 is notoriously difficult to determine,[62] Paul seems to contrast those who love God in the citation with οἱ ἄρχοντες τοῦ αἰῶνος τούτου (2:6). In 2:9-10, therefore, Paul is saying that the πνεῦμα, who is capable of searching everything, *revealed* to "us" the "things" (ἅ) which οἱ ἄρχοντες were not able to see, hear, and perceive. Paul's intention here is to show that his ability to speak the wisdom of God and hidden mystery depends on the revelatory activity of πνεῦμα, because the πνεῦμα he has received is not τὸ πνεῦμα τοῦ κόσμου but τὸ πνεῦμα τὸ ἐκ τοῦ θεοῦ (2:12). This enables Paul to see himself as true πνευματικός who has the *mind of Christ* and is capable of understanding and discerning *pneumatic gifts and truths* (2:13-16).[63]

So 1 Corinthians 2:11 should not be understood differently from the immediate context. On the contrary, Jewett argues that Paul's intention in introducing a dualistic concept of πνεῦμα in the passage is polemical. That is, Paul aims to show the inferiority of the Gnostics' claim that their possession of the divine spirit enabled them to become true πνευματικοί and hence to question whether Paul was πνευματικός.[64] For Jewett, "the τὸ πνεῦμα τοῦ ἀνθρώπου is definable, therefore, only in a negative sense as utterly incommensurate with God's spirit, as related to the πνεῦμα τοῦ κόσμου and a characteristic of ψυχικὸς ἄνθρωπος."[65] Jewett is right in that Paul may be setting a polemic against his critics' desire to submit some kind of judgment to determine whether he was πνευματικός or ψυχικός. But Jewett is wrong in talking about the Gnostics' claim because there is not any conclusive evidence about the existence of Gnosticism in the first century CE. He is also probably wrong in viewing τὸ πνεῦμα τοῦ ἀνθρώπου and τὸ πνεῦμα τοῦ θεοῦ in our text as *an analogy of opposites* for at least two reasons. First, the analogy is not utilized primarily in prepa-

---

62. But cf. Isa. 64:4, Sir. 1:10; *Asc. Isa.* 11.34; and G. Fee, *The First Epistle to the Corinthians*, New International Commentary on the New Testament (Grand Rapids: Eerdmans, 1987), p. 109.

63. See also A. Munzinger, *Discerning the Spirits: Theological and Ethical Hermeneutics in Paul* (Cambridge: Cambridge University Press, 2007), pp. 141-87.

64. Jewett, *Terms*, p. 188.

65. Jewett, *Terms*, pp. 188-89.

ration for the subsequent denial and affirmation of verse 12, but to provide confirmation for Pauline assertions regarding *the Spirit's revelatory operation* in 1 Corinthians 2:10. Second, Paul does not say that his critics' possession of human spirit resulted in them being ψυχικοί and ignorant of the mystery of God. That is, the analogy gives us no clue regarding Paul's intention to disqualify the critics' belief that their capability to know the mystery of God was based on their possession of τὸ πνεῦμα τοῦ ἀνθρώπου that is incommensurate with τὸ πνεῦμα τοῦ θεοῦ.[66]

So could Paul's analogy in 1 Corinthians 2:11 have been intended to emphasize the existence of a *consubstantiality* between human spirit and divine spirit?[67] If yes, Paul's use of πνεῦμα with human and divine associations in our passage may not necessarily suggest that he viewed them as two different entities within the divine-human relationship in the Christian context. This, of course, leaves us with several questions. Did Paul understand πνεῦμα as a constitutive component divinely breathed out in creation so as to realize an ontological possibility for all humanity?[68] Or did he understand it as God's eschatological gift, which — through revelation — enables human beings to cross the chasm between human existence and pneumatic existence?[69] Or did he understand it as *a physical entity* that is at the same time instrumental in generating understanding as *a cognitive power*?[70]

These questions cannot be answered in this short article, but going back to the context of 1 Corinthians 2:11, it is important to note that Paul's Corinthian critics had probably cast doubt on his possession of πνεῦμα and his being πνευματικός. That makes Paul say, "We have not received the spirit of the world but the Spirit who is from God" (2:12a); "But we have the mind of Christ" (2:16); "But I have the Spirit of God" (7:40b). Paul seems to attempt to reverse his critics' claim by categorizing them as ψυχικοί. In doing so, he accuses them of acting as those who do not have the spirit from God, the mind of Christ. For Paul, it seems,

---

66. So J. A. Davies, *Wisdom and Spirit: An Investigation of 1 Corinthians 1:18–3:20 against the Background of Jewish Sapiential Traditions in the Greco-Roman Period* (Lanham: University Press of America, 1984), p. 111.

67. B. A. Pearson, *The Pneumatikos-Psychikos Terminology in 1 Corinthians* (Missoula: Scholars Press, 1973), p. 41.

68. Pearson, *Terminology*, p. 39.

69. G. Sterling, "'Wisdom Among the Perfect': Creation Traditions in Alexandrian Judaism and Corinthian Christianity," *NovT* 37 (1995): 355-84.

70. Engberg-Pedersen, *Cosmology*, pp. 62-67.

πνεῦμα defines, marks, and represents the new life and identity of a Christian. For example, in 1 Corinthians 2:16, where Isaiah 40:13 from the LXX is quoted, the *mind of Christ*, for Paul, represents Christ, who is now *in the Christian*, as *the mind or spirit of the Lord* represents the Lord for Isaiah. Similarly, the "one spirit" that Christians *become* through their union with Christ (1 Cor. 6:17; cf. 12:1-6) is the "holy spirit" that indwells the Christian (1 Cor. 6:19; cf. 3:16). In both *union* and *temple-dwelling* metaphors, the πνεῦμα marks a renewed life and identity for the community of believers. As a result, Paul can say that every believer in the community has *the same spirit . . . the same Lord . . . the same God* (1 Cor. 12:4-6).

6. Synthesis

We set out in this article to answer the question as to whether or not Paul's use of πνεῦμα with human association and divine association suggests that he understood human spirit and divine spirit as two different entities. Our exegetical analysis of Romans 8:16 and 1 Corinthians 2:11 showed that for Paul πνεῦμα *is divine spirit and that the use of human spirit and divine spirit should probably be understood as a conventional linguistic expression that originated from Scriptural traditions*. But neither Stoic nor biblical-Jewish traditions show that the use of רוח/πνεῦμα with human and divine associations implies that the depictions of divine spirit and human spirit are to be understood in terms of two different entities.

While we cannot be certain about the extent to which Paul was dependent on the Stoic and biblical-Jewish traditions we considered, our studies of the traditions and textual readings showed that what Paul describes as "human spirit" *within* a Christian (1 Cor. 2:11) or "our spirit" (Rom. 8:16) probably stands for the divine spirit that indwells the Christian and has become the *life-giving spirit*. Like the Old Testament writers, who borrowed the term רוח/πνεῦμα from the natural world and gave it different nuances in accordance with the demand of the context in which they used it, Paul too associated πνεῦμα with different "things" or "beings" and that association resulted in different expressions: sometimes theological, sometimes anthropological, sometimes christological, sometimes cosmological. But for him, πνεῦμα, in Romans 8:16 and 1 Corinthians 2:11, *is divine spirit*, although this is not to deny that the term could have a different sense elsewhere in his corpus.

There is very little question that Paul's thinking in both Romans and 1 Corinthians is influenced by Genesis 2:7 at different levels.[71] That influence runs through the history of Israel and Judaism well into the Second Temple period and beyond. Indeed, Adam's reception of the *breath of life* for his actuality and identity in Genesis serves as a defining framework of Israel's relationship with Yhwh and its true life and existence. So in the Old Testament, the *breath of life* is the *divine spirit* expressed generally in contexts where human existence or divine-human relationship — rather than display of mighty phenomena — is in focus. So the depictions of spirit with human and divine categories in the Old Testament do not necessarily have different meanings. We noted a similar perspective in the Jewish literature of the Second Temple period.

Thus, when biblical writers speak about the divine spirit and human spirit as two different categories, they may have done so only at a linguistic level.[72] Paul, for example, speaks about God's spirit and human spirit in 1 Corinthians 2:11 and "the spirit [of sonship]" bearing witness with "our spirit" in Romans 8:16. But at the same time he can say "I serve God with my spirit" (Rom. 1:9), the person "who is united with the Lord is one spirit" (1 Cor. 6:17). He also talks about "one spirit" in which Jews, Greeks, slaves, and free "were baptized into one body" and of which they were "all made to drink" (1 Cor. 12:13). In the course of using such linguistic expressions and imageries to describe his new understanding of πνεῦμα, Paul — like others before, during and after him — uses divine and human categories but without implying the existence of two separate, distinct (metaphysical) entities.[73]

Paul's new understanding of πνεῦμα centres on the risen Christ. For him, a person can acquire new or renewed life and identity through Christ, which is marked by πνεῦμα that is *in the Christian*. The πνεῦμα that indwells the Christian is referred to as the *spirit of life*, the spirit of God, the spirit of Christ, etc. (Rom. 8:2-11). But Paul also talks about Christ residing *in the Christian* (Rom 8:9-10) as the *life-giving Spirit* (1 Cor. 15:45; cf. Rom. 5:17-21). So it seems to us to be more akin to Paul's thinking to understand his talk about human spirit and divine spirit in Romans 8:16 and 1 Corinthians 2:11 from the standpoint of Christ residing in the believer as and through the *life-giving Spirit*.

71. So Levison, *Filled with the Spirit*, pp. 313-16.
72. See also Bennema, *Power*, p. 98 and n. 221.
73. See also J. Ziesler, *Pauline Christianity* (Oxford: Oxford University Press, 1990), pp. 99-100; Dunn, *Theology*, pp. 76-77; Bennema, *Power*, pp. 95-98; Engberg-Pedersen, *Cosmology*, p. 66.

Ephesians and Divine-Christology

Chris Tilling

1. Introduction

Would the earliest Christians have agreed that Christ is "on the divine side of the line which monotheism must draw between God and creatures"?[1] This question has generated concentrated debate for centuries, not least in recent decades, with reference to the writings of Paul the Apostle. As its Pauline authorship remains disputed,[2] Ephesians has not been a focus of Christological debate. However, analysis of contemporary scholarly recourse to this letter, in terms of the Christology debate, is illuminating, as shall be seen. Indeed, this analysis will suggest that time is ripe for fresh analysis of the Christological language of

---

1. Richard J. Bauckham, "The Worship of Jesus in Apocalyptic Christianity," *NTS* 27 (1981): 335.
2. I will not, in this article, take sides on that debate. I will occasionally refer to "Paul" as the author for the sake of simplicity.

As most scholars think that Ephesians knew and drew upon Colossians, some reflection on the way in which Ephesians precisely does this would be desirable. However, for reasons of space this will not be undertaken in the following chapter. This is a strategic decision underscored by the fact that the scholarly Colossians-priority-consensus has been challenged in Best's important commentary (Ernest Best, *A Critical and Exegetical Commentary on Ephesians*, International Critical Commentary [Edinburgh: T&T Clark, 1998], pp. 20-36), and so would require more detailed discussion than space permits. What is more, in this chapter we hope to clarify the sometimes underestimated Christological import of the text of Ephesians itself, something which requires focused attention. The results of the following engagement with Ephesians can then open up a second stage of inquiry, in dialogue with Colossians. But that is a task for another essay.

Chris Tilling

Ephesians, with a view to clarifying wider debates surrounding the question of an early divine-Christology.

2. Ephesians in Recent New Testament Christological Studies

2.1. Richard Bauckham

Bauckham's contributions to the early divine-Christology debate are perhaps the most imaginative and intellectually stimulating. His main offering to the debate has been succinctly summarized in his small but influential monograph, *God Crucified*,[3] now reprinted together with a number of important essays, in his 2008 book, *Jesus and the God of Israel*.[4] In it Bauckham maintains that Jews focused on certain matters to identify the absolute uniqueness of God. A "strict" monotheism is posited by focusing on God's *identity*, one asserted in terms of God's relationship, first, *to Israel* as the one who reveals the divine name, YHWH, and as one who is known through "the consistency of his acts and character."[5] Second, God is identified in his relationship *to all reality* "most especially [in] that he is Creator of all things and sovereign Ruler of all things."[6] Alongside "these two principal ways of characterizing God's unique identity" there is a third: "monolatry, the exclusive worship of the one God."[7] In practice, when turning to New Testament Christology, Bauckham tends to focus on the second "principal way," and the matter of monolatry. He finds that, as a pattern of evidence, early Christology, when read in the light of these identifying categories, "included Jesus, precisely and unambiguously, within the unique identity of the one God of Israel."[8] For Bauckham, Christ is understood as eternal, as associated with creation and sovereign rule, as worshipped etc., and is thus on the "divine side of the line."

This is all reflected in Bauckham's engagement with Ephesians.

---

3. Richard J. Bauckham, *God Crucified: Monotheism and Christology in the New Testament* (Carlisle: Paternoster, 1998).
4. Richard J. Bauckham, *Jesus and the God of Israel* (Milton Keynes: Paternoster, 2008).
5. Bauckham, *Jesus*, p. 8.
6. Bauckham, *Jesus*, p. 8.
7. Bauckham, *Jesus*, p. 11.
8. Bauckham, *God Crucified*, p. vii.

Ephesians and Divine-Christology

Hence he points out the significance of "singing of hymns 'to the Lord' [i.e., to Christ]" as "attested in Eph 5:19."[9] He also maintains that Ephesians is witness to Jesus' sharing "God's exaltation above all the angelic powers," citing Ephesians 1:21-22 as evidence.[10] In particular, Bauckham perceives considerable significance in the language of Christ's exaltation "*far above* all rule and authority," which prompts engagement with spatial imagery in Ephesians (e.g. 4:10).[11] But Bauckham also casts his Christological net wider by noting "YHWH texts with Jesus as referent,"[12] referencing in this case Ephesians 4:8 and 6:19, and he understands the repeated use of "one" language in Ephesians 4:4-5 in terms of the *Shema*.[13]

2.2. Larry Hurtado

The focus of Larry Hurtado's work has been "the religious devotion to the figure of Christ in first-century Christianity, especially the reverencing of Christ in ways that connote a view of him as in some way divine."[14] Given this focus, it is natural that his major work, *Lord Jesus Christ*, has made reference to Ephesians 5:18-20.[15] Though Hurtado's emphasis in examining Christ-devotion has been "the *pattern* of early Christian devotional *practice*,"[16] his understanding of "devotion" also includes appreciation of early Christian beliefs.[17] In this respect, his relatively brief treatment of Ephesians has focused on Christ's centrality in redemption (referencing Eph. 1:3-14 and much material in Eph. 2). Further, he notes that Ephesians "sought to shape . . . everyday social behavior out of devotion to Christ. That is, 'devotion' to Jesus clearly extended beyond Christological beliefs and worship prac-

---

9. Richard J. Bauckham, "The Worship of Jesus," *ABD*, 3:814.
10. Bauckham, *Jesus*, p. 23.
11. Bauckham, *Jesus*, pp. 24, 177, 238.
12. Bauckham, *Jesus*, pp. 219-21.
13. Bauckham, *Jesus*, pp. 104-5.
14. Larry W. Hurtado, *One God, One Lord*, 2nd ed. (Edinburgh: T&T Clark, 1998), p. vii; Larry W. Hurtado, *Lord Jesus Christ: Devotion to Jesus in Earliest Christianity* (Grand Rapids: Eerdmans, 2003), p. xiii.
15. Hurtado, *Lord Jesus Christ*, pp. 146-47.
16. Larry W. Hurtado, *How on Earth Did Jesus Become a God?* (Grand Rapids: Eerdmans, 2005), p. 27, italics mine.
17. Hurtado, *Lord Jesus Christ*, p. 3.

Chris Tilling

tice."[18] Hurtado argues that Paul "wrote of the exalted Christ and reverenced him in ways that seem to require us to conclude that Paul treated him as divine."[19] His overview of Ephesians and other — what he calls — "Later Pauline Texts"[20] leads to the conclusion that "in the traditions that these texts reaffirm, Jesus is revered as divine."[21]

2.3. Gordon Fee

The most thorough analysis of the Christology of Ephesians is offered by Gordon Fee in his 2007 tome, *Pauline Christology*.[22] The structure of the work as a whole is reflected in his chapter on Ephesians, so it again makes sense to summarize briefly his basic approach. Drawing on the work of Bauckham and Hurtado, Fee attempts to realize two goals. First, he wants to perform a detailed exegesis of "those texts deemed to have or, in some cases, not to have Christological significance."[23] Second, he seeks to provide a thematic analysis, in light of this exegetical work, with the goal of "determining how we might best speak *theologically* about Paul's Christology."[24] In conscious distinction from what he calls a narrative or titular method of Christological analysis, Fee calls his own "primarily exegetical."[25] Corresponding to this approach, the book is divided into two parts, an exegetical analysis (part 1), which contains his chapter on Ephesians, and a thematic synthesis (part 2).

That said, his exegetical section tends to examine the Pauline material according to titular subsections. Under Paul's supposed "Son of God Christology," Fee typically spends time assessing to what extent this is meant messianically, and to what extent pre-existence is implied. Fee's second major subdivision in his exegetical chapters involves examination of Paul's supposed "Κύριος Christology." Third, Fee spends

---

18. Hurtado, *Lord Jesus Christ*, pp. 511-12.
19. Hurtado, *One God*, p. 4.
20. Hurtado, *Lord Jesus Christ*, p. 504.
21. Hurtado, *Lord Jesus Christ*, p. 518.
22. Gordon D. Fee, *Pauline Christology: An Exegetical-Theological Study* (Peabody: Hendrickson, 2007).
23. Fee, *Christology*, p. 10.
24. Fee, *Christology*, p. 10, italics his.
25. Fee, *Christology*, p. 4.

considerable space examining the divine roles and prerogatives adopted by Christ, and notes the times Paul appears deliberately to apply "Yhwh texts" to the risen Christ. In his opening comments he defines "Christology" as concerned with the "person" and not "work" of Christ. Indeed, given that Paul, Fee maintains, does not write about Christology as such, Fee's task is formulated as an attempt "to try to tease out what Paul himself understood *presuppositionally* about Christ, and to do so on the basis of his explicit and incidental references to Christ."[26] Corresponding to these distinctions in his exegetical work, Fee, in the synthesis section (part 2), concludes that "Christ is, first of all, the messianic/eternal Son of God . . . ; and second, Christ is the messianic, now exalted 'Lord' . . . , who for Paul has come to be identified with κύριος *(Lord)* = Yahweh."[27]

This general approach is very clearly reflected in Fee's engagement with Christology in Ephesians. Under the heading "Jesus as Messianic/Eternal Son of God,"[28] he examines the nature of the relationship between God the Father and the Lord as Son by seeking to explain the "subordination" texts (especially 1:17) not as statements which distinguish Christ from divinity, but rather as evidence of "a christological identification of God the Father."[29] While God is praised in Ephesians 1:3-14, 15-23, "the praise is for what the Father has done through the Son, resulting in adoration of the Son as the primary content of [these] . . . passages."[30] This all demonstrates, Fee argues, Paul's "deeply rooted, presuppositional Son of God Christology,"[31] which is further designated as (presuppositionally) a Christology of pre-existence.[32]

Under the heading "Christ as Κύριος,"[33] Fee analyses a number of passages to demonstrate that Paul uses language which would ordinarily belong to God alone (cf. his exegesis of Eph. 1:20-23), that Paul

26. Fee, *Christology*, pp. 3-4.
27. Fee, *Christology*, p. 482, italics his.
28. Fee, *Christology*, pp. 342-51.
29. Fee, *Christology*, p. 344. One is also reminded of the arguments proffered in Francis Watson, "The Triune Divine Identity: Reflections on Pauline God-Language, in Disagreement with J. D. G. Dunn," *JSNT* 80 (2000): 99-124. Recently, cf. also Larry W. Hurtado, *God in New Testament Theology* (Nashville: Abingdon Press, 2010), p. 38.
30. Fee, *Christology*, p. 343.
31. Fee, *Christology*, p. 344.
32. Cf. Fee, *Christology*, p. 344 in reference to Eph. 1:4, and p. 350 with reference to Eph. 5:20.
33. Fee, *Christology*, pp. 351-59.

applies YHWH texts to Christ (cf. his exegesis of Eph. 4:7-13), and that God's identity now includes both Son and Spirit (cf. his exegesis of Eph. 4:4-6). This leads into a final section which lists ways in which Christ assumes divine prerogatives.[34]

2.4. James D. G. Dunn

Though Dunn, contrary to the expectations of some, asserts an early "high-Christology,"[35] he nevertheless tries to demonstrate that the evidence is more ambiguous than many claim. Dunn is well aware that much material in Paul suggests a divine-Christology, such as the application of YHWH texts to the risen Lord. But he will also note aspects of Paul's theology that would seem to counter a divine-Christology, and he thus prefers to urge attention to the variety of Christological language. In practice, however, Dunn tends to emphasize Christological language and themes that seem to speak against a divine-Christology. Hence, Dunn focuses on the ways in which Paul's letters distinguish God and Christ,[36] and he emphasizes verses that state Christ is, in one way or another, subordinate to God. Indeed, at times he stresses the latter verses so much that he struggles to explain passages that seem to affirm a divine-Christology. In reflecting on Romans 9:5, Dunn even argues that Paul could only refer to Christ as God, here, if "Paul's own [christological] reserve . . . slipped at this point." It should thus not be taken "as a considered expression of his theology."[37]

This general approach is reflected in Dunn's engagement with Ephesians. In his recent 2010 book on this theme, *Did the First Christians Worship Jesus?*,[38] his engagement with Ephesians begins by noting language in Ephesians which subordinates Christ to God, namely Ephesians 1:3 and 17 which speak of God as "the God . . . of our Lord Jesus Christ." "God is *the God of Jesus*," Dunn stresses, "even of Jesus as

---

34. Fee, *Christology*, pp. 359-63.
35. James D. G. Dunn, *The Theology of Paul the Apostle* (Grand Rapids: Eerdmans, 1998), p. 258.
36. James D. G. Dunn, "Was Christianity a Monotheistic Faith from the Beginning?," in *The Christ and the Spirit: Christology* (Edinburgh: T&T Clark, 1998), pp. 337-38.
37. Dunn, *Theology*, p. 257.
38. James D. G. Dunn, *Did the First Christians Worship Jesus?: The New Testament Evidence* (London: SPCK, 2010).

Lord."[39] He also, and quite correctly, refers to Ephesians as part of his task of distinguishing the kind of praise and prayer language used in reference to God, from that used in terms of Christ.[40] Less poignantly, he also cites Ephesians 1:17 as evidence that Paul "refrains from speaking of the Spirit as given by Jesus, whereas he regularly describes *God* as the one who gives the Spirit."[41] When he must admit evidence which points in a different direction, such as songs sung *to Christ* (Eph. 5:19), he tries to offer an alternative reading. On this theme, he suggests that "the readiness to see Christ in or referred to in the Psalms may be better understood as evidence of hermeneutical more than liturgical practice." "Once again," Dunn insists, "the data is more complex and the implications not so clearly drawn."[42] Or again, contra Bauckham's claim that Christ's universal lordship, in Ephesians 1:20-22, is evidence of a divine-Christology, Dunn retorts that reference to Psalms 110:1 and 8:6 in Ephesians merely shows that this lordship is a type of "Adam Christology," which confirms Christ's exaltation as the fulfillment of God's purpose for *humankind*.[43] In contrast to Bauckham's claim that the "one" language in Ephesians 4:4-5 should be understood in terms of the *Shema*, Dunn attempts again to "muddy the water," this time noting that God the Father is the source, origin and goal, while Christ the Lord is simply the "mediating agency."[44] With respect to Ephesians, Dunn at least admits that language in Ephesians 5:21, 32 and 6:5 does indicate "a reverential fear of Christ, a usage entirely appropriate within a context of worship," though this is, he adds, "an isolated case."[45]

---

39. Dunn, *Worship*, p. 3, italics his.
40. Cf., e.g., Dunn, *Worship*, pp. 19-20, 26, 33.
41. Dunn, *Worship*, p. 127; James D. G. Dunn, *Christology in the Making: A New Testament Inquiry into the Origins of the Doctrine of the Incarnation*, 2nd ed. (London: SCM Press, 1989), p. 143. For critique of this point, cf. Mehrdad Fatehi, *The Spirit's Relation to the Risen Lord in Paul: An Examination of Its Christological Implications* (Tübingen: Mohr Siebeck, 2000), pp. 326-30.
42. Dunn, *Worship*, p. 39.
43. Dunn, *Worship*, p. 139; Dunn, *Christology*, p. 109.
44. Dunn, *Worship*, p. 109.
45. Dunn, *Worship*, p. 19.

3. Criticism of These Recent Scholarly Appropriations of Ephesians in Christological Debate

This is not the place for a detailed critical engagement with the claims of these scholars generally,[46] but a number of points can be made. Beginning with Bauckham, one must ask whether his categories for identifying the unique divine identity would have been as obvious to Roman-era Jews as he suggests, especially in light of material in both *1 Enoch* and Philo.[47] Is, then, Bauckham trying to make Ephesians 1:21-22 say too much? Some will also want to challenge whether the "one" language in Ephesians 4:4-5 is best understood in terms of an inclusion of Christ in the *Shema*.[48]

Turning to Hurtado's contributions, unlike his work on the undisputed Pauline letters, where his grasp of devotion arguably lacks a certain appreciation of the richness and color of Paul's language (e.g. he does not sufficiently account for the passionate nature of Christ devotion in Paul, and misses many relevant texts in his analysis of Paul),[49] in Ephesians he does examine material which he describes as a "devotion" which extends "beyond christological beliefs and worship practice."[50] However, while Hurtado examines Christ-devotion to "do full justice to the way in which Jesus figures in early Christian circles,"[51] his grasp of the best pattern of evidence necessary to accomplish this aim, though helpful, is not entirely without problems. I have argued elsewhere in detail that Christ-devotion is itself better understood as part of a larger, more Pauline, pattern of data, namely that concerning the relation between risen Lord and believers (which includes, alongside Christ-devotion, other matters such as the experience of the presence and absence of Christ, the ways in which Christ is

---

46. For this, see my forthcoming *Paul's Divine Christology* (Tübingen: Mohr Siebeck, 2012).

47. Cf. the valid points raised in Andrew Chester, *Messiah and Exaltation: Jewish Messianic and Visionary Traditions and New Testament Christology* (Tübingen: Mohr Siebeck, 2007), pp. 20-27.

48. Cf. James F. McGrath, *The Only True God: Early Christian Monotheism in Its Jewish Context* (Urbana: University of Illinois Press, 2009), pp. 38-54. McGrath's arguments are, however, not overly compelling, and they are even less so in terms of 1 Cor. 8:6 (cf. Tilling, *Christology*, forthcoming).

49. Cf. Tilling, *Christology*, forthcoming.

50. Hurtado, *Lord Jesus Christ*, p. 512.

51. Hurtado, *Lord Jesus Christ*, p. 4.

characterized, etc.).[52] This way of approaching the task of Christological investigation is suggested by a number of factors, not least Pauline monotheism and epistemology, which are arguably best understood in relational terms,[53] but also by the very shape of Paul's individual arguments. Importantly, when Ephesians is so examined, it will yield more relevant Christological data than was discovered in light of Hurtado's project.[54] In other words, one has a better chance of doing "full justice" to the sources when they are approached in relational terms, something that will arguably be demonstrated in section 4, below. Certainly, Hurtado did not mean to engage exhaustively with Ephesians, and so one cannot complain too vigorously that he did not discuss enough material. But that is not the main point of contention. Rather, it is Hurtado's "Christ-devotion" approach which has arguably encouraged some blind spots when actually engaging the primary sources, a criticism at least not refuted by his contributions to analyzing "the way in which Jesus figures" in Ephesians.

Though Hurtado's analysis of Ephesians was short, the same cannot be said of Fee's contribution. There is much in Fee's thorough analysis that is helpful, and recourse to some of his exegetical observations will facilitate our own overview below of relevant themes in Ephesians. Yet a number of serious questions must be raised. First, one won-

52. Tilling, *Christology*, forthcoming.

53. As Dunn puts it: "To know God is to worship him ... to know God is to be known by him, a two-way relationship of acknowledgment and obligation (Gal. 4.9). As in the (Jewish) scriptures, the 'knowledge of God' includes experience of God's dealings, the two-way knowing of personal relationship" (James D. G. Dunn, "'The Body of Christ' in Paul," in *Worship, Theology and Ministry in the Early Church*, ed. Michael J. Wilkins and Terence Paige [Sheffield: Sheffield Academic Press, 1992], p. 47). Cf. also, among other points, how Paul reuses (Erik Waaler, *The Shema and the First Commandment in First Corinthians: An Intertextual Approach to Paul's Re-Reading of Deuteronomy* [Tübingen: Mohr Siebeck, 2008]) the relational (Nathan MacDonald, *Deuteronomy and the Meaning of "Monotheism"* [Tübingen: Mohr Siebeck, 2003]) *Shema* in key ways in his theological thinking (Suzanne Nicholson, *Dynamic Oneness: The Significance and Flexibility of Paul's One-God Language* [Eugene: Pickwick, 2010]).

For examination of Paul's relational epistemology, cf. Ian W. Scott, *Implicit Epistemology in the Letters of Paul: Story, Experience and the Spirit* (Tübingen: Mohr Siebeck, 2006); Mary Healy, "Knowledge of the Mystery: A Study of Pauline Epistemology," in *The Bible and Epistemology*, ed. Mary Healy and Robin Parry (Milton Keynes: Paternoster, 2007), pp. 134-57.

54. For this approach applied to the undisputed letters of Paul, cf. Tilling, *Christology*, forthcoming.

ders whether Fee's implied ontological commitments are appropriate. He conceives of Christology in arguably rather Aristotelian terms, with a consequent emphasis on the substance or essence of Christ (hence the inordinate focus on pre-existence in his argument generally, but also Ephesians specifically [cf. his claims with respect to Eph. 1:4 and 5:20][55]). Concurrently, this ontology involves a suppression of "relation" as "accidental" to a thing;[56] hence Fee tends to fail to grasp the importance of relational language as part of his wider thematically synthesizing conclusions.[57] This is also seen in the way he categorizes material in his "exegetical" sections. For example, he includes under the heading "Christ and Divine Prerogatives"[58] the following: "living to please the Lord," "singing to the Lord," "obedience to Christ" and "being strong in the Lord." But are these not better described as aspects of relation to Christ, rather than Christ's prerogatives? Arguably, this mislabeling of aspects of Christ-language in Ephesians is representative of a more basic problem, an ontological misstep, one evidenced also in his claim that Christology is about the Person and *not* work of Christ.[59] Arguably, this (problematic) metaphysical substructure powerfully shapes Fee's exegesis of Paul and because of this, though Fee's analysis of Christology in Ephesians is by far and away the most thorough to date, it contains quite a few blind spots. This is perhaps one reason why Fee asserts that, after Galatians, Ephesians "has the least amount of Christological data in the church corpus,"[60] a remark which arguably only demonstrates Fee's inappropriate analytical posture. Ontology is perhaps a key reason why Fee appears to write defensively when engaging with subordination texts. Thus his analysis of Ephesians 1:17, that God is "God of our Lord Jesus Christ," can say a lot about the Christological identification of God, and very little about

---

55. Cf. Fee, *Christology*, pp. 344-45, 350-51.

56. Cf. the explication of Aristotle, metaphysics, ontology and relations in the various publications of Shults (e.g. F. LeRon Shults, *Reforming Theological Anthropology: After the Philosophical Turn to Relationality* [Grand Rapids: Eerdmans, 2003]; F. LeRon Shults, *Reforming the Doctrine of God* [Grand Rapids: Eerdmans, 2005]; F. LeRon Shults, *Christology and Science* [Aldershot: Ashgate, 2008]).

57. Various strands of evidence for this claim are catalogued in Tilling, *Christology*, forthcoming.

58. Fee, *Christology*, pp. 359-63.

59. Fee, *Christology*, p. 1.

60. Fee, *Christology*, p. 363.

the Lord Jesus having a God (the Father). If Christology is about static "being,"[61] subordination will be difficult to accommodate.[62]

Though Fee's often skillful analysis of evidence in Ephesians *for* a divine-Christology is matched by a less satisfying engagement with texts which seem to speak *against* it, the opposite can be said about Dunn's contributions. That is, Dunn gives central stage to texts which make a divine-Christology ambiguous, whereas those which seem to speak for such a Christology are unconvincingly sidestepped. For example, "singing and making melody to the Lord in your hearts" (5:19) is hardly best understood here as a hermeneutical *rather than* liturgical practice, as he claims (see above).[63] He notes evidence for the "reverential fear" of Christ (see above), but then asserts that this material in Ephesians is "isolated." But what about 2 Corinthians 5:11 ("knowing the fear of the Lord"), together with the copious references to aspects of vigorous Christ-devotion in the undisputed Pauline letters?

In terms of the divine-Christology debate, two basic perspectives are represented above. On the one hand, Dunn can be understood to represent a position which pleads for Christological ambiguity when it involves affirmation of full divinity in Ephesians. On the other hand, scholars such as Fee, Hurtado, and Bauckham maintain, in one way or another, a divine-Christology in Ephesians. Given the overview above, one suspects that these scholars often simply speak past one another by focusing on different passages, as suits their ends. Not infrequently, the "difficult" texts for their respective positions are either ignored or dealt with as part of an "explain away" procedure.

4. Ephesians and Christology: A Fresh Look

In light of these critical observations, a fresh analysis of Christological language in Ephesians is suggested. A fresh analysis of these scholars and those aspects where their approaches are arguably problematic will (i) be more ontologically appropriate/self-aware (i.e., relational), (ii) take seriously material supportive of both sides of the divine-

---

61. Cf. his telling recourse to the language of "being" in, e.g., Fee, *Christology*, pp. 142-43, 267, 269. But cf. his opaque comments on "ontology" and "choice" in p. 503 n. 8.

62. Cf. his comments in Fee, *Christology*, pp. 113, 142-43.

63. One also wonders why Hurtado has not made more of this passage, given his own focus.

Christology debate, (iii) do justice to the breadth of relevant material in Ephesians, as Fee and Hurtado urge, and (iv) account for general patterns of material as both Hurtado and Bauckham correctly insist. In practice, this will therefore mean an analysis of material in Ephesians which concerns God and Christ in relation to each other, the world and, as Ephesians emphasizes, especially to believers. This next section overviews much of the important material in this respect.[64]

4.1. Important God Language in Ephesians

New Testament Christology involves language both about God and Christ; one cannot be discussed without the other as they are inextricably bound together. Hence, we begin this overview of relevant language in Ephesians by examining its (relational) God-language. It can be divided into the following categories. Sadly, space permits no more than a summary of relevant texts, rather than detailed exegetical engagement.

4.1.1. God is present and active in the world, ruling by his power and his Spirit. "Grace . . . and peace," for the Ephesian believers, comes from "God our Father" (1:2). It is God who blessed, chose and destined believers for such things as adoption, holiness etc. (1:3-5). God can do this as he is the one "who accomplishes all things according to his counsel and will" (1:11). Paul prays to God to "give you a spirit of wisdom and revelation" and he speaks of "the immeasurable greatness of his power for us who believe, according to the working of his great power." This power, Paul continues, was put into effect when God raised Jesus from the dead (1:20). The redeemed become a "holy temple" which is "a dwelling place for God" (2:22). Paul speaks of his own ministry as the result of "the working of his [God's] power" (3:7). When Paul prays to God in chapter 3 for an inner strengthening, it is accomplished "through his Spirit" (3:16). The answer is given "by the power [of God's Spirit] at work within us" which is "able to accomplish abundantly far more than all we can ask or imagine" (3:20).

---

64. The meaning of "relational" in this paragraph should become clear as the analysis is undertaken. It simply means to indicate an examination of texts concerning God and Christ *in relation* — usually to humans, but also more generally to the cosmos.

The universal scope of God's sovereign power is affirmed in a number of ways. God is also the one "who created all things" (3:9), and it is from the Father that "every family in heaven and on earth takes its name" (3:15). Likewise, there is "one God and Father *of all,* who is above all and through all and in all" (4:6).

4.1.2. God is central to Paul's ultimate goals. Believers are destined by God for adoption "to the praise of his glorious grace" (1:6), to "live for the praise of his [God's] glory" (1:12). Redemption is likewise "to the praise of his glory" (1:14). Paul's prayer to the Father in chapter 3 is ultimately that the believers all "be filled with all the fullness of God" (3:19), a prayer which ends with a word of praise ("to him be glory in the church and in Christ Jesus to all generations, forever and ever" [3:21]).

4.1.3. Devotion is expressed toward God in numerous ways. While praise of and devotion to God are associated with Paul's ultimate goals (cf. the previous point), in portions of the letter Paul explicitly uses praise language in speaking of God. So he writes "blessed be . . . God." Humans become, in redemption, "God's own people" (1:14), arguably indicating a particular relationship to God enjoyed by the redeemed. Paul also prays to God (1:17), and in that prayer speaks of coming "to know him [God]" (1:17). Negatively, the state of those not "in Christ" is described as existence without "hope and without God in the world" (2:12), suggesting, albeit negatively, that living with God is understood, again, as relationship with God. This is affirmed a little later when Paul speaks of reconciliation "to God" (τῷ θεῷ, 2:16), and of the access available through Christ and in the Spirit *to the Father* (2:18), and by Paul's description of the Gentiles as "alienated from the life of God" in 4:18. In related language, the Spirit of God can be grieved and disobedience invites "God's wrath" (5:6). Paul prays to God again in chapter 3, and states that he bows his knees "before the Father" in intercession (3:14-19). He likewise encourages believers to give "thanks to God the Father at all times and for everything" (5:20).

4.1.4. God is characterized in certain ways. God is depicted as the source of grace, peace, love, and faith (1:2; 6:23; cf. also 3:7), and his activity of election leads to the praise of "his glorious grace that he freely bestowed on us" (1:6). Forgiveness is "according to the riches of his [God's] grace that he lavished on us" (1:7-8; cf. also 4:32). Chapter 2 details the character of God even further. Paul writes of God as "rich (πλούσιος) in mercy" and of his salvific activity as done "out of the great love with which he loved us" (2:4). God's salvific activity is made known with "all wisdom and insight" (1:8), and his election of humans "before the foundation of the world" (1:4) speaks of God's eternity (cf. also 3:11, "eternal purpose"). Finally, while the emphasis in Ephesians is on God's grace and love, he is also characterized in terms of "wrath" when confronted by disobedience (5:6).

4.1.5. God is related to Christ in specific ways. On the one hand, God is "the God of our Lord Jesus Christ" (1:17). On the other hand, it is "God in Christ" who has forgiven sinners (4:32). God blesses and chooses "in Christ" (1:3-4) and grace is bestowed "in the Beloved" (1:6). The kingdom is both "of Christ and of God" (5:5). Precise explication of the exact relationship between the God and Christ language in Ephesians must await the result of the examination of the latter in the following section.

4.1.6. Summary. In light of the above, it is difficult to be entirely sympathetic with Fee's claim that the emphasis in Ephesians "is so thoroughly on the role of Christ that it becomes emphatically christocentric," as opposed to "theocentric" Romans.[65] God, in Ephesians, is conceived in overtly relational terms, and in this respect is known in terms of certain characteristics, such as love, grace, mercy, and as powerfully present and active. Devotion to God is expressed in a variety of ways, including association of God with ultimate goals. God is also understood to be present and active in the world. This pattern is entirely predictable and reflects the sort of God-language found across Paul's undisputed letters and beyond.[66] Indeed, this pattern of God-relation data constitutes the way God was conceived as unique in Second Temple texts generally, as well as in Paul in particular, that is, the God-relation pattern was never, as a pattern, used to describe any other figure, however highly exalted (including the "Son of Man" in *1 En.*).[67]

---

65. Fee, *Christology*, p. 339.
66. Cf. Paul A. Rainbow, "Monotheism and Christology in 1 Corinthians 8:4-6," unpublished DPhil diss. (Oxford, 1987).
67. Cf. Tilling, *Christology*, forthcoming.

Ephesians and Divine-Christology

4.2. Key Christ Language in Ephesians

Generally speaking, the first half of Ephesians is dominated more by God-language, whereas the second half concentrates more on Christ-language. Once again, it shall be seen that certain themes emerge, and they can be categorized as follows.

4.2.1. Christ is in the heavens, "above all." God raised Christ from the dead "and seated him at his right hand in the heavenly places, *far above* all rule and authority," etc. (1:20-21). As Andrew Lincoln insightfully observes: With reference to Christ's place of exaltation "the writer sets a symbolic phrase, 'at his right hand,' next to a spatial one, 'in the heavenly realms.'"[68] Christ is in the heavenly realms, as are other rulers and authorities (3:10), also evil ones (6:12), but he is "far above" them all. Spatially, then, Christ is distinguished from the world and sphere of mortals, and even spiritual powers, a point stressed, as noted above, by Bauckham. It is difficult to be sure precisely what is meant by referring to Christ as the ἀκρογωνιαῖος ("key- or corner-stone" 2:20), but Lincoln argues it is language best understood in terms of Christ's heavenly lordship.[69] Either way, Christ is, in Ephesians, the "heavenly Lord."[70] So Paul writes in 4:10 that Christ has "ascended far above all the heavens."

4.2.2. Christ as present and active in the world by the Spirit. What is noteworthy is that Christ, in Ephesians, is not simply in heaven, but also, and at the same time, present and active in the world. Just as grace and peace was "from God" it is equally from "the Lord Jesus Christ" (1:2; cf. also 6:23). The implication is that Christ is active in the community of believers as the source of grace and peace. It could be argued that these verses simply speak of the past Christ-event, but most interpreters understand grace as practically synonymous with "power."[71]

In a less than obvious claim, Paul writes that Christ, now seated by God in heaven at God's right hand (1:20), is "far above all rule and authority and power and dominion . . . and [God] has put all things un-

---

68. Andrew T. Lincoln, *Ephesians*, Word Biblical Commentary 42 (Dallas: Word, 1990), p. 62.
69. Best, *Ephesians*, p. 286, is less confident about the precise meaning of the word.
70. Lincoln, *Ephesians*, p. 156.
71. Rudolf Bultmann, *Theology of the New Testament* (London: SCM Press, 1952), vol. 1, p. 291, a perspective repeated by Dunn, *Theology*, p. 48.

der his feet and has made him the head over all things for the church, which is his body, the fullness of him who fills[72] all in all" (1:21-23). As Fee comments:

> Christ [is] . . . described in language that ordinarily belongs to God alone. Through his church, Christ's own fullness now fills τὰ πάντα ἐν πᾶσιν. . . . This is precisely the kind of thing said . . . about God the Father — in this letter in 4:6.[73]

What is more, each member of the body, Ephesians maintains, is given grace "according to the measure of the gift of Christ" (κατὰ τὸ μέτρον τῆς δωρεᾶς τοῦ Χριστοῦ [4:7]). This potentially ambiguous Greek is clarified as one reads on: Christ "gave gifts to his people" (4:7), gifts such as apostles, prophets and evangelists, as Paul lists in 4:11. Precisely as he ascends, Christ gives these gifts (4:8). Put in more cosmic terms, though Christ has "ascended far above all the heavens," this happens "so that [ἵνα] he [Christ] might fill all things" (4:10). As Lincoln puts it: "Christ can be said to fill the universe in every respect as he pervades it with his rule."[74] However this phrase is to be exactly understood, Christ is portrayed at some level as present in, or pervading, all things. Further, this is an example of the application of an Old Testament passage, originally referring to Yhwh, to Christ (which could be taken as an expression of Christ-devotion).[75]

Finally, the church is exhorted to be strong, to resist "cosmic powers" etc. "in the Lord and in the strength of his power" (6:10). This is not simply that Ephesians understands Christ "as in the divine role otherwise attributed to God the Father,"[76] but further evidence that Christ, according to this letter, is present and active in the world even though he is exalted to the right hand of God in heaven.

4.2.3. Christ is associated with central goals.

In 3:8 Paul speaks of his motivations in mission to the Gentiles, one driven by the "boundless

---

72. Fee notes that the vast majority of interpreters read the participle as a middle (Fee, *Christology*, p. 354 n. 33).

73. Fee, *Christology*, p. 354.

74. Lincoln, *Ephesians*, p. 248.

75. For an approach to Christology which takes this kind of data seriously, cf. David B. Capes, *Old Testament Yahweh Texts in Paul's Christology* (Tübingen: J. C. B. Mohr [Paul Siebeck], 1992). Also cf. Fee, *Christology*, p. 358.

76. Fee, *Christology*, p. 363.

riches of Christ" (3:8). Paul portrays Christ's activity in giving gifts to the church as undertaken "until all of us come to . . . the knowledge of the Son of God" (4:13).[77] The purpose of the church is, at some level, to grow into its head, Christ (4:15). What is more, Christ loved the church and gave himself for it precisely "to present the church to *himself* in splendor" (5:27).

4.2.4. Christ-devotion is expressed in a variety of ways. It is those who set their "hope on Christ" who live for the glory of God (1:12). 1:15 (cf. also 3:12) speaks of the faith of this community "in the Lord Jesus" (πίστιν ἐν τῷ κυρίῳ Ἰησοῦ). Paul speaks of himself as "the prisoner in the Lord" and of Christ (cf. 4:1 and 3:1). As Lincoln observes, this language speaks of "spiritual captivity to Christ" and of "unconditional allegiance to his Lord."[78] In Paul's prayer to the Father in Ephesians 3, the power of God exercised through the Spirit is precisely so that "Christ may dwell in your hearts" (3:17). In 3:19, being filled with the fullness of God is conditioned on knowing (γνῶναί) "the love of Christ which surpasses knowledge." In 4:13 Paul picks up on this theme again, speaking of the future maturity of the "knowledge of the Son of God." Fee argues that language concerning "the knowledge of the Son of God" (4:13) implies a divine-Christology. As he explains:

> Full knowledge of the Son of God is, in this passage, the equivalent of full knowledge of God himself, since the word has to do not so much with the accumulation of facts and data but with the kind of knowing that people who know each other well have of one another.[79]

The church must try "to find out what is pleasing to the Lord" (5:10), to "understand what the will of the Lord is" (5:17). Being filled with the Spirit is associated with "singing and making melody to the Lord in your hearts" (5:19). In this context, Paul reminds the Ephesians: "Rise from the dead and Christ will shine on you" (5:14). "The association of Christ with a shining light," Lincoln notes, has a dominant back-

---

77. As Best notes, "καταντάω with εἰς points to a goal" (*Ephesians,* p. 399).
78. Lincoln, *Ephesians,* p. 173.
79. Fee, *Christology,* p. 347. Cf. also Harold W. Hoehner, *Ephesians: An Exegetical Commentary* (Grand Rapids: Baker Academic, 2002), p. 554.

Chris Tilling

ground, namely its use as an image "for Yahweh coming to save or help his people."⁸⁰

The so-called *Haustafeln* are centered on devotion to Christ. Being "subject to one another" is done "out of reverence for Christ" (5:21). Further, wives are to be subject to their husbands as "to the Lord" (5:22), just as the church is subject to Christ (5:24). As part of these comparisons between Christ's relationship with the church and human relations, Paul expresses their nature in terms of a husband and a wife becoming "one flesh" (5:31). Further, slaves are to obey earthly masters as they obey Christ, as slaves ultimately *of Christ* (6:6). Grace, finally, is with all those who specifically love the Lord Jesus (πάντων τῶν ἀγαπώντων [6:24]). As Lincoln observes: "the letter closes with a stress on believers' personal relationship and commitment to Christ."⁸¹

4.2.5. Christ-devotion is passionate. As noted above, Paul's concern for the church is that it grows into the head, who is Christ. What is more, this growth is to be seen "in every way" (4:15). Slaves are to obey earthly masters as they would obey Christ, "in singleness of heart" (ἐν ἁπλότητι τῆς καρδίας, 6:5), while their service is to be given "with enthusiasm" (μετ' εὐνοίας, 6:7). Finally, grace is with all who love the Lord Jesus Christ, as Paul puts it in 6:24, with an "undying love."

As Lincoln remarks:

> This is a Christological adaptation of the common expression "those who love God," found in the Old Testament, Second Temple Judaism, and the New Testament (cf., e.g., Exod. 20:6; Deut. 5:10; 7:9; *Pss. Sol.* 4.25; 6.6; *T. Sim.* 3.6; *1 En.* 108.8; Rom. 8:28; 1 Cor. 2:9; 8:3; Jas. 1:12; 2:5).⁸²

It only needs to be added that love for God, as detailed in these texts, is an exclusive love and devotion over against idolatry. It is an undying love.⁸³

---

80. Lincoln, *Ephesians*, p. 332. He notes, among other passages, Deut. 33:2; Pss. 50:2; 80:1-3, 7, 19; 1QHᵃ 4.5, 6, 23; 9.31; CD 20.25, 26. One will likely also remember the Benediction, from Num. 6.

81. Lincoln, *Ephesians*, p. 466.

82. Lincoln, *Ephesians*, p. 466.

83. Admittedly, this is a contentious reading of the Greek as it is not entirely clear what ἐν ἀφθαρσίᾳ belongs with. Most major commentators, however, opt for our reading, or something like it. Best notes that ἀγαπώντων is the "main word in the verse,"

4.2.6. Christ is characterized in specific ways. As noted above, Paul speaks of the "boundless riches [πλοῦτος] of Christ" (3:8). In Paul's chapter 3 prayer, his concern is that the believers may know Christ's *love* (3:19). In 4:5-6 Paul speaks of "one faith," "one God," etc., also mentioning the "one Lord." Christ is also portrayed as the "gift giver" in 4:7-12, active with the purpose of building up the church. This is part of the picture of Christ as "caring" for his church, as stated explicitly in 5:29. Likewise, Christ "loved us and gave himself for us" (5:1). Again, in the context of the so-called *Haustafeln,* Paul exhorts the behavior of husbands in terms of the love with which Christ "loved the church and gave himself up for her" (5:25). As noted above, Christ does this "to present the church to himself in splendor" (5:27). Christ is thus the loving bridegroom, a common metaphor used to describe the relationship between God and his people.[84] Christ is likewise the *Savior* of the church.[85] Finally, Ephesians makes an illuminating distinction in 6:7. Service is to be rendered "as to the Lord" with enthusiasm, *and not* ἀνθρώποις. What is Christ if he is contrasted with that which is "human"? What is more, the service must be rendered well as "we will receive the same again from the Lord" (6:8). Is the implication that the risen Christ sees what good deeds are done, so he can judge appropriately? Either way, Christ is the one to whom all are accountable, and with him "there is no partiality" (6:9).

4.2.7. Summary Christ is present and active in the world, and especially in the church, in a variety of ways, despite the fact that he is also, in some sense, spatially exalted. He is associated with Paul's central goals, and devotion to Christ is expressed in a variety of other ways: knowing, loving, living to please etc. At the same time, this relation with the gracious, loving, rich, impartial Lord is to be lived with passion and deep vigor.

---

thus making the association of ἐν ἀφθαρσίᾳ with the love more likely. What is more, Best suggests that, read like this, the verse "picks up and concludes the conflict of 6:10-17 in which those conquer who stand firm for ever" (Best, *Ephesians,* p. 620).

84. Cf. Raymond C. Ortlund Jr., *Whoredom: God's Unfaithful Wife in Biblical Theology* (Leicester: Apollos, 1996).

85. Eph. 5:23. This is, of course, a common way of speaking of God's relation to Israel in the Scriptures. Cf., e.g., 2 Sam. 22:3; 2 Kgs. 13:5; Pss. 17:7; 106:21; Isa. 19:20; 43:3, 11; 45:15, 21; 49:26; 60:16; 63:8; Jer. 14:8; Hos. 13:4.

5. Concluding Reflections

In order to assess the status of the material in Ephesians relevant to the divine-Christology debate, it is suggested that approaching the letter in terms of the Christ-relation will help to specify more precise questions and, ultimately, to clarify matters. It will prove illuminating to finish these reflections in dialogue with the great Wilhelm Bousset, who once argued that, in Paul's letters, there is a complication of the God-human relationship by "a peculiar thoroughgoing duplication" of the object of religious faith and veneration.[86] Further, he suggested that this implies a Pauline divine-Christology.[87] Bousset ultimately refused to accept that line of reasoning because of certain titular considerations (Christ was not, he thought, called θεός by Paul, and therefore he could not affirm a divine-Christology).[88] To what extent is Ephesians evidence for or against Bousset's claims?

First, is there such a "duplication" in Ephesians? Arguably, what Bousset began to see was the extensive *overlap* between the themes associated with the God- and Christ-relations. The overview of Ephesians above can confirm his intuition: while various differences of emphasis between specific elements of the Christ- and God-relations in Ephesians can be isolated (as emphasized, for example, by Dunn), the same basic pattern of language is used, and certainly both relations evidence the same shape and cover many similar themes, as the structure of the analysis above has shown. What is more, this overlap appears to some extent to be a deliberate move by Ephesians, as is suggested by the use of YHWH texts and metaphors in terms of Christ (Eph. 4:8 and 6:19; Christ as bridegroom and savior etc.), and repetition of specific God language in Ephesians in terms of Christ (such as God and Christ filling all [cf. 1:21-23 and 4:6]).

Is Bousset correct, however, to prioritize titular concerns over against such duplication or overlap? Arguably not. If Paul's epistemology is relational, did not Bousset prioritize the wrong element? Paul's "way of knowing" would have resonated with the kind of material Bousset deemed theologically less significant, and this was an unfortu-

---

86. W. Bousset, *Kyrios Christos: Geschichte des Christusglaubens von den Anfängen des Christentums bis Irenaeus* (New York: Abingdon, 1970), p. 205, translation mine.

87. Bousset, *Kyrios,* p. 209 n. 150.

88. Bousset, *Kyrios,* p. 210.

nate move. Further, it is not as if Bousset needed to wait for clarification of the nature of Pauline epistemology in recent research. As William Wrede put it over a century ago: *"[t]he religion of the apostle is theological through and through: his theology is his religion."*[89] In other words, if one is Pauline, such relational "overlap" should be seen as evidence with divine-Christological import.

To put things differently, if the pattern of God-relation data constitutes the way God was conceived as unique in Second Temple texts generally, and in Paul in particular (as further witnessed in Ephesians), then describing the Christ-relation in Ephesians in a way which, as a pattern, reflects that unique God-relation suggests a divine-Christology, albeit a relational one. That is, Ephesians is further evidence of a divine-Christology, though one expressed as relationship. This coheres with Paul's likely relational epistemology, and offers an ontology for conceptualizing the coexistence of evidence, in Ephesians, which scholars such as Fee and Dunn would unnecessarily set in opposition. What is more, and as is so important to Max Turner, it reminds the guild of New Testament scholars that the world of New Testament studies should not, and arguably cannot, be neatly separated from the wider life and health of the church. It reminds us that, for Ephesians, "doing christology is a practice of disciples, not spectators."[90]

---

89. William Wrede, *Paul,* trans. Edward Lummis, reprint, 1908 (Eugene: Wipf & Stock, 2001), p. 76, italics his. Cf. also Adolf Deissmann, *Paul: A Study in Social and Religious History,* trans. William E. Wilson (New York: Harper & Row, 1957 [orig. 1912]).

90. Terrence W. Tilley, *The Disciples' Jesus: Christology as Reconciling Practice* (Maryknoll: Orbis Books, 2008), p. 15.

Salvation's Bath by the Spirit:
A Study of Titus 3:5b-6 in Its Canonical Setting

Robert W. Wall

One of the most important Pauline formulae about the Holy Spirit is also one of the most neglected in the Pauline corpus. Found as the centerpiece of a "faithful saying," Titus 3:4-7, the text is an elaboration of Paul's core beliefs about the apocalypse of God's salvation in which the Spirit performs a strategic role. The neglect of this saying by scholars during the last two centuries can mostly be explained by its canonical location in one of the so-called "Pastoral Epistles" (PE), and the presumed theological disparity between this collection and the seven-letter Pauline corpus of critical orthodoxy. The PE have been effectively banished from the Pauline corpus, if not yet from the biblical canon, because scholars have generally concluded they are not productions of the real Paul, so are deemed "inauthentic" and therefore deutero-apostolic.[1] And the effect of the modern academy's decisions about the

---

1. The recent spate of superb commentaries on the PE from church-centered scholars who are unwilling to toss these letters on the garbage dump of modern criticism's other rejects, mostly because they defend Paul's authorship of them, has been a gift of God in due season. Included among these is the commentary of I. Howard Marshall (International Critical Commentary), who does question Paul's direct involvement in the production of 1 Tim., and another by his student, P. Towner, for the New International Commentary on the New Testament series. To these may be added Luke T. Johnson's contribution on 1-2 Tim. to the Anchor Bible and W. Mounce's exhaustive study on the PE for the Word Biblical Commentary. Still, however, these works along with the many monographs written on the PE over the last two decades to support this renewed interest, continue to slog forward based upon decisions about authorship and social location, both ecclesial and cultural.

PE upon the church's clergy, who rarely use them any longer in preaching or catechesis, has been nothing short of catastrophic.

In particular, scholars sometimes call attention to the sparse and ambiguous mention of "spirit" in the PE, where reference to the Holy Spirit relates to the ministry of congregation's leaders in preserving Pauline tradition (e.g., 2 Tim. 1:6-7, 14) rather than to spiritual gifts given to the congregation to empower ministry toward one another (e.g., 1 Cor. 12-14). This datum is sometimes listed among the evidence of a post-Pauline date where certain groups of Paulinists have replaced the charismatic apocalypticism of the real Paul for a more domesticated religion or one closer to the speculations and social ethos of the later era of Apostolic Fathers.[2]

Any climate change in the current environment must first clear away the debris of modern criticism's shabby treatment of the PE collection in order to rediscover what it might offer its current readers who seek to understand Paul better (cf. 2 Pet. 3:15-16!). In the case of Titus 3:5b-6, I will argue this offering is a definitive synthesis and "canonical harmony" of Pauline pneumatology, not only then to underwrite the congregation's experience of God's saving mercy as Paul interprets it but also to help relate the distinctive elements of the Pauline tradition to the broader apostolic tradition.

1. Clearing the Debris Away:
The Pastoral Epistles in Canonical Context

A shift of the reader's interest from their composition to their canonization breaks open a new hermeneutical horizon for the study of PE.

---

2. But see I. Howard Marshall, "The Holy Spirit in the Pastoral Epistles and the Apostolic Fathers," in *Holy Spirit and Christian Origins*, ed. G. N. Stanton, B. W. Longenecker, S. G. Barton (Grand Rapids: Eerdmans, 2004), pp. 257-69, who concludes that the PE "represent a stage on the way to the AF [Apostolic Fathers], in which, although the endowment of all believers with the Spirit is strongly affirmed, there is less attention to the role of the Spirit in ministry in the congregation and more on the Spirit's role in relations to leaders" (p. 269). In this same volume, Paul Trebilco makes the additional case that the PE are no different than other Pauline letters in which the apostle's core beliefs (including about the Spirit of the risen One) are adapted to the aims of the letter in response to the crisis at hand. In this sense, then, the PE definition of the Spirit's role and work in Christian existence is of a piece with the undisputed letters, even if with a different coloring and contour that fits the pastoral purpose of the PE ("The Significance and Relevance of the Spirit in the Pastoral Epistles," pp. 241-56).

Robert W. Wall

The formation of whole collections of writings during the canonical process creates another kind of literary aesthetic that is substantively and functionally different than those corpora scholars compose according to their historical critical constructions of authorship and social location. The seven-letter Pauline canon of most modern historical critics differs in shape and substance from the thirteen-letter Pauline corpus that was fashioned and fixed during the church's canonical process. Even though the canonical approach should not be considered a substitute for critical reconstructions (or deconstructions) of the Pauline letter collection, the priority of the canonical Paul at Scripture's ecclesial address compels the biblical interpreter to exploit the hermeneutical importance of that later moment when the collection of PE were received by the ancient church and added to its extant ten-letter Pauline collection to complete it as canonical for the one holy catholic and apostolic church.

In making this shift to the point of canonization, the essential structure of criticism's approach to the developing theology of the historical Paul is retained. That is, the standard critical approach to the core beliefs of Pauline pneumatology does not assume a static conception but a dynamic one, such that Paul's conception of the Spirit's role unfolded over time as a consequence of various factors, personal and environmental. Assuming this, scholars reconstitute the genuine Pauline letters into a chronology of compositions in order to investigate Paul's developing pneumatology. For example, F. W. Horn famously writes of three different stages in the formation of his idea of the Spirit, the details of which have been vigorously challenged but not the essential structure of his historical construction.[3] And most would agree that the details of Paul's view of the Spirit unfolded along a similar line with his developing Christology.

My reading of Titus 3:5b-6 within its canonical context does not require a departure from this historical critical approach. In fact, this same approach is useful in framing my hypothesis: the church's reception of the canonical Paul's memory and message is first of all mediated through the 10-letter Pauline corpus, which was in wide circulation for most if not all of the second century; but then the canonical and enduring deposit of Pauline tradition is completed toward the end of the cen-

---

3. However, see Volker Rabens, "The Development of Pauline Pneumatology: A Response to F. W. Horn," *BZ* 43 (1999): 161-79, esp. pp. 174-79.

tury by the addition of the PE collection.⁴ To put the matter more pointedly, the normative understanding of Pauline pneumatology that unfolds across the antecedent ten-letter Pauline collection is made complete in this final redaction of the Pauline corpus when the rich formulation of the Spirit's outpouring in Titus 3:5b-6 is added.

While it is standard fare for scholars to consider the PE as post-Pauline interpretations of antecedent Pauline letters, ironically their removal from the Pauline canon has rendered them irrelevant for interpreting the Pauline corpus! The addition of the PE collection to the ten-letter Pauline corpus forms and fixes a collection of "aesthetic excellence" that brings to completion core themes of the Pauline tradition and so can more effectively guide the church's formation.⁵

Two historical reminders are noted in brief to frame this programmatic idea before moving to the Titus text. First, while the exact moment of the church's earliest reception of the PE remains indeterminate for lack of evidence, most scholars interested in this phenomenon have concluded that the reception of the apostolic tradition within earliest Christianity was concentrated by a debate between rival teachers over Paul's extraordinary legacy, which created a kind of epistemic crisis among his tradents: who then is the official carrier of the canonical Paul that will help forge the future of the church? The church had already decided that an emergent collection of his letters would be the principal vehicle by which his message and memory would be made known to subsequent generations of Christians (Irenaeus); the relevant question facing the early church regarded the final shape of this collection.⁶

---

4. For this construction, see R. W. Wall, "The Function of the Pastoral Letters within the Pauline Canon of the New Testament: A Canonical Approach," in *The Pauline Canon*, ed. S. E. Porter (Leiden: Brill, 2004), pp. 27-44, which will be revised and expanded in the introduction to my forthcoming commentary on the PE in The Two Horizons New Testament Commentary, ed. Joel B. Green and Max Turner (Eerdmans).

5. The idea of a canonical collection's "aesthetic excellence" is borrowed from Nicholas Wolterstorff, *Art in Action* (Grand Rapids: Eerdmans, 1980), whose definition of good art is more functional: the artistic excellence of a piece is judged by its capacity to effect its public according to the purpose intended. The church's recognition of the final form of the Pauline collection with the addition of the PE is based upon the observed excellence of the thirteen-letter Pauline canon in making people wise about God's salvation and mature in doing God's work (so 2 Tim. 3:15-17). I develop this idea more fully in the introduction to my forthcoming commentary.

6. Other than P³², which includes a fragment of Titus, other early papyri from the second and third centuries that include Pauline letters do not mention the PE. Possible

2 Peter 3:15-16 remains a pivotal text for understanding the continuing role of the PE within the Pauline corpus. Depending on the date of this text, it seems likely from this passage that the valorization of the Pauline corpus, which 2 Peter claims is a fount of spiritual "wisdom" (3:15), shares the same effect as Israel's Scripture, which conveys "wisdom" necessary for salvation (2 Tim. 3:15). But 2 Peter also indicates that Paul's letters' lack of clarity opens them up to potential abuse by the very teachers it castigates. This passing reference to a Pauline collection hints at a hermeneutical crisis that might threaten the future of the community.

The addition of the PE collection to the extant Pauline corpus subsequent to the cautionary note sounded in 2 Peter may therefore be understood as a response to such a crisis. Not only does its portrait of a canonical Paul respond decisively to the battle over Paul's legacy within Pauline Christianity, the canonical sayings and the theological formulae that fashion a Pauline rule of faith, along with the instructions about personal and congregational practices that illustrate how the rule is applied, are spread across its pages to commend a particular version of Pauline Christianity that chooses sides — we would argue at the Holy Spirit's bidding — in a challenging and contested succession.

Allusions to antecedent Pauline texts found in the PE may have been useful as hermeneutical props in a community responding to the intellectual crisis provoked by disagreements over the canonical Paul during the second century. Vivid memories of Paul's body of work scattered across these letters exemplify what is expected of his successors (see 2 Tim. 2:1-7; 3:10-14). Well known are the canonical sayings (cf. 1 Tim. 1:15; 2:15-3:1a; 4:8-9; 2 Tim. 2:11-13; Titus 3:4-8a) and other important theological formulae (for example, 1 Tim. 2:3-7; 3:16; Titus 2:11-14; 3:4-8) that fashion a Pauline rule of faith that regulates how the post-Pauline community should adapt Paul's gospel to everyday life. This same rule, which focuses on the pattern of God's redemption of the world, also guides the community's use of Israel's Scripture in search of

---

allusions to the PE from the second century, most clearly from Polycarp (ca. 120), may be of oral tradition rather than Pauline texts. In any case, maintaining a distinction between the possible dates of composition and, subsequently, of canonization enables one to explain the broad circulation of the ten-letter Pauline corpus, exclusive of the PE, throughout most of the second century. The relevant issue in the reception of the PE into the Pauline canon is their catholicity, then, and not their apostolicity; see my forthcoming Two Horizons Commentary on the PE for an elaboration of this point.

wisdom for salvation (so 2 Tim. 3:15). Still other memorable aphorisms and one-liners found throughout these letters aid to this day in the catechism of new believers.

The effect of our hypothesis is this: rather than approaching the PE as a marginal collection of questionable ancestry and theological value, its teaching should be considered of decisive importance precisely because these books guide readers when using the Pauline corpus as Scripture to understand the apostle's distinctive and ongoing witness to God's gospel in his absence.

2. Salvation's Bath by the Spirit: A Study of Titus 3:5b-6

The studied passage is the centerpiece of the letter's second grand theological formulation of the epiphany of God's salvation (3:4-7), which constitutes the last of five canonical sayings spread across the PE (cf. 3:8a). Its similarity with the first epiphany saying (2:11-14) suggests the two function together as a mutually-glossing pair: both provide instruction and exhortation for both leaders and congregation by combining highly compressed doctrinal formulations about the apocalypse of God's salvation that in turn is foundational for the present experience of God's salvation. As in the first instance, this text also concludes with an exhortation to "give careful attention to good works" (3:8bc par. 2:14b). Salvation is confirmed by its concrete, moral effect upon those who experience the Spirit's outpouring.

The theological affirmation about the Spirit's work is framed by a dense and syntactically uncertain confession that this "God our Savior appeared . . . God saved us" (3:4). This is a core belief of the Pauline apostolate and it encloses yet another core belief that contrasts humanity's failed attempts to earn God's salvation by "works of moral rectitude" with the ultimate triumph of "God's mercy" (3:5a). Of course, this very contrast is made famous in Romans as the central claim of Paul's gospel (e.g., Rom. 1:16-17; 3:21-31; 4:1-5; 9:30–10:13). In this instance, the conflict between human works and divine mercy is made even more emphatic in the Greek text by placing the main verbal idea, "God saved us," *after* the contrast with works asserted (rather than before it as in most translations). That is, the rhetorical design of this letter's reformulation of the centerpiece of the Pauline gospel has the appearance and act of God's salvation enclosing and glossing the contrast between works and mercy in terms of the divine nature. In this sense, then, humanity's "works of moral rectitude" does not work as the means of our salvation because it is at odds with who God is. Against the backdrop of a letter that makes clear God's delight in good works (2:4, 14; 3:1, 8, 14), the idea is sharpened that God befriends us not because we get things right but because a merciful God rights things.

What follows this main idea that God has appeared to save us is an expansive prepositional phrase that conceives of salvation as a corporate experience mediated "through" (διά of agency) the Holy Spirit. "Nowhere else does Scripture speak as fully and explicitly about the content and activity of the means of salvation as it does here."[7] The phrase unravels a string of three nouns, all indefinite genitives and each a metaphor of salvation that together set out in bold relief the comprehensive work performed by the Spirit poured out at Pentecost "through Jesus Christ our Savior" to conduct and complete God's rescue operation of sinners. The key exegetical question regards the relationship between these three nouns and their relationship to the Holy Spirit.[8]

Prior to this explanation, however, is to clarify the occasion of the Spirit's reception by the community. The aorist of the verb ἐκχέω, "poured out" (3:6), is used figuratively in Romans 5:5 of the Spirit who "pours out" God's love into the heart of every believer. While most interpreters agree that this allusion is in play here, it more likely trades on an extant Pentecost tradition that lies behind Acts 2. The main verb of Joel's prophecy of the Day of the Lord is the "pouring out" of the Spirit "upon all flesh" to cue a day of judgment as means to Israel's repentance and survival (LXX Joel 3:1-4). Romans 5:5 envisages the Spirit's work in the individual's salvation and the benefaction of love suggests the inward cultivation of intimate fellowship with God. In continuity with Pentecost, this passage imagines the community receives the Spirit through agency of Christ who pours out the Spirit "on

---

7. George W. Knight, *Pastoral Epistles: A Commentary on the Greek Text* (Grand Rapids: Eerdmans, 1992), p. 342.

8. For a recent history-of-religion treatment of Scripture's pneumatology and an appraisal of Paul's distinctive contribution, see now John R. Levison's superb study, *Filled with the Spirit* (Grand Rapids: Eerdmans, 2009). Also, P. H. Towner, *The Letters to Timothy and Titus*, New International Commentary on the New Testament (Grand Rapids: Eerdmans, 2006), pp. 779-86, who sees an intertextual link with Ezek. 36 as backdrop for hearing the echo of Joel 3:1-2.

us." According to Acts 2, the Spirit's reception inaugurates salvation's "last days" (Acts 2:17-18; cf. 10:45), and so the change of tense from future (Joel 3:1 par. Acts 2:17) to aorist (Titus 3:6) indicates what Acts makes clear: those who receive the eschatological Spirit "hope for eternal life" (Acts 2:21 as interpreted by Acts 2:22-41).[9]

The subsequent διά phrase, "by Jesus Christ our Savior" (3:6), picks up the close connection of Spirit and Christ in Pauline theology: for Paul, the Spirit is the Spirit of Christ (so Rom. 8:9-11). As M. Turner puts the matter, "receiving Christ and receiving the Spirit are simply two ways of speaking of essentially the same reality, for Christ cannot be received except in the gift of the Spirit who brings him, and the Spirit comes as the Spirit of Christ, to unite us with Christ, and to lead us deeper into Christ, and to empower us to serve Christ until finally the Spirit conforms us fully to Christ in resurrection."[10] But the shift of preposition from ἐν Χριστῷ to διὰ Ἰησοῦ Χριστοῦ brings this formula into contact with the Christology of Acts 2:33 that the crucified and exalted Jesus is the agent by whom God's prophecy of the Spirit's outpouring is fulfilled (Acts 1:4-5). The relationship between God our Savior and Jesus Christ our Savior is thereby cast in Acts by prophecy-fulfillment: Jesus fulfills what God has promised according to Israel's Scripture. Read against this canonical backdrop, the double use of "savior" in this saying carries this same theological freight: the promise of eternal life made by God our Savior "before time began" (Titus 1:2) has now been fulfilled by Jesus Christ our Savior, who pours out the Spirit upon the "elect ones" as the bath of salvation. Although to presume that a fully Nicaean conception of a triune Deity stands behind this Pauline confession is surely anachronistic, the shared responsibility of "God our Savior" who "pours out" the Holy Spirit "by Jesus Christ our Savior" coheres closely to a trinitarian conception of salvation.[11]

What must be allowed when constructing this intertext between

---

9. See R. W. Wall, "Acts," *NIB*, 10:60-70.

10. Max Turner, "Receiving Christ and Receiving the Spirit: In Dialogue with David Pawson," *JPT* 15 (1999): 30.

11. Max Turner has made an important contribution to the connection of Pauline Christology and Pneumatology by insisting that the presence of the indwelling Spirit explains the community's worship of the divine Jesus: Jesus' gift of the Spirit is the turning point of the church's recognition of him as Son. See now his "'Trinitarian' Pneumatology in the New Testament — Towards an Explanation of the Worship of Jesus," *ATJ* 57/58 (2002/2003): 167-86.

Acts 2 and Titus 3 are the different conceptions of the Spirit at play in each text. According to Acts, the Lord pours out God's Spirit to empower a ministry that continues what he had begun to do and say according to the Gospel (so Acts 1:1-2). The Spirit's entry into the community is marked by signs and wonders, by extraordinary feats of biblical interpretation, by persuasive preaching all of which confirm the Gospel narrative about the risen Jesus is true. But in this narrative world the Spirit of Acts is not a broker of God's salvation who transforms the sinner into a saint. While Luke's conception of a vocation-minded Spirit is certainly present in a passage like 2 Timothy 1:6-7, within the bounds of this epiphany saying, God poured out the Spirit through Jesus Christ in order to bathe believers in regeneration and renewal, not to empower their mission to the end of the earth.[12]

The single preposition διά indicates a singular Spirit reception but one that has a complex effect envisaged by a pair of results: παλιγγενεσία, "rebirth," and ἀνακαίνωσις, "renewal."[13] The noun παλιγγενεσία is rarely used in the New Testament (only in Matt. 19:28) and most commentators pin its meaning to its general use in antiquity to express rebirth or restoration.[14] The Matthean passage, however, may help define its distinctively Christian sense in play here. In the Gospel pericope, Matthew's Jesus responds ironically to Peter's question regarding the future reward of the community of disciples who have given up material goods to follow Jesus. Jesus responds that the reward given the apostles ("the twelve") is the task of "judging [κρίνοντες] the twelve tribes of Israel" in the παλιγγενεσία — an expansive exercise of authority that doubtless includes Israel's restoration. The meaning of the phrase ἐν τῇ παλιγγενεσίᾳ in Matthew's redaction of this saying has been variously understood and translated, but probably refers to an extended period of time "until the end of the age" (Matt. 28:20). That is, it makes little sense to place the apostolic practice of κρίνοντες in the eschaton when it is too late to matter. Rather it seems best to understand the παλιγγενεσία as a hopeful figuration of the present age when apostolic authority will be exercised on God's be-

---

12. This point does not suggest the believer's reception of the Spirit is delayed to a "baptism in the Spirit" that follows salvation, sonship, and new birth; see Turner's response to Pawson for this (see note 10 above).

13. Cf. Towner, *Letters to Timothy and Titus*, p. 783.

14. For a survey, see William D. Mounce, *Pastoral Epistles* (Nashville: Nelson, 2000), pp. 449-50.

half to bring about the promise of a restored Israel.[15] Such is what the Spirit's coming at Pentecost inaugurates according to Acts.

But how does this vague connection of apostolic authority during the παλιγγενεσία gloss the Spirit's cleansing bath, if it does at all? The answer to this question helps to clarify how this expansive reference to the Spirit is hermeneutical of the Pauline corpus. Perhaps the washing away of the community's total lawlessness and its performance of good works (see 2:14) testify not only to the presence of the indwelling Spirit but also to the fulfillment of God's promise of a restored Israel. Read within the Pauline canon, παλιγγενεσία may cue Pauline teaching in Romans 9-11 that God's promise now extends to repentant Gentiles, represented here by Titus, who have been grafted into the restored Israel to receive the eschatological blessings promised by God (so Rom. 11:11-24). Implicit in this new reality is the authority of the Pauline apostolate to bring the "word of faith" near so that those who call upon the name of the Lord will be saved (so Rom. 10:9-13). The instruction of the PE to mind the Pauline apostolate ultimately targets this redemptive plan.

The final in this triad of nouns is ἀνακαίνωσις: God pours out the Spirit through Jesus Christ to bathe believers in rebirth "and renewal." This same word is used in Romans 12:2 of a transformed way a graced community thinks about God's will (cf. Col. 3:10) but also cues the root word καινός, which is used in the Pauline canon to denote the creation of something "new" in Christ Jesus (2 Cor. 5:17; Gal. 6:15; Eph. 2:15; 4:24), and καινότης in Romans 6:4 of the "new life" that results from participating in the death and resurrection of Christ. Significantly, καινότης is then used with the Spirit (Rom. 7:6) in a formulation that denotes the Spirit-led manner of the covenant community's slavery to God.[16] The issue at stake in this pastoral letter is the congregation's moral and spiritual transformation from a life of vice to one of virtue initiated by God's epiphany (3:3-4; cf. Gal. 5:16-26) and conducted under the direction of the Holy Spirit that God has poured out upon it. In this regard, the combined meaning of "rebirth and renewal" seems to envisage transformed existence, however vaguely, as the end-product of a maturing process in God's direction (cf. 2:11-12) — some even think consisting

---

15. W. D. Davies and D. C. Allison, *A Critical and Exegetical Commentary on the Gospel According to Saint Matthew*, International Critical Commentary (Edinburgh: T&T Clark, 1988), vol. 3, pp. 57-58.

16. Nicholas T. Wright, "Romans," *NIB*, 10:560-61.

of two discrete stages ("rebirth" then "renewal") — by which every believer becomes a morally competent person.

The ultimate purpose (ἵνα, "so that") of God's epiphany for the work of salvation is finally stated: "having been made righteous by that grace, we may become heirs of the hope for eternal life" (3:7). In the first place, the application of God's saving grace makes sinners righteous. This affirmation evokes one of the most contested features in Pauline studies today: the meaning of δικαιόω in a Pauline pattern of salvation, which is put into play by the opening chapters of Romans (and so of the Pauline canon). Our translation of this passive participle tips our hand in the debate. As is well known, the metaphor comes from the law court where a judge renders a verdict of acquittal based upon evidence of the innocence of the accused. Of course, the verdict of "not guilty" is made by God on the sole basis of Christ's faithfulness (Rom. 3:21-31). But if this verdict is then applied individualistically as an internal matter of the heart, and thereby detached from any real change that takes place in the way one lives, then we would suggest it is far wide of the mark. According to this "core belief," the pouring out and reception of the Spirit issue in the "rebirth and renewal" — that is, the transformation — of human existence. While a righteousness of works is not a precondition for God's rescue operation of sinners (so 3:5a), a righteousness of works is its certain outcome.

This observation leads us naturally to the second purpose of God's epiphany to save the world: so that "we may become heirs of the hope for eternal life" (3:7). The metaphor of a future inheritance, well used in the New Testament, has its background in the Old Testament land promise. An inheritance of a replenished and sanctified land — a "new creation" — is home to a restored Israel and therefore an essential blessing promised to God's covenant people.[17] In this case, "eternal life" is the covenant blessing promised by God to the "elect ones" (see 1:1-3) and destiny of those on whom God has presently poured out the Spirit for παλιγγενεσία — an extended process of regeneration and renewal directed by the church's apostolate (cf. 1:1-3). The catchphrase, "eternal life," is thematic of the PE (1 Tim. 1:16; 6:12; Titus 1:2) and, significantly, is used with "hope" in Titus 1:2. The literary effect of repeating this combination of a community's hope for eternal life at the beginning and ending of the letter is

---

17. For the programmatic treatment of this motif, see W. Brueggemann, *The Land* (Philadelphia: Fortress Press, 1977).

Salvation's Bath by the Spirit

to form a kind of *inclusio* that helps to focus Paul's exhortation and instruction about the present situation and status of his apostolate upon salvation history's endgame: "a future ending life with God."[18]

3. The Canonical Effect of Titus 3:5b-6

The Titus 3 formula about the work of the Spirit at the apocalypse of God's salvation is hermeneutical of Pauline pneumatology in two different ways. (1) The repetition of core beliefs about the Spirit secures them as canonical for the Pauline tradition. Clarification of this matter would have been important at the point of completing and finalizing the Pauline canon when controversy over the role of the Spirit among Christians had been provoked by the "New Prophecy" movement. Very little is known about this movement and what is known is mediated by others in response to its different stages or emphases. Tertullian, for example, even though committed to the church's core theological agreements, defended the phenomenon of ecstatic prophecy and the moral rigorism it motivated. Not only did he emphasize the distinctive importance of the *Paracletus* in making preparations for the Lord's coming epiphany but also, more critically, its present role in witnessing to and confirming the apostolic tradition within the church (so *De Ieiunio* 10.6). None of this disagrees with Paul.[19] The fact that Tertullian's support of New Prophecy for mostly moralistic and epistemic reasons was so widely misunderstood by the ancient church suggests the church's reflection on an apostolic doctrine of the Spirit was still in a somewhat fluid state.[20] Against this backdrop, then, this

---

18. Knight, *Pastoral Epistles*, p. 347.
19. See now David E. Wilhite, *Tertullian the African* (Berlin: W. de Gruyter, 2007), pp. 167-76.
20. Richard Pervo, among others, claims the Paul of the apocryphal *Acts of Paul* (AP) reflects some of the interests of the New Prophecy movement, including its "charismatic element," but strangely does not mention the Spirit as the source of Thecla's religious zeal and moral rigorism (Richard I. Pervo, *The Making of Paul: Constructions of the Apostle in Early Christianity* [Minneapolis: Fortress Press, 2010], pp. 163-64). Although the point remains contested, the lack of references to an active Spirit in the extant AP — "Holy Spirit" is only mentioned in trinitarian refrains — suggests to me that an interest in moral rigor and spiritual discipline has replaced the reception of the Spirit as the primary marker of salvation; cf. W. Schneemelcher, "The Acts of Paul," in *New Testament Apocrypha*, ed. W. Schneemelcher (Louisville: Westminster John Knox Press, 1992), vol. 2, pp. 213-70.

saying, which features the congregation's reception of God's Spirit by "Jesus Christ our Savior," is strategic for securing the limits of a correct Pauline pneumatology.

The fact that the Titus saying resists any separation of the Spirit from God's normal pattern of salvation serves to underwrite the traditional Pauline conception. In fact, the trigger mechanism of the Spirit's reception is not "works of moral rectitude but because of God's mercy" (3:5a). That is, the Spirit is given by God before it is received by covenant heirs.[21] Neither should it strike one as odd that the Spirit's reception is logically linked to the community's "hope for eternal life" (Rom. 8). Moreover, the experience of "renewal" (and I take this idiom as such) echoes Paul's decisive introduction to his description of Christian existence in Rom 12:2 (cf. 1 Cor. 2:6-16). Whether soteriological, eschatological, Christological, or the experience of God's salvation, the community's life in the Spirit is canonically underwritten by this formula, again to secure its place for those who "hold to a pattern of healthy teaching heard from (Paul)" (2 Tim. 1:13).

The variation of this repetition of traditional ideas suggests that this affirmation of Pauline teaching does not come at the expense of a dynamism that adapts its theological grammar to changing circumstance and crisis. This quality of a canonical heritage may be envisaged by the claim that the Spirit is "poured out [ἐκκέχυται] upon us by [διά] Jesus Christ." Whilst this affirmation certainly sounds a Pauline tone (cf. Rom. 5:5; see above), the experience of rebirth and renewal that results is "upon us" — a corporate filling rather than one that is inward and individual, reminiscent of Luke's Pentecost tradition (see above). And rather than an experience of divine love poured out into the realm of Christ by the Spirit, the referent here is of those expansive experiences of rebirth and renewal poured out "upon us" by the risen Jesus (cf. Luke 3:16). This elaboration of the activities of the risen Jesus to include the gift of the eschatological Spirit to prepare heirs for eternal life brings Easter and Pentecost together as integral of the gospel's power. This Christological reworking of the gift of the Spirit — it is "by Jesus Christ" that the Spirit is given to the covenant community who then can experience rebirth and renewal because of its presence — makes more firm the Christological shape of that experience (cf. Rom.

---

21. For the importance of this distinction and the collocation of key Pauline texts it envisages, see Levison, *Filled with the Spirit,* pp. 253-67 ("giving") and pp. 267-72 ("receiving").

Salvation's Bath by the Spirit

8:9-17). The community's reception of the Spirit not only helps it remember those crucial beliefs about Christ formulated for the PE (1 Tim. 3:16; 2 Tim. 2:8) but also to produce a manner of life that bears the image of Christ. It is for Paul the Spirit of Christ who enlivens the community in accordance with the image of God in Christ. And this newly released, transformational power is concurrent with the entire process of salvation, from new birth to eternal life.[22]

(2) This formula glosses the Pauline tradition in a way that creates a kind of canonical harmony that links the distinctive contribution of a Pauline pneumatology to other traditions within the broader apostolic community also included in its biblical canon.[23] The hermeneutics of the canonical process goes against the grain of modernity's familiar reductionisms — of a parochial Pauline canon within the Canon or pitting Pauline conceptions against other biblical conceptions to defend an insoluble and adversarial diversity or the facile harmonizations that seek to rid Scripture of its diversity altogether. This robust formulation of the Spirit's work in salvation introduces non-Pauline properties into a traditional Pauline rubric in a way that forms a seamless, complementary whole. I would argue this reflects the conception of apostolicity that guided the canonical process and is finally instantiated in the church's single biblical canon. There the reader finds the gospels of different apostolates, which are bound together to form an illuminating whole that is greater than the sum of its parts.

To illustrate: I have mentioned already the allusion to Luke's Pentecost tradition that reimages the pouring out of the Spirit by Christ for a Pauline setting (see above). Another example of canonical harmonization is the pair of experiences that the Spirit's reception effects when poured out "upon us." Once again the more traditional Pauline conception of "renewal" is combined with "rebirth" (παλιγγενεσία), a

---

22. See Volker Rabens, *The Holy Spirit and Ethics in Paul: Transformation and Empowering for Religious-Ethical Life* (Tübingen: Mohr Siebeck, 2010), chs. 4 and 6; also James D. G. Dunn, *The Theology of Paul the Apostle* (Grand Rapids: Eerdmans, 1998), pp. 413-41, 94-95.

23. The stimulating discussion by Brevard S. Childs on a canonical approach to a "gospel harmony" in *The New Testament as Canon* (Minneapolis: Fortress Press, 1984), pp. 157-209, provides a hermeneutical model for what I have in mind here. See in particular his discussion of the longer ending of Mark as a biblical example of harmonization (pp. 205-9) in which different bits and pieces of disparate gospel traditions are pulled together to form a new coherent whole "to function as a formal device to aid the reader in linking the parts" (p. 207).

conception of Christian existence not found in the ten-letter Pauline corpus.[24] Rather this noun echoes the extraordinary use of γεννάω in the Johannine tradition to speak of believers as God's children, reborn of God (John 3:3-8; 1 John 2:29; 3:9; 4:7; 5:1, 3-4, 18). At first glance, the evident creational sense of this new birth idiom shares much in common with the Pauline new creation motif, which is more eschatological and communal in scope.[25] In John, however, new birth initiates *individual* Christians into the presence of the Spirit to live with the purity of Jesus — real children do not practice sin! — in preparation for the imminent apocalypse of God's kingdom (John 3:3; 1 John 2:28–3:3).[26] This passing nod in the direction of John also allows the reader to expand the meaning of "bath" within this Pauline setting to include water baptism, since both the Fourth Gospel and 1 John combine the gift of the Spirit and water baptism as markers of this new birth (John 3:5; 1 John 5:6; cf. Acts 19:1-7). In this sense, then, Christian baptism confirms or perhaps symbolizes the filling of the Spirit in regeneration and for renewal.

Finally, then, the grammar of the Titus saying focuses the apocalypse of God's salvation upon the Holy Spirit's "bath of rebirth and renewal" rather than the traditional Pauline formulation of justification — "not because we had done works of moral rectitude but because of God's mercy." Doing so may correct a tendency to separate the two: God's pardon of sin and our purity from sin are of a piece with the Spirit's work in salvation. In fact, such a work envisages the concluding ἵνα clause that "those who have come to believe in God (for pardon of sin) may give careful attention to good works (for purity from sin)" (3:8c; so also 1 Cor. 6:9-11).

---

24. References to a nine/ten- or thirteen-letter Pauline corpus in this essay are canonical constructions; rather than cuing the conclusions of authorship made by historians (i.e., distinctions between "authentic" and "inauthentic" Pauline compositions), comment on a "ten-letter Pauline corpus" refers to its shape prior to its final redaction and canonization toward the end of the second century; see my fuller discussion of this point in the Introduction to my Two Horizons Commentary on the Pastoral Epistles (forthcoming).

25. Although now see Levison's discussion of Paul's "new creation" motif (*Filled with the Spirit*, pp. 307-16), esp. in comparison with his discussion of the same motif in the Fourth Gospel (pp. 367-72).

26. C. K. Barrett points out that at Qumran, water and Spirit were linked to a community's purification rather than to its regeneration but offers no opinion whether Qumran influenced Johannine tradition at this point (*The Gospel According to St. John*, 2nd ed. [Louisville: Westminster John Knox Press, 1978], p. 209).

The Spirit in Hebrews: No Longer Forgotten?

Steve Motyer

1. Introduction: Turner on Hebrews, and a New Interest

Max Turner has been a much-valued and admired colleague at the London School of Theology for over twenty years, and I am delighted to have this opportunity to make a small contribution, in homage to Max, to the area which he has so much made his scholarly *pied-à-terre,* namely New Testament pneumatology.

One of the distinctive features of Max's scholarship has been the way in which he has sought to bridge the gap between his technical studies on the Spirit in the biblical traditions and second-temple Judaism, and the development of pneumatology and trinitarian theology in subsequent Christianity. This interest motivates the first of the two passing references that Turner makes to the Spirit in Hebrews, in his magisterial *The Holy Spirit and Spiritual Gifts — Then and Now.*[1] He refers to the work of Larry Hurtado,[2] and comments that, along with other New Testament texts, Hebrews contains clear references to "the Christological confession of Jesus' unity with God as the 'one Lord' of creation and redemption," but adds that generally "no such attention . . . was paid to the Spirit," so that according to some the New Testament is "properly binitarian rather than trinitarian."[3]

---

1. Max Turner, *The Holy Spirit and Spiritual Gifts — Then and Now* (Carlisle: Paternoster, 1996).

2. At that time, referring to Larry W. Hurtado, *One God, One Lord* (London: SCM Press, 1988). Hurtado subsequently greatly developed his ideas in *Lord Jesus Christ: Devotion to Jesus in Earliest Christianity* (Grand Rapids: Eerdmans, 2003).

3. Turner, *Holy Spirit,* pp. 169-70.

Turner then argues against this judgment for other sections of the New Testament (Paul, John, Luke-Acts), but does not return to Hebrews — thus leaving open the possibility that he might see Hebrews as "properly binitarian." And it is certainly the case that Hebrews does not develop a theology of the Spirit such that we could easily draw "trinitarian" conclusions of the sort for which Turner so ably then argues for those other parts of the New Testament.[4] In fact, the standard view in Hebrews scholarship is, as Lindars puts it, that in Hebrews "there is no emphasis on the Spirit, and in fact the Spirit plays no part in the argument of the letter."[5] No wonder Turner ignores Hebrews, as he explores the pneumatology of the New Testament.

But there are signs of an awakening interest, and the focus of this essay will be to interact with a significant recent article on the Spirit in Hebrews by David Allen,[6] and to argue, beyond Allen, that Hebrews is certainly congruent with a "trinitarian" approach to the Spirit, and might even contribute something distinctive to the New Testament range on this. Our strategy, after some opening remarks about the addressees of Hebrews, will be to survey the seven "Spirit" references in Hebrews, in dialogue with Allen and with wider scholarship.

2. The Spirit and the "Hebrews"

The significance of charismatic experience as a defining feature of the addressees of Hebrews has also been generally overlooked. Turner himself — in his second reference to Hebrews — argues against the "cessationist" reading of Hebrews 2:3-4, which asserts that, in these verses, "signs and wonders and various powers, and distributions of the Holy Spirit" were limited to the apostles, "those who heard the Lord" (2:3). Quite rightly, in my view, Turner argues that 2:4 "does not suggest that similar confirmation would be lacking when others preached."[7]

---

4. See, in outline, Turner, *Holy Spirit*, pp. 172-80. Cf. Max Turner, "'Trinitarian' Pneumatology in the New Testament? — Towards an Explanation of the Worship of Jesus," *ATJ* 57/58 (2002/2003): 167-86.

5. Barnabas Lindars, *The Theology of the Letter to the Hebrews* (Cambridge: Cambridge University Press, 1991), pp. 55-56.

6. David M. Allen, "'The Forgotten Spirit': A Pentecostal Reading of the Letter to the Hebrews?" *JPT* 18 (2009): 51-66.

7. Turner, *Holy Spirit*, pp. 292-93.

The verse therefore suggests that "distributions of Holy Spirit," attested by "signs and wonders and various powers," were a regular, maybe even a prominent, part of the addressees' experience. Certainly we can say that this is the evidence to which the author appeals, when wanting to convince his readers that "the salvation declared at first through the Lord" is *so great* that it cannot be simply "neglected" (2:3). Paul makes a similar argument in Galatians 3:5.

The debate about the readers' situation is huge and I do not intend to summarize it here. But I think that this "Spirit" dimension of their situation has generally been overlooked.[8] As Allen notes, it must be significant that "the Spirit is referred to in four of Hebrews' five so-called warning passages."[9] A scenario readily suggests itself: we have here a group of Jewish Christians, who still belong to the synagogue wherever they are, but who also meet as messianic believers to exercise the gifts of the Spirit in worship ("the powers of the age to come," 6:5). They are somewhat separate from the wider Christian congregation (many have seen this as an implication of the repeated "all" in 13:24), and quite possibly under renewed threat of persecution (10:32-34; 12:4) they are now tempted just to slip back into Judaism — that is, to "neglect" their distinctive meeting together (10:25).

We can imagine the theological arguments that might have supported this merging back into the synagogue, and significantly *at their heart is a separation between Jesus as Christ and the Holy Spirit, the giver of the gifts they enjoy.* "Don't we believe that the Abrahamic covenant is what secures our salvation?" they tell each other. "Our Jewish upbringing gave us the fundamentals about repentance, faith, purity, worship, and final judgment and resurrection (6:1-2). None of that changes, if we confess Jesus to be the Christ. So we could subtract the confession, and still enjoy the covenant. And doesn't the same apply to our experience of the Spirit of prophecy? God has given us this wonderful gift — but isn't it exactly what the prophets enjoyed? An immediate sense of *God speaking*, accompanied by miraculous signs of his grace? Has this gift — this 'Spirit of grace' (10:29) — not in fact been given to us *irrespective* of our faith in Jesus as the Christ? So can we not continue to experience and enjoy the Spirit of prophecy just as 'ordinary' synagogue members?"

---

8. See for instance Lindars, *Theology*, pp. 4-15. He does not mention the Spirit in his long discussion.

9. Allen, "Forgotten Spirit," p. 59.

The author's fundamental strategy in response, as is well known and shown, is to argue passionately for the inadequacy of the Abrahamic covenant apart from the further "speaking" of God through his Son, Jesus Christ. The whole structure of the letter is shaped around this conviction and the pastoral passion arising from it, and the arguments are creative and powerful — treading a careful path between emphasizing the wonderful newness of what God has done in Christ, on the one hand, and deeply affirming the necessary continuity with the old covenant and people on the other. It is a magnificent theological *tour de force*.

But what about the Spirit as an element within this argument? It fits beautifully with this overall strategy, if we see the author as likewise affirming *the inseparability of Christ and the Spirit*. Just as covenant and Christ cannot be prized apart, so neither can Spirit and Christ. And it is this feature of Hebrews' argument which can point towards later trinitarian developments, in concert with other parts of the New Testament which do the same, albeit in different ways. And this is what we will now explore.

3. The Spirit and Christ in 2:1-4

Lindars, having asserted that the Spirit is irrelevant to the argument of Hebrews, then spends three pages nicely classifying the two distinctive ways in which Hebrews refers to the Spirit: as God's active power, giving gifts of grace to his people (2:4, 6:4, 9:14, and 10:29), and as the author of Scripture (3:7, 9:8, and 10:15).[10] He notes that "holy spirit" tends to be anarthrous in the first category (except in 10:29), and arthrous in the second, and draws from this the conclusion that the first group represents an undeveloped view of "spirit" as God's active power in the world — a divine *attribute* which, as in the Old Testament, is "objectified as almost a separate being."[11] In the second (arthrous) category, the article secures the view that it is *God's* Spirit that speaks in Scripture. However, it is doubtful whether the presence or absence of the article can bear so much weight, particularly in as stylistically creative a work as Hebrews.[12]

---

10. Lindars, *Theology*, pp. 56-58.
11. Lindars, *Theology*, p. 56.
12. See Stanley E. Porter, *Idioms of the Greek New Testament* (Sheffield: Sheffield Academic Press, 1994), pp. 103-4.

After Pentecost, in any branch of the church, it must surely be the case that the expression πνεύματος ἁγίου μερισμοί (2:4, "distributions of the Holy Spirit"), with its possible echo of the verb that Luke chooses to describe the "distribution" of the tongues of fire (Acts 2:3, διαμερίζεσθαι), would connote those amazing and special experiences in which *God himself* was felt to be immediately present in some new way, because of Jesus: more than just an experience of God's "power."

Allen boldly calls these μερισμοί of the Holy Spirit "repeated Pentecosts for the communities who have received the message of salvation,"[13] and seeks to develop a third category, according to which, for the author of Hebrews, the Holy Spirit is "the one who brings revelation by validating, in self-representative fashion, the efficacy of the new covenant dispensation."[14] This certainly fits with what we find in 2:1-4, the first "Spirit" reference, where the author says that the salvation first spoken through the Lord "was confirmed to us" (εἰς ἡμᾶς ἐβεβαιώθη) through God's own testimony expressed through signs, wonders, powers and distributions of the Spirit. This matches the way in which the old covenant likewise "was confirmed" (ἐγένετο βέβαιος, 2:2). This usage of βέβαιος and βεβαιοῦσθαι, as Schlier points out,[15] has a semi-technical legal quality, pointing to the way in which, when a transaction was disputed, one of the parties might be asked to "confirm" it, that is, make it legally binding and secure. In Leviticus 25:23 the sale of the land cannot be εἰς βεβαίωσιν, that is, it cannot be finally legally binding before God. So in Hebrews 2:4 the *testimony of God*, expressed through signs, wonders, powers and "distributions" of the Holy Spirit, puts the new covenant legally in force.

"Signs and wonders" are a regular dyad in connection with the Exodus — in no fewer than seventeen passages, in fact, and always in this order.[16] They are joined by δύναμις to form a triad referring to the Exodus only in Baruch 2:11 (and there δύναμις is in the singular). Basically, it is only in the New Testament that the plural δυνάμεις ("powers") becomes a regular term, possibly coordinated with "signs and wonders," to refer to the miracles typical of Jesus or of the work of the Spirit. Grässer suggests that the three occur together sufficiently for us to regard them as a "feste

---

13. Allen, "Forgotten Spirit," p. 56.
14. Allen, "Forgotten Spirit," p. 55.
15. Heinrich Schlier, "βέβαιος, βεβαιόω, βεβαίωσις," *TDNT*, 1:600-603, here p. 602.
16. See, e.g., Deut. 4:34; 7:19; 26:8 and Jer. 32:21.

Formel" in the New Testament,[17] but actually only in 2 Corinthians 12:12 do we meet them in the same order. The order is reversed in Acts 2:22, and they occur together in modified form in Romans 15:19. So the evidence hardly supports Grässer's "fixed formula."

The point is this: a fixed formula connoting the Exodus — "signs and wonders" — is supplemented and expanded by two further expressions which underline the newness and "greater-ness" of the new dispensation: "various powers" and "distributions of the Holy Spirit." The last phrase is particularly powerful against the background of the material about angels in Hebrews 1. In 1:14 the *catena* of quotations is brought to a conclusion with the comment about angels, "Are they not all ministering spirits (λειτουργικὰ πνεύματα) sent out to serve, for the sake of those who are to inherit salvation?" This then leads straight (διὰ τοῦτο . . .) into the comparison between the covenants in 2:1-4, with its climax in the "distributions" of the Spirit. The best the old covenant can offer is λειτουργικὰ πνεύματα — occasional visitations from angels sent to serve the people of God when in need. But now — ! The will of God is still the determining factor (κατὰ τὴν αὐτοῦ θέλησιν, 2:4, "according to his will"), but now, instead of sending an angel with a message — even bearing the law itself, 2:2 — God distributes his own πνεῦμα ἅγιον.

This difference in *degree* matches the contrast between the Son and the angels in chapter 1. God is doing something altogether greater, now, to which he himself testifies by adding "powers" to "signs and wonders" and by lavishly distributing his own Spirit. The author prepares the way for this extension of the contrast between the angels and the Son with his quotation of Psalm 104:4 (LXX 103:4) in 1:7, "who makes his angels spirits. . . ." As ἄγγελοι, they represent the execution of God's will in the world, sent to speak for him, especially in the giving of the law — but are now put into the shade by the coming of the Son, who enters the world as God's πρωτότοκος (1:6); as πνεύματα, they represent God's service personnel, doing his will to equip his people — but they are now put into the shade by the ἅγιον πνεῦμα, a gift of surpassing and wonderful greatness.

This way of reading 2:1-4 in context amply supports Allen's view that, for the author of Hebrews, the Holy Spirit comes to *validate the ef-*

---

17. Erich Grässer, *An die Hebräer (Hebr. 1–6)*, Evangelisch-Katholischer Kommentar zum Neuen Testament 17:1 (Zürich: Benziger/Neukirchen: Neukirchener Verlag, 1990), p. 107.

ficacy of the new covenant, and that the *experience* of the "signs, wonders and various powers" is crucial to this validation. But it is vital that we keep in sight the connection between Christ and the Spirit implicit here. Two recent major studies of the relationship between Christ and the Spirit, both produced by research students working under Max Turner's supervision at the London School of Theology, have underlined the way in which both the Christology and the pneumatology of the New Testament draw upon Old Testament and intertestamental "wisdom" themes and metaphors, so that we cannot rightly understand both unless we bear in mind their common roots in this aspect of the conceptuality of Second Temple Judaism.[18] And that is precisely what we have here in Hebrews: a deep drawing upon wisdom themes in order to give depth and imagery to what God has done in and through his "Son" (especially, of course, in 1:2-3), which then naturally — because it is part of the same tradition — moves into talk of the Spirit of God. For wisdom is not only the "reflection (ἀπαύγασμα) of eternal light" (Wis. 7:26; cf. Heb. 1:3),[19] but is also πνεῦμα ἅγιον (Wis. 7:22), "the breath of the power (δύναμις) of God" (Wis. 7:25).

Against this shared wisdom background, Christ and the Spirit are intimately coordinated, and *this is right at the heart of what the author wants to communicate to his readers*. They cannot have the Spirit without Christ. It is only through the coming of the Son and the "speaking" of this salvation through him, that this gift of the Holy Spirit is possible. Even *Moses*, the receiver and giver of the Law, had only λειτουργικὰ πνεύματα, "angels," to speak the word to him (2:2). How much greater is the gift they now have *because of the Son!*

A final, vital, comment is necessary before we move on from 2:4. Commentators on this passage tend to restrict the exercise of the "powers" to the missionaries who brought the gospel to the "Hebrews." Their message needed validation, and the powers served this function. Generally, therefore, the implication is not drawn that the "Hebrews" themselves started to exercise "powers" when they received the gospel. Only Lane cautiously ventures an implication: "It is presumably the

---

18. I refer to Mehrdad Fatehi, *The Spirit's Relation to the Risen Lord in Paul: An Examination of Its Christological Implications* (Tübingen: Mohr Siebeck, 2000), and to Cornelis Bennema, *The Power of Saving Wisdom: An Investigation of Spirit and Wisdom in Relation to the Soteriology of the Fourth Gospel* (Tübingen: Mohr Siebeck, 2002).

19. It has often been noted that the striking word ἀπαύγασμα ("reflection, radiance") is only used in Wis. 7:26 and Heb. 1:3 in the entire Bible.

perpetuation of the charisma in the life of the community . . . that provides indisputable evidence of God's seal upon the word received by the congregation."[20] But there can be no "presumably" about it, following the use of the word μερισμοί: this surely *requires* that, with the receiving of the Spirit, "the congregation" began to exercise the "powers" that are the hallmark of the Spirit's presence. Allen's comment about "repeated Pentecosts" is undoubtedly right.[21]

4. "Partners of the Holy Spirit" (6:4)

As Allen notes, the reference to the Holy Spirit in 6:4 is often grouped with 2:4.[22] Here again we find a link between the Spirit and power. There are two ways of structuring the list of five new covenant blessings in 6:4-5, and either way the Holy Spirit is emphasized. Mathias Rissi argues that the list of five is structured in such a way that the third element, the Spirit reference, is highlighted as the basis of the other four. He points out that the first two and the last two are coordinated with τε, whereas the third is introduced and followed by καί.[23] So "through the Spirit people enter the experience to which these four realities point."[24] Alternatively — and perhaps more satisfactorily — the first item ("once enlightened") can be seen as basic or introductory to the other four, which then unpack what this "enlightenment" actually is.[25] In this case, the following items form two pairs, both introduced by the verb "taste," and we can analyze them as follows:

---

20. William L. Lane, *Hebrews 1–8,* Word Biblical Commentary 47A (Dallas: Word Books, 1991), p. 40.
21. Allen, "Forgotten Spirit," p. 56.
22. Allen, "Forgotten Spirit," p. 56.
23. Τε and καί may both be used in Greek to co-ordinate items (English "and"), and are sometimes used in combination (English "both . . . and").
24. Mathias Rissi, *Die Theologie des Hebräerbriefs* (Tübingen: J. C. B. Mohr [Paul Siebeck], 1987), p. 5: "durch dem Geist wird erlebt, was diese vier Wirklichkeiten anzeigen."
25. So Hans-Friedrich Weiss, *Der Brief an die Hebräer,* Meyers Kritisch-Exegetischer Kommentar über das Neue Testament 13 (Göttingen: Vandenhoeck & Ruprecht, 1991), p. 341, although Weiss does not wish to exclude Rissi's highlighting of the third element (p. 341 n. 57). This analysis is also adopted by Dunn (James D. G. Dunn, *Baptism in the Holy Spirit* [London: SCM Press, 1970], pp. 208-9), and by Lane, *Hebrews 1–8,* p. 141.

A. 6:4, items 2 & 3, tasting the heavenly gift and becoming partners of the Holy Spirit: *the fundamental experience at the heart of this "enlightenment."*
B. 6:5, items 4 & 5, tasting God's good word and the powers of the coming age: *the headline blessings enjoyed by partners of the Holy Spirit.*

This analysis treats the list sequentially, pointing first to the basic experience of the Spirit as "heavenly gift," and then to the experiences and benefits that arrive with the Spirit — hearing the word, and feeling the power.

Thus either analysis puts the Spirit center-stage, as the author of the experiences listed here. And so here too we notice the intense connection between the Spirit and Christ, which underlies the argument: *those who fall away, after becoming partners of the Spirit, recrucify the Son of God on their own account.* They cannot retain the Spirit, and lose the Christ. This intimate link is a consistent feature of the warning passages, as we see also in 10:29, where to "spurn the Son of God" is also to "outrage the Spirit of grace." The theological substructure here, I argue, is provided by the "wisdom" background that informs the author's thinking both about Christ and about the Spirit, as in 1:1-2:4.

But there is another feature of the list in 6:4-5 which is largely overlooked by commentators: just as in 2:4, this list requires that the "Hebrews" were themselves experiencing "the good word of God" and "the powers of the coming age." Generally, commentators see a reference to their initial reception of the gospel in "tasting the good word of God,"[26] and this is reflected in the translations that turn the focus onto the "goodness of the word of God,"[27] or introduce the word "message."[28] Similarly commentators generally refer "the powers of the coming age" back to 2:4, where the δυνάμεις have been taken to refer exclusively to the initial signs and wonders that accompanied the first preaching of the gospel to the "Hebrews."

I suggest that this is fundamentally mistaken. If the list is read se-

---

26. So, e.g., Donald Guthrie, *Hebrews*, Tyndale New Testament Commentaries (Leicester: IVP, 1983), p. 143; Craig R. Koester, *Hebrews*, Anchor Bible 36 (New York: Doubleday, 2001), p. 314; Harold W. Attridge, *The Epistle to the Hebrews*, Hermeneia (Philadelphia: Fortress Press, 1989), p. 170.

27. So, e.g., NIV and NRSV.

28. So, e.g., JB and CEV. JB is typical: the translation "appreciated the good message of God" makes the phrase refer to their conversion.

quentially, with item one ("once enlightened") unpacked successively by the following two pairs, then the second "tasting" in 6:5 refers directly to *the Hebrews' own experience* of the good word of God, and of the "powers" of the coming kingdom.[29] Yes, they have learned to hear God speak immediately to them, in the context of entering *now* into the experience of things which properly belong to the age to come. They have not just learned that the gospel is good. They have heard "God's good word" for themselves — like Zechariah, who may be in the background here. The same phrase, though in the plural, is used in Zechariah 1:13 to describe the "good words" (ῥήματα καλά) with which the Lord addresses Zechariah. But fascinatingly, in that context, God's "good words" are mediated to Zechariah through an angel, who passes them on to the prophet. But for the author of this letter, and for the "Hebrews" themselves, there is no question of any such mediation. God speaks directly, and the powers of the coming age are breaking in, and the "Hebrews" have "tasted" this fully.

Thus a substantial case can be made that the spirituality of the "Hebrews" included the prominent exercise of charismatic gifts, and that the response of the author to their (understandable) desire to retain these just as members of the synagogue, dropping their messianic confession of Jesus, is to underline the intimate connection between Christ and the Spirit. They come as a pair, and they are lost as a pair.

5. The Spirit and Scripture

I believe that this insight helps our understanding of the three references where the Spirit is identified as the author of Scripture — Lindars's second category: 3:7, 9:8 and 10:15. For Lindars this is incidental to the argument of Hebrews, and simply illustrates the general New Testament "tendency to think of the Scriptures almost as a divine oracle" — written by God rather than by human beings.[30]

But it is not incidental to the argument of Hebrews, and in fact

---

29. The first "tasting" pair refers to their inner, heart experience: they have become "partners," "companions" (cf. 1:9) of the Holy Spirit. The second "tasting" pair then follows with the matching outward experience — prophetic revelation and the "powers" of the Kingdom. This contrast between inner and outer is noticed by Dunn, *Baptism*, p. 209, and by Lane, *Hebrews 1–8*, p. 141.

30. Lindars, *Theology*, p. 57.

The Spirit in Hebrews

fits with what we have already seen of Hebrews' pneumatology. It illustrates a view, not of the *authorship* of Scripture, but of the *use* of Scripture, and is a feature of Hebrews' use of the Old Testament which has not yet received sufficient attention, in my view. That lack cannot be supplied here, but we can develop some preliminary reflections by looking at each passage in turn.

5.1. "As the Holy Spirit Says . . ." (3:7)

In 3:7, the author hears the voice of the Holy Spirit in Psalm 95:7-11, even though he is well aware that the Psalm is by David (4:7). Lindars points to the oddness of this.[31] But it is only odd if 3:7 asserts the kind of "oracular" view of Scripture that Lindars finds there. Key to our reading of it is the present tense in 3:7: "as the Holy Spirit says (λέγει). . . ." The present tense is repeated when the author returns to Psalm 95 in 4:7, and David is cited as the author of the Psalm: "Again he sets a certain day, 'Today,' saying through David [ἐν Δαυὶδ λέγων]. . . ." It is interesting to speculate (not much more is possible) whether this present tense points to a "charismatic" use of this text. The Holy Spirit has "given" this text and this reading of it to the author, so that he can deliver it to the "Hebrews" as a *new* word from God — a word made present by new insight and application.

Several commentators find in the present tense a sense of the *present voice* of the Spirit,[32] reinforcing here the point the author wants to make from Psalm 95 about the present "day," the "today" when God's voice may be heard.[33] But I want to suggest a little more: that this *present hearing* of Scripture itself proceeds from a theology of the charismatic Spirit, who "gives" Scriptures with powerful interpreted meanings through prophetic revelation, and that this theology is shared by author and readers alike. The evidence for this is not strong, in relation to 3:7, but there are a couple of hints: (a) the author chooses to quote *three times* Psalm 95:7, "Today, if you would hear his voice, do not harden your hearts . . ." (3:7-8; 3:15; 4:7): does this reflect a group culture in which members *expected* to be hearing God's voice regularly, so that the

---

31. Lindars, *Theology*, p. 57.
32. E.g. Lane, *Hebrews 1-8*, p. 85; Koester, *Hebrews*, p. 254.
33. So Weiss, *Hebräer*, pp. 258-59.

author is using Scripture to warn them that, if they "harden their hearts" against Jesus, they will lose this experience? And (b) this view of prophetically interpreted and applied Scripture fits beautifully with the author's powerful concluding statement about the way in which he has used Psalm 95 — "the word of God is living and active, sharper than any two-edged sword . . ." (4:12).

Further evidence in support of this view comes from the other two "Spirit and Scripture" passages.

5.2. The Witness of the Spirit (10:15)

In 10:15 the author repeats part of his long citation from Jeremiah 31, with the introduction "The Holy Spirit bears witness to us, for after saying . . ." — and then follows Jeremiah 31:33-34, quoted in 10:16-17. At first sight it looks as though the Holy Spirit is simply (as at first sight also in 3:7) being treated as the real "author" of Scripture. But all is not as appears, and the clue here is to attend to the strange grammar of this citation. The introduction "for after saying . . ." (μετὰ γὰρ τὸ εἰρηκέναι) makes the quotation start off as a subordinate clause, and leaves us looking for a main verb to follow. Where is it? Puzzlement ensues — a puzzlement which led some scribes to supply "he later says" (ὕστερον λέγει) at the beginning of 10:17, before the end of the quotation. However light dawns when we reflect that this text would have been encountered aurally, and was written with that in mind. *Listeners* (rather than readers) would hear "says the Lord" (λέγει κύριος) at the end of the first line of the quotation as supplying the missing main verb.[34]

The effect of this on our understanding of the witness of the Spirit (10:15) is subtle and profound. It means that the Spirit is *not* being called to testify as the author of Scripture. Technically, as Grässer points out,[35] if "the Lord" is the subject of the main verb in the sen-

---

34. So Erich Grässer, *An die Hebräer (Hebr 7,1–10,18)*, Evangelisch-Katholischer Kommentar zum Neuen Testament 17:2 (Zürich: Benziger/Neukirchen: Neukirchener Verlag, 1993), p. 232; Attridge, *Hebrews*, p. 281; Weiss, *Hebräer*, pp. 513-14. Amongst translations only JB follows this construal of the grammar, although Attridge maintains that this has been the view of "most commentators since Bengel" (Attridge, *Hebrews*, p. 281 n. 44).

35. Grässer, *Hebräer (Hebr 7,1–10,18)*, p. 232 n. 56.

tence that begins with "For after saying . . . ," then "the Lord" is also the implied subject of "saying." "The Lord" is the speaker of this whole scriptural quotation. The witness of the Spirit, then, is the real, inner experience of the "law in the heart" accompanied by a deep consciousness of the forgiveness of sins (10:16b-17): the structure of the sentence highlights these two experiences as the heart of the new covenant promise, and the author wants to lead the "Hebrews" to recognize that, *assured by the Spirit's inner witness, they have already entered into the fulfillment of that promise.* They already have the "confidence" (10:19, παρρησία) which belongs to people who *know* that their sins are remembered no more.

So here, certainly (I contend), we have a prophetic reading of Scripture which starts with profound spiritual experience and then, under the leading of the Spirit, finds that experience described in Scripture.

5.3. "By this the Holy Spirit makes clear . . ." (9:8)

However, something rather different and even more striking is going on in 9:8. The focus here is not on a particular spiritual experience, but on a creative reading of the geography of the tabernacle. It is a subtle and complex reading, in which the twofold structure of the tabernacle, with an inner and an outer "tent," is understood as a picture of the two tabernacles, the earthly (belonging to the old covenant) and the heavenly, into which Christ has now entered (9:11-14). This double-tent structure, with the second tent entered only by the High Priest on the Day of Atonement (9:7), is what the Holy Spirit then explains: "By this the Holy Spirit is making clear that the way into the Most Holy Place has not yet been opened, as long as the first tent is still standing" (9:8).

Some commentators pass over this with bland comments like that of Bruce, "the Holy Spirit has a lesson to teach," or of Koester, "the Spirit that speaks through the Scriptures . . . gives insight into the Scriptures."[36] Others comment on the way in which here too, as in 3:7, the Spirit gives the Scriptures a *contemporary* meaning.[37] But more is

---

36. Frederick F. Bruce, *The Epistle to the Hebrews*, New International Commentary on the New Testament (Grand Rapids: Eerdmans, 1964), p. 164; Koester, *Hebrews*, p. 397.

37. So Attridge, *Hebrews*, p. 240; Grässer, *Hebräer (Hebr 7,1-10,18)*, p. 133.

going on, I suggest. Lane adds that we meet here "a claim to special insight which was not previously available to readers of the Old Testament. . . . *The Holy Spirit disclosed to the writer that*, so long as the front compartment of the tabernacle enjoyed cultic status, access to the presence of God was not yet available."[38] This is moving in the right direction, with its acknowledgement that we encounter here a claim to special scriptural interpretation, given by the Spirit. But it is more than just adding another, this time Spirit-led, interpretation to the range of attempts to understand the "real," or original, meaning of the Scriptures. In this case, the interpretation is so radical that it amounts virtually to a *reversal* of the original meaning. The "Tent of Meeting" was meant to be just that — a place of meeting between God and his people. The Holy Spirit has revealed to the author of Hebrews that, far from facilitating meeting, it actually constituted a barrier to connection between God and humankind — "pending the time of restoration" (9:10). *Only the priests* could enter the first tent (9:6), and *only the High Priest* could enter the second (9:7). What kind of "meeting" is this?

Of course there are textual indicators that this prophetic reading is not completely "off the wall" — particularly to do with the Day of Atonement. But it is clear (a) that this is a "backwards" reading, starting from the fact of the experience of the new covenant in Christ, and (b) — especially important for us — that this is a "given" reading, one "made clear" by the Holy Spirit. The fact that the author includes such a reading in his letter must indicate that the "Hebrews" were open to such interpretative revelations, and ready to listen to them, even if they sounded hugely radical (as this one must have done).

6. Finally "the Eternal Spirit" (9:14)

I have essentially argued for three things in this article: (a) that in the background to the letter lies shared charismatic experience, common both to the author and the addressees, a shared experience of the Holy Spirit present to them in "powers" and in revelation, (b) that a sense of Spirit-empowered prophetic interpretation underlies the radical and creative handling of Scripture that we meet here, and (c) that the au-

---

38. William B. Lane, *Hebrews 9–13*, Word Biblical Commentary 47B (Dallas: Word Books, 1991), p. 223 (my emphasis).

thor is passionately convinced, and passionately argues, that the Holy Spirit now only comes with Christ the Son of God. The "Hebrews" cannot keep their charismatic gifts just as Jews, no longer attached to Jesus. This last point is particularly the point that begins to move us, from Hebrews, in the direction of trinitarian theology.

And it significantly underlies and illumines the seventh reference to the Spirit in Hebrews, in 9:14. This is a stunning and powerful statement, and is the only one that brings the Spirit into direct relation with Christ. I have argued that that relationship is implicit throughout — but here it becomes explicit. Christ "offered himself blameless to God through the eternal Spirit (διὰ πνεύματος αἰωνίου)." This certainly looks back to the phrase "eternal redemption" in 9:12: by his blood, offered through the eternal Spirit, Christ gains eternal redemption for his people. But we need to bear in mind that "eternal" (αἰώνιος) means "of the age to come," and thus also naturally reminds us of the "powers of the coming age" (6:5, δυνάμεις . . . μέλλοντος αἰῶνος) which the Spirit has brought to the lives of the "Hebrews." This prompts an interesting reflection. Paul tends to associate the resurrection with the Holy Spirit (e.g. Rom. 1:3; 7:5-6; 8:2), thus opening the door to a triumphalist view of the Spirit, an over-realized eschatology against which he argues particularly in 1 Corinthians. Rissi has suggested that the "Hebrews" too had an over-realized eschatology, a super-confidence in their possession of the Spirit.[39] Here at the heart of the letter,[40] the author insists that the *flesh* of Christ is offered by the *Spirit* to God, and thus lays the foundation for the kind of spiritual discipleship *in the flesh* which he then expounds so powerfully in Hebrews 11-13.

Max Turner has always lived by the conviction that discipleship must rest on scholarship, and that both must be animated by the Spirit, and that the Spirit-filled life is a life lived faithfully *in the flesh*. I think that the author of Hebrews would agree profoundly with all this.

---

39. Rissi, *Theologie*, p. 9.
40. Vanhoye famously argued that Hebrews has a concentric structure, and that 9:11-14 is at the heart of the whole thing: Albert Vanhoye, *Structure and Message of the Epistle to the Hebrews* (Rome: Pontifical Biblical Institute, 1989).

New Jerusalem and the Conversion of the Nations: An Exercise in Pneumatic Discernment (Rev. 21:1–22:5)

John Christopher Thomas

Just over twenty years ago, when I first arrived in Sheffield, I was constantly asked, "Do you know Max Turner?" When I would ask why, the response was invariably, "I think you two would get on well." When our mutual friend Bob Willoughby brought me from Cambridge to London Bible College a couple of years later, I understood full well why so many people thought we should meet. Within seconds of our introduction we were deep in non-stop conversation about all things pneumatological. In fact at one point I thought to apologize for not making room for normal points of introduction, to which Max revealed that we were very much on the same wavelength. In some ways that initial conversation has never stopped but has continued over hospitality shown to me by Max and Lucy on numerous occasions, the editing of one another's books, and a whole host of intense dialogues characterized by respect and love. The life and ministry of Max Turner is quite significant indeed, and my life would be all the poorer without it. It is indeed my honor to contribute a piece to this *Festschrift* in his honor.

The topic of the conversion of the nations in the Apocalypse is a well-known and much disputed issue. Interpretive options range from minimalist views that deny much of any place for the conversion of the nations, owing to their largely negative function in the book, to views that embrace some sort of modified or fully fledged universalism, owing in part to the symbolic nature of the book.

Before offering my thoughts on this topic perhaps a few words of orientation are in order. First, this study comes from my commentary

New Jerusalem and the Conversion of the Nations

work on the Apocalypse for the Two Horizons Series, in which methodologically I employ a combination of narrative and intertextual analyses, by which to determine, as nearly as possible, the effect of the text upon the hearers. By this means I seek to honor both the visionary nature of the book and the clear priority given in the book itself to hearing the words of this prophecy (1:3). Thus, in what follows, I have sought to allow my own reflection to be informed and controlled by the text itself and its clear intertexts, with minimal interference or imposition by things extra-textual. Second, as a Pentecostal reader or hearer I have been and continue to be shaped and formed by the worshipping Pentecostal communities of which I am part, in the parish (the Woodward Ave Church of God in Athens, TN) and the academy (the Pentecostal Theological Seminary), where the fivefold gospel (Jesus is Savior, Sanctifier, Holy Ghost Baptizer, Healer, and Soon Coming King) serves as the theological heart of the tradition. While the eschatology of earliest Pentecostalism was anything but monolithic, being characterized primarily by a discerning reflection upon the meaning of Jesus as Soon Coming King as part of the fivefold gospel, in North America dispensational thought soon tended to become the dominant tutor on things eschatological — though dissenting voices continued to be found.[1] In such a dispensational environment little attention was given to the idea of the conversion of the nations, for as the lines of demarcation were drawn, it was quite clear how the nations functioned — as antagonists of God and his people. It might be safe to say that while it was thought that a few individuals might be converted during the period of "the great tribulation," there was little possibility that any of the nations would be converted. While my own initial thoughts on this subject were, no doubt, colored by such pessimism with regard to the nations' soteriological chances, as I began my interpretive journey through the Apocalypse, I began to discover that the text of the Apocalypse continually subverted such pessimism. Happily, during the course of my interpretive journey I have discovered a number of fellow travelers for recently a number of Pentecostal scholars have been devoting their attention to the academic study of the Apocalypse.

A final point of orientation is related to certain interpretive convictions to which my intensive engagement with the Apocalypse over

---

1. On this topic, see the ground-breaking work of Larry R. McQueen, *Toward a Pentecostal Eschatology: Discerning the Way Forward* (Blandford Forum: Deo, 2012).

the last decade has led me. First, I have become convinced that the document is a narrative with a discernible linear development, for example the way in which the theophanic elements introduced in 4:5 reappear with increasing intensity at the conclusion of each of the series of sevens (seals 8:5, trumpets 11:19, and bowls 16:18-21). Second, I have learned that the cyclical aspects of the book do not necessarily undermine the narrative's linear development but rather add dimensions of meaning in ways that drive the hearers to appreciate better its dialectical qualities. Third, I have come to appreciate the psychedelic nature of the text where things and individuals morph from one form into another form before the eyes (and ears!) of the hearers and where things and people that appear to be destroyed at a certain point can reappear with little or no explanation. In such cases it seems that the (implied) hearers do not become stuck in their reflection by such linear incongruities but rather continue their narrative journey informed (and formed) by such tensions and dissonances at even deeper levels (e.g. the affective) than the cognitive. Fourth, I have come to think of the Apocalypse more and more as a kind of kaleidoscope where one seeks to discern meaning through a variety of sensory perceptions experienced. But, pushing this imagery a bit further, it seems to me that the Apocalypse is like a kaleidoscope that one can actually enter into and experience from the inside out. Specifically, I have found that as the interpreter makes one's way through the book one discovers that the images earlier encountered begin to change in appearance, and as one enters further into the book and looks backwards the images earlier encountered take on additional dimensions and nuances not earlier discernable. Thus, in the world of the Apocalypse the meaning of different concepts, terms, and themes continues to grow and develop — looking different the further into the kaleidoscope one goes. Fifth, a word should perhaps be offered about the subtitle of this study as it is integral to my understanding of how one should approach the Apocalypse and thus it is not just an attempt to make this essay relevant to the title of the book in which it appears! One of the results of making an interpretive journey through the Apocalypse is the discovery that pneumatic discernment is explicitly called for at numerous points along the way. Owing to the limitations of space only a few examples are here noted. (a) John begins his own journey whilst "in the Spirit on the Lord's day" (1:10), a journey that continues "in the Spirit" at each major transition point (4:2; 17:3; 21:10). (b) In his initial encounter with the resurrected Jesus John is provided supernatural assistance by Jesus himself as to the meaning of the mystery of the seven stars and the seven golden lampstands (1:19-20). (c) Each of the seven prophetic messages spoken by the resurrected Jesus concludes with a call for the hearers to engage in pneumatic discernment — "the one who has an ear let that one hear what the Spirit is saying to the churches" (2:7, 11, 17, 29; 3:6, 13, 22). (d) John and his hearers are given special assistance, this time by one of the twenty-four elders, with regard to the identity of those clothed in white who "are coming out of the great tribulation" (7:13-14). (e) The identity of the Great City in which the two witnesses offer their prophetic testimony is revealed to the hearers by means of the Spirit, for its identity is given πνευματικῶς ("pneumatically") as Sodom, Egypt, the place where their Lord was crucified (11:8). (f) Still another call for the hearers' pneumatic discernment, "if anyone has an ear let that one hear," prefaces words of exhortation about the nature of the patient endurance of the saints (13:9-10). (g) This call is followed in the text by, "The one who has understanding let that one calculate the number of the beast" (13:18). (h) Interpretive assistance is also given in 17:9-10 with regard to the identity of the seven heads and their relationship to the Great Whore and the beast where a call for pneumatic discernment is implied as to the seven kings, "five who have fallen, one who is, and one who is not yet." These numerous explicit and implicit calls for pneumatic discernment within the Apocalypse itself suggest that its interpreters should attempt to engage it by means of such pneumatic discernment. With these words of prolegomenon, I now turn to the topic at hand.

As the third major section of the Apocalypse (17:1–21:8) draws to a close, the attention of the hearers is directed to the New Jerusalem coming down out of heaven, "And the holy city New Jerusalem I saw coming down out of heaven from God, prepared as a bride adorned for her husband" (21:2). At this point the hearers encounter the by now familiar words καὶ εἶδον ("and I saw"), though for the first and only time in the Apocalypse here the conjunction and verb are separated by the direct object,[2] a construction that adds further emphasis to and focus upon the object, "the holy city New Jerusalem." How would the hearers understand this holy city, this New Jerusalem? Perhaps the first hint comes earlier in the book where the people of God have metaphorically been

---

2. D. E. Aune, *Revelation 17–22*, Word Biblical Commentary 52C (Nashville: Nelson, 1998), p. 1120.

called the holy city (11:2), which was to be trampled for forty-two months. Thus, perhaps the hearers would immediately detect some degree of continuity between this holy city and the people of God here in 21:2. At the same time, they would also be aware that this is the second time that they have encountered the name New Jerusalem in the Apocalypse, with the first occurrence coming in the prophetic message to the church in Philadelphia in the form of a promise from the resurrected Jesus to the one who overcomes — "I will write upon him the name of my God and the name of the city of my God, the New Jerusalem" (3:12),[3] thus further underscoring the identity of the city as closely connected if not identical to the people of God. As in its first mention in the book, so too here New Jerusalem is identified as "coming down out of heaven from God," words that make clear to the hearers that New Jerusalem is, unlike the Jerusalem of old, an entity that is of divine origin, coming from God himself. It would be difficult to imagine that the hearers would not pick up on the fact that this two-fold attribution makes clear the divine origin of this holy city. The fact that in both references to this point in the Apocalypse New Jerusalem is identified as "coming down out of heaven from God" might well lead the hearers to understand this phrase as a defining attribute of the city, underscoring its ongoing divine origin. If the hearers have suspicions that this holy city New Jerusalem is closely identified with the people of God, the last phrase in 21:2 makes such a connection clear, for she is "prepared as a bride adorned for her husband." Such language would be significant to the hearers for at least two reasons. First, the description of New Jerusalem as a bride would remind them of the radical difference between this city, described as a bride, and fallen Babylon in which the voice (or sound) of the bride will be heard no longer (18:23), contrasting (yet again) the impotency of the Great Whore with the promise of the Bride. Second, the language of 21:2 could not help but call to mind the marriage supper of the Lamb and his bride, γυνή ("woman") in this instance, who has prepared herself for her marriage by means of her righteous acts (19:7-8). Thus, it would be difficult for the hearers not to take the holy city New Jerusalem as the bride of the Lamb,[4] indicating that the marriage supper of the Lamb

---

3. R. H. Mounce, *The Book of Revelation,* New International Commentary on the New Testament (Grand Rapids: Eerdmans, 1977), p. 370.

4. R. Zimmermann, "Nuptial Imagery in the Revelation of John," *Bib* 84 (2003): 169.

New Jerusalem and the Conversion of the Nations

has indeed come at last.[5] If so, her preparations, which consist of her righteous acts, might be understood further in the light of her designation as the holy city. Her preparations are coterminous with her having adorned herself for her husband, an activity that is now past, the effects of which are still felt, as the perfect κεκοσμημένην ("adorned") indicates, standing in stark contrast to the adornment of the Great Whore in chapters 17-18. Finally, the hearers might additionally discern that the kind of discontinuity that exists between the first heaven and first earth and the New Heaven and New Earth (21:1) would likely also exist between the Jerusalem of old and the holy city New Jerusalem. For this is not another Jerusalem of the same kind as the first; rather it is a New Jerusalem. The hearers might well wonder, since some of the eschatological promises found earlier in the Apocalypse appear to be fulfilled in the New Heaven and New Earth, is it not possible that the eschatological promises with regard to eschatological Jerusalem, scattered throughout the biblical tradition, would be fulfilled in New Jerusalem?[6]

The first hints with regard to the conversion of the nations and New Jerusalem are found in verse 3. Whatever reflection the words of verse 2 generate within the hearers, it is interrupted by even more extraordinary words, "And I heard a great voice out of the throne saying, 'Behold the dwelling of God is with men, and he will dwell with them, and they will be his peoples, and God himself will be with them.'" A number of aspects of these words would be significant for the hearers. First, while they will have by this time encountered a number of voices from heaven, and even a voice from the throne (19:5), this is the first great voice from the throne that they have encountered. The combination of the adjective "great" with the fact that this voice originates from the throne would heighten the dramatic quality of the narration and lead the hearers to expect that the words to be heard are indeed significant and of great eschatological consequence.[7] As these divine words from the throne are made known, (once again) they take on third person form, being words spoken about God. Second, the first words from the throne, "Behold the dwelling of God is with men," serve to confirm the hearers' earlier suspicions that the nature of the relationship between God and his people in the New Creation will be more direct and

---

5. G. E. Ladd, *Revelation* (Grand Rapids: Eerdmans, 1972), p. 277.
6. S. S. Smalley, *The Revelation to John* (Downers Grove: IVP, 2005), p. 535.
7. Smalley, *Revelation*, p. 537.

unhindered than before.[8] These words would be of great significance for the hearers, as a number of Old Testament texts appear to converge before their eyes and ears at this point. The language of dwelling could hardly help but point to the presence of God in the tabernacle amongst Israel during her wilderness wanderings (Lev. 26:11-12), (once again) echoing the continuity between God's past salvific activity and what lies ahead.[9] At the same time, discerning Johannine hearers would be well aware of the fact that in the life and ministry of Jesus the presence of God amongst them was made even more immediate, for "the Word became flesh and dwelt among us, and we beheld his glory, the glory of the unique Son of God" (John 1:14). They would also likely be quite impressed by the fact that the dwelling of God, previously encountered in heaven (Rev. 15:5), is now amongst human beings, confirming that divine access is now more immediate and direct. Third, the fact that the dwelling of God is said to be "with men" would perhaps remind the hearers of the wideness in God's mercy, for despite the fact that significant numbers of "men" have perished earlier in the Apocalypse (8:11; 9:15, 18), the dwelling of God "with men" at this point would appear to give additional hope amongst the hearers for the conversion of the nations.[10] Fourth, the next line, "and he will dwell with them," also echoes numerous Old Testament texts and reinforces the words of the previous line, with the verb σκηνώσει ("will dwell") appearing here, where the noun σκηνή ("dwelling") had earlier appeared. In the Apocalypse the hearers would know that such language points to the fulfillment of the eschatological promises for those who come out of the great tribulation where the One Who Sits upon the throne "will dwell upon them" (7:15). Such linguistic repetition leaves no doubt that the nature of God's relationship to the faithful is immediate and unveiled. It is on a new level and order. Fifth, the next line, "and they will be his peoples," drives the point home even further, again underscoring the fulfillment of the eschatological promises of many Old Testament texts, while at the same time again affirming the large scope of the soteriological reality.[11]

---

8. G. R. Beasley-Murray, *Revelation* (Grand Rapids: Eerdmans, 1981), p. 311.

9. R. H. Gause, *Revelation: God's Stamp of Sovereignty on History* (Cleveland: Pathway, 1984), p. 265.

10. D. Mathewson, "The Destiny of the Nations in Revelation 21:1–22:5: A Reconsideration," *TynBul* 53 (2002): 128.

11. R. Bauckham, *Climax of Prophecy: Studies on the Book of Revelation* (Edinburgh: T&T Clark, 1993), pp. 311-13.

Among other things the hearers might well pick up on the fact that here the term "peoples" is plural, rather than singular as in Leviticus 26:12 and Jeremiah 24:7, perhaps suggesting to the readers that the eschatological people of God, Israel, has expanded to include all peoples,[12] in accord with John's earlier vision of the crowd from every tribe and tongue and people and nation around the throne (Rev. 5:9), and the innumerable crowd out of all nations and tribes and peoples and tongues who are coming out of the great tribulation (7:9).[13] Sixth, the emphasis upon the intimate relationship between God and his peoples continues to be made clear in the final line of verse 3, where it is emphatically stated that "God himself will be with them," the emphatic construction αὐτὸς ὁ θεός ("God himself") occurring here alone in the whole of the Apocalypse.[14] It is difficult to imagine how the personal eschatological presence of God amongst his peoples could be conveyed more powerfully. It is he of the dwelling of God, he who will dwell with them, he whose peoples they are; it is this very God himself who will be with them! At the same time, the warning of verse 8 reminds the hearers that not everyone will participate in the eschatological rewards given to those who overcome and, thus, it would be mistaken to think that universal salvation as such will be extended to the nations.

The next hint as to the relationship between the conversion of the nations and New Jerusalem appears to occur in the description of the holy city which has ". . . a wall great and high, having twelve gates, and upon these gates twelve angels, and names have been written which are of the twelve tribes of the sons of Israel; from the east three gates and from the north three gates and from the south three gates and from the west three gates" (21:12-13). With these words the hearers begin to learn of the physical attributes of the holy city. Several details would be of significance for them. First, the hearers discover that the city John sees is described exactly like the mountain to which he is taken, as great and high, suggesting that the wall is in keeping with the mountain upon which the city apparently sits. As the description continues the hearers could not help but be impressed by the various combinations of the number twelve that they encounter, each occurrence re-

---

12. S. Pattemore, *The People of God in the Apocalypse: Discourse, Structure and Exegesis* (Cambridge: Cambridge University Press, 2004), p. 201.

13. R. H. Gundry, "The New Jerusalem: People as Place, not Place for People," *NovT* 29 (1987): 257.

14. Smalley, *Revelation*, p. 538.

minding them of the theologically significant ways in which they have encountered the multiples of the number twelve previously (4:4, 10; 5:8; 7:4-8; 11:16; 12:1; 14:1, 3; 19:4). This theologically significant number is in some ways indistinguishable from the city itself, for it is deeply embedded in its very essence and being. Such emphasis would likely suggest to the hearers perfection in all details. In this case the wall of the city has the perfect number of (twelve) gates, attended by the perfect number of (twelve) angels, with the names of the perfect number of the (twelve) tribes of the sons of Israel! The twelve gates suggest perfect access,[15] while the twelve angels convey the idea of divinely appointed perfect oversight of access. The names that have been written on the gates include all the names of those encountered earlier when the 144,000 of the tribes of the sons of Israel were divinely sealed (Rev. 7:4-8). As the hearers ponder these names perhaps they would remember the strong connection between their own community and the 144,000: the messianic character of this group; that these are the heirs to what God has done through Israel, owing in part to the presence of the historically important tribes; that this group is marked in part by its priestly identity; that this group has a prophetic identity; and that this group is clearly one marked out as belonging to God and protected by him. Thus, twelve gates, each of which bears the name of one of the tribes of the sons of Israel, would testify to the way in which God's people and the holy city are identical.[16]

The gates, the hearers discover, are symmetrically distributed around the city with three gates on each side, but in the peculiar geographical order — East, North, South, and West.[17] At the least, the enumeration of these twelve gates that open in all directions would suggest universal access,[18] as no corner of existence stands without three entrances to the holy city. However, it is not altogether clear what the hearers would make of the peculiar order found here, as normally such a description would follow a North, East, South, West direction (e.g. Ezek. 48:30-35). What might such an order suggest to the hearers? Perhaps it would not be overlooked that the place of prominence is given to the East and that it is in this direction that the door of the Jerusalem

---

15. P. Lee, *The New Jerusalem in the Book of Revelation* (Tübingen: Mohr Siebeck, 2001), p. 281.
16. Gause, *Revelation*, p. 271.
17. J. Sweet, *Revelation* (London: SCM Press, 1990), p. 304.
18. Smalley, *Revelation*, p. 548.

temple faced.[19] Would such a theological-geographical detail suggest to the hearers that this city, which the wall encloses, is itself a temple, owing to the brilliant radiance of the glory of God present in it and its eastern orientation? Would the hearers also remember that when the sixth bowl was poured out a way was prepared for the kings of the east to make their way to the war of the great day of God the All Powerful One (16:12-16)? If so, would the three gates on the East wall of the holy city suggest to the hearers that there is even hope for these kings from the East, kings who violently opposed God, to enter the holy city? When pondering about the gates on the North would the hearers think of the ways in which Gog and Magog, the traditional enemies from the North (Ezek. 38:2), gathered together to make war with the camp of the saints, God's beloved city (Rev. 20:8)? If so, would they be inclined to think that these gates are opened to them and all others from the four points of the earth (20:8) that have opposed God? When contemplating the gates on the South side of the wall, would they be reminded of the city pneumatically called Sodom and Egypt that humiliates the two Spirit-inspired prophets (11:8)? Is it possible that there exists access to the holy city even for these? And would thoughts of the three gates on the West remind them of the great sea, which is no more? Is there hope even for those that are in its grip? While it is impossible to know what the hearers would make of the peculiar geographical orientation of the description of these gates, it is almost certain that these details would not be passed over without discerning reflection.

The next relevant stretch of text comes in verse 24 after a description of the way in which God and the Lamb is the temple and in which the glory of God enlightens the city and the Lamb is its lamp, "And the nations will walk by means of its light, and the kings of the earth bring their glory into it." The hearers would find these words significant for the following reasons. First, the words' content could not help but remind the hearers of an Isaianic promise with regard to the ideal age to come, where (once again) near identical wording occurs (Isa. 60:3). Second, there could be little doubt that the hearers would understand this language to mean that the nations who walk in the light are those who have experienced his salvation, owing in part to the fact that in Johannine thought the word περιπατέω ("walk") functions metaphorically as a description of one's relationship to or fellowship with God, Jesus,

---

19. An observation for which I am indebted to my colleague L. R. Martin.

and/or the Light (John 6:66; 8:12; 11:9-10; 12:35; 1 John 1:6-7; 2:6, 11; 2 John 4, 6; 3 John 3, 4) and this very word has been encountered earlier in the Apocalypse to describe fellowship with the resurrected Jesus (Rev. 2:1), eschatological reward (3:4), and ethical conduct (16:15). Third, in some ways the words of 21:24 follow on quite naturally from the optimistic impression left by the perfect and universal access to the holy city conveyed by the twelve gates that open in all directions (21:13). The hearers would well recall from that context the questions raised with regard to the possible conversion of the enemies of God and his people from the East (the kings from the east), the North (Gog and Magog, traditional enemies from the north), the South (the great city pneumatically known as Sodom and Egypt), and the West (the sea that is no more). Thus, it appears that the hearers would discern a further reason to believe that the rebellious nations will find a place in God's salvific light that fills the holy city, fulfilling their previous expectations based upon descriptions of the nations in precisely these terms (5:9; 7:9; 11:9-13; 15:3-4), nations that are the specific objects of faithful witness and prophecy (10:11; 11:9-13; 14:6). Fourth, at the same time, the hearers would know full well that the nations have been previously spoken of as being opposed to God and his people (11:9-13, 18), as being under the authority of the Beast (13:7), as being intoxicated with the wine of the Great Whore's sexual immorality (14:8; 18:3) — under her domination (17:15) — deceived by her magic (18:23), being deceived by Satan (20:3, 8), and as being judged by God and the Rider on the white horse (16:17; 19:15). The fact that the nations, perhaps these very nations, are spoken of as walking in the light of the holy city, the very glory of God, would stretch the imaginative abilities of the hearers to their limits as they are forced to hold these dialectical possibilities together, the possible implication being that God is even more gracious and longsuffering than they could have ever imagined! These first words of 21:24 would clearly suggest to the hearers that the nations who walk in the light of the holy city are indeed converted, but these words would go further, being pregnant with meaning, causing them to reflect on the incongruities of these two ends of the dialectic — that perhaps those who have expressed such open hostility and opposition to God and his people somehow experience his salvific light! If the hearers are uneasy and reluctant to consider such possibilities, the rest of the words in 21:24 almost demand that they give them serious reflection, as the hearers continue to engage in pneumatic discernment, for not only are the nations said to walk in the light of the holy city, but it is also said that "the kings of the earth bring their glory into it"! These words, as those that precede, would be significant for the hearers. First, as with the previous words in this verse, these that follow could not help but remind the hearers of the same Isaianic promise with regard to the ideal age to come, where near identical wording occurs (Isa. 60:3). Second, it is clear that the kings of the earth in this verse are seen not only as entering the holy city, but also as bringing their glory into it, a word that in the Apocalypse is closely associated with worship (1:6; 4:9, 11; 5:12, 13; 7:12; 11:13; 14:7; 16:9; 19:1, 7),[20] indicating that the kings of the earth too are engaged in the worship of the God whose own glory enlightens the entire city. Third, in some ways these words would appear to be even more challenging to the hearers than those with regard to the nations, for aside from the first reference to the kings of the earth, where Jesus is referred to as the ruler of the kings of the earth (1:5), there is no other place in the whole of the Apocalypse where the kings of the earth do not function as the enemies of God (6:15; 17:2, 18; 18:3, 9; 19:19) save here in 21:24,[21] but in point of fact appear to have been destroyed by the Rider on the white horse! And yet, here they are spoken of as bringing their own objects of worship into the holy city.[22] Would not such an inversion suggest that a remarkable conversion takes place amongst the kings of the earth whose idolatrous greed and self-serving pursuit of power, whose opposition to God and his people have been transformed so that these kings now worship God with the very things they had formally sought for themselves?[23] As with the nations, it would be clear to the hearers that these kings of the earth have indeed been converted as a result of the faithful witness of God's people, but would the absolute polarities and incongruities encountered in the text not push the hearers to contemplate a greater wideness in God's mercy than they have hitherto been prepared to explore or for which even to hope?[24] If so, would not such a marvelous optimism serve to encourage their faithful pneumatic witness all the more[25] — that the conversion of the nations

---

20. Mathewson, "Destiny," p. 130.
21. Aune, *Revelation 17–22*, p. 1171.
22. G. B. Caird, *The Revelation of Saint John* (London: Black, 1966), p. 279.
23. Beasley-Murray, *Revelation*, p. 328; Sweet, *Revelation*, p. 308; Bauckham, *Climax*, p. 315.
24. Pattemore, *People of God*, p. 202.
25. As R. Herms notes, ". . . universal language does not necessarily presuppose

and their kings might possibly include even greater numbers than the hearers are able to see or have heard in the words of this prophecy and that, therefore, they cannot begin to calculate its importance? If so, the significant fact that the two positive references to the kings of the earth in the Apocalypse (1:5; 21:24) envelop all the negative references would not be lost on the hearers.

The perfect access to the holy city is made even clearer in the words the hearers next encounter, "And its gates are never closed by day, for night is not there, and they will bring the glory and honor of the nations into it" (21:25-26). Not only do the twelve gates provide perfect access to the holy city from all directions, but they also provide immediate access, for unlike the city gates of the ancient world, where gates would close for security purposes especially at night, these gates never close during the day owing to the fact that the angelic sentries and God himself ensure its security. In point of fact, these gates would appear to provide around-the-clock access to the holy city, in accord with the Isaianic promises of the ideal days to come (Isa. 60:11),[26] for there is no night there! These words would likely convey at least two things to the hearers. First, they would no doubt take them to indicate that the radiance of the glory of God means that darkness is never manifested in the holy city, which is enlightened at all times. Confirming this interpretation is the fact that whenever the words day and night occur in close proximity in the Apocalypse (4:8; 7:15; 12:10; 14:11; 20:10), with one exception (8:12), the meaning conveys the idea of around-the-clock activity or access. Second, discerning Johannine hearers might well detect here a still deeper meaning owing to how in Johannine thought both night (John 3:2; 9:4; 11:10; 13:30; 19:39) and darkness (1:5; 6:17; 8:12; 12:35, 46; 1 John 1:5; 2:8, 9, 11) often have ominous spiritual connotations. If the hearers pick up on these associations in Revelation 21:25 it would be further proof that there is no place in the holy city for the unbelief and doubt of night and/or darkness — for all is light in it.[27] Thus, this around-the-clock, immediate access to the holy city means that the kings of the earth will have ample opportunity

---

universal salvation; rather, it serves to vindicate the faithful community, and validate their present circumstances in light of a future reversal" (*An Apocalypse for the Church and the World: The Narrative Function of Universal Language in the Book of Revelation* [Berlin: W. de Gruyter, 2006], p. 260).

26. Beasley-Murray, *Revelation*, p. 329.
27. Smalley, *Revelation*, p. 560.

to bring into it the glory and honor of the nations. The combination of the words glory and honor would well remind the hearers of that particular combination in 4:9, 11 and 5:12-13 where they stand together to describe the worship given to the One Who Sits on the throne and to the Lamb,[28] indicating once again that the kings and nations offer genuine worship to God as they enter into the holy city. Perhaps the hearers would also see here a contrast between the earthly kings who brought their glory into the Babylon of old[29] and, as yet another sign of the conversion of the nations, the kings of the earth that bring in their glory in accord with the eschatological hopes found in various places in the Old Testament (Isa. 45:20, 22, 24; Zech. 2:11; 8:23; Dan. 7:14), further reinforcing the dialectical relationship confronting the hearers between the conversion of the nations and the judgment of those who fail to repent,[30] who appear to be punished in the lake of fire (20:15).

If the hope for the conversion of the nations is nurtured in the hearers by the words found in 21:24-26, the other end of the dialectic is underscored in the very next words they encounter, "And every impure thing and the one who engages in abominations and falsehood will never enter into it, except those who have been written in the Lamb's book of life" (21:27). While the previous verses have made clear that the nations and the kings of the earth will be present in the holy city, they do not make explicit at what point these entities convert nor do they explain how these opponents of God, who apparently are punished by God in the lake of burning sulfur forever and ever (21:8), are transformed into those worthy to gain admission to the holy city. Without resolving such tensions for the hearers, the words of 21:27 reveal that however such a transformation comes about, those who enter the holy city, including the nations and the kings of the earth, will not enter it as impure entities or as those who are characterized by abominations, like the Great Whore (17:4-5; 21:8), or falsehood, like the Beast (21:8). Rather, just like all others who overcome, they too must of necessity have their names written in the Lamb's book of life (3:5; 13:8; 17:8; 20:12, 15),[31] an indication that they too have experienced the salvation offered by the Lamb who had been slaughtered (5:6) and whose blood has

---

28. Smalley, *Revelation*, p. 558.
29. Sweet, *Revelation*, p. 310.
30. Aune, *Revelation 17–22*, p. 1173.
31. J. R. Michaels, *Revelation*, IVP New Testament Commentary 20 (Downers Grove: IVP, 1997), p. 246.

loosed them from their sin (1:5; 5:9), and thus have rejected the Beast and joined in offering faithful witness to the Lamb!

The next text directly relevant to our topic comes when the hearers learn more about the river of life and its effects in the words of 22:2, "and on either side of the river a tree of life bearing twelve fruits, each month giving its fruit, and the leaves of the tree for healing of the nations." The potency of the river of living water is underscored by the fact that it is surrounded by plantings of the tree of life on either side of the river.[32] Mention of the tree of life, in conjunction with the river of living water, could not help but remind the hearers of the tree of life found in the Garden of Eden. They would well remember how human access to the fruit of this tree was prohibited after Adam and Eve ate the fruit of the tree of the knowledge of good and evil, lest they take the fruit of the tree of life and live forever (Gen. 3:22-24), with Cherubim placed at the entrance of the Garden with a flaming sword to protect this tree of life. But the appearance of the tree of life in Revelation 22:2 would not take the hearers completely by surprise for in the very first prophetic message given by the resurrected Jesus to the seven churches the hearers learn that the one who overcomes will be given to eat of the tree of life in the paradise of God (2:7)![33] Therefore, the anticipation created by this initial eschatological promise of life, given by the resurrected living one (!), is finally fulfilled. The presence of this tree signals the reversal of the curse brought on by the disobedience of Adam and Eve while again making clear the immediate and direct access the overcomers have to God, for this tree is a sign that the previous separation and enmity between God and humankind is now completely removed.[34] Thus, the fruit of the tree of life that had been prohibited for human consumption by divine initiative is now freely available to those who inhabit the New Jerusalem. At the same time, owing to the close association between the tree of life and the paradise of God, the hearers would perhaps suspect that this holy city bears the characteristics of a garden. Something of the inexhaustible supply of eternal life in this New Jerusalem is exhibited by the fact that the tree of life brings forth a

---

32. Gause, *Revelation*, p. 276. The Greek expression ξύλον ζωῆς ("tree of life") is a collective, standing for this whole genus of trees.

33. M. Kiddle, *The Revelation of St John* (London: Hodder & Stoughton, 1940), pp. 441-42.

34. P. Mayo, *"Those Who Call Themselves Jews": The Church and Judaism in the Apocalypse of John* (Eugene: Pickwick, 2006), p. 196.

New Jerusalem and the Conversion of the Nations

staggering amount of fruit, far exceeding even that described in Ezekiel's vision (Ezek. 47:12).[35] For in keeping with the other characteristics of the holy city, the tree produces the perfect amount of eternal sustenance — as it generates twelve crops, with these twelve crops of fruit given not just once or even twice a year, but every month — twelve times a year! This supply of eternal life, like that of the river, is more than enough and never ending. But in some ways perhaps the most surprising detail about this remarkable part of this vision are the words, "and the leaves of the tree are for the healing of the nations." Several aspects of this statement would be of significance for the hearers. First, it would be clear that the leaves of this tree of life, a tree that stands on both sides of the river of life, are closely associated with eternal life and, consequently, are signs of its bestowal. Second, these words stand with the other statements in the description of New Jerusalem that underscore a view of a wideness in God's mercy that includes the conversion of the nations (21:3, 12-13, 24-26).[36] Third, discerning Johannine hearers would also likely find a deeper soteriological significance in these words, for in the Fourth Gospel there is an almost indistinguishable connection between signs of healing and salvation, that is belief in Jesus. In point of fact, each physical healing described in the Fourth Gospel is directly connected to the experience of eternal life based in the atoning life and death of Jesus (John 4:46-54; 5:1-18; 9:1-41; 11:1-57).[37] Thus, when the hearers learn that the leaves of the tree are for the healing of the nations, they would likely understand healing in its most holistic and comprehensive fashion, encompassing both physical and spiritual healing for both are part of the salvific work of Jesus. Fourth, owing to this comprehensive understanding of the healing of the nations, the hearers might well discern in these words some additional insight into the conversion of the nations, for while they still are not told exactly when and how such a conversion takes place, they now learn that provision is indeed made for such and is part of the very fabric of the New Jerusalem! Perhaps they would understand this healing to include the healing of the wounds of the nations incurred in their rebellion against God and the Lamb.[38] Thus, not only is the eternal life

---

35. Aune, *Revelation 17–22*, p. 1178.
36. Mathewson, "Destiny," p. 139
37. Cf. J. C. Thomas, "Healing in the Atonement: A Johannine Perspective," in *The Spirit of the New Testament* (Blandford Forum: Deo, 2006), pp. 175-89.
38. Sweet, *Revelation*, p. 311.

that flows in this river and is available in the fruit of the tree of life inexhaustible, but it is also comprehensive for all who will respond to its offer.

This focus appears to continue in the next words the hearers encounter, "And there is no curse any longer" (22:3). Owing to the thoughts about the tree of life in the Garden of Eden generated by reference to the tree of life on either side of the river of life in the New Jerusalem and the implications of the mention of the leaves of the tree for the conversion of the nations, the first words in 22:3 "and there is no curse any longer" would likely have at least a double meaning for the hearers. On the one hand, it is very difficult to imagine that the lifting of the restriction to the fruit of the tree of life and its immediate availability in the New Jerusalem could be seen as anything other than the removal of the curse incurred by humanity via the disobedience of Adam and Eve.[39] On the other hand, the recent emphasis upon the healing of the nations would likely suggest that reference to the absence of a curse in 22:3 would convey to the hearers the sense that the nations are also in mind, specifically, that the ban of destruction placed upon the enemies of God has now been lifted (Zech. 14:11).[40] No curse remains upon humanity or the nations in New Jerusalem, for eternal life is available to all there.

What are the results of this hearing of the Apocalypse? First, it has shown that the conversion of the nations is indeed a theme of major importance in the Apocalypse. The evidence for this conclusion comes in the form of subtle hints ("peoples" rather than "people"), calls to pneumatic discernment (the theological significance of the geographical directions of the 12 gates of the city), and explicit statements about the presence of the kings of the earth and the nations in the New Jerusalem. Second, at the same time, these affirmations with regard to the conversion of the nations are accompanied by warnings that not all will enter into the holy city (21:8, 27), but only those who overcome. Third, these two emphases stand in some tension with one another and are never fully reconciled in the Apocalypse. Fourth, though the hearers come away from the Apocalypse with the knowledge that the conversion of the nations is a foregone conclusion, they

---

39. F. J. Murphy, *Fallen Is Babylon: The Revelation to John* (Harrisburg: Trinity Press International, 1998), p. 429.

40. Mathewson, "Destiny," pp. 139-41.

never learn at which point such a conversion takes place or even how it occurs. It is treated simply as part of the terrain. Fifth, rather than seeking to gain leverage on this topic by extra-textual evidence or by allowing the power of one of the images (the conversion of the nations) to override and even obliterate the exclusion passages (those who cannot enter into the holy city), this hearing has sought to allow meaning to emerge from the theological dialectic of the text that forms the hearers — that is to say, it seeks to allow each end of this seemingly irreconcilable dialectic to have its say. Sixth, as such, this hearing suggests that these seemingly disparate emphases would serve to form the hearers as they seek to offer faithful witness to a hostile world. Following the lead of Jesus ("the faithful witness"), Antipas ("my faithful witness"), and the two prophetic witnesses in chapter 11, the hearers realize that they are called to bear pneumatic faithful witness even unto death. Though there are occasional hints in the text of the Apocalypse that such witness will be met by the conversion of the nations (as in chapter 11), for the most part the vision has described near wholesale rejection of their prophetic message and it includes description after description of the eternal punishment of those who oppose God and his people. Given this context, the incredible scenes of New Jerusalem would stretch their discerning abilities to their limits, suggesting that despite the opposition to and rejection of their faithful witness that surrounds them, their faithful witness is not as ineffective as it may appear. Rather, an unbelievable harvest awaits; one that they have not heretofore expected nor even been able to envision. For despite the fact that kings and nations will no doubt be slain, dying in their obstinate refusal to repent for the works of their hands, kings and nations will have access to New Jerusalem, where they will worship God and the Lamb, walk in their light, drink of the river of life, find healing in the leaves of the tree of life. Such a vision could not help but encourage the hearers to continue their faithful witness to a hostile unbelieving world, for despite the opposition and rejection of their witness, their faithful witness will bear fruit; unbelievable fruit; fruit they could not imagine; fruit they will not see until they themselves are part of the New Jerusalem. Indeed, their works will follow them (14:13b).

Moses as "God" in Philo of Alexandria: A Precedent for Christology?

Richard Bauckham

In the attempt to understand the origins of early Christology in its Jewish context, scholars have given considerable attention to figures, both human and angelic, who are alleged to be accorded divine or at least semi-divine status in early Jewish literature. Among these figures is Moses, in whose case the writings of Philo are of interest. Moses is the only human individual to whom Philo actually applies the term "god" (θεός). This rather remarkable usage, along with some related statements about Moses by Philo, has been found relevant to Christology in two rather contrasting ways. Some scholars have understood Philo to be speaking about a real deification of Moses: the transformation of the human Moses into a heavenly divine being (subordinate to the supreme God). As Crispin Fletcher-Louis puts it, "It is well known that in the second Temple period Philo deified Moses."[1] The work of Wayne Meeks has been particularly influential in advancing this view.[2] This would make Philo's Moses a precedent for a Christology that attributes some kind of ontological divinity to Jesus. But other scholars have

---

[1] Crispin H. T. Fletcher-Louis, *Luke-Acts: Angels, Christology and Soteriology* (Tübingen: Mohr Siebeck, 1997), p. 173; cf. also Crispin H. T. Fletcher-Louis, "4Q374: A Discourse on the Sinai Tradition: The Deification of Moses and Early Christology," *DSD* 3 (1996): pp. 236-52, here pp. 242-43. Other scholars who take this view of Philo's Moses and relate it to Christology include Wayne A. Meeks, *The Prophet-King: Moses Traditions and the Johannine Christology* (Leiden: Brill, 1967), p. 296; Charles A. Gieschen, *Angelomorphic Christology: Antecedents and Early Evidence* (Leiden: Brill, 1998), p. 165.

[2] Especially Wayne A. Meeks, "Moses as God and King," in *Religions in Antiquity*, ed. Jacob Neusner (Leiden: Brill, 1968), pp. 354-71.

taken Philo's use of the term "god" for Moses to be figurative or metaphorical. Recently, James Dunn finds it significant that Philo, despite being a monotheist, "had no apparent difficulty in using such language hyperbolically or in symbolic terms." It shows that adherence to the *Shema* "did not prevent" Jews of that period "from using god-language metaphorically or with poetic flourish."[3] The implication is that similarly "divine" language about Jesus in the New Testament may not be intended too literally.

Finally, Larry Hurtado's discussion should be mentioned specifically, because he relates his interpretation of Philo to his general claim that in early Judaism there was a notion of "exalted patriarchs," humans given power and glory in heaven, where they remain figures distinct from God, but rule the cosmos as God's plenipotentiary or vicegerent. Hurtado has learned from Carl Holladay's work that when Philo portrays Moses as "god" his meaning is predominantly figurative and ethical, but he gives sufficient credence to Meeks' arguments to suppose that behind Philo's work there must have been a tradition of regarding Moses as God's chief agent in his sovereignty over the world.[4]

Philo's usage deserves a more careful investigation.[5] A good place to begin is with recognizing that, whether Philo's use of the term "god" for Moses is literal or metaphorical or figurative or poetic, it is most certainly *exegetical*, in that in every case Philo is echoing the biblical text. The word "god" (אלהים) is used of Moses in the Hebrew Bible on two occasions (Exod. 4:16; 7:1), but the Septuagint Greek avoids calling Moses "god" (θεός) on the first of these occasions. So, in Philo's Bible, the relevant text is Exodus 7:1, where God says to Moses, "Look, I have appointed (δέδωκα) you a god to Pharaoh [or: Pharaoh's god] and Aaron will be your prophet."

Philo quotes or makes clear allusion to Exodus 7:1 at least ten

---

3. James D. G. Dunn, *Did the First Christians Worship Jesus? The New Testament Evidence* (London: SPCK/Louisville: Westminster John Knox Press, 2010), p. 66.

4. Larry W. Hurtado, *One God, One Lord: Early Christian Devotion and Ancient Jewish Monotheism* (Philadelphia: Fortress Press, 1988), pp. 59-63.

5. The fullest and the most important study is Carl R. Holladay, *Theios Aner in Hellenistic Judaism: A Critique of the Use of This Category in New Testament Christology* (Missoula: Scholars Press, 1977), pp. 108-63, to which I am much indebted. It is oriented to the question of whether Philo uses the alleged existing category of "divine man" to portray Moses. The achievement of his book was thoroughly to deconstruct this category. Consequently I do not regard it as a relevant issue in the present discussion.

times (in the order in which we shall discuss them: *Quod omnis probus liber sit* 43-44; *De somniis* 2.189; *De mutatione nominum* 19, 125-129; *De migratione Abrahami* 84, 169; *De sacrificiis Abelis et Caini* 9; *Quod deterius potiori insidiari soleat* 161-162; *Legum allegoriae* 1.40; *De vita Mosis* 1.158).[6] There is also a probable case of implicit allusion (*Opif.* 69, which will be discussed in connexion with *Leg.* 1.40). For our purposes the two most interesting texts are *Quod omnis probus liber sit* 43-44 and *De vita Mosis* 1.158, and we shall give detailed attention to these, while discussing the other nine texts more briefly.

1. *Quod omnis probus liber sit* 42-44

(42) And, in addition to this, who would not agree that the friends of God (τοὺς φίλους τοῦ θεοῦ) are free? For, unless it is conceded that not only freedom but also dominion (ἀρχήν) belongs to close companions (ἑταίροις) of kings, inasmuch as they share in the oversight and management of the realm, then one must ascribe slavery to those (companions) of the Olympian gods who, because they are lovers of God(s) (φιλόθεον), have thereby become loved by God(s) (θεοφιλεῖς), having been honored in return with goodwill that is truly justified, and are, as the poets say, rulers of all (πανάρχοντες), indeed, kings of kings. (43) But the legislator of the Jews, with even more audacity, went a step further, as if he were a naked Cynic, and was presumptuous enough to say that the one who is possessed by divine love (ἔρωτι θείῳ) and worships only the Existent One (τὸ ὄν μόνον θεραπεύοντα) is no longer "man" but "god," but, mind you, a "god" of humans, not a "god" of the natural order, thereby reserving for the Father of all the position of being King and God of gods (τὸ θεῶν εἶναι βασιλεῖ καὶ θεῷ). (44) Now, I ask you, does one who has obtained such a privilege as this deserve to be regarded as a slave, or as free and free alone? Even if he has not been deemed worthy of divine status in his own right (θείας οὐκ ἠξίωται μοίρας καθ'

---

6. There is also a quotation in a Greek fragment of the *Quaestiones in Exodum* (book 2, fragment 6, in Ralph Marcus, *Philo: Supplement II: Questions and Answers on Exodus*, Loeb Classical Library [London: Heinemann/Cambridge, Mass.: Harvard University Press, 1953], pp. 241-42), which appears to take Exodus 7:1 as an example of the figurative use of language for a ruler. But there is too little context to make much of this reference and it is impossible to be sure how far the text really preserves what Philo wrote.

αὐτόν), at least, because he was treated as a friend by God (διὰ τὸ φίλῳ θεῷ), he was bound to have absolute and continuous happiness. For God, since he is companionable (φιλικῶν), is neither a frail champion nor one who neglects friendship rights, and he oversees those affairs that pertain to his companions (ἑταίρους).[7]

Philo's *Quod omnis probus liber sit* ("Every good man is free") is a philosophical treatise defending the Stoic "paradox" that only the wise man is free. For Stoic thought in this period, the truly wise man is also the truly good man, the one who understands and practises virtue. Thus Philo's own version of the paradox is: "only the good man (ὁ ἀστεῖος) is free" (*Prob.* 1), but he also makes use of parallel paradoxes: that only the wise (good) man is a king and that only the wise (good) man is happy. (There is allusion to both of these in the passage quoted above.) Also from Stoic discussion comes the notion that the wise or good are "friends of God," the notion that holds together the quoted passage.

Unlike many of Philo's works, the *Quod omnis probus* is not an exegetical but a purely philosophical treatise, but he does occasionally support his argument from the Pentateuch, assuming that the good man according to Moses closely resembles the Stoic ideal. On these few occasions he is doing what he does at great length in other works: expounding the Pentateuch by means of Hellenistic philosophy. Given the rarity of these passages in *Quod omnis probus* (cf. 29, 57, 68-69) it is striking that the one quoted above (42-44) turns on two texts about Moses — Exodus 7:1 (where Moses is called "God") and Exodus 33:11 (where Moses is called God's "friend") — as well as alluding to the *Shema* and the first commandment ("the one who is possessed by divine love and worships only the Existent One") and citing the biblical divine title "God of gods" (Deut. 10:17). The density of biblical reference in this short section contradicts the supposition that this work dates from an early period when Philo "still had the dialectic of the philosophical schools fresh in mind and before he had settled down to his life's work of interpreting the Pentateuch."[8] Such a view of Philo's intellectual development has been refuted on other evidence also.[9]

---

7. Translation from Holladay, *Theios Aner*, pp. 132-33, with minor alterations.
8. F. H. Colson in *Philo*, Loeb Classical Library 9 (Cambridge, Mass./London: Harvard University Press, 1941), p. 2; cf. also Holladay, *Theios Aner*, pp. 129-52.
9. Abraham Terian, "A Critical Introduction to Philo's Dialogues," *ANRW* 2.21.1 (1984): 272-94, here pp. 292-94.

In the quoted passage, Philo presents both an argument from Gentile Hellenistic thought (42) and an argument from Jewish Scripture (43-44). Starting from the accepted view that the virtuous man is a "friend of God," he presents an analogy from the close companions of an earthly monarch, who participate in the government of the realm. By analogy the friends of God participate in God's rule, and are called by the Greek poets "rulers of all" and "kings of kings." The meaning is not that they literally take part in the government of the cosmos, but the Stoic idea that the virtuous man, being master of himself and not a slave to his passions, conforms to the universal law of nature and so possesses natural authority over the ignorant and wicked (for Philo's use of this Stoic idea, cf. *Prob.* 20; *Mut.* 151-153; *Sobr.* 57; *Migr.* 197; *Somn.* 2.244; *Abr.* 261). As Philo says of Abraham: "by those among whom he settled he was regarded as a king, not because of the outward state that surrounded him, for he was merely a commoner (ἰδιώτης), but because of his greatness of soul, for his spirit was the spirit of a king" (*Virt.* 216).[10]

From the Gentile poets Philo turns to the writings of Moses and points out that they are daring enough to call the virtuous man not only "friend of God" but also "god." In the Pentateuch these terms apply only to Moses himself, but evidently presupposed by Philo here is the idea that Moses was the ideal virtuous man, so that the terms Moses applies to himself also apply to other virtuous men (whom Philo thinks are rare but far from non-existent, cf. *Prob.* 62-74). Philo makes a point here of giving the virtuous man a distinctively Jewish definition: "the one who is possessed by divine love [i.e. love for God, cf. Deut. 6:5] and worships only the Existent One [cf. Exod. 20:4-5; Deut. 5:8-9; 6:13]." The definition echoes both the *Shema* and the first commandment of the Decalogue, referring to the exclusive worship of and devotion to the God of Israel that marked Jews out from pagans. This characterization of the virtuous man according to Moses is directly related to the way Philo goes on to qualify carefully the sense in which Moses calls the virtuous man "god." Unlike the Greek poets, Philo cannot call him "ruler of all" or "king of kings," for sovereignty over the whole cosmos is the exclusive prerogative of the Existent One, for whom Philo uses both the Stoic term "Father of all" and the scriptural term "king and God of gods" (cf. Deut. 10:17: "God of gods and Lord of lords"). The vir-

---

10. Translation from F. H. Colson, *Philo*, Loeb Classical Library 8 (Cambridge, Mass./London: Harvard University Press, 1939), p. 297, with minor alterations.

tuous man can therefore be called a god only in relation to humans, not in relation to the rest of creation. It is notable that, even though Philo is not referring to literal government but to the ethical superiority of the virtuous man (as in, e.g., *Mut.* 151-153), he finds it necessary to insist that sovereignty over the whole cosmos belongs only to God. It is also notable that he makes this point in the context of a philosophical treatise whose general argument applies to Jew and Gentile without distinction.

Thus Philo stresses both the remarkable nature of the use of the term "god" for a man in the Jewish Scriptures, but also the restricted sense in which it is used. That the virtuous man "is no longer 'man' but 'god'" is not a claim to transformation of nature but to the privileged status God grants his "friends." Like the companions of a monarch, the virtuous man is not a slave to God. He is subordinate but free. The presupposition in this argument is that friendship implies likemindedness. The virtuous man reflects the goodness of God voluntarily, not under constraint, as a slave does.

A feature of most of Philo's interpretations of "god" in Exodus 7:1 is that he associates the term with rule. In this passage the most obvious point is that he takes it to be equivalent to "friend of God," but the connotation of rule is certainly also present, carried over from the preceding discussion of the non-Jewish understanding of "friend of God." That the virtuous man is "a god of humans" must mean that he exercises some kind of rule over them, viz. the inherent authority of the virtuous man over the ignorant and wicked. But this is something much less than participation in God's supreme sovereignty over all things.

Philo's exegesis of Exodus 7:1 in *Quod omnis probus liber sit* 43-44 is allegorical in that he is not concerned with Moses as a historical individual but with the generic category of "the virtuous man," of whom he implicitly regards Moses as a notable example. This is only one of many allegorical uses of the text that Philo propounds in other passages, as can be briefly demonstrated by a survey of other passages in which Philo interprets Exodus 7:1.

2. Other Passages

In *De somniis* 2.189, he takes the high priest Aaron as an allegorical symbol of the Logos, whom he situates on the boundary between God and humanity, neither God nor a human. This is shown by two texts about the high priest. Leviticus 16:17 (according to Philo's curious reading of the Greek text) shows that, while he was in the holy of holies, the high priest was not a man, while Exodus 7:1 shows that he was not God either, for in Exodus 7:1 the title "god" is given not to Aaron but to Moses. Thus, in that verse read allegorically, Moses stands for God (the Existent One himself) and Aaron for the Logos.

In *De mutatione nominum* 19, Philo again allegorizes the characters in Exodus 7:1, but this time Moses and Pharaoh. He is arguing that God does not call himself God of the wicked, but only Lord and Master of them (whereas he does call himself God of good people). This is proved by the fact that in Exodus 7:1, where Pharaoh represents the wicked, God does not call himself "God of Pharaoh" but gives that title to Moses.

Pharaoh is again taken to represent the wicked in *De mutatione nominum* 125-129. Just as in Stoic thought it is the wise man who is virtuous, so the wicked is a fool. So, in Exodus 7:1, Moses, representing the good man, is called the god of Pharaoh "because he is wise and therefore the ruler (ἄρχων) of every fool." Philo goes on to say that, just as "the Ruler of all" (God) exercises his judgment with mercy, so the virtuous man shows beneficence, a quality that belongs to kings (see also *Spec.* 4.187-188). So in this text Philo combines the idea that the virtuous man is called "god" because, by virtue of his ethical superiority, he "rules over" fools, with the idea that the virtuous man is called "god" because he resembles God in virtue. Needless to say Philo says nothing in this passage that applies to Moses in particular, rather than virtuous people in general.

Philo deploys yet another kind of allegory in *De migratione Abrahami* 84, where he takes up the relationship in which Exodus 7:1 puts Aaron as prophet or spokesman for Moses. Aaron speaks what Moses thinks. Moses represents God, while Aaron represents the prophet who speaks the mind of God. Later in the same work (169) Philo makes the same relationship between Moses and Abraham an allegory of the relation of human reason to human speech.

In *De sacrificiis Abelis et Caini* 9, Philo is again discussing the ideal wise man, the super-sage. To enable such a perfect human to govern the passions of the soul God has not merely given the "common excellence" (κοινὴν τινα ἀρετήν) that rulers and kings (such as Pharaoh) have, but has "appointed him as god, putting all the bodily region and the mind that rules it (τὸν ἡγεμόνα αὐτῆς νοῦν) in subjection and slavery to him." Once again, in quoting Exodus 7:1 to establish this, Philo reads the text as referring, not to Moses as a unique individual, but to Moses as representing a very select class of people that God raises above the ordinary human level, and once more he employs the Stoic paradox that the wise man is the true king, though the point here is that he has total sovereignty over his own being, body and mind, experiencing no passions whatsoever. Once again "god" is understood to function as ethical allegory, not as a matter of metaphysical nature. Philo does say of Moses or the wise man that God "loaned him to the inhabitants of earth and allowed him to get acquainted with them" (τοῖς περιγείοις χρήσας αὐτὸν εἴασεν ἐνομιλεῖν),[11] but Philo thought all rational souls were pre-existent. In this case, according to David Winston, Philo is referring to "that category of rational souls that ordinarily never leave the supernal regions for embodiment below"[12] — an exceptional class of souls to which Moses belongs.

In *Quod deterius potiori insidiari soleat* 161-162, Philo is arguing that, since God alone has true being, human virtue can be only "a copy and likeness" of God's virtue. Consequently, when God appointed Moses "a god to Pharaoh," Moses did not become such "in reality" (πρὸς ἀλήθειαν) but only "in a manner of speaking" (δόξῃ). The point is proved by the observation that God cannot be the passive recipient of an action (as Moses is in Exodus 7:1) but only active. Moses is no more truly a god than a counterfeit coin is an authentic coin. But when, as a wise man, he is put alongside a fool (represented in the text by Pharaoh), the contrast is such that he may appear to be a god in the opinion of humans. This interpretation of the text is essentially the view we have met already: that the virtuous man is called a god because his virtue reflects the virtue of God. But here Philo is particularly concerned to stress the metaphysical divide between Creator and creation, such that human virtue can be no more than a reflection of God's.

In *Legum allegoriae* 1.40, Philo finds an anthropological allegory in Exodus 7:1: Moses represents the human mind (νοῦς), while Pharaoh apparently represents the irrational part of the soul. The reason Philo

---

11. The meaning of this clause is not entirely clear, but my translation takes a cue from David Winston, "Judaism and Hellenism: Hidden Tensions in Philo's Thought," *SPhilo* 2 (1990): 1-19, here p. 11.

12. Winston, "Judaism," p. 11.

gives here for the use of the term "god" for Moses and therefore, by means of the allegory, for the human mind, is that God, in creating the human being, breathed life directly into the mind, whereas it is the mind that imparts life to the irrational part of the soul. (The argument reflects Philo's pervasive concern not to place God in a direct relationship with anything material and mortal.) This particular allegorization of Exodus 7:1 is also facilitated by the familiar association of "god" with rule, for Philo tells us that the mind is the dominant element (ἡγεμονικόν) of the soul (39).

Philo's argument in *Legum allegoriae* 1.40 makes it very likely that Exodus 7:1 has also influenced his thinking in *De opificio mundi* 69, although there is no explicit allusion there. Philo is interpreting the statement in Genesis 1:26 that humanity was made "after the image and likeness of God." The word "image" does not refer to the body, but to the human mind, the ruling element (ἡγεμονικόν) of the soul, which is "after a fashion (τρόπον τινὰ) a god to the one who carries and bears it as a divine image (ἀγαλματοφοροῦντος),[13] for the human mind evidently occupies a position in humans resembling that which the great Ruler (ἡγεμών) occupies in the whole universe." The human mind (νοῦς) can thus be called "god" in that it rules and so reflects the ruling character of the cosmic νοῦς, the Logos.[14]

From our survey of these texts, it is evident that, while Exodus 7:1 was evidently a favorite text (perhaps because of Philo's particular interest in the significance of names and titles), Philo has no consistent interpretation of it (even within a single work). We can, however, say that Philo's interpretation of "god" in this verse is usually connected with rule, such that the human person or component of a person to whom he understands the word to apply can be called "god" because they or it rules, in a way that reflects, on a limited scale, the supreme God's rule over the universe. It is surprising that when Philo interprets the verse by means of an allegory in which Moses stands for God himself (*Somn.* 2.189; *Mut.* 19; *Migr.* 84) the connotation of rule is absent. But the connexion between human and divine rule is present in *Quod omnis probus liber sit* 42-44 and *De opificio mundi* 69. Philo does not think that

---

13. Philo uses the same word with reference to the mind of Moses in *Mos.* 1.27. In the light of *Opif.* 69, this usage in *Mos.* 1.27 is perhaps less significant than has sometimes been thought.

14. Wendy E. Helleman, "Philo of Alexandria on Deification or Assimilation to God," *SPhilo* 2 (1990): 51-71, here pp. 66-67.

humans can literally share in the divine nature, and so the word "god" can be justified only in an analogical sense, indicating ways in which a virtuous human can imperfectly reflect the virtues of God. Whenever Philo takes the text to refer to humans, he thinks of the Stoic ideal of the wise and virtuous man who is king, not in the ordinary sense of the ruler of a state or nation, but in the sense of ethical superiority over others or in the sense, also ethical, of being in control of his passions. Philo's exegesis is always allegorical. He is never in these texts concerned with Moses as a unique historical individual. At most he takes Moses in the text to be a (perhaps the best) representative of a select class of outstandingly wise men. However, the remaining text we have to consider belongs to Philo's biography of Moses, and so it is overtly concerned with the historical individual Moses.

3. *De vita Mosis* 1.155-158

> (155) And so, as he abjured the accumulation of lucre, and the wealth whose influence is mighty among humans, God rewarded him by giving him instead the greatest and most perfect wealth. That is the wealth of the whole earth and sea and rivers, and of all the other elements and the combinations that they form. For, since God judged him worthy to appear as a partner (κοινωνόν) of his own possessions, he gave into his hands the whole world as a portion well fitted for his heir. (156) Therefore, each of the elements obeyed him as its master (δεσπότῃ), changed its natural properties and submitted to his command, and this perhaps is no wonder.[15] For if, as the proverb says, what belongs to friends is common (κοινὰ τὰ φίλων),[16] and the prophet is called the friend of God, it would follow that he shares also God's possessions, so far as he has need. (157) For God possesses all things and needs nothing; whereas the good man (ὁ σπουδαῖος ἄνθρωπος), though he possesses nothing in the proper sense (κυρίως), not even himself, partakes of the treasures of God so far as he is capable. And that is only reasonable, for he is a world citizen (κοσμοπολίτης), and therefore not on the

---

15. On the translation of this last phrase, see David Lenz Tiede, *The Charismatic Figure as Miracle Worker* (Missoula: SBL, 1972), p. 126 n. 45.

16. This maxim is found in Plato, Aristotle, Dio Chrysostom, and others; see Holladay, *Theios Aner*, p. 120.

roll of any city of the world, rightly so because he has received no mere piece of land but the whole world as his portion (κλῆρον). (158) Again, did he not enjoy greater fellowship (κοινωνίας) with the Father and Maker of the universe, seeing that he was deemed worthy to bear the same title (προσρήσεως τῆς αὐτῆς ἀξιωθείς)? For he was named god and king of the whole nation (ὅλου τοῦ ἔθνους θεὸς καὶ βασιλεύς), and entered, we are told, into the darkness where God was, that is into the unseen, invisible, incorporeal and archetypal essence of existing things, perceiving (κατανοῶν) what is invisible to mortal nature, and, in himself and his life displayed for all to see, he has set before us, like some well-wrought picture, a piece of work beautiful and godlike (θεοειδὲς), a model (παράδειγμα) for those who are willing to copy it (μιμεῖσθαι).[17]

In a work written primarily for a non-Jewish audience,[18] Philo is here presenting Moses as the ideal philosopher-king. (Elsewhere in the work he presents him also as the ideal priest, the best-qualified lawgiver, and the greatest prophet.) This entails portraying him as the ideal sage or virtuous man, according to Stoic principles, but with an admixture also of the Platonic ideal of the philosopher-king, the ideal king who governs well because he is also a philosopher. (Philo actually quotes Plato on this point at *Mos.* 2.2, paraphrasing *Resp.* 473c-d.) The Stoic element in the portrait is similar to the way Philo understands the representative figure of Moses in *Quod omnis probus liber sit* 42-44 and other passages, but the Platonic element is a useful addition because here Philo wants to depict Moses as a ruler, not just in the figurative-ethical sense of the Stoic sage, but also as literally the ruler of the Israelite people.

As in *Quod omnis probus liber sit* 42-44, Philo brings to the discussion not only Exodus 7:1 but also Exodus 33:11, where Moses is called "friend of God." Again he exploits the Stoic-Cynic use of that term by appealing to the well-known maxim, "Friends have all things in common," with the implication that a friend of God shares in God's possessions, which, of course, are the whole cosmos. Philo's statements are here very close to those of Diogenes the Cynic, as reported by Diogenes

---

17. Translation from F. H. Colson, *Philo*, Loeb Classical Library 6 (London: Heinemann/Cambridge, Mass.: Harvard University Press, 1935), pp. 357, 359, with minor alterations.

18. Louis H. Feldman, *Philo's Portrayal of Moses in the Context of Ancient Judaism* (Notre Dame: University of Notre Dame Press, 2007), pp. 11-16, though the point is disputed.

Laertius: "All things belong to the gods. The gods are friends to the wise, and friends share all property in common; therefore all things are the property of the wise."[19] The fact that the Stoic-Cynic wise man was understood to possess all things through his friendship with the gods suggests that we should not take Philo's language about Moses' possession of the whole cosmos as literally as some scholars have done.[20] We should also notice the qualifications that Philo introduces, even though his purpose is clearly to magnify the figure of Moses as much as possible. Moses shares God's possessions "as far as he has need" and partakes of God's treasures "so far as he is capable." This does not sound like the cosmic rule of God's vicegerent, which is the role that Wayne Meeks and others have found in this text,[21] but rather Moses had the privilege of access to divine resources when he needed and so far as he was able to deploy them.

In fact, it would probably be a mistake to take this part of Philo's portrait of Moses (155-157) as referring to Moses' literal kingship. Like Philo's account of Moses' virtues, which qualify him for kingship but are themselves the virtues to which every sage aspires, so his account of Moses' enjoyment of the whole cosmos as his God-given "wealth" is the privilege of the sage, not a unique gift to Moses. Philo, in fact, explicitly generalizes the point, as he does so regularly in the other passages about Moses as "god" that we have already considered: "*the good man . . . partakes of the treasures of God so far as he is capable*" (157). Philo goes on to say that this is reasonable since the good man is a citizen of the world (κοσμοπολίτης), a standard Stoic understanding of the virtuous or wise person. So, despite the fact that Philo is explicitly describing the historical individual Moses, he has not discarded his usual habit of treating Moses as representative of the wise or virtuous man as such. He seems to want, here as elsewhere in *De vita Mosis,* to portray Moses as the most wise and most virtuous of all, the super-sage, but the difference from other outstandingly wise men is one of degree. Moses does not differ radically in kind from the ideal Stoic sage, as he would if we were to suppose that Philo here depicts him as exalted to participate in God's cosmic sovereignty. The only kind of kingship Philo could envis-

---

19. Diogenes Laertius 6.72, quoted in Holladay, *Theios Aner,* p. 121.

20. E.g. P. Maurice Casey, *From Jewish Prophet to Gentile God: The Origins and Development of New Testament Christology* (Cambridge: James Clarke/Louisville: Westminster John Knox Press, 1991), p. 84.

21. Meeks, "Moses as God and King," p. 359.

age in this part of his argument is that of the Stoic sage whose moral superiority constitutes a metaphorical sort of rule.

This understanding of this section (155-157) removes what would otherwise be a puzzling incoherence, in that in the wider context, where Philo does refer to Moses' literal kingship, it is kingship of the nation of Israel, not rule over the cosmos, that is in view (147-151, 158, 163). Certainly, this rule over Israel has a kind of universal dimension:

> the kingship of a nation more populous and mightier [than Egypt], a nation destined to be consecrated above all others to offer prayers for ever on behalf of the human race that it may be delivered from evil and participate in what is good (*Mos.* 1.149).[22]

This expresses Philo's rather strong sense of the unique role of Israel in bringing benefit to all peoples, but it does not make Moses ruler of the nations, let alone of the whole cosmos. Even more significant, however, is that when Philo comes to the title "god" from Exodus 7:1 and interprets it as kingship, he makes no attempt to give it a universal or cosmic scope: "he was named god and king of the whole nation" (158). (The English is perhaps ambiguous, but in the Greek it is clear that Philo calls Moses god of the whole nation and king of the whole nation.) If Philo were concerned to portray Moses as God's cosmic vicegerent, it would surely be here, in relation to the title "god," that the point could be most effectively made. Instead, he interprets it as meaning no more than king of Israel.

Within the description of God's gift of the whole cosmos to Moses, there remains to be discussed the rather obscure statement:

> Therefore, each of the elements (στοιχείων) obeyed him as its master (δεσπότη), changed its natural properties and submitted to his command, and this perhaps is no wonder (*Mos.* 1.156).

Whatever precisely this means, we should note at once that, like the rest of its context, it does not claim to state something unique to Moses, for Philo goes on to explain the reason it is no wonder: friends of God share in God's possessions. The statement that the elements obeyed Moses has generally been understood to refer to Moses' miracles, but Carl Holladay, arguing for a wholly ethical, rather than thaumaturgical, reading of the

---

22. Translation from Colson, *Philo,* vol. 6, p. 355.

Moses as "God" in Philo of Alexandria

passage, argues that Stoic physics allows Moses' command of the elements to refer to his mastery of his human nature.[23] This would certainly cohere with other passages in Philo that we have discussed, but even David Runia, who otherwise agrees with Holladay's interpretation of the passage, is not convinced by this particular argument.[24]

A reference to Moses' miracles would be consistent with Philo's statement that Moses, as a friend of God, shares in God's possessions "so far as he has need" (156). A comparison with Philo's actual account of the ten plagues of Egypt (earlier in *De vita Mosis*) may teach us not to exaggerate what he means at this point. He sees the plagues as judgments carried out by the four elements (στοιχεῖα, as in 156) of the universe: earth, fire, air and water (96).

> He [God] distributed the punishments in this way: three belonging to the denser elements, earth and water, which have gone to make our bodily qualities what they are, he committed to the brother of Moses; another set of three, belonging to air and fire, the two most productive of life, he gave to Moses alone; one, the seventh, he committed to both in common; and the other three that go to complete the ten he reserved to himself.[25]

Though Moses is here, as we should expect, superior to Aaron, what is envisaged is far from a wholesale delegation of God's cosmic powers to Moses. On the contrary, God merely permits Moses to exercise some power over the elements on specific occasions at his command.

Having portrayed Moses as super-sage, with a friend's access to God's treasures, Philo goes on to a "greater" instance of Moses' fellowship with God his friend. He even shares the same title: "God and king" (158). (That this is something "greater" than what Philo has just described confirms our view that not until this point in the passage we are discussing does Philo refer to Moses' actual kingship, for which his virtue and wisdom qualify him.) Holladay and Runia agree that, in Philo's phrase "God and king," the second noun explicates the first.[26] We have already seen how regularly Philo's various interpretations of Exodus 7:1 associate the term "god" with rule. Here Philo is actually us-

---

23. Holladay, *Theios Aner*, pp. 121-22.
24. David T. Runia, "God and Man in Philo of Alexandria," *JTS* 39 (1988): 48-75, here p. 55 and n. 29.
25. Translation from Colson, *Philo*, vol. 6, pp. 325, 327, with minor alterations.
26. Holladay, *Theios Aner*, pp. 123-25; Runia, "God and Man," p. 54.

ing Exodus 7:1 to demonstrate that God appointed Moses as king (a term that the Pentateuch itself never applies to Moses).[27] That he refers to Moses as king of Israel, rather than as king in relation to Pharaoh (as we might expect from Exod. 7:1), is not surprising in view of Philo's flexible approach to exegesis. He could well, on this occasion, have understood the text to mean, not that Moses was to rule over Pharaoh, but that Moses should speak and act towards Pharaoh with the authority of the divinely appointed ruler of Israel.

At this point in Philo's discussion occurs also a transition from the model of the Stoic wise man to the model of the Platonic philosopher-king. When Philo writes that Moses "entered . . . into the darkness where God was, that is into the unseen, invisible, incorporeal and archetypal essence of existing things, perceiving (κατανοῶν) what is invisible to mortal nature," he alludes to Moses' ascent of Mount Sinai (Exod. 20:21: "Moses entered the darkness where God was"), but interprets it as the philosopher-king's intellectual perception of Plato's noumenal world, the paradigms of true virtue. As a result Moses was able to embody true virtue in his own life, becoming a model for his people to imitate, as Plato's ideal required.[28] At the same time it is entirely typical of Philo's thought that, at this high point of Moses' qualifications for ideal kingship, it is with moral excellence that he is concerned. Moses is the ideal king because he is the closest possible approximation to the Platonic idea of the Good and thereby enables his people also to reflect the Good to a lesser degree by imitating him. This focus on virtue makes it entirely inappropriate to postulate that a Jewish apocalyptic idea of an ascent of Moses to heaven, his heavenly enthronement and transformation into godlike form, lies behind Philo's text, as Meeks[29] and Peder Borgen[30] have supposed.[31] What Philo says is entirely ade-

---

27. Philo could well have understood Deut. 33:5 to use the word king of Moses.
28. Holladay, *Theios Aner*, pp. 126-27.
29. Meeks, "Moses as God and King," p. 355: "Philo is uniting the Hellenistic ideology of kingship with an existing midrashic tradition that interpreted Moses' ascent of Sinai as an ascension to heaven." Meeks reconstructs this tradition from a variety of rabbinic and Samaritan sources, a dubious procedure in itself. Even more dubious is the use of such a reconstructed tradition to interpret Philo. See also Meeks, *The Prophet-King*, pp. 111, 130.
30. Peder Borgen, *Philo of Alexandria: An Exegete for His Time* (Leiden: Brill, 1997), pp. 202-3.
31. Ian W. Scott, "Is Philo's Moses a Divine Man?," *SPhilo* 14 (2002): 87-111, here p. 107, objects to Holladay's reduction of "this passage to a hyperbolic description of

quately explained from the Hellenistic philosophical ideas that are his usual resources for exegesis of the Pentateuch. He betrays no knowledge of an enthronement of Moses and the only kind of transformation he recognizes is an ethical assimilation to the divine virtues.[32]

4. The Meaning of θεός

In order to assess the significance of Philo's interpretation of the word "god" (θεός) in Exodus 7:1, we should note some features of Philo's general use of the words θεός and θεῖος. Following common Hellenistic usage, Philo uses θεός not only of the one supreme God, but sometimes also for any of the incorporeal, intelligible beings: the Logos, angels, heavenly bodies and δαίμονες.[33] In a sense Philo must regard the term "god" as more appropriate to these heavenly beings than to the one God. It can only be applied to the one God "improperly" (according to κατάχρησις), since God is essentially nameless. As he says to Moses, "no name at all can properly be used of me, to whom alone existence belongs" (*Mos.* 1.75; cf., more fully, *Mut.* 11-15). God allows humans to use such terms as θεός and κύριος only because they must have some way of referring to him. This inappropriateness of θεός when used of the one God makes Philo's wider use of the term less significant than it might otherwise be. It certainly does not serve to put the one God in a category that includes all incorporeal beings. However, aside from the passages based on Exodus 7:1 that we have discussed, Philo never uses the term θεός to refer to humans in their embodied state. Incorporeality seems essential to his normal usage of the word.

The adjective θεῖος has a wider application.[34] It can mean "godlike"

Moses' kingship or his philosophical virtue," but his reference to *Mos.* 2.70, where Philo is merely paraphrasing the biblical text (Exod. 34:29-35), is a slender argument against it. He wishes to take Moses' title "god" as referring to a mediatorial role given to Moses by his mystical experience on Sinai, but Philo understands the title only in relation to Moses' kingship. As the king who mirrors the divine virtues for his people's imitation, Moses may be said to be a mediator, but this is the only mediatorial sense Philo seems to give to the term "god." Essentially Scott seems to agree ("Philo's Moses," pp. 106-9).

32. See especially Helleman, "Philo of Alexandria." She discusses other passages in which Philo speaks of some sort of "divinization" of Moses or other humans.

33. See Helleman, "Philo of Alexandria," p. 70; Runia, "God and Man," p. 56.

34. See the survey of Philo's usage in Holladay, *Theios Aner,* pp. 177-83.

or simply "associated with God," when it is more or less interchangeable with τοῦ θεοῦ. Even so it is rarely applied to human persons. When Moses is once called "the divine prophet" (*Mos.* 2.188: τοῦ θείου προφήτου), the meaning is no more than "the prophet of God," with θεῖος used in place of τοῦ θεοῦ probably only for the sake of stylistic variation. In his early work, *De providentia*, which lacks any distinctively Jewish content, Philo evidently adopted the use of the term "divine men" (the relevant passages are extant only in Armenian) as a technical term for philosophers,[35] but in his works extant in Greek, where the word θεῖος occurs 555 times,[36] he never couples it with ἄνθρωπος and only once with ἀνήρ.[37] (The exceptional case is *Virt.* 177: "absolute sinlessness belongs to God alone, or possibly to a divine man.") While he frequently uses the biblical term "man of God" (ἄνθρωπος θεοῦ) for Moses, he never turns this into θεῖος ἄνθρωπος. In view of the common use of θεῖος as an epithet of humans in Greek literature,[38] Philo's avoidance of such terminology must be deliberate and significant. It is most likely connected with his Jewish concern, especially in relation to the imperial cult (see *Legat.* 114-118, on Caligula), that humans, even eminent humans, should not be worshipped. In discussing the claims of emperors to divinity, Philo can say that "sooner could God (θεόν) change into a human than a human into God" (*Legat.* 118).

In the light of all this evidence, Philo must have found the scriptural use of "god" with reference to Moses (Exod. 7:1) entirely out of line with his own usage of θεός. This explains why he does not give it, in his interpretations of that text, the meaning he ordinarily gives the word. Instead he takes it in this context to mean "ruler" or "king," a meaning he does not attribute to θεός in any other context. He has evidently concluded that, since Moses could not be called θεός in either his own or the common uses of that word, the word in Exodus 7:1 must be used in a special sense. Therefore we entirely misread Philo if we associate his use of the word θεός for Moses or for the wise and virtuous man of whom Moses is a good example or even for the human mind as the ruling element within humans with his use of the word θεός in other contexts. Notably Philo does not even adopt the term θεός from

---

35. Holladay, *Theios Aner*, pp. 183-86.
36. Feldman, *Philo's Portrayal*, p. 339.
37. Holladay, *Theios Aner*, p. 182.
38. Feldman, *Philo's Portrayal*, pp. 331-32.

its use in Exodus 7:1 and employ it with reference to Moses or the wise man in general when he is not actually engaged in interpretation of the text of Exodus 7:1. The usage of that verse is one that Philo employs only when he is actually interpreting that text.

5. A Precedent for Christology?

For the issue of relevance to Christology, the following findings of our study are the most significant:

(1) When Philo interprets the word "god" in Exodus 7:1 as a reference to humans (rather than as an allegory of some other kind), he always makes it refer to a class of people, of whom Moses is no more than an outstanding example. In these passages it does not refer to a unique role of Moses in the purposes of God, but rather to the character and status of the wise and virtuous man. This is even the case in *De vita Mosis* 1.155-157.

(2) In his interpretations of the word "god" in Exodus 7:1 it usually has a connotation of rule, but, in keeping with the reference to the wise and virtuous man in general, this rule has a figurative-ethical meaning, as it had for the Stoic thought on which Philo is drawing. It does not refer to literal participation in God's rule over the cosmos or to literal government on earth.

(3) Only in *De vita Mosis* 1.158 does Philo use the words of Exodus 7:1 to say something unique about Moses. There he paraphrases "god" in the text as "god of the whole nation (of Israel)" and takes this to mean that Moses is "king of the whole nation." Here the application to Moses is unique and the rule literal, but it refers to no more than Moses' leadership of the people of Israel on earth, as Philo narrates it in the rest of his biography.

(4) Representing Moses as the Platonic philosopher-king, Philo also, in *De vita Mosis* 1.158, interprets his ascent of Mount Sinai as a mystical-intellectual perception of the Platonic realm of Ideas, which enables Moses to embody them in his own life and thereby provide a model of virtue for his people. Philo connects this with his interpretation of Exodus 7:1 not because he thinks Moses was enthroned as king on Mount Sinai but because Moses' mystical-intellectual perception of the Ideas qualified him to be the ideal king.

(5) There is no indication here of a heavenly enthronement or

transformation into godlike form. Philo's thought is ethical and philosophical, mystical only in a Platonic philosophical way, quite unrelated to the Jewish apocalyptic tradition of visionary ascent to heaven or to the later tradition of Merkavah mysticism (however these two may be related to each other).

(6) Philo never takes "god" in Exodus 7:1 to refer to deification in the sense of elevation to divine status or transformation into divine nature. The deification in question is only that of the virtuous man who reflects the divine virtues in his understanding and life.

(7) In all his various interpretations of "god" in Exodus 7:1, Philo always finds a sense that is in some way allegorical or metaphorical. In that sense, Dunn is right to see the language as metaphorical, though "poetic flourish" is not something I would associate with Philo. What Dunn neglects, however, is that the usage is always strictly *exegetical*. It is only because the Pentateuch uses the word "god" in this text (and nowhere else with reference to a human being) that Philo uses it at all. It does not conform at all to his usage of the word elsewhere. Since it tells us nothing about the way Philo uses the word outside these eleven passages, it can also tell us very little about the attitude of Jews of this period to the use of god-language. The fact that Philo never uses the word "god" to refer to human beings outside these eleven passages, where he takes up a specific scriptural usage and gives it a special meaning, actually suggests that Jews would be very wary of using god-language of human beings.

(8) Properly understood, Philo does not portray Moses as God's vicegerent or exalted agent, and there is nothing to suggest that a tradition of regarding Moses in those terms lies anywhere behind his work (whether or not such a tradition existed). For Philo, Moses' role in God's purposes was purely and simply what the Pentateuch narrates. Certainly Philo portrays Moses as realising the highest ideals of virtue and wisdom, so that his leadership of his people and especially his role as legislator for his people are supremely exemplary, but he is an earthly king, not a cosmic viceroy.

Thus the implications for New Testament Christology are largely negative. Philo's use of the word "god" with reference to Moses provides no precedent for the attribution of divine nature or status to Jesus. Moses, for Philo, is neither deified ontologically nor exalted to a position of cosmic rule. Philo's figurative use of the term "god" for humans (in most of these cases wise and virtuous people generally, only

Moses as "God" in Philo of Alexandria

once Moses individually) is strictly limited to his explanations of the sole such use of the term in the Septuagint Pentateuch: Exodus 7:1. The figurative meaning he gives it there ("ruler") is not a meaning he gives the word anywhere else in his work. His usage can hardly be used as evidence for a figurative use of "god" other than in exegesis of Exodus 7:1.

Jesus and the Spirit in Biblical and Theological Perspective: Messianic Empowering, Saving Wisdom, and the Limits of Biblical Theology

Mark L. Strauss

It is a joy to offer this article in honor of my mentor and friend, Professor Max Turner. Few have written with greater insight and clarity than Max on the role of the Holy Spirit in Luke-Acts in particular, and in the life of Jesus and the early church in general. It is therefore a privilege to offer a very small contribution in an area so well-trodden by my distinguished mentor and colleague.

This short study has three parts. The first two summarize briefly the state of research on the role of the Spirit in Jesus' ministry in the Synoptic Gospels (especially Luke) and the Gospel of John, respectively. Much important work has been done on the empowering presence of the Spirit in the narrative theology of the Gospels. The third part has a more precarious purpose, which is to seek to cross the fragile bridge between biblical and systematic theology by exploring this role of the Spirit with reference to the humanity and deity of the incarnate Christ.

1. Jesus and the Spirit in the Synoptic Gospels (especially Luke-Acts)

Research on Jesus and the Spirit over the last century has centered on the nature of Jesus' Spirit-endowment and the relationship of his experience of the Spirit to that of the early church.[1] In his groundbreaking

---

1. For a detailed survey of the debate over the last century see Max Turner, *Power from on High: The Spirit in Israel's Restoration and Witness in Luke-Acts* (Sheffield: Sheffield Academic Press, 1996), pp. 20-79.

Jesus and the Spirit in Biblical and Theological Perspective

work, *Baptism in the Holy Spirit,* James D. G. Dunn argued that Jesus' experience of the Spirit at his baptism was more than just an empowerment to accomplish his messianic task. It was a decisive moment in his experience of sonship to God, marking his own entrance into the new creation and the inauguration of the kingdom of God. Jesus' experience thus became the model and archetype for all Christians, whose reception of the Spirit marks their entrance into new covenant life and blessings of the kingdom of God. As Dunn puts it, "What Jordan was to Jesus, Pentecost was to the disciples. As Jesus entered the new age and covenant by being baptized in the Spirit at Jordan, so the disciples followed him in like manner at Pentecost."[2]

Dunn's claims ran counter to traditional Pentecostal theology (to which he was in part responding), which viewed the Spirit as a *donum superadditum* ("subsequent gift") of prophetic empowerment that comes at some time *after* salvation. The Spirit's work for Dunn was essentially soteriological, bringing new covenant life and eschatological sonship to all who believed. In this way Luke and Paul share similar perspectives, since for Paul the Spirit is the regenerating agent who provides believers with eschatological sonship and entrance into the new age (Rom. 8:13-16).

Dunn's views have been challenged by various scholars, most comprehensively by Robert Menzies.[3] Building on the work of Eduard Schweizer,[4] Menzies argued that the Judaism of Jesus' day viewed the Spirit almost exclusively as the "Spirit of prophecy," meaning the power of revelation or inspired speech. Only rarely is the Spirit portrayed as

---

2. James D. G. Dunn, *Baptism in the Holy Spirit: A Re-examination of the New Testament Teaching on the Gift of the Spirit in relation to Pentecostalism Today* (Philadelphia: Westminster, 1970), p. 40. Cf. James D. G. Dunn, *Jesus and the Spirit: A Study of the Religious and Charismatic Experience of Jesus and the First Christians as Reflected in the New Testament* (Grand Rapids: Eerdmans, 1975), esp. pp. 41-67, 135-96. Dunn builds on the earlier work of H. von Baer, *Der Heilige Geist in den Lukasschriften* (Stuttgart: Kohlhammer, 1926), p. 167.

3. Robert P. Menzies, *The Development of Early Christian Pneumatology with Special Reference to Luke-Acts* (Sheffield: JSOT Press, 1991); Robert P. Menzies, *Empowered for Witness: The Spirit in Luke-Acts* (Sheffield: Sheffield Academic Press, 1994). Similar views have been developed (with some variation) by Roger Stronstad, *The Charismatic Theology of Saint Luke* (Peabody: Hendrickson, 1984) and G. Haya-Prats, *L'Esprit force de l'église* (Paris: Cerf, 1975).

4. E. Schweizer, "πνεῦμα, πνευματικός," *TDNT,* 6:405ff.; E. Schweizer, *The Holy Spirit* (London: SCM Press, 1981).

the power behind miracles and almost never as imparting salvation.[5] According to Menzies, for Jesus and the earliest church the Spirit was the power for Jesus' preaching and miracles and, after Jesus' resurrection, the power for prophetic witness by the church. It was Paul who first identified the Spirit with the gift of salvation and eschatological restoration. While for Paul the Spirit is the agent of salvation and entrance into the new age, providing new covenant life and sonship, the church before him viewed the Spirit as exclusively the power for mission and witness. Luke himself took up this early Christian view of the Spirit, but stressed even more strongly the Spirit of prophecy and downplayed the connection between the Spirit and miracles (found in Matthew and Mark). An example of this can be seen in the Q saying about the power behind Jesus' exorcisms, where Luke alters Matthew's (= Q's) "by the Spirit of God" (Matt. 12:28) to read "by the finger of God" (Luke 11:20).[6] Against Dunn, who sees the promise of the Spirit against the background of the covenant renewal and eschatological salvation found in Ezekiel 36 and Jeremiah 31, Menzies claims that Luke himself sets the Spirit's coming in the context of Joel 2:28-32, a promise of prophetic empowerment for witness, not miracles or eschatological salvation.

Between the views of Dunn and Menzies, Max Turner has charted a mediating course.[7] To establish common ground, he notes five areas of broad consensus concerning Lukan pneumatology.[8] These are significant and so worth listing: (1) *The essential background for Luke's pneumatological material is Jewish and deeply rooted in the Old Testament.* The attempts by H. Leisegang and others from the History of Religions school to derive Lukan pneumatology from Greek mysticism or Mantic prophetism have been largely rejected. (2) *The Spirit is the uniting motif and the driving force within the Lukan salvation history, and provides the legitimization of the mission in which this leads.* It is this theme that holds to-

---

5. Menzies, *Development*, pp. 52-111. For Menzies, only in 1QH[a] and Wisdom of Solomon do we see the reception of saving wisdom through the Spirit as necessary for salvation.

6. Menzies, *Development*, pp. 185-90.

7. Turner, *Power*, passim; Max Turner, *The Holy Spirit and Spiritual Gifts — Then and Now*, rev. ed. (Carlisle: Paternoster, 1999), pp. 19-56; Max Turner, "The Spirit and Salvation in Luke-Acts," in *The Holy Spirit and Christian Origins. Essays in Honor of James D. G. Dunn*, ed. G. N. Stanton, B. W. Longenecker, and S. C. Barton (Grand Rapids: Eerdmans, 2004), pp. 103-16.

8. Turner, *Holy Spirit*, pp. 37-41; repeated in Turner, "Spirit and Salvation," p. 105.

Jesus and the Spirit in Biblical and Theological Perspective

gether the theological narrative of Luke-Acts, including the birth narrative, the messianic mission of Jesus, and the proclamation of messianic salvation in Acts. (3) *For Luke the Spirit is largely the "Spirit of prophecy"; in Acts especially as an "empowering for mission."* This priority is even conceded by Dunn in his later work, that is, that the Spirit for Luke is preeminently (though not exclusively) Joel's "Spirit of prophecy."[9] (4) *Correspondingly, Luke shows relatively little interest in the Spirit as the power for spiritual, ethical, and religious renewal of the individual.* The Spirit is portrayed by Luke primarily as charismatic empowering rather than ethical renewal. (5) *Luke's pneumatology develops beyond Judaism in giving the Spirit Christocentric functions.* In Acts the exalted and enthroned Messiah pours out the Spirit in God's place (Acts 2:33) and becomes present and known to the disciples *in* the Spirit. The "Spirit of the Lord" can be identified with the "Spirit of Jesus" (Acts 16:6-7).[10] In his later work, Turner identifies a sixth point of near consensus: that the Spirit is "normally" or "ideally" given at or in close temporal proximity to conversion-initiation.[11]

The major issue that remains in dispute is whether the Spirit in Luke-Acts is *exclusively* Joel's "Spirit of prophecy" and a *donum superadditum,* or whether the Spirit has moral, ethical, and soteriological functions. Here is where Turner charts a mediating course. With Schweizer and Menzies (and against Dunn), he affirms that the Spirit at Jesus' baptism provides him with messianic empowerment rather than new creation life (which is bestowed already at 1:35). Yet contrary to their view, he claims that this Spirit of prophecy is a "unique messianic version of this endowment," based especially on Isaiah 11:1-4 and the broader framework of the Isaianic New Exodus:

> The traditions of the Messiah of the Spirit expected the one endowed to be empowered by the Spirit to liberate Israel, and within the context of Isaianic New Exodus hope this "liberation" was readily extended to miracles of healing and deliverance. Equally (again *contra* Schweizer and Menzies) the traditions of the Messiah of the Spirit expected the one so endowed to exhibit a robust righ-

---

9. See James D. G. Dunn, "Baptism in the Spirit: A Response to Pentecostal Scholarship on Luke-Acts," *JPT* 3 (1993): 3-27, esp. p. 8. Statements to this effect can already be seen in his earlier *Jesus and the Spirit,* pp. 189-93.
10. Turner, *Holy Spirit,* pp. 40-41.
11. Turner, "Spirit and Salvation," p. 105.

teousness through the wisdom, knowledge, and fear of the Lord upon him (he was to purge Israel by it), and Luke 4:1b echoes this.[12]

It is this view, in my opinion, that best fits the broader historical context and the narrative theology of Luke-Acts. Even before his baptism, the Spirit's role in the conception (Luke 1:35) and the growth in wisdom (2:40, 52; cf. Isa. 11:1-4) of the messianic Son of God is placed in the context of Isaianic eschatological salvation (2:29-34; Isa. 40:5; 42:6; 49:6, 9). In Acts, the inauguration of the messianic reign at the exaltation/enthronement of the Messiah (Acts 2:30-36) is directly connected by Luke to the pouring out of the Spirit at Pentecost. This, in turn, is viewed by Luke through the lens of the Isaianic New Exodus, a theme that various commentators (including myself) have found central for Luke's soteriological, ecclesiological and Christological purposes.[13] Though Joel 2:28-32 is the only text explicitly cited by Luke with reference to the pouring out of the Spirit at Pentecost, from the birth narrative onward Luke has been drawing on a whole constellation of images related to Isaiah's portrait of eschatological salvation. Most significantly, perhaps, is Luke's reference to "power/Spirit from on high" at the key transitional point between the Gospel and Acts (Luke 24:49; Acts 1:8). The phrase echoes Isaiah 32:15-16 (cf. 44:3-5), which links the pouring out of the Spirit to the restoration of creation and the spiritual renewal of the people of God. With this reference, *"Luke appears to be pointing readers back to Isaiah himself for any answer to the question of by what power Israel's New Exodus eschatological restoration/salvation becomes richly present to the post-ascension community."*[14] Luke surely views the Spirit's role here as more than mere empowerment for witness.

2. Jesus and the Spirit in the Fourth Gospel

John's Gospel's has both similarities with and differences from the Synoptics with reference to the role of the Spirit in Jesus' life. As in the

---

12. Turner, *Holy Spirit*, pp. 34-35.
13. See David W. Pao, *Acts and the Isaianic New Exodus* (Grand Rapids: Baker, 2000), *passim*; Mark L. Strauss, *The Davidic Messiah in Luke-Acts: The Promise and Its Fulfillment in Lukan Christology* (Sheffield: Sheffield Academic Press, 1995), ch. 6; Turner, *Power*, pp. 140-315.
14. Turner, "Spirit and Salvation," p. 110 (italics his).

Jesus and the Spirit in Biblical and Theological Perspective

Synoptics, Jesus is the Spirit-endowed Messiah of Isaiah 11:1-4 who mediates the Spirit to his disciples as an empowerment for witness. Yet in John the Spirit is not identified as the means of miraculous powers for exorcism and healing, but rather the agent of revelatory wisdom.[15] Since in the Fourth Gospel such revelation is the means of salvation, the Spirit is by implication the agent of this salvation.

Some scholars have claimed that John's exalted Logos Christology so emphasizes the intimacy of relationship between the Father and the Son that the Spirit plays no significant role in Jesus' life.[16] This, however, is an overstatement. Gary Burge and others[17] have demonstrated that the Spirit continues to play a critical role in Johannine Christology and soteriology. Although John's Gospel does not narrate the baptismal anointing of Jesus, John the Baptist describes the event: "I saw the Spirit come down from heaven as a dove and remain on him" (1:32). The language of resting or remaining echoes Isaiah 11:2, so that the Spirit upon Jesus is presented as the empowerment of the Davidic Messiah.[18] Bennema concludes that "Jesus' experience at the Jordan is an endowment as Messiah and the allusions to Isaiah 11.2 (and 42.1) would naturally assume that *Jesus would be equipped by the Spirit to accomplish his ministry exactly through the gifts of charismatic wisdom, understanding, knowledge and liberating power.*"[19]

A second key reference to the Spirit in relation to Jesus in the Fourth Gospel is 3:34, the context of which is the superiority of Jesus' testimony over John the Baptist's and all previous revelation (3:31-36).[20]

---

15. Turner, *Holy Spirit*, p. 57.

16. Rudolf Bultmann, *The Gospel of John,* trans. G. R. Beasley-Murray (Oxford: Blackwell, 1971), p. 92 n. 4; E. Käsemann, *The Testament of Jesus: A Study of the Gospel of John in the Light of Chapter 17* (Philadelphia: Fortress Press, 1968), pp. 20-26; W. G. Kümmel, *The Theology of the New Testament: According to Its Major Witnesses, Jesus, Paul, John,* trans. John E. Steely (London: SCM Press, 1974), p. 314; E. Schweizer, "Πνεῦμα, πνευματικός," *TDNT,* 6:483.

17. Gary Burge, *The Anointed Community: The Holy Spirit in the Johannine Community* (Grand Rapids: Eerdmans, 1987), pp. 71-72, 81-110; cf. Felix Porsch, *Pneuma und Wort: Ein exegetischer Beitrag zur Pneumatologie des Johannesevangeliums* (Frankfurt: Knecht, 1974); Turner, *Holy Spirit,* pp. 58-59; Cornelis Bennema, *The Power of Saving Wisdom: An Investigation of Spirit and Wisdom in Relation to the Soteriology of the Fourth Gospel* (Tübingen: Mohr Siebeck, 2002), pp. 161-67.

18. Burge, *Anointed Community,* pp. 53-58; Turner, *Holy Spirit,* pp. 58-59.

19. Bennema, *Power,* p. 163. Cf. Turner, *Holy Spirit,* p. 59.

20. Craig S. Keener, *The Gospel of John: A Commentary,* 2 vols. (Peabody: Hendrickson, 2003), pp. 581-83.

While the subject of "*he* gives the Spirit without limit" could grammatically be either Jesus or God, it is almost certainly God, since "it can hardly be that Jesus speaks the word of God because *Jesus* gives the Spirit without measure."[21] The point is that "the *immeasurable* gift of the Spirit (of revelation) *to* Jesus corresponds to the perfection of revelation *through Jesus* — it provides a revelation which *transcends* the Law and the Prophets."[22] Jesus speaks the words of God because "God gives [him] the Spirit without limit" (3:34). A contrast may be intended with the Old Testament prophets, of whom it was said that "The Holy Spirit . . . rests on them only by measure" (*Lev. Rab.* 15.2). With this foundation in view, we can see that the Spirit plays a more prominent role in Jesus' life in the Fourth Gospel than is sometimes supposed. It is by virtue of this immeasurable revelatory gift of the Spirit that Jesus bestows the gift on others.

This understanding of the Spirit as revelatory and salvific wisdom from God provides the interpretive key to other passages in John 1–12. To be born "of water and the Spirit" (3:5) is likely a hendiadys, alluding to the water-and-Spirit eschatological cleansing predicted in Ezekiel 36:25-27.[23] The "living water" that brings eternal life in 4:10, 13-14 is clarified in 7:37-39 to be "the Spirit, which those who believed in him were to receive" (cf. 4:23). In 6:63 the life that the Spirit gives is appropriated through the words that Jesus has spoken, which are themselves "Spirit and life." This eternal life, though only fully realized after Jesus' death and resurrection, is available even now to those who respond in faith to Jesus, the true Wisdom from God.[24]

In summary, the common feature in the presentation of Jesus' relationship to the Spirit in the four Gospels is that the Spirit functions as the essential empowering and revelatory agent for Jesus to accomplish his messianic task. In the Synoptics Jesus heals the sick, casts out demons, and proclaims the kingdom of God — all in the

---

21. Turner, *Holy Spirit*, p. 59. So most commentators. See, e.g., Bultmann, *Gospel of John*, p. 164; C. K. Barrett, *The Gospel according to St. John*, 2nd ed. (Philadelphia: Westminster, 1978), p. 226; Burge, *Anointed Community*, pp. 83-84; G. R. Beasley-Murray, *John*, 2nd ed., Word Biblical Commentary 36 (Waco: Word, 1999), pp. 53-54; Andreas J. Köstenberger, *John*, Baker Exegetical Commentary on the New Testament (Grand Rapids: Baker, 2004), p. 139; Bennema, *Power*, pp. 164-65; Keener, *Gospel*, pp. 582-83.

22. Turner, *Holy Spirit*, p. 59; cf. Beasley-Murray, *John*, pp. 53-54.

23. Linda Belleville, "'Born of Water and Spirit': John 3:5," *TJ* 1 (1980): 125-41.

24. See further Turner, *Holy Spirit*, ch. 4; Bennema, *Power*, ch. 4.

power of the Spirit. In the Fourth Gospel the Spirit is the essential agent of revelatory wisdom, through which Jesus perfectly knows the Father and his will and reveals him to the world, providing salvation for all who believe.

This brief summary of the Spirit's role in Jesus' life raises intriguing questions when we move from biblical to systematic (dogmatic) theology. If Jesus in his incarnate state was fully divine, did he not have perfect knowledge and absolute power even apart from the Spirit? Why would he rely on the Spirit to know and reveal the Father or to perform miraculous deeds? It is to this question that we turn in the next section.

3. From Biblical to Systematic Theology: Jesus, the Spirit, and Incarnational Theology

The subtitle of Max Turner's *The Holy Spirit and Spiritual Gifts — Then and Now* indicates that his task is not just to describe the perspective of the biblical authors (i.e., "biblical theology"), but to contextualize the message for today. This, of course, is an essential part of biblical interpretation for those who view these documents not just as artifacts of religious experience, but as the authoritative Word of God, a message for believers today. Turner's concerns are primarily pneumatological, and so in subsequent chapters he investigates a theology of the Spirit, including such issues as whether the New Testament can be shown to justify a Trinitarian pneumatology and the nature and contemporary significance of spiritual gifts like tongues, prophecy, and healing.

But another theological question related to the Spirit is the intriguing relationship between pneumatology and Christology in the earthly life of Jesus. Orthodox Christians affirm that Jesus is "perfect in Godhead and also perfect in manhood; truly God and truly man" (Creed of Chalcedon) and Jesus' words and deeds in the Gospels are often appealed to in defense of Christ's true humanity and true divinity. But if the Spirit was the source of Jesus' miraculous powers and divine knowledge, what role did Jesus' divine nature play during his earthly ministry? Did the Son exercise personal authority as the Second Person of the Trinity, or did he act fully in his humanity, wholly dependent on the Spirit?

Mark L. Strauss

3.1. The Spirit as Mediator of Jesus' Divine Power and Insight

One New Testament scholar who has addressed this issue is Gerald Hawthorne. In his 1991 work, *The Presence & the Power,* Hawthorne investigates the role of the Spirit in Jesus' ministry. While the study is primarily a historical Jesus enquiry, from the outset Hawthorne has in mind the larger theological question of the relationship of the Spirit to Christ's deity. After a study of the Spirit's role in the conception, birth, boyhood, baptism, temptation, and ministry of Jesus, Hawthorne concludes that although Jesus possessed divine power and authority,

> by a preincarnate deliberate decision the eternal Son of God chose that all his intrinsic power, all his attributes, would remain latent within him during the days of his flesh and that he would become truly human and limit himself to the abilities and powers common to all other human beings. Therefore he depended upon the Holy Spirit for wisdom and knowledge and for power to perform the signs and wonders that marked the days of his years.[25]

In other words, according to Hawthorne, during his earthly ministry Jesus never acted in the power of his intrinsic deity, but rather lived a life of complete dependence on the Spirit to accomplish his messianic mission. Hawthorne does not deny the full humanity and deity of Christ and spends considerable time defending it. His point, rather, is that Jesus never acted in the power of that deity during his earthly life.

Hawthorne's views on the nature of the incarnation are not new. He aligns himself with a moderate version of kenotic theory[26] associated with thinkers like Austin Farrer, P. T. Forsyth, H. R. Mackintosh, O. C. Quick, Vincent Taylor, and Brian Hebblethwaite.[27] These writers assert, in one form or another, that when Jesus "emptied" himself, he gave up nothing of his divine attributes. He did not become any less God. The incarnation was not a subtraction but an addition, as he took

---

25. Gerald F. Hawthorne, *The Presence & the Power: The Significance of the Holy Spirit in the Life and Ministry of the Historical Jesus* (Dallas: Word, 1991), p. 218.

26. Hawthorne rejects the more radical kenotic theory of G. Thomasius, W. F. Gess, and F. Godet, who believe that the eternal Logos emptied himself of the "relative" attributes that belong to deity, including omniscience, omnipotence, and omnipresence but not of the "essential" attributes of holiness, love, and justice (*Presence,* p. 206).

27. Hawthorne, *Presence,* p. 207. Hawthorne follows especially V. Taylor, *The Person of Christ in New Testament Teaching* (London: Macmillan, 1958).

on true humanity. Yet those divine attributes remained latent during his earthly life. Hawthorne writes:

> Divine attributes, including those of omniscience, omnipotence and omnipresence, are not to be thought of as being laid aside when the eternal Son became human but rather thought of as becoming potential or latent within this incarnate One — present in Jesus in all their fullness, but no longer in exercise. Knowledge of who he was and of what his mission in life was to be was given to him as he developed by revelation and intuition, especially at times of crisis in his life, and during times of prayer and communion with his Heavenly Father.[28]

What is new about Hawthorne's thesis is not his emphasis on the functionality of the humanity of Christ, which is common to kenotic theory, but his emphasis that the Spirit mediated divine knowledge and authority to Jesus. "The Spirit who was present and active even in the conception of Jesus, in his boyhood and youth, throughout all of his adult ministry, in his death and resurrection was what might be called — dare I say it? — the 'Holy Synapse' by which the truly human Jesus was made aware, made conscious, of the fact that he *was* indeed the Unique Son of God."[29]

Theologian Bruce Ware takes up much of Hawthorne's thesis, arguing for the critical, and often under-appreciated, significance of the humanity of Jesus. According to Ware, while we must see Jesus living his life as the true God-man rather than isolating either his deity or his humanity, "the emphasis must be placed on the humanity of Christ as the primary reality he expressed in his day-by-day life, ministry, and work."[30]

While Hawthorne's primary interest is the role of the Spirit in Jesus' life, Ware's is the relationship between the humanity and impeccability of Christ. Theologians through the centuries have wrestled with the conundrum of how Jesus could be fully human (and so susceptible to temptation) yet incapable of committing sin. After discussing various views, Ware proposes a solution that separates the question of why Jesus *could not* sin from the question of why he *did not* sin. Jesus *could not*

---

28. Hawthorne, *Presence*, pp. 208-9.
29. Hawthorne, *Presence*, p. 215.
30. Bruce A. Ware, "The Man Christ Jesus," *JETS* 53 (2010): 5-18; quote from p. 5.

sin because he was divine. But in the context of his earthly life, he *did not* sin because he lived a life of complete dependence on the Holy Spirit.[31] Jesus' temptations were therefore real and (as in Hawthorne's proposal) Jesus' dependence on the Spirit has direct application for our lives. Since the pouring out of the Spirit on the Day of Pentecost, we have the same Spirit of God living in us, empowering us to accomplish God's purpose in our lives.

While asserting that Jesus' humanity was the primary reality through which he lived his life, Ware backs away from Hawthorne's contention that Jesus' divine attributes were fully latent during his earthly ministry. He suggests instead that "some of the works of Jesus ... displayed his deity," such as forgiving sins, the transfiguration, raising Lazarus from the dead, and, most importantly, the efficacy of the atonement as an eternal payment for our sins. Nevertheless, "the predominant reality he experienced day by day, and the predominant means by which he fulfilled his calling, was that of his genuine and full humanity."[32]

Hawthorne's proposal is appealing and seems at first sight an ideal solution to the vexing question of the convergence of the human and divine in the person of Christ. There is certainly a great deal of biblical evidence that Jesus acted in full dependence on the Holy Spirit:

(1) Isaiah 11:1-4 presents the coming messianic king as one who will live a life of complete dependence on God. He will not "judge ... with his eyes" or "decide ... with his ears," but will depend on God for wisdom and understanding. Though Isaiah 11 is not cited explicitly in the Gospels, it provides the conceptual background to Jesus' dependence on the Spirit. In the angelic annunciation to Mary, Luke introduces Jesus as the messianic king whose conception by the Holy Spirit establishes a unique Father/Son relationship with God (Luke 1:32-35). Luke then frames the story of the boy Jesus in the temple — where Jesus recognizes this unique relationship to the Father — with two statements about his early growth in wisdom (σοφία) and grace/favor (χάρις) with God and human beings (2:40, 52).[33] H. J. de Jonge rightly concludes that "Luke ii.41-51 is a biographical rendering of the tradi-

---

31. Ware, "The Man Christ Jesus," pp. 13-17.
32. Ware, "The Man Christ Jesus," p. 5; cf. K. Issler, "Jesus' Example: Prototype of the Dependent, Spirit-Filled Life," in *Jesus in Trinitarian Perspective* (Nashville: B&H Academic, 2007), pp. 189-225.
33. See Strauss, *Davidic Messiah*, pp. 87-97, 117-23.

tional conception that the messiah would be endowed by God with wisdom and understanding."[34]

(2) In all three Synoptics, the descent of the Spirit at Jesus' baptism marks the beginning of his public ministry and his empowerment for teaching, exorcism, and healing (Matt. 3:13-17; Mark 1:9-11; Luke 3:21-22). The divine voice from heaven alludes to Psalm 2:7 ("you are my son") — a royal Davidic psalm — and Isaiah 42:1 ("in whom I delight"), merging imagery related to the Spirit-endowed messianic king (cf. Isa. 11:1-4) and the Servant of the LORD (Isa. 42:1). Luke draws the most explicit connection between the descent of the Spirit and Jesus' messianic anointing. Jesus returns from the Jordan "full of the Holy Spirit" and is "led by the Spirit" for his testing/temptation in the wilderness (4:1). He then returns to Galilee "in the power of the Spirit" (4:14) and enters his hometown synagogue in Nazareth, where he reads from Isaiah 61:1-2: "The Spirit of the Lord has anointed me." In this way Luke confirms the descent of the Spirit as Jesus' "anointing" as Messiah and the Spirit as the power through which he will accomplish his messianic task: preaching good news to the poor, giving sight to the blind, and setting free the oppressed (Isa 58:6). It becomes clear in the narrative that follows that this refers to Jesus' proclamation of the kingdom of God (4:31, 36, 43), his healings (4:38-40), and his exorcisms, as freedom from demonic oppression (4:31-37, 41).[35]

(3) When the religious leaders accuse Jesus of casting out demons by the power of Satan, Jesus first points out the illogic that Satan would cast out his own demons, and then affirms the source of his own power: "But if it is by the Spirit of God that I drive out demons, then the kingdom of God has come upon you" (Matt. 12:28).[36] Similarly, in his introduction to the account of the healing of the paralyzed man, Luke points out that "the power of the Lord was with Jesus to heal the sick" (Luke 5:17). Jesus heals not in his own power, but by virtue of the power of God at work within him.

(4) The role of the Spirit in Jesus' miracles also appears in the apostolic preaching in Acts. At the home of Cornelius, Peter points out

34. H. J. de Jonge, "Sonship, Wisdom, Infancy: Luke II.41-51a," *NTS* 24 (1978): 349.

35. Hawthorne, *Presence,* p. 133: "According to the Gospel writers, Jesus, from the moment the Spirit descended to him, became aware of a new power within him, a power to save, to heal, to bind the strong man and overturn his evil designs (Matt. 12:29)."

36. Although Luke has the "finger of God" (Luke 11:20; cf. Exod. 8:19), Turner convincingly argues that the referent remains the Spirit (*Power from on High,* pp. 256-59).

that, "You know what has happened . . . how God anointed Jesus of Nazareth with the Holy Spirit and power, and how he went around doing good and healing all who were under the power of the devil, because God was with him" (Acts 10:37-38). Jesus performed his healings and exorcism through the power of God's Spirit at work in him.

(5) Further evidence of Jesus' complete dependence on the Spirit is his limited knowledge during his earthly life. In Mark 13:32 (par. Matt. 24:36) Jesus makes a remarkable statement about the coming of the Son of Man: "But about that day or hour no one knows, not even the angels in heaven, nor the Son, but only the Father." The passage caused consternation in the early church and continues to perplex readers. Some manuscripts omit "the Son" from the parallel in Matthew, evidence of the embarrassment caused by this passage in the church.[37] Some interpreters, citing passages like Matthew 11:27, John 10:15; 16:15, and Acts 1:7, have claimed that this passage is being misunderstood, and that Jesus did, in fact, know the time of the end.[38] Augustine, for example, said that the meaning of the verse was that Jesus knew the time, but that he withheld this information from his disciples (*On the Trinity* 1.12.1).[39] Athanasius claimed, on the other hand, that Christ knew the time of his return *in his divine nature,* but not in his human one (*Four Discourses Against the Arians* 3.46), a view supported by Wayne Grudem.[40] Yet this interpretation not only creates the strange scenario that Jesus had two centers of consciousness at once, but is also contrary to the plain meaning of the text. As Stein points out, Jesus' words move beyond his humanity alone by emphasizing that it is the divine Son who does not know the time of his return.[41] It is not one half of a schizophrenic Jesus, but rather the whole of the incarnate Christ who is unaware. The progression in the text makes this clear: from humanity ("no one knows"), to the angels, to the Son, to the Fa-

---

37. Robert H. Stein, *Mark,* Baker Exegetical Commentary on the New Testament (Grand Rapids: Baker, 2008), p. 623.

38. Joel Marcus, *Mark 8–16: A New Translation with Introduction and Commentary,* Anchor Bible 27A (New Haven/London: Yale University Press, 2009), p. 913; T. C. Oden and C. A. Hall, eds., *Mark,* Ancient Christian Commentary on Scripture. New Testament 2 (Downers Grove: IVP, 1998), pp. 191-93.

39. Cited by Marcus, *Mark 8–16,* p. 914.

40. Wayne Grudem, *Systematic Theology: An Introduction to Biblical Doctrine* (Grand Rapids: Zondervan, 1994), p. 561.

41. Stein, *Mark,* p. 623 n. 4.

ther. The Son's ignorance was therefore real, and was "a necessary part of his participation in the limitation of human existence."[42] This statement would seem to affirm Hawthorne's assertion that during his earthly life Jesus voluntarily gave up the exercise of his omniscience and lived in full dependence on the Spirit for divine insight and power.

(6) In John's Gospel, too, Jesus is presented as living a life of full dependence on the Spirit. While strongly stressing the deity of Christ (1:1, 18; 5:17-18; 8:58; 14:7-9; 20:28), John consistently affirms Jesus' submission to the will of the Father. In 5:19, Jesus says that "the Son can do nothing by himself; he can do only what he sees his Father doing." Similarly, in John 8:28 he affirms that "I do nothing on my own but speak just what the Father has taught me." Jesus speaks what he hears from the Father (8:26) and what he has seen in the Father's presence (8:38). Whatever Jesus says "is just what the Father has told me to say" (12:50). The words he speaks "are not my own; they belong to the Father who sent me" (14:24). Everything he has learned from his Father "I have made known to you" (15:15). Not only do Jesus' words come from the Father, but also his actions. He "can do nothing by himself [ἀφ' ἑαυτοῦ]; he can do only what he sees his Father doing" (5:19). As we have seen, John presents this revelatory wisdom and power as coming through the fullness of the Spirit given to Jesus by the Father (1:32-34; 3:34).

3.2. Acts of Intrinsic Divine Authority?

This evidence would seem to support Hawthorne's view. As predicted in Isaiah 11, Jesus the Messiah acts not by his own initiative and power, but in complete submission to the Father's will and with the power and insight given to him by the Holy Spirit. But has Hawthorne dealt sufficiently with *all* of the evidence? There are certain events in the Gospel tradition that seem to go beyond *mediated* knowledge and authority. To clarify, we are not referring to statements that *assert* Jesus' divine status or essential nature. Examples of these would include statements about Jesus by the Evangelists (John 1:1, 18), Jesus' self-identification as the "I AM" (John 8:58) or his claim to be the future judge of all people (John 5:22). These would not seem to contradict Hawthorne's claims since Je-

---

42. Marcus, *Mark 8–16*, p. 914, citing G. Ebeling, *Dogmatik des christlichen Glaubens* (Tübingen: J. C. B. Mohr [Paul Siebeck], 1979), vol. 2, p. 473.

sus would be asserting his divine nature or referring to his preincarnate or post-resurrection status without actually *exercising divine attributes* during his earthly ministry. From Hawthorne's perspective, these divine attributes would have been present *but latent* during Jesus' earthly life. Similarly, the transfiguration (Mark 9:2-8 and parallels) would be a revelation or unveiling of Jesus' divine identity, but not an exercise of divine power. What we are seeking instead are words or deeds that entail Jesus' own exercise of divine insight or authority.[43] Here are some texts and themes that seem problematic to Hawthorne's case:

(1) *Supernatural knowledge.* Jesus demonstrates supernatural knowledge throughout the Gospel tradition. He is frequently said to know the thoughts and intentions of his opponents (Matt. 9:4; 12:25; 22:18; Mark 2:8; Luke 5:22; 6:8; 9:47; 11:17). He predicts the destruction of Jerusalem (Luke 19:43-44; 21:20-24, etc.) and knows about his coming arrest, trial and crucifixion (Mark 8:31-32; 9:31; 10:33-34, and parallels). He is aware of his betrayer (Matt. 13:25; John 13:11, 21) and that Peter will deny him (Matt. 26:31-35 and parallels). In John's Gospel, Jesus "sees" Nathanael from afar (1:48), knows the past of the Samaritan woman (4:16-18) and is aware when the crowds are intending to make him king by force (6:15). Jesus knows "from the beginning" who truly believes in him and who will betray him (6:64). Though many miles away, he knows when Lazarus has died (11:11-14). He is aware of "all that is going to happen to him" concerning his arrest, trial and crucifixion (18:4; cf. 8:14; 13:1-3, 11; 19:28).

Of course all this knowledge could have come through the Holy Spirit. As we have seen, the constant refrain throughout John's Gospel is that the Father reveals all things to the Son. Everything Jesus says "is just what the Father has told me to say" (12:50), and his words "are not my own; they belong to the Father who sent me" (14:24). Yet some statements seem to go beyond mediated knowledge to personal omniscience. In John 2:24-25, for example, the narrator says that Jesus "did not need any testimony about mankind (ἀνθρώπου), for he knew what was in each person (ἀνθρώπῳ)" (John 2:25 NIV). Two interpretations of this statement, however, are possible. As the NIV suggests, it could mean that Jesus knew every human heart, an apparent claim to omniscience. The other possibility, however, is that Jesus "knew what was in

---

43. Of course we are dealing with fine nuances here, since the Johannine Jesus acts in complete dependence on and in unison with the Father.

man" (cf. NASB; ESV; HCSB; NKJV), that is, "He knew what people were really like" (God's Word; cf. NLT; CEV). The passage may be more about Jesus' intimate knowledge of the human condition than knowledge of every human thought. John 16:30 is also ambiguous. Jesus' disciples say, "Now we can see that you know all things and that you do not even need to have anyone ask you questions. This makes us believe that you came from God." Is Jesus' knowledge of "all things" a claim of omniscience or of mediated knowledge through the Holy Spirit?

(2) *Forgiving sins.* Another context where Jesus appears to exercise divine authority is in the Synoptic account of the healing of the paralyzed man (Mark 2:3-12 and parallels). When Jesus says to the man, "your sins are forgiven," the religious leaders respond, "Why does this fellow talk like that? He's blaspheming! Who can forgive sins but God alone?" (2:7). Jesus responds by healing the man, demonstrating that "the Son of Man has authority on earth to forgive sins" (2:10). Was this an exercise of divine authority? Many interpreters treat "are forgiven" (ἀφίενται) as a divine passive, where Jesus pronounces *God's* forgiveness (cf. 2 Sam. 12:13).[44] In this case Jesus would be acting with mediated authority and the religious leaders would be angry because he is claiming to be God's representative. This is possible, but less likely in light of the response of the religious leaders. They seem to interpret Jesus' statement "as the exercising of a divine prerogative, the power to actually forgive sins."[45]

(3) *The power to give life.* Jesus' authority to raise the dead would seem to be an exercise of divine authority. Twice in the Synoptics (Mark 5:21-24, 35-43 and parallels; Luke 7:11-17) and once in John (John 11:1-44), Jesus raises the dead with an authoritative command. In the latter context, Jesus is seen praying and thanking God for hearing and responding to him (11:41-42). This may indicate that Jesus is not raising Lazarus through his own divine power, but that the Father raised Lazarus in answer to Jesus' prayer. Yet John's theology appears to go beyond this. Jesus says "I am the resurrection and the life" (11:25) and John 1:4 asserts that "in him was life" in a context with allusions to the Genesis creation account. John 5:26 claims that "the Father has life in himself and

---

44. See Robert A. Guelich, *Mark 1–8:26,* Word Biblical Commentary 34A (Dallas: Word, 1989), pp. 85-86, 93-95.

45. Robert Stein, *The Method and Message of Jesus' Teaching* (Philadelphia: Westminster, 1978), p. 114.

has granted the Son to have life in himself." Life "in himself" certainly sounds as though the Son is imparting life by virtue of *his own* divine authority, even if that authority ultimately came from the Father. John 5:21 similarly says, "For just as the Father raises the dead and gives them life, even so the Son gives life to whom he is pleased to give it." Jesus appears to be claiming divine authority to raise the dead.

Jesus' own resurrection is similarly attributed to both the power of the Father and the power of the Son himself. Concerning his own life, Jesus says, "No one takes it from me, but I lay it down of my own accord. I have authority to lay it down and authority to take it up again. This command I received from my Father" (John 10:18). Though this authority (like all authority) comes from the Father, it is viewed as a divine prerogative that Jesus presently possesses.

(4) *Nature miracles.* Another category that bears closer investigation with regard to Jesus' actions are his nature miracles, such as turning water to wine, feeding the multitudes, walking on water, and calming the storm. Of course nature miracles performed by God through a human agent appear in the Old Testament. Although Moses commanded the rock in the wilderness to produce water (Num. 20:8; cf. Exod. 17:6), it was God who performed the miracle. Similarly, Moses stretched out his hand over the Red Sea, but it was the power of God that made the water recede (Exod. 14:26-28). Jesus could be performing these miracles as the prophets did, through the power of the Holy Spirit at work in him.

Yet, again, some of these Gospel miracles seem to be viewed by the Evangelists as demonstrations of Jesus' own divine authority. When Jesus turns water to wine at Cana, the narrator concludes by noting that through this first sign, Jesus "revealed his glory," and "his disciples believed in him." The miracle is identified as a revelation of *Jesus'* glory, not the glory of the Father or the Spirit.[46] In Mark 4, when Jesus and his disciples are caught in a storm on the sea of Galilee, Jesus rebukes the wind and the waves, and they immediately calm. An attentive first-century reader would certainly know Old Testament passages like Psalm 89:9, where Yahweh demonstrates authority over the sea's primeval chaos: "You rule over the surging sea; when its waves mount up, you still them" (cf. Pss. 65:5-7; 107:23-29). The disciples are terrified and ask, "Who is this? Even the wind and the sea obey him!" (Mark 4:35-41; and

---

46. Grudem, *Systematic Theology,* p. 547.

parallels Matt. 8:23-27; Luke 8:22-25). Since, in the disciples' conceptual world, only God controls the sea,[47] Jesus' action is apparently presented as an act of divine authority.

Similarly, when Jesus walks on water in Mark 6:45-51, he appears to be acting with divine authority, since God alone "treads on the waves of the sea" (Job 9:8; cf. Isa. 43:16; 51:10; Ps. 77:19; Sir. 24:5-6). This implication is reinforced when the narrator makes the puzzling statement that as Jesus approached the boat, "he was about to pass them by" (6:48). A growing number of commentators consider this to be an intentional echo of Old Testament language of theophany, where God reveals himself to his people by "passing before" them (cf. Exod. 33:18-23; 1 Kgs. 19:10-12).[48] Again, the Evangelist appears to present Jesus' actions as evidence of his own divine power and authority.

4. Conclusion: The Limits of Biblical Theology

It seems the conundrum of the incarnation remains. The biblical evidence apparently asserts Jesus' full humanity and complete dependence on the Spirit, but (contra Hawthorne) also implies acts of intrinsic divine power and authority. Ware's claim that Jesus performed occasional acts of divine authority appears to fit the biblical data better, but it raises significant theological (and logical) difficulties. If the soteriological significance of Jesus' person and work is inextricably tied to his true humanity (Heb. 2:14-18) and if the Son voluntarily gave up the right to exercise these attributes, why would he *occasionally* act with his own divine authority? And in what contexts and situations

---

47. The Qumran fragment *4QMessianic Apocalypse* (4Q521) includes the line, "[for the heav]ens and the earth will listen to his anointed one, [and all th]at is in them will not turn away from the precepts of the holy ones" (4Q521 fr. 2 2.1; F. G. Martínez and E. J. C. Tigchelaar, *The Dead Sea Scrolls: Study Edition,* 2 vols. [Grand Rapids: Eerdmans, 1997], vol. 2, p. 1045). Joel Marcus suggests that here we find Second Temple expectations that the Messiah will control nature (*Mark 1–8: A New Translation with Introduction and Commentary,* Anchor Bible 27 [New Haven/London: Yale University Press, 2000], p. 335). But the Qumran text seems more like a hyperbolic description of the obedience of the nations to the Messiah (cf. Gen. 49:10) than his control over the wind and the waves. People, not nature, obey "the precepts of the holy ones."

48. So Guelich, *Mark,* p. 350; Stein, *Mark,* p. 325; Marcus, *Mark 1–8,* p. 426; W. Lane, *The Gospel According to Mark,* New International Commentary on the New Testament (Grand Rapids: Eerdmans, 1974), p. 236.

would this have been permissible? Would not the purpose of Christ's humanity be compromised if he occasionally "cheated" by calling on his divine knowledge and power?

I would suggest that the main problem is that we are trying to answer philosophical and theological questions that these texts were never intended to answer. The Synoptics are seeking to show that Jesus is the Spirit-endowed Messiah, whose coming marks the dawn of eschatological salvation, the inauguration of the kingdom of God, and true forgiveness of sins. Empowered by the Spirit, Jesus accomplishes the signs of eschatological salvation — casting out demons, healing the sick, and proclaiming the good news. The question of how Jesus' full dependence on the Spirit relates to his essential identity as the Eternal Son of God and the Second Person of the Trinity is not addressed, since the Synoptic Evangelists are not operating from the backdrop of a Nicean or Chalcedonian Christology. The "high" or divine Christology that occasionally shines through in their narrative is an implicit one, resulting from their insistence that in Jesus, God has visited and brought redemption to his people (Luke 1:68).

John's theological purpose is more Christologically-focused, but is still not intended to answer the question of the relationship between the human and the divine in the life of the incarnate Christ. Rather, the Fourth Evangelist seeks to show that Jesus the Son is the self-revelation of Father, the Eternal Logos, and Wisdom of God who has come to bring eternal life to all who believe. The Spirit's role for John is to mediate the presence and power of the Father to the Son, and through the Son, to the people of God.

In the end, the New Testament interpreter must admit that some questions cannot be answered through exegesis alone and that the baton must be passed to those engaged in philosophical and speculative theology. These are the limits of biblical theology.

Cyril of Alexandria and the Incarnation

Anthony N. S. Lane

Max Turner and I first met at the end of 1969 as fellow residents at Tyndale House in Cambridge. Five years later he came to join me on the staff at London Bible College, as it then was. Fast forward a few decades and we were the first two faculty members there to be awarded professorial status — not that we were better than our predecessors, but such a facility did not previously exist. So our paths have crossed through no less than six decades, counting the late 1960s and the early 2010s!

During our early years at London Bible College we used to discuss whether contemporary biblical studies were all that was needed and what was the role of historical theological studies. In the spirit of those early debates I would like to offer this modest study of Cyril's Christology. My argument is that the brutal clarity of Cyril's grasp of the Incarnation is a valuable reminder of something that is always in danger of being obscured. My aim is to make it accessible to those without much of the historical background, like New Testament professors!

I have tackled themes similar to those in this essay twice previously: "Christology Beyond Chalcedon," in *Christ the Lord*, ed. Harold H. Rowdon (Leicester: IVP, 1982), pp. 257-81; "Cyril's *Twelve Anathemas:* An Exercise in Theological Moderation," in *The Only Hope: Jesus Yesterday • Today • Forever*, ed. Mark Elliott and John L. McPake (Fearn: Christian Focus Publications/Mentor, 2001), pp. 39-58. In places there will be some overlap in content. I am grateful to Graham Gould and to Richard Price for helpful comments on earlier drafts of this paper.

Anthony N. S. Lane

1. The Chalcedonian Definition[1]

For the Western Church the classic statement of the person of Christ is the *Definition of Faith* produced at the Council of Chalcedon in 451. The Chalcedonian Definition offers a well-balanced statement of the person of Christ. It is not surprising that it was so popular in the West as this had been the western formula ever since Tertullian in the early third century. While it may have merit as a balanced formula it has the drawback that it can appear lifeless and analytical and out of touch with the dynamic picture of Christ in the New Testament. It is precisely at this point that Cyril has much to offer.

Before turning to Cyril we should briefly review the teaching of Chalcedon. The first four councils each condemned a heresy about the person of Christ and made a positive affirmation in opposition to it. The Chalcedonian Definition affirmed these four positive points. In order to demonstrate this, the key section of the Definition is printed below with the four points in four different styles, as follows:

1. <u>The full deity of Christ</u>. This was affirmed in response to Arius at the Council of Nicea (325). Arius held that the Son is the one through whom the Father created the universe, but nonetheless he is only a creature made out of nothing, not God.

2. <u>The full humanity of Christ</u>. This was affirmed in response to Apollinaris of Laodicea, who believed firmly in the full deity of Christ and his incarnation, but held these at the expense of his full humanity. He established the unity of the incarnate Christ by teaching that the divine Word replaced the highest part of humanity in Christ, the mind or the rational soul. This teaching was condemned at Rome in 377 and at the Council of Constantinople in 381.

3. **The indivisible unity of Christ**. This was affirmed in response to Nestorius, to whom we will pay more attention below. He held firmly to the full deity of the divine Word and the full humanity of the man Jesus. But despite his attempt to weld these together into one Christ he never fully escaped from what has been called the "pantomime horse" theory of the incarnation, in which Christ appears to be one, but at the deepest level remains two. Nestorius was opposed by Cyril and condemned at the Council of Ephesus in 431, to which we will return.

---

1. On Chalcedon, see, e.g., Robert V. Sellers, *The Council of Chalcedon* (London: SPCK, 1961).

4. *Christ's humanity and deity remain distinct.* This was affirmed in response to Eutyches. Where Nestorius was accused of dividing Christ into two people, Eutyches was accused of blurring his two natures (deity and humanity) into one and creating a mixture. If yellow paint is mixed with blue, the outcome is green paint, which is neither yellow nor blue; if a horse is mated with a donkey, the outcome is a mule, which is neither a horse nor a donkey. Likewise, Eutyches was accused of making of Jesus Christ a mixture of deity and humanity, a *tertium quid* or third entity, which is neither God nor man but a sort of mongrel. Eutyches was condemned at the Council of Chalcedon in 451.

> Following the holy fathers, we confess with one voice **the one and the same Son**, our Lord Jesus Christ, and **the same one** perfect in Godhead, **the same one** perfect in manhood, truly God and truly man, the same one with a rational soul and a body. He is of one substance [*homoousios*] with the Father *as God*, and **the same one** is of one substance [*homoousios*] with us *as man*. He is like us in all things except sin. He was begotten of his Father before the ages *as God*, but in these last days and for our salvation he was born of Mary the virgin, **the** *theotokos*, *as man*.
>
> This **one and the same Christ, Son, Lord, Only-begotten** *is made known in two natures [which exist] without confusion, without change,* **without division, without separation.** *The distinction of the natures is in no way taken away by their union, but rather the distinctive properties of each nature are preserved.* **[Both natures] unite into one person and one hypostasis. They are not separated or divided into two persons but [they form] one and the same Son, Only-begotten, God, Word, Lord Jesus Christ**, just as the prophets of old [have spoken] concerning him and as the Lord Jesus Christ himself has taught us and as the creed of the fathers has delivered to us.

The Chalcedonian Definition can be summed up in the statement that Christ is one person made known in two natures. What does this actually mean? Does it mean denying that Christ was a human person? The problem is that today we think of "person" in largely psychological terms, but this was not the way it was seen in the fifth century. A simple rule of thumb is to say that "person" is the answer to the question "who is he?" and nature is the answer to the question "what is he?" Who is Christ? There is a single answer to this. He is the eternal Word, who is eternally God and who (the same one) for our salvation in time became a man. What is Christ? There is a twofold answer to this. Eternally he is God, in time he becomes human. So did he have a human personality? Yes, because psychology is an aspect of human *nature*. The doctrine of the incarnation does not deny that Jesus was fully a human person in our sense of the term, but affirms that this human person was none other than the Word made flesh.[2]

It must be admitted, though, that Chalcedon has not always been read this way. After the council there were those who sought to interpret it differently and to deny that the "one person" of Christ was none other than the eternal Word. Here is not the place to pursue this, but in line with most of the recent scholarship I am persuaded that this was never a valid interpretation of the Definition. Furthermore, it was clearly repudiated by the following council, at Constantinople in 553, which significantly did so by emphasizing the teaching of Cyril. This makes my point that the precise formulation of Chalcedon needs the safeguard of the dynamic Christology of Cyril.[3] Without that there has always been a danger that it will be interpreted in a way that effectually denies that "the Word became flesh," a danger that is very live today.

2. Cyril's Controversy with Nestorius

Nestorius was a popular preacher who in 428 became patriarch of Constantinople. While he may have been a gifted preacher, his actions as patriarch demonstrated a lack both of diplomacy and of political prudence. He preached against the doctrine, by now well-established amongst the Alexandrians, that the Virgin Mary was *theotokos*, the one who gave birth to God. He soon found himself in trouble with Cyril, who since 412 had been the patriarch of Alexandria. Cyril acted decisively against Nestorius.

What was Cyril's motivation? There had long been a power struggle between the ancient see of Alexandria and the upstart see of Constantinople which had usurped the status of being second to Rome.

---

2. On this, see Thomas G. Weinandy, "Cyril and the Mystery of the Incarnation," in *The Theology of St Cyril of Alexandria*, ed. Thomas G. Weinandy and Daniel A. Keating (London/New York: T&T Clark, 2003), p. 45.

3. A conviction shared with Weinandy, "Cyril and the Mystery of the Incarnation," pp. 23, 43-44.

Cyril's uncle and predecessor Theophilus had engineered the exile of the saintly John Chrysostom, Cyril had Nestorius branded a heretic, and Cyril's successor Dioscorus did the same for Flavian of Constantinople. But while this ecclesiastical political dimension should not be forgotten, it would be mistaken to suppose that Cyril was simply out to humiliate his rival. The controversy with Nestorius involved serious christological issues about which both parties were deeply concerned.[4]

2.1. Nestorius's Christology

Nestorius stood within the Antiochene tradition, though with his own distinctives. He aimed to protect both the full deity and the true humanity of Christ. He stressed the transcendence, immutability and impassibility of the eternal Word, in order to safeguard his deity. This led him to make a sharp contrast between God the Word and Jesus the human being. He saw Christ as Jesus the man indwelt by God the Word. They are two agents in the sense that some of the things recorded in the gospels are done by Jesus (e.g. sleeping) while others are done by the Word (e.g. miracles). It was Jesus and not the Word who was born of Mary, suffered and died for us. The Word experienced the sufferings of Jesus indirectly, just as the emperor is dishonored if someone throws rotten apples at his statue. This sharp contrast between Jesus and the Word is maintained because of Nestorius's concern to protect the transcendence and impassibility of the divine Word. Unfortunately the price for this protection is to all intents and purposes an abandonment of the doctrine of the incarnation. This was not a price that Cyril was prepared to pay.

Nestorius wished to affirm the unity of Christ and attempted to do so. There is the closest possible conjunction between Jesus the man and God the Word — they are united in purpose and will. But when all is said and done, despite Nestorius's attempts to unite them, they remain two individuals — "they" rather than "he." Nestorius affirmed in Christ not just two natures or two substances (human and divine) but also two beings or hypostases and two persons (Jesus and the Word). It

---

4. As is argued by Henry Chadwick, "Eucharist and Christology in the Nestorian Controversy," *JTS* 2 (1951): 145-64. Weinandy, "Cyril and the Mystery of the Incarnation," pp. 24-27, also highlights the soteriological concern underlying Cyril's Christology.

is not surprising that having ascribed to Christ two of each of the four entities discussed in the christological debates (nature, substance, hypostasis, and person), he should have found it hard to express the unity of Christ.[5] He did not wish to end with an Adoptionist view of Christ and sought to defend himself against the charge, but how effectively? In 1910 a long-lost work of Nestorius, *The Bazaar of Heracleides*, was discovered. This confirms Nestorius's *desire* to be orthodox and to affirm the unity of Jesus Christ, but not his success in this aim. Cyril certainly did not feel that Nestorius had safeguarded the unity of Christ. Donald Fairbairn argues that in denying that it was the Word that was born of Mary Nestorius was opposing not a specifically Alexandrian doctrine but one that was held by all but a tiny number at that time. This is why John of Antioch and others of the Antiochene school were willing to accept his condemnation as a heretic.[6]

2.2. Cyril's Christology

Nestorius's Christology began with the human Jesus and the divine Word. For Nestorius these two persons or two agents are united in one Christ, but it is questionable whether any real unity can be achieved this way. For Cyril the only way to arrive at one Christ is to recognize that it is God the Word who is the sole agent or subject in Christ. What does that mean? Take the incident when Christ raised Lazarus. As a human being he wept over Lazarus, as God he raised him from the dead. But it was the same "he" each time. Both were actions of the Word — acting in his own nature as God and acting in the flesh as human. Christ is one not because (as Nestorius suggested) the two persons Jesus and the Word are closely conjoined and united in purpose and will, but because Jesus *is* the Word, made flesh.

It is not that the Word inspires, indwells, or cooperates with a human being (as some Antiochenes at times suggested) but rather that the Word *becomes* a human being (without ceasing to be God). Unless the Word is the one subject of Christ, there is no true incarnation. It

---

5. See Norman Russell, *Cyril of Alexandria* (London/New York: Routledge, 2000), pp. 40-41, for the fluidity of these technical terms at that stage.

6. Donald Fairbairn, *Grace and Christology in the Early Church* (Oxford: Oxford University Press, 2003), pp. 200-224.

follows simply that Mary is *theotokos*.[7] Who was born of Mary? Jesus. Who is Jesus? The Word made flesh. As the Nicene Creed states, the "one Lord Jesus Christ" is "the Son of God, begotten from the Father before all ages" and he (the same "he") "for us and for our salvation came down, was made flesh from the Holy Spirit and the virgin Mary and became man." Mary therefore bore the Word. He has a double birth: in eternity as God, in time as human. *Theotokos* affirms the fact that Jesus, who was born of Mary, is the incarnate Word, not just a human being who was indwelt by the Word. Again, it was the Word who suffered, died, and rose again. These things are true of him not (as Nestorius professed to believe Cyril to be saying) as God, in his divine nature, but as human.

Christ is not a conjunction (nor even a union) of Jesus and the Word. Instead, the divine Word became flesh (John 1:14) — that is he took flesh animated with a rational soul and became a human being. He takes complete humanity (Cyril has learned from the condemnation of Apollinaris) but not an already existing human being. The Word and his humanity are united to form a single reality, a single hypostasis. Thus Cyril talks of the "hypostatic union" of the Word with his flesh. Cyril also took over a formula that had been coined by Apollinaris: "the one incarnate nature of the Word." Apollinaris's works were banned after his condemnation, but a number of them continued to circulate under the name of Athanasius. Thus Cyril came to adopt Apollinaris's formula, being unaware of its true origin. But while Cyril used an Apollinarian formula, it does not follow that he was guilty of Apollinarianism. On the point for which Apollinaris was condemned (denying the full humanity of Christ) Cyril is carefully orthodox.

For Cyril, the Word becomes flesh/a human being. But this does not involve any change in or diminution of the divine nature. It is not incarnation by mutation — the Word does not exchange a human for a divine nature, like a prince turning into a frog. Nor is it incarnation by diminution or subtraction — the Word's divine nature does not shrink to the size of human nature, like a balloon being deflated. Instead it is incarnation by addition — the Word takes human nature in addition to

---

7. On this, see Frances Young, "*Theotokos:* Mary and the Pattern of Fall and Redemption in the Theology of Cyril of Alexandria," in *The Theology of St Cyril of Alexandria,* ed. Thomas G. Weinandy and Daniel A. Keating (London/New York: T&T Clark, 2003), pp. 55-74.

his divine nature, as a company might open up a new branch.[8] Thus the incarnation involves no interruption of the divine life of the Word. While *as human* he was a baby in his mother's arms, he was still filling the universe *as God*.

2.3. The Controversy

In the late summer of 429, when he heard of Nestorius's preaching, Cyril wrote his *First Letter to Nestorius*, urging him to accept that Mary was *theotokos*. Nestorius sent an evasive reply. Cyril responded with his *Second Letter to Nestorius*, one of the texts that was officially approved at the Council of Chalcedon. At that stage Cyril had yet to win the support of Rome. This letter is carefully written. Nestorius had accused Cyril of teaching that it was the divine nature of the Word that was born of Mary, suffered and died. Cyril devotes as much space to refuting this charge as he does to attacking Nestorius. He takes care to adopt a reasonable and courteous tone towards Nestorius. On June 15th 430 Nestorius responded. He did not seem to have grasped Cyril's point, still accusing him of teaching that the divine nature of the Word is passible and had its beginning with the Virgin Mary.

In the summer of 430 Cyril wrote to Rome against Nestorius. On August 11th a synod met there and decided against Nestorius. He was required to recant within ten days of being informed, Cyril being entrusted with the execution of this. Early in November Cyril wrote his *Third Letter to Nestorius*. The tone of this letter is very different from the previous one. Now that Cyril has the support of Rome he need no longer tread softly. Nestorius is simply required to recant. *Twelve Anathemas* are appended to the letter for Nestorius to sign. These are aggressive and provocative in their tone and "summarize the Cyrilline Christology in uncompromising terms."[9]

Cyril's letter and anathemas brought the controversy to a head. Nestorius circulated the anathemas to a number of leading Antiochene theologians, who attacked them. Cyril responded. At Nestorius's request, the emperor called a council to meet at Ephesus. This was due to

---

8. These three analogies are mine, not Cyril's. None of them should be pushed too far.

9. John N. D. Kelly, *Early Christian Doctrines*, 5th ed. (London: Black, 1977), p. 324.

open on June 7th 431 but the Antiochenes were late arriving. On the 22nd Cyril proceeded without them and held a council which condemned Nestorius. Four days later the Antiochenes arrived and held a minority council which condemned Cyril and his anathemas. On July 10th the Roman delegates arrived and endorsed Cyril's council. For nearly two years there was a serious split between the Alexandrian and Antiochene parties in the East. This was brought to a conclusion by the Antiochenes accepting the condemnation of Nestorius and Cyril accepting an Antiochene declaration of faith called the *Formula of Reunion*, which significantly influenced the Chalcedonian Definition.

3. Cyril's Twelve Anathemas

The *Twelve Anathemas* have not had a good press. They were sent to Nestorius appended to Cyril's *Third Letter*, but they were forwarded to two leading Antiochene theologians, Theodoret and Andrew, on their own, separated from the letter. They understandably reacted vehemently to the anathemas, reading into them all sorts of ideas which are clearly rejected in the accompanying letter.[10] This hostile interpretation has been continued over the ages by those who are unsympathetic to Cyril. Since, however, the anathemas as sent were appended to the letter they will be (and have been) misinterpreted unless they are interpreted in the context of and against the background of the letter.

What is the precise relationship between the letter and the anathemas? As is often noted, the subject matter is not totally identical and the order of the anathemas does not altogether correspond to the order of topics in the letter. Wickham offers a convincing explanation.[11] Pope Celestine charged Cyril to lay two distinct but related requirements before Nestorius: to affirm the Catholic faith and to condemn his own errors. The letter, with its exposition of the Nicene Creed, presents him with the Catholic faith; the anathemas present him with his errors.

---

10. Joseph Mahé notes: "Il me semble que Nestorius envoya à Antioche les Anathématismes *sans la lettre* qui les développait et les justifiait. On ne s'expliquerait guère autrement les objections, qui étaient presque toutes résolues à l'avance dans la lettre en question" ("Les Anathématismes de Saint Cyrille d'Alexandrie," *Revue d'Histoire Ecclésiastique* 7 [1906]: p. 506 [his emphasis]).

11. Lionel R. Wickham, "Cyril of Alexandria and the Apple of Discord," *Studia Patristica* 15:I, p. 390.

Essentially the message of both the letter and the anathemas is very simple: Jesus of Nazareth is none other than the Word incarnate. The sole subject of the human life of Jesus is the Word. In a real sense the anathemas do no more than state this fact and draw out some of its implications. If such a belief is extreme, then so are the anathemas; otherwise they are not. Frances Young concludes her discussion of the debate over the anathemas with an apposite comment: "The essential difference remains: the Antiochenes could not make the Logos directly the subject of incarnation, passion, and death, whereas that was precisely what Cyril was trying to do."[12] Cyril is repeating one basic point, which he expresses in many different ways: Jesus Christ is not a human being who was in a unique relationship with God the Word, but he is himself the divine Word, made flesh. In other words, rather than speak of Jesus *and* the Word we must confess that Jesus *is* the Word. It is this point that comes up in all of the issues that Cyril tackles. There are not twelve different errors but one error that has implications in twelve different areas, twelve different "presenting symptoms."[13] Cyril responds not with twelve different doctrines but with one doctrine which has implications in all twelve areas. We will examine the anathemas in turn, illustrating this point.[14]

1. If anyone does not acknowledge that Emmanuel is truly God and therefore that the holy Virgin is *theotokos* (for she gave fleshly birth to the Word of God made flesh): let him be anathema.

Cyril starts with the issue that had provoked the controversy in the first place: *theotokos*. At stake was the status of Christ rather than Mary.[15] Who was the baby born of Mary? According to the historian Socrates, Nestorius stated that he could not call a two- or three-month-

---

12. Frances Young, *From Nicaea to Chalcedon* (London: SCM Press, 1983), p. 228.

13. We will not examine here the extent to which Nestorius actually held the views condemned. Cyril presents them not as an account of Nestorius's teaching but as errors to be rejected, though clearly he thought they were either taught by Nestorius or were possible implications of his teaching.

14. The translation of the anathemas is my own, paying heed to earlier translations, as also are quotations from Cyril's *Third Letter* and his *Letter to John of Antioch*.

15. Richard M. Price, "The Theotokos and the Council of Ephesus," in *Origins of the Cult of the Virgin Mary*, ed. Chris Maunder (London: Burns & Oates, 2008), pp. 89-103. Cyril does, however, report that Nestorius warned against the danger of making Mary a goddess and *theotokos* did in due course give a stimulus to the cult of Mary.

old baby God.[16] The baby born of Mary was Jesus, but who was Jesus? Was he a human being who was especially closely connected to God? For Cyril he was much more than this — he was the eternal Word, made flesh. As he put it in his *Letter to John of Antioch*, "To whom did [Mary] give birth if it is not true that she bore Immanuel after the flesh?"

2. If anyone does not acknowledge that the Word of God the Father has been hypostatically united with flesh and that he is one Christ with one flesh, so that the same one [Christ] is at once both God and human, let him be anathema.

Cyril called upon Nestorius to accept the (new) term "hypostatic union." Christological terminology was still fluid at this stage and Cyril was called upon to justify his new formula. In response to Theodoret he states that it means "nothing else . . . than only that the nature of the Logos — that is, the hypostasis, which is the Logos himself — was truly united to human nature, without any change or confusion."[17] The union that takes place is between the Word and human *nature*, not between the Word and a human *being*. The upshot is not that the Word is intimately linked to a human being called Jesus but that the Word *becomes* a human being.

Responding to Theodoret, Cyril denied that the incarnation involved any change or confusion, charges repeatedly brought against him by the Antiochenes. As has already been seen, Cyril was adamant that the incarnation involves no change at all in the nature of Godhead or the divine nature of the Word. In his reply to these accusations Cyril again emphasizes that the incarnation does not involve any confusion or mixture of deity and humanity in Christ.[18] In his *Letter to John of Antioch* accepting the *Formula of Reunion* Cyril protests against the charge:

---

16. Socrates, *Ecclesiastical History* 7:34 (*NPNF* 2:172).

17. *Contra Theodoretum* 20 [on anathema 2] (*ACO* 1.1.6, p. 115), cited by Robert A. Norris, "Christological Models in Cyril of Alexandria," *Studia Patristica* 13:II, p. 263. Cyril's aim here was to make his language acceptable to Theodoret and not too much must be read into the "nothing else." In particular, it is wrong to take it as evidence of Cyril's innocence of technical terminology, as is argued by Wickham, "Cyril of Alexandria and the Apple of Discord," p. 388; Cyril of Alexandria, *Select Letters*, ed./trans. Lionel R. Wickham (Oxford: Oxford University Press, 1983), p. xxxiv.

18. *Contra Theodoretum* 35-36 [on anathema 4] (*ACO* 1.1.6, p. 123).

As for those who say that there was a mixture or confusion or blending of God the Word with the flesh, let your holiness vouchsafe to stop their mouths. For it is likely that some are spreading false rumours about me, as though I had either thought or said this. But so far am I from thinking any such thing that I reckon those who can for a moment suppose it possible for a shadow of turning to take place in respect of the divine nature of the Word to be out of their minds. For it remains what it always was and has not been changed, nor indeed could it ever be changed or be capable of variation.

3. If anyone [when talking of] the one Christ divides the hypostases after the [hypostatic] union, joining them together merely in a conjunction on the basis of dignity, authority or power, instead of combining them into a natural union, let him be anathema.

Nestorius is wrong to portray Christ as two beings or hypostases conjoined together "on the basis of dignity, authority or power." Such language suggests the "pantomime horse" picture of two beings cooperating together very closely, while for Cyril there are not two beings, only the one Word of God who has taken flesh and become a human being.

Cyril does not call upon Nestorius to renounce the traditional Antiochene talk of the two *natures* of Christ, but he does here refer to a "natural union." This phrase offended the Antiochenes who took it to imply that the union was inevitable to the Word and not a voluntary expression of his love. In his reply to Theodoret, Cyril explains that "natural" implies a "real" union as opposed to a merely "moral" or "acquired" union, such as Nestorius taught.[19] By affirming one hypostasis and person, hypostatic union, natural union, Cyril is simply expressing in different terms his basic conviction that there is a union between the Word and his flesh/manhood such that the Word is the sole subject of all the experiences of Jesus Christ.

4. If anyone divides between two persons or hypostases the terms contained in the Gospels and apostolic writings or applied to Christ by

---

19. *Contra Theodoretum* 27-28, 30 (ACO 1.1.6, pp. 118-20). On Cyril's explanation, see the comments in n. 17, above. On Cyril's ambiguous use of the term "nature" see Weinandy, "Cyril and the Mystery of the Incarnation," pp. 32-41.

the saints or by himself, and applies some to the man considered separately from the Word of God and others to the Word of God the Father alone (on the grounds that they are divine), let him be anathema.

Jesus Christ is called the Son of David and clearly this relates to his humanity, since he was not Son of David before his incarnation. He is also called the Word, and this explicitly relates to his eternal deity. There is nothing wrong with distinguishing between sayings in this way and Cyril does so in his *Third Letter to Nestorius*. What is wrong, according to this anathema, is to apply some to the human Jesus *separately from* the eternal Word and others to the eternal Word *separately from* the human Jesus. Instead we have what is called the *communicatio idiomatum*, the "communication of properties" or "exchange of attributes." We do not only say that the human Jesus suffered and died but also (as in anathema 12) that the eternal Word suffered (in the flesh). Conversely, it is not just the deity but Christ's human flesh that is life-giving, as Cyril states in anathema 11. The reason for this is that there is only one Christ. The human flesh of Jesus is the flesh of the Word, since Jesus is the Word made flesh. The suffering of the human Jesus is God's suffering since there is no one other than the Word to be the subject of this suffering.[20]

5. If anyone has the nerve to state that Christ is a God-bearing man [i.e. indwelt by God] instead of saying that he is truly God, being [God's] one Son by nature because "the Word became flesh" [John 1:14] and "shared in flesh and blood like us" [Heb. 2:14], let him be anathema.

This anathema makes the same basic point as all the others. Jesus Christ is not a human being who is somehow "God-bearing." Such language starts from the premise that there are a human Jesus and a divine Word and then seeks to unify them. The truth is much simpler. Jesus is not "God-bearing" because he is himself God, the Word made flesh.

The most commonly repeated of the charges that the Antiochenes brought against the anathemas, found in response to no fewer than seven of them including this one, is that the Word is *changed into* flesh. Apart from the fact that the anathemas never state this, the charge is clearly denied in the *Third Letter*:

---

20. It has been disputed since the fifth century whether Cyril contradicted this anathema by signing the Antiochene *Formula of Reunion* in 433. I have discussed this in "Cyril's *Twelve Anathemas*," pp. 55-58.

> And we say neither that the flesh was changed into the nature of Godhead, nor indeed that the inexpressible nature of God the Word was converted into that of flesh, for he is immutable and unalterable, ever abiding the same, according to the Scriptures.

It can safely be said that Cyril rejected no less vehemently than the Antiochenes any suggestion that Christ's deity was changed into humanity.

6. If anyone says that the Word of God the Father is Christ's God or Lord instead of acknowledging the same [Christ] as at once God and human, on the scriptural ground that "the Word became flesh" [John 1:14], let him be anathema.

This anathema again opposes the idea that there is a human being Jesus Christ who is distinct from the divine Word. This time the "presenting symptom" is the idea that the eternal Word is the God or Lord of the human Jesus. This is wrong because the human Jesus is himself none other than the eternal Word, made flesh.

7. If anyone says that the human Jesus is merely energized by God the Word and that the glory of the Only-begotten is attributed to Jesus [not as his own but] as given to him by someone else [i.e. the Word], let him be anathema.

This anathema again clearly focuses on the same one point. Jesus is not some human being who is especially energized and glorified by God the Word, but is himself the Word made flesh. A similar point is made in anathema 9 about glorification by the Spirit.

8. If anyone has the nerve to state that we should worship the "assumed man" [Jesus] along with God the Word, and that the one [Jesus] should be praised and called God along with the other [the Word] (for to add "along with" will always imply this), instead of worshipping Emmanuel with a single worship and ascribing to him a single act of praise because "the Word became flesh" [John 1:14], let him be anathema.

In this anathema an Adoptionist view is yet again directly opposed. There are not two people to be worshipped, the human Jesus and the divine Word, but only the single person, the incarnate Word.

Cyril of Alexandria and the Incarnation

9. If anyone says that the one Lord Jesus Christ has been glorified by the Spirit in such a way that (1) the power which Jesus exercised was someone's else received through the Spirit and (2) his power over unclean spirits and his power to perform miracles on people came from the Spirit, instead of saying that the Spirit by which he performed these miracles was his own Spirit, let him be anathema.

This anathema could easily be misread as affirming that Jesus performed his miracles by his own divine power rather than by the Holy Spirit. It is true that in the Early Church the miracles of Jesus were often attributed to the divine power of the eternal Word rather than the Holy Spirit, but it would be mistaken to see Cyril as denying the latter. So in his commentary on Luke 11:20 he states that the "finger of God" by which Jesus cast out demons is the Holy Spirit. He goes on to explain that the Son does everything by the Spirit.[21] Again, on Luke 4:14, Jesus "is glorified, therefore, by exercising as His own proper might and power that of the consubstantial Spirit."[22] What the anathema rejects is the idea that the Son is glorified by the Spirit *in such a way that* the power of the Spirit is someone else's. In other words, it is not the case of a man Jesus performing miracles by someone else's Spirit but rather Jesus, being himself the incarnate Word, performs miracles by his *own* [Holy] Spirit. Cyril's explanation of this anathema at the Council of Ephesus makes clear that the "Spirit" by which Jesus performed miracles is the Holy Spirit.[23]

10. The divine Scripture states that Christ has been made "the high priest and apostle of our confession" [Heb. 3:1] and that he "gave himself up for us as a fragrant sacrifice to God the Father" [Eph. 5:2]. So if anyone says that it was not the Word of God himself who was made our high priest and apostle when he became flesh and a human being like us but another distinct from him, a man born of a woman yet separate from him, or if anyone says that [Jesus] offered

---

21. Cyril of Alexandria, *Commentary on the Gospel of Saint Luke* (Long Island, NY: Studion, 1983), p. 331 (Homily 81).

22. Cyril, *Commentary*, p. 91.

23. ACO 1.1.5, p. 23; Russell, *Cyril of Alexandria*, pp. 186-87. For more on the role of the Spirit in the ministry of Jesus, see Daniel A. Keating, "Divinisation in Cyril," in *The Theology of St Cyril of Alexandria*, ed. Thomas G. Weinandy and Daniel A. Keating (London/New York: T&T Clark, 2003), pp. 152-60, which is spelt out more fully in his *The Appropriation of Divine Life in Cyril of Alexandria* (Oxford: Oxford University Press, 2004).

his sacrifice not just for us alone but for himself as well (for he who knew no sin needed no sacrifice), let him be anathema.

The central point of this anathema is the same as all the others. The human Jesus Christ who became our high priest is the Word of God himself, not a human being distinct from the Word. It is not a case of Jesus and the Word but rather Jesus is himself the Word, incarnate.

Fourteen times in these anathemas the humanity of Christ is referred to as "flesh." The Antiochenes feared that Cyril's talk of the Word and the flesh implied an incomplete humanity, devoid of a rational soul, which is Apollinarianism. More recently, Hans von Campenhausen claims that the anathemas "were *rightly* interpreted as Apollinarian by the Antiochenes."[24] This is grossly unfair, for a number of reasons. First, in the *Third Letter* Cyril qualifies "he became flesh" with the addition of "that is, a human being endowed with a rational soul." Cyril retained the traditional Word-flesh terminology of Alexandria, while qualifying it in a suitably anti-Apollinarian way. In this anathema the same point is made less explicitly: "he became flesh and a human being like us."[25] In his reply to Theodoret, Cyril states that he, like John in 1:14, was using flesh to mean the whole of humanity.[26] Of the fourteen occurrences of "flesh" in the anathemas, five come in quotations from or allusions to John 1:14.

11. If anyone does not acknowledge that the Lord's flesh is life-giving and that it belongs to the very Word of God the Father, but instead says that it belongs to someone different joined to him [the Word] by dignity or merely indwelt by God, rather than being (as we said) life-giving because it has become the flesh of the Word who is able to give life to all, let him be anathema.

For Cyril, as for all of the early fathers, the doctrine of the person of Christ is important for the doctrine of salvation. Like Apollinaris, he stresses that we receive life from the life-giving flesh of Christ (John 6). This is possible because the flesh of Christ is not just that of a human

---

24. Hans von Campenhausen, *The Fathers of the Greek Church* (London: Black, 1963), p. 166 (my emphasis). William H. C. Frend, *Saints and Sinners in the Early Church* (Wilmington: Michael Glazier, 1985), p. 153 considers some of the anathemas "obviously Apollinarian in inspiration."

25. I recant my concession, in "Cyril's *Twelve Anathemas*," p. 54, that there is nothing in the anathemas themselves to refute the charge of Apollinarianism.

26. *Contra Theodoretum* 87 [on anathema 11] (*ACO* 1.1.6, p. 143).

being closely united to the Word but is itself the flesh of the Word incarnate. Henry Chadwick argued that this was *the* central concern for Cyril, whose "fundamental objections to Antiochene doctrine lay rather in the repercussions of such thought upon the doctrines of the eucharist and the atonement."[27] He is right to draw attention to the importance of these doctrines, but overstates it. They are not mentioned in Cyril's *Second Letter* and in the *Third Letter* are not especially emphasized. They do appear in anathemas 10 and 11, but there is no indication that they are of greater importance than his other concerns.[28]

12. **If anyone does not acknowledge that the Word of God suffered in the flesh, was crucified in the flesh, tasted death in the flesh and became first-born from the dead because as God he is life and lifegiving, let him be anathema.**

The twelfth anathema clearly states that the Word suffered. Cyril believed, together with all of the early church, that the Word as God is impassible, incapable of suffering.[29] But his doctrine of the incarnation, his belief that the Word is the one subject in Christ, means that the same Word suffered in the flesh, as a human being. Here Cyril is often unfairly treated. Frances Young, for instance, states that "*without qualification,* suffering and death were predicated of the Logos."[30] This is simply not true. There is the thrice-repeated qualification "in the flesh." If we read this in the light of his *Second* and *Third Letters to Nestorius,* it is clear that Cyril held to the impassibility of the Word in his own divine nature. In the *Third Letter* he refers to the Word "impassibly making his own the sufferings of his own flesh" and the affirmation of impassibility is more explicit in the previous letter. The element of paradox comes out well in Cyril's statement that "he suffered impassibly."[31]

---

27. Chadwick, "Eucharist and Christology in the Nestorian Controversy," quotation at p. 153.

28. Indeed, Mark Edwards, *Catholicity and Heresy in the Early Church* (Farnham: Ashgate, 2009), p. 161, points out that Theodoret in his response makes no mention of the Eucharist.

29. Many modern theologians would deny that God is impassible in his divine nature. If they are right it does not alter the point being made here since all agree that God, as God, cannot be nailed to a tree. The whole point of the incarnation is that Christ should experience *human* suffering.

30. Young, *Nicaea to Chalcedon,* p. 227 (my emphasis).

31. *Scholia on the Incarnation* 37 in John A. McGuckin, *St. Cyril of Alexandria: The*

In affirming that it was the Word who suffered, was crucified and tasted death Cyril is again defending the doctrine of the incarnation. Who was it who suffered? Jesus. Who was Jesus? The Word made flesh. It follows that it was the incarnate Word who experienced the suffering. There is no human Jesus, separate from the Word, to experience the suffering in his place.

The issue of *theotokos* was resolved through the Nestorian controversy, in that this was thereafter accepted throughout the Catholic Church. Resistance to the idea that suffering could be ascribed to the Word proved to be more obstinate and flared up in the sixth century in what is called the "Theopaschite" controversy. This was resolved in the Second Council of Constantinople, the tenth anathema of which stated: "If anyone does not confess that our Lord Jesus Christ who was crucified in the flesh is true God and the Lord of Glory and one of the Holy Trinity, let him be anathema."[32]

4. Conclusion

We have looked at a controversy from the past involving points of detail which may not appear very relevant today. Yet at the same time we have merely watched one episode of an ongoing struggle between those who do and do not believe in the incarnation. Cyril reduces the various detailed issues to one simple point. The human being Jesus is none other than the Word made flesh. We must never speak of Jesus *and* the Word because Jesus *is* the Word, made flesh. As Lionel Wickham comments, in Cyril's anathemas, "the delicate veil of nuanced provisos is torn away, and we are presented with the logical consequences of what we have been saying all along, if, that is, we have been speaking of Incarnation."[33] They expose with brutal clarity the weak point of Nestorius's Christology. They also remind us today of the need to ensure that underneath the complex language of many contemporary Christologies there lies indeed the core belief that in Christ "the Word became flesh."

Christological Controversy (New York: St Vladimir's Seminary Press, 2004), p. 332 (where it is numbered 35).

32. John H. Leith, ed., *Creeds of the Churches*, 3rd ed. (Louisville: Westminster John Knox Press, 1982), p. 50.

33. Cyril of Alexandria, *Select Letters*, p. xlii.

"By the Washing of Regeneration and Renewal in the Holy Spirit": Towards a Pneumatological Theology of Justification

Veli-Matti Kärkkäinen

> *But when the goodness and loving kindness of God our Savior appeared, he saved us, not because of deeds done by us in righteousness, but in virtue of his own mercy, by the washing of regeneration and renewal in the Holy Spirit, which he poured out upon us richly through Jesus Christ our Savior.*
>
> Titus 3:4-6

> *But ye are washed; but ye are justified; but ye are sanctified in the name of our Lord Jesus Christ, and by the Spirit of our God.*
>
> Cyprian, On the Lord's Prayer 12

> *Through the Holy Spirit comes our restoration to paradise, our ascension into the kingdom of heaven, our return to the adoption of sons, our liberty to call God our Father, our being made partakers of the grace of Christ, our being called children of light, our sharing in eternal glory, and, in a word, our being brought into a state of all fulness of blessing, both in this world and in the world to come.*
>
> St. Basil, On the Holy Spirit 15.36

> *All the works of God end in the presence of the Spirit.*
>
> Jürgen Moltmann, God in Creation[1]

---

1. Moltmann, *God in Creation: A New Theology of Creation and the Spirit of God*, trans. Margaret Kohl (New York: Harper & Row, 1985), p. 96.

Veli-Matti Kärkkäinen

1. First Words: The Key Reformation Doctrine in Need of "Reformation"

In this essay I seek to revise and reconceptualize the traditional Protestant/Lutheran doctrine of justification by recasting it in a robust pneumatological and trinitarian framework. By doing so I am not necessarily attempting to replace the more traditional account of justification nor arguing that the older way is "wrong." Rather, learning from a number of exciting and inspiring advancements in biblical, historical, systematic, and ecumenical studies, I submit to the continuing international and ecumenical conversation the thesis that a proper, fully worked-out doctrine of justification, as presented by Reformation theologians and adopted by post-Reformation Protestant churches, is in need of "reformation." Not least in my mind are the needs of the multicultural, complex, and religiously pluralistic world. Having lived and taught theology in Asia (Thailand) — in addition to the United States and Europe — I have become deeply convinced of the relativity and limitations of any particular doctrinal formulation and consequently of the need to continue working towards a more "globally" and culturally appropriate formulation (or perhaps, formulations, in the plural).[2] What makes the received Protestant formulation of justification problematic is that it claims too much when it is made *the* right formulation.

The resources I have in my mind for this exploration include the following perspectives and developments:

- The "New Perspective" in Pauline and biblical theological studies, with a changed/changing view of what key terms such as "law," "gospel," "justice," and "righteousness" may mean.
- Ecumenical convergences and investigations readdressing the problem of allegedly differing views of justification in Lutheran and Roman Catholic traditions as well as the relation of justifica-

---

2. The often-used term "global" theology in the conversations engaging contextuality is a term that has to be used with great care. The term "global" may easily fall into the trap of being understood in the sense of modernist "universal" ideas. The only meaning of the term "global" that contemporary theology can accept is the "communion" of "local" interpretations in mutual dialogue with each other. In other words, the only "global" is "local." See further, Veli-Matti Kärkkäinen and William Dyrness, "Introduction" to *Global Dictionary of Theology*, ed. William Dyrness and Veli-Matti Kärkkäinen, with Simon Chan and Juan Martinez (Downers Grove: IVP, 2008), pp. vii-xiv.

tion (particularly in Protestant theologies) to the Eastern Orthodox concept of *theosis*. The groundbreaking work has been carried out by Finnish Lutheran scholars under the leadership of my *Doktorvater* Tuomo Mannermaa and his school.
- The criticism and revision of the Lutheran doctrine of salvation by the Lutheran systematician Wolfhart Pannenberg.
- The need to seek to expose the highly "contextual" situation of the Reformation era in order to, on the one hand, gain a deeper insight into why the Lutheran doctrine of justification became what it is and, on the other hand, relativize and reshape it in light of the contemporary global context.

With these resources at my disposal, I seek to make the doctrine of justification more authentically pneumatological-trinitarian and so complement the predominantly Christological orientation. This orientation also helps bring the communal and participatory aspects of soteriology into a proper view.

Since such a task of revision would require much more space than is available here, I will limit my investigation significantly. My argument will be developed in the following interrelated phases: First, in order to show the possibility and the need for such a revisionary work, I will attempt to expose the highly "contextual" view of the Protestant doctrine of justification and thus relativize its status as *the* only and right doctrine; in other words, alongside the "official" interpretation of the Protestant view of salvation, I seek to offer another complementary formulation. In the second moment of the essay, I seek to show that the need for such revisionary work is based first and foremost on the rediscovery of the biblical insights into key topics such as justification/justice, righteousness, covenant, law, and so forth. Writing in the company of several leading international biblical scholars, there is hardly any need to attempt any kind of comprehensive study of the wide variety of biblical viewpoints; rather, as a systematician I just add a few remarks on the work of the biblical scholars to tell them how much my guild has learned from their work.

These two preliminary tasks would then, third, allow me to focus on the main task of the essay, namely, to construct a pneumatologically framed view of justification in a trinitarian framework. Fourth, I will briefly look at the most recent ecumenical advancements in the discussion of justification as conducted between Lutherans and Roman

Catholics, on the one hand, and Lutherans and Orthodox, on the other hand, and how those developments both anticipated and gained from the kinds of revisions attempted in the essay. Finally, I will offer a few reflections as to further tasks awaiting continuing ecumenical and constructive work in soteriology.

Now, before proceeding to the material presentation, let me add a note concerning the highly "contextual" nature of the Reformation formulation of justification.[3]

2. The *Relative* Value of the Protestant Formulation of Justification

The way the doctrine of justification was formulated during the Reformation times — as *the* defining form of soteriology — is undoubtedly related to the late medieval culture with a divinely sanctified hierarchical culture; the prominence of guilt, condemnation, and judgment; as well a deep penitential attitude.[4] That culture, however, has passed away. We live in a different world in the beginning of the third millennium. Hence, says the Brazilian Lutheran Liberationist Walter Altmann, "Contemporary existential concerns have changed, they are couched less in terms of guilt and condemnation and more in terms of the meaning of life and the prospects for material survival."[5] It is not that guilt and condemnation do not matter anymore, they do; but most people in the Global North (Europe, USA) not only after the advent of postmodernism but even much before seem not to be bothered by these concerns primarily — for better or for worse! Let alone, when you think of the peoples in the Global South, other issues such as shame, belonging, and sanctity of life appear to be on the forefront.

---

3. I am well aware of the fact that to speak of "the Reformation formulation of justification" as if there were only one fixed doctrine can only be done heuristically and for the sake of the clarity of conversation. Of course, not only among the Lutheran theologians but especially among the various branches of Reformation there were a number of formulations. That said, for the sake of my argumentation here, the shorthand phrase "Reformation formulation" seems to be legitimate.

4. See further, Wolfhart Pannenberg, *Systematic Theology,* trans. Geoffrey W. Bromiley, 3 vols. (Grand Rapids: Eerdmans, 1991, 1994, 1998), vol. 3, p. 81.

5. Walter Altmann, *Luther and Liberation: A Latin American Perspective,* trans. Mary M. Solberg (Minneapolis: Fortress Press, 1992), pp. 4-5.

"By the Washing of Regeneration and Renewal in the Holy Spirit"

Although the Bible happened to be printed during the time of the Reformation, it was written much before! For biblical authors, themes, motifs, and concerns evident in the cultures of the current Global South and post-Enlightenment North — including among postmodern young adults — such as those just mentioned, from meaning of life to belonging to affirmation of the value of life, were not unfamiliar. In that respect, the continuing reworking of the doctrine of justification in the changing cultural contexts of our pluralistic world is but a call to "Go back to the Bible!"

Behind the Reformation formula of justification lies a certain kind of understanding of the relation of Law to Gospel. Indeed, that distinction served as the hermeneutical device behind much of both Lutheran and Calvinistic doctrines of justification. That template is also in need of revision. As the Lutheran Pannenberg has convincingly shown, the Reformers mistakenly "viewed the law as an expression of God's demand in antithesis to the gospel as promise and pronouncement of the forgiveness of sins." Whereas for Paul, "we have in the law on the one side, and faith in Christ, on the other, two realities in salvation history that belong to two different epochs in what God does in history. The coming of Christ ended the epoch of the law (Gal. 3:24-25; Rom. 10:4)."[6] While it is understandable that Luther, against the penitential mentality of his times, mistakenly contrasted with each other the law as the demand of God (telling us what to do and what not) and the gospel as the forgiveness of sins, that distinction cannot be maintained anymore. Among other problems, that kind of distinction blurs the wider context of the biblical idea of forgiveness of sins that "has its basis in the proximity of the divine rule" of God and thus links together forgiveness and God's righteous demands.[7] In other words, we should understand the integral relationship between forgiveness of sins and the desire of the forgiven person to submit one's life under the demands of the rule of God. Thus, there is also the eschatological orientation: Since the turn from the law to grace has happened definitely in Christ, this turn "must always be related to the broad context of world history in its movement by divine world rule toward the future of

---

6. Pannenberg, *Systematic Theology*, vol. 3, p. 61; for the whole discussion, including a careful engagement of biblical scholarship and tracing of historical developments, see pp. 58-96.

7. Pannenberg, *Systematic Theology*, vol. 3, pp. 82-83 (82).

God."[8] All of these implications stemming from the reworked relationship between the Law and Gospel bear on the reinterpretation of the doctrine of justification.

The term *relative* in the heading should be taken in an inclusive sense. On the one hand, it means "relative" as in contrast to "absolute." Hence, the Reformation formulation of justification in the beginning of the third millennium cannot be considered a fixed, nonalterable doctrine but rather a limited, in some way narrow formula — as such important and normative but not final and absolute. On the other hand, the term *relative* in the heading also means "in relation to": the doctrine functions best in relation to the context it was meant for. Thus it should be considered "occasional," having been occasioned by the context of the times. When divorced from that cultural, societal, epistemological, and religious context, its lacunae appear evident.

A main impetus in contemporary ecumenical and systematic theology to revisit the doctrine of justification has been the many new insights gained in biblical studies, with regard to both the Old and New Testaments, into concepts such as justification, righteousness, and covenant. To those we turn next.

3. The "Justification of God" and "Making Things Right" in the World

Already some time ago, James D. G. Dunn summarized many of the concerns and challenges concerning the traditional notion of the doctrine of justification by faith among biblical scholars:

> Luther's conversion experience and the insight which it gave him also began a tradition in Biblical interpretation, which has resulted for many in the loss or neglect of other crucial Biblical insights related to the same theme of divine justice. And particularly in the case of Paul, Luther's discovery of "justification by faith" and the theological impetus it gave especially to Lutheran theology has involved a significant misunderstanding of Paul, not least in relation to "justification by faith" itself.[9]

---

8. Pannenberg, *Systematic Theology*, vol. 3, p. 87.
9. James D. G. Dunn, "The Justice of God: A Renewed Perspective on Justification by Faith," *JTS* 43 (1992): 2. In my *One with God: Salvation as Deification and Justification*

In keeping with this revisiting of the Reformation doctrine, some biblical scholars maintain that that traditional view has made the doctrine too much a function of a personal, at times even existential experience rather than looking at the biblical perspective of the need to "justify" God. Furthermore, they say, the Lutheran doctrine is too individualistic and thus misses the communal ramifications. Part of the criticism against the traditional view is that the traditional doctrine sets Paul and Judaism in antithesis, making the religion of Israel virtually a degenerate religion. It is also mentioned that faith and good works, or declarative and effective righteousness, are not only separated (as in the Protestant distinction between justification and sanctification) but also set in opposition to each other (allegedly to protect the gratuitous nature of justification by faith). And so forth.

Consequently, current biblical scholarship has helped systematic theologians to reconsider and correct the traditional meaning and context of the terms "justification" and "righteousness." E. P. Sanders famously recommended the term "righteousing" (rather than the old English "rightwising") as the more proper way of speaking of "justification" as the gift of righteousness, putting things and people in right relation to God and to each other.[10] This means moving away from the predominantly forensic understanding toward an understanding of "saving righteousness" with a view to setting things right for the whole creation and between creation and God.[11] This redemptive justice, while not totally lacking forensic aspects, is more about "justifying" God's saving deeds with the world in a way that is in keeping with his faithfulness, holiness, love, and integrity.[12]

Righteousness is thus a relational concept: it speaks of the way

---

(Collegeville: Liturgical Press, 2004), ch. 1, I have offered a more comprehensive discussion of the implications of the biblical studies for the doctrine of justification. A highly useful recent book is, N. T. Wright, *Justification: God's Plan & Paul's Vision* (Downers Grove: IVP, 2009).

10. E. P. Sanders, *Paul, the Law, and the Jewish People* (Philadelphia: Fortress Press, 1983), p. 6.

11. For a helpful brief discussion, see Frank Macchia, "Justification through New Creation: The Holy Spirit and the Doctrine by which the Church Stands or Falls," *ThTo* 58 (2001): 207-11. Macchia fittingly titles this section "Justification as Redemptive Justice in Christ and New Creation."

12. See, e.g., Karl Barth, *Church Dogmatics*, vol. 4/2, ed. Geoffrey W. Bromiley and Thomas F. Torrance (Edinburgh: T&T Clark, 1958), p. 562.

Yahweh and the Father of Jesus Christ relates to creation and humanity, and how humanity, redeemed in Christ, should relate to God and other people. Consequently, this terminology is more communal than individualistic. Being relational and communal, the talk about justice and righteousness is focused on the covenant and covenant faithfulness. The forensic court-driven mentality of the times of the Reformation has a hard time envisioning the justice of God through the lens of the merciful and holy faithfulness of the covenant. Yet a focus on covenant and on God's own faithfulness and justice also helps rediscover the key biblical insight of the integral relation of justification to justice. In the words of Kathryn Tanner, "a modification promoted by biblical theology has to do with the way mercy and justice are woven together in Christian theologies of justification. Mercy and justice will no longer be merely juxtaposed but will instead be brought to bear on one another to produce a radically altered sense of both but especially a radically altered sense of justice."[13]

At the same time, learning from biblical scholars, a growing number of systematicians are convinced that the metaphor of justification is just that, *a metaphor*, and therefore cannot be considered the normative symbol of salvation. It simply is not true that in the Pauline soteriology, let alone in the midst of the diversity of New Testament interpretations, justification or any other one single metaphor should be considered the normative one. As Pannenberg rightly notes, "The doctrine of justification is but one of many ways of expounding the theme of" the salvation of God in Christ. He reminds us that, for example, the Johannine traditions speak of salvation in very different ways. "Even for Paul himself," Pannenberg adds, the doctrine of justification "is not the only center of his theology that controls all else."[14] The conclusion thus is inevitable:

> The many early Christian approaches to a theological explanation of the salvation that is accessible to faith by and in Jesus Christ help us to grasp the various ways of understanding salvation in the history of Christianity right up to our present ecumenical situa-

---

13. Kathryn Tanner, "Justification and Justice in a Theology of Grace," *ThTo* 55 (1999): 513. For a fairly detailed summary statement concerning the main results of the New Perspective on key concepts related to the doctrine of justification, see Kärkkäinen, *One with God*, p. 16.

14. Pannenberg, *Systematic Theology*, vol. 3, p. 213.

tion, and this fact should warn us not to single out any one form of understanding, even the doctrine of justification, as the only legitimate one, as though, were this lacking, no authentic Christian faith could be present. Instead, the various ways of understanding salvation are calculated to correct the one-sidedness that can arise with each one of them.[15]

In sum: we are now in a better place to see the highly "contextual" and thus limited meaning of the traditional doctrine of justification as developed during the Reformation times. This penitential, courtroom-driven, forensic formulation, while having its own important place in the development of the doctrine, thus has to be relativized against the multiplicity of biblical metaphors of salvation. It is but one way of speaking of the gift of righteousness given to humanity by the Triune God. Furthermore, even when using this metaphor, its inclusive, relational, communal, and trinitarian network of meanings should be duly recognized. Taking this insight seriously means that ecumenical and constructive theology has to work intentionally to parse these implications and their significance for the newly revised doctrine. The task that is closest to my heart for the purposes of this essay is the trinitarian and pneumatological aspect of the concept of justification and righteousness. Indeed, this is again something systematicians have learned from biblical scholars — and from the early tradition of doctrinal theology.

4. The "Objective" Work of the Holy Spirit

To summarize much of what has been argued so far, on the basis of the biblical investigation of justification and righteousness and the need to continue anchoring that doctrine in a healthy trinitarian-pneumatological framework, the statement by the Pentecostal theologian Frank Macchia puts it well:

> This gift of righteousness involves God's self-justification as the faithful Creator and covenant partner to creation; but it also involves the participation of the creature, for the kingdom of God is "righteousness, peace, and joy in the Holy Spirit" (Rom. 14:17). Seen

---

15. Pannenberg, *Systematic Theology*, vol. 3, p. 214.

from the lens of the Spirit, this right relationship is a *mutual indwelling* that has communion and the "swallowing up" of mortality by life as its substance (2 Cor. 5:4). It is based on the self-giving embrace of the triune God and is manifested in the new birth, witness, and, ultimately, resurrection. There is no lens through which to view salvation that is not realized and perfected in the presence of the Spirit.[16]

As is well known, one of the main differences between Eastern and Western theologies has been the prominence of a pneumatological/trinitarian outlook in the East.[17] This goes back all the way to the robust pneumatological theology of the Eastern Fathers.[18] Somewhat ironically, the Protestant *ordo salutis*, while usually under pneumatology, has tended to be one-sidedly built on Christological categories in the sense that the Holy Spirit has to do only with the "subjective" reception of the "objective" work wrought about by Christ. This is, however, "soteriological subordinationism." Several contemporary Protestant theologians are well aware of this lacuna and are working towards rectifying it. Pannenberg places the talk about soteriology under the telling heading

---

16. Frank D. Macchia, *Justified in the Spirit: Creation, Redemption, and the Triune God* (Grand Rapids: Eerdmans, 2010), p. 3.

17. This statement is of course one-sided and highly unnuanced — it should be taken merely as a heuristic remark. While it is of course true that the soteriology of the Christian West is often — rightly! — blamed by Eastern theologians for its lack of pneumatological orientation, this is not to say that, for theologians such as St. Augustine, the Spirit does not play an important role in salvation and soteriology. Indeed, for Augustine the Holy Spirit is the uncreated grace *(gratia increata)* given to humans (see, e.g., *On the Spirit and Letter*). Thus, grace and justification are understood as the actual effect of the Holy Spirit. It was rather in later theology, most prominently in medieval times, that the distinction between the Holy Spirit and grace became a norm. Thomas Aquinas (differently from Peter Lombard) was critical of Augustine's view of the identification of grace with the Spirit given to the heart of the believer (see, e.g., *Summa Theologicae* II-II, 23, 2 in which Thomas responds to Augustine, *On the Trinity* 15, 17). While for Augustine, God/Spirit is not only the giver but also the gift, i.e., the personal presence of God in the heart of the believer, for Thomas grace (and love) springs from the Holy Spirit, who then sets the soul in motion acquiring the justifying grace. This development of course helped blur the meaning of the robustly pneumatological (and trinitarian) view of salvation.

18. For representative examples, see Veli-Matti Kärkkäinen, *Holy Spirit and Salvation*, The Westminster Collection of Sources of Christian Theology, ed. John McGuckin, Joseph Wawrykow, Timothy George, and Lois Malcolm (Louisville: Westminster John Knox Press, 2010), ch. 2 particularly.

"The Basic Saving Works of the Spirit in Individual Christians" in his discussion of pneumatology and ecclesiology.[19] Moltmann similarly has criticized the traditional Reformation view for not paying due attention to the role of the Spirit in salvation. Referring to passages such as Titus 3:5-7, which speaks about the "washing of regeneration and renewal in the Holy Spirit, which he poured out upon us richly," Moltmann emphasizes that "'regeneration' as 'renewal' comes about through the Holy Spirit' when the "Spirit is 'poured out.'"[20] By making further reference to John 4:14, the metaphor of the divine "wellspring of life" that begins to flow in a human being, he contends that "through this experience of the Spirit, who comes upon us from the Father through the Son, we become 'justified through grace.'"[21]

While in no way diminishing the work of the Son, the Spirit's work cannot only be considered "subjective" as in traditional presentations of the *ordo salutis*. It was through the Spirit that the Father raised Jesus from the dead (Rom. 1:4), the act that led to our justification (Rom. 4:25). Christ's cross requires resurrection by the Spirit and vice versa. In a qualified sense of the word, the Spirit's work is thus as "objective" as that of Christ, albeit differently. Hence, it would do good to speak of "objective pneumatology," following this somewhat idiosyncratic expression of John Thompson in relation to Karl Barth's doctrine of the Holy Spirit.[22] That expression can be used to speak of the necessary and mutually conditioning role of the Spirit in everything having to do with Christ (and of course, vice versa): Christ's coming, ministry, self-surrender all the way to the point of death on the cross, resurrection, and current "teaching" ministry through the Paraclete — all call for the "objective" work of the Spirit. Even more: this objective pneumatology "also involves the Spirit's mission to indwell the creation by first indwelling the Son. The embrace of the Spirit thus takes ambiguous creaturely life into the circle of love and justice enjoyed within God as Father, Son, and Spirit."[23]

---

19. The heading is on p. 135 of Pannenberg, *Systematic Theology*, vol. 3.

20. Moltmann, *The Spirit of Life* (Minneapolis: Fortress, 1992), p. 146.

21. Moltmann, *Spirit of Life*, p. 146. See also Kenneth L. Bakken, "Holy Spirit and Theosis: Toward a Lutheran Theology of Healing," *SVTQ* 38 (1994): 410-11.

22. John Thompson, *The Holy Spirit in the Theology of Karl Barth*, Princeton Theological Monograph Series (Kent: Pickwick, 1991).

23. Macchia, *Justified in the Spirit*, p. 133. The whole section (pp. 131-35) is titled "Objective Pneumatology: Preliminary Thoughts."

Only thus can we come to the place in which the mutually conditioning work of the Spirit and Christ is understood in an inclusive way of both justifying God, in his faithfulness to creation, and making it possible for the creatures to truly participate in the life divine through and in the Spirit. Following that grammar, the justification goes far beyond the contours of a legal, forensic pronouncement of "innocence," as in a courtroom, although there is no reason to leave behind that aspect as one of the many metaphors of salvation. A trinitarian, pneumatological account of justification has so much more to offer. And indeed, Macchia reminds us, "If justification is to offer a liberating word in an increasingly graceless world, the doctrine must be reworked precisely at this point of neglect, namely, at the relationship between justification and the work of the Spirit as the giver of new life." Therefore, he suggests, an attempt has to be made to open "the doctrine to the full breadth of the Spirit's work in and through Christ to make all things new."[24] What Macchia is rightly aiming at is a vision of justification that — in a properly trinitarian framework[25] — would empower and energize the justified and renewed person to work in fulfillment of the demands of the kingdom in all areas of life, with a view towards final consummation. I would add one more important task for such a constructive work: justification should be framed in a way that would help link the individual person's union with Christ with the fellowship of believers, thus including communal aspects as well.

Indeed, one of the key reasons pneumatology has to be introduced into the center of soteriological discourse is that otherwise the Spirit's work is seen as something "external" and thus secondary. Again, this is not a matter of in any way diminishing the function of the Christ as Savior; nor is it only a matter of finding a balance as much it is also a way to make Christ's work of salvation more inclusive and robust. The way this participation in Christ's reconciliation through the Holy Spirit happens can be explained with the help of the term "ecstasy" (*ek-stasis;* "standing outside oneself"). In the Spirit the justified believer is being "lifted up," as it were, into Christ and finds

24. Macchia, "Justification through New Creation," pp. 202-3.
25. Robert Jenson makes the interesting observation that whereas the "Pauline" understanding of justification is focused on God the Father and the maintenance of divine righteousness in the act of redemption, the "Protestant" view is focused on the grace of Christ, and the "Catholic" understanding centers on the Spirit's transformative work. Robert Jenson, "Justification as a Triune Event," *Modern Theology* 11 (1995): 422-23.

"By the Washing of Regeneration and Renewal in the Holy Spirit"

new identity in Christ. Faith — as in Luther's own theology — is an ecstatic experience, finding one's existence in Christ.[26] The following lengthier citation from Pannenberg explains this in some detail:

> But how can others share in the reconciliation that was achieved in exemplary fashion by the incarnation and death of the Son in Jesus Christ? They can do so only as they are taken up into fellowship with the Father of the Son who became man in Jesus Christ (cf. Gal. 3:26f.; 4:5; Rom. 8:14f.). This taking up is not merely in the sense of something that happens to them from outside but as a liberation to their own identity, though not in their own power. This takes place through the Spirit. Through the Spirit reconciliation with God no longer comes upon us solely from outside. We ourselves enter into it. The Spirit lifts us above our own finitude, so that in faith we share in him who is outside us, Jesus Christ, and in the event of reconciliation that God accomplished in his death. Believers are "ecstatic," i.e., outside themselves, as they are in Christ (Rom. 6:6, 11).[27]

By virtue of this lifting up by the Spirit into Christ, the dynamic tension between individual and community in the church can also be explained — an ancient ecclesiological problem not as thoroughly discussed in theology as it should have been:

> In "ecstatic" being with Christ, believers are not in bondage to another, for Jesus as the Son of the Father is for his part fully God and therefore the man who gives himself up for others. As believers through the Spirit are with Jesus, they participate in the filial relation of Jesus to the Father, in his acceptance of the world in virtue of the goodness of God as Creator, in his love for the world. Those who believe in Jesus are thus not estranged from themselves, for with Jesus they are with God, who is the origin of the finite existence of all creatures and their specific destiny. For this reason being outside the self through the Spirit and in faith in Jesus Christ means liberation, not merely in the sense of elevation above our own finitude, but also in the sense of attaining afresh by this eleva-

---

26. See, e.g., Pannenberg, *Systematic Theology*, vol. 2, pp. 451-53; for this theme in Luther, see, e.g., Pannenberg, *Systematic Theology*, vol. 3, pp. 217-29.

27. Pannenberg, *Systematic Theology*, vol. 2, p. 450.

tion to our own existence as the Creator has affirmed it and reconciled it to himself. It means liberation from the bondage of the world, sin, and the devil for a life in the world in the power of the Spirit.[28]

Although it has to be left to ecclesiological reflections to parse the many implications of this statement on the communal meaning of the "ecstatic" existence in Christ, let it suffice to mention that that is an appropriate way to systematically explain the biblical idea of the relational (and thus trinitarian) and *koinonia*-driven view of salvation. As long as the work of the Spirit is conceived only as "subjective" or "external" as in an "imputed righteousness" scheme, the gift of salvation is in danger of being diminished, as it were.

In current ecumenical advancements the theme of justification as participation in the life of the Triune God through the Spirit has found fruitful expressions as some Lutheran theologians have revisited the doctrine of justification and engaged Catholic and Eastern traditions.

5. "*In ipsa fide Christus adest*": The Indwelling of Christ through the Spirit in the Believer

Against the typical suspicion according to which the Lutheran doctrine of justification must be set in opposition to the Eastern Orthodox notion of *theosis* in which salvation is conceived in terms of "real" participation through Spirit in the life divine, the following statement by the Lutheran team in an Orthodox-Lutheran dialogue represents the New Interpretation of the Reformer's doctrine of justification:

> This life of the Christian in Christ is called in the Lutheran tradition participation in God, although it is often expressed in different terms. The sacramental word and sacraments and faith firstly bring it about that Christ joins himself in a real, but hidden way to the sinner. Participation in Christ and the divine nature means then that in the sinner there takes place a profound and fundamental renewal. From this wells forth true love of God and one's

---

28. Pannenberg, *Systematic Theology*, vol. 2, p. 452. Behind this pneumatological recasting of soteriology is also a highly pneumatological concept of the gospel; Pannenberg, *Systematic Theology*, vol. 1, pp. 249-50.

neighbour. In Lutheranism, this is called by the name, new birth, justification, adoption by God, deification of man.[29]

With regard to the traditional juxtaposition of Reformation and Roman Catholic understandings — the former being a matter of merely a forensic action, God declaring the sinner righteous in God's sight, whereas for Catholics it is making the person righteous — recent ecumenical advancements are opening up new venues, as illustrated in the highly significant recent joint statement by the Lutheran World Federation and the Vatican.

This New Interpretation of Luther studies has emerged and could become a major influence on the future of the Christian ecumenical movement. The New Interpretation of Luther's theology, as advanced by the so-called Mannermaa School at the University of Helsinki, has challenged the traditional view.[30] While not without its critics,[31] the

---

29. From the 1977 conversations between the Russian Orthodox Church and the Lutheran Church of Finland, cited in Risto Saarinen, *Faith and Holiness: Lutheran-Orthodox Dialogue, 1959-1994* (Göttingen: Vandenhoeck & Ruprecht, 1997), p. 74. For details of that groundbreaking dialogue, see Hannu Kamppuri, ed., *Dialogue between Neighbours: The Theological Conversations between the Evangelical-Lutheran Church of Finland and the Russian Orthodox Church, 1970-1986* (Helsinki: Luther-Agricola Society, 1986).

30. The publications of the Mannermaa School are written mainly in German (and Scandinavian languages). Not until 1998 was the first English monograph, a collection of essays by Finnish Luther scholars and edited by two leading American Lutheran experts, offered to the English-speaking world: *Union with Christ: The New Finnish Interpretation of Luther,* ed. Carl E. Braaten and Robert W. Jenson (Grand Rapids: Eerdmans, 1998). Recently, the key work by Mannermaa himself was made available for the English-speaking audience: Tuomo Mannermaa, *Christ Present in Faith: Luther's View of Justification,* ed./trans. Kirsti Stjerna (Minneapolis: Augsburg Fortress, 2005 [orig. 1979]). A succinct introduction to the methodological orientations and the main results of the Mannermaa School can be found in Tuomo Mannermaa's essay, "Why Is Luther So Fascinating? Modern Finnish Luther Research," in *Union with Christ* (Grand Rapids: Eerdmans, 1998), pp. 1-20.

31. For some aspects of criticism, see my "Salvation as Justification and *Theosis:* The Contribution of the New Finnish Luther Interpretation to Our Ecumenical Future," *Dialog* 45 (2006): 74-82. While I think that the Mannermaa School should engage the criticism, particularly by the German-speaking Lutheran scholarship, what I do not find helpful or constructive is the virtual dismissal of the whole New Interpretation (Bernhard Lohse, *Martin Luther's Theology: Its Historical and Systematic Development* [Minneapolis: Fortress Press, 1999], p. 221) or the leveling of fancy charges such as that of "Osianderism" (Robert Kolb and Charles P. Arand, *The Genius of Luther's Theology: A Wittenberg Way of Thinking for the Contemporary Church* [Grand Rapids: Baker Academic, 2008], p. 48).

Finnish interpretation has profoundly energized the conversation at the global and ecumenical levels. Having offered a detailed documentation and argumentation elsewhere,[32] let me here just summarize the main insights of the New Interpretation with a view to the topic under discussion.

Luther's own understanding[33] of salvation can be expressed not only in terms of the doctrine of justification, but also in terms of *theosis*. Thus, while there are differences between the Eastern and Lutheran understandings of soteriology, over questions such as free will and understandings of the effects of the Fall, Luther's own theology cannot be set in opposition to the ancient Eastern idea of deification. Even in light of the fact that Luther himself used the term *theosis* sparingly, there are a number of other ways he refers to the same reality, such as when he speaks of union and participation.

In contrast to the confessional writings,[34] for Luther, the main idea of justification is Christ present in faith *(in ipsa fide Christus adest)*. In other words, Luther saw justification as the union between Christ

---

32. My *One with God* contains detailed discussion and documentation of various aspects of the New Interpretation by the Mannermaa School. For my other contributions on various aspects of the topics, see my "Justification as Forgiveness of Sins and Making Righteous: The Ecumenical Promise of a New Interpretation of Luther," *One in Christ* 37 (2002): 32-45; "The Ecumenical Potential of Theosis: Emerging Convergences between Eastern Orthodox, Protestant, and Pentecostal Soteriologies," *Sobornost/ECR* 23 (2002): 45-77; "The Holy Spirit and Justification: The Ecumenical Significance of Luther's Doctrine of Justification," *Pneuma* 24 (2002): 26-39; "Salvation as Justification and Deification: The Ecumenical Potential of a New Perspective on Luther," in *Theology between West and East: Honoring the Radical Legacy of Professor Dr. Jan M. Lochman*, ed. Frank Macchia and Paul Chung (Lanham: University Press of America, 2002), pp. 59-76.

33. The distinction between "Luther's theology" (denoting the theology of the Reformer himself) and "Lutheran theology" (the subsequent theology of the confessional documents of the Lutheran Church, as drafted under the leadership of Philipp Melanchthon) is vital for Helsinki scholars. They argue that one of the weaknesses of the older Luther research, as conducted mainly in the German academy, is the neglect of this vital distinction. Indeed, one of the main motifs of the New Interpretation is to dig into core themes of Martin Luther's own theology and not hasten to read Luther in light of his later interpreters or vice versa. (Of course I leave it to the Lutheran confessional family to decide whether the Lutheran *denominational* identity should be based on the confessions rather than on the founder's theology.)

34. I am of course aware of the fact that even in the confessions justification is at times talked about in terms of the change of life — or at least an implication is there. However, in the main they insist, and often, in contradistinction to the Roman position, on the forensic interpretation.

and the believer as Christ through faith abides in the Christian through the Spirit. Another way of saying the same thing is that "Ecstatic fellowship with Christ, to whom believers entrust themselves, forms the basis of Luther's understanding of justification. He starts here with his view of the act of faith that takes believers out of themselves and sets them in Christ."[35] Being in Christ, one with him, the believer participates and shares in Christ and all his "goods."[36]

Consequently, justification is more than a declaration, it means a "real-ontic" (a somewhat controversial term used by the Mannermaa School) participation in God through the indwelling of Christ in the heart of the believer through the Spirit. Therefore, again in contrast to the theology of the Lutheran Confessions, Luther does not make a distinction between forensic and effective justification, but rather argues that justification includes both. In other words, in line with Catholic theology, justification means both declaring righteous and making righteous. This happens because Christ living in the heart of the believer makes the Christian a "christ" to the neighbor. The renewed believer begins to act like Christ. This is not to say that Luther leaves behind the idea of *simul iustus et peccator*, but that this idea is put in the context of Christ "absorbing" all sin in a moment and beginning the renewal which, in the daily repentance and return to the grace of baptism, continues the rest of one's life. In other words, the "new identity that believers have outside themselves in Christ . . . [is] gradually changing the empirical reality of their lives, though for Luther these effects will always be incomplete in this life, and hence they are consequences, not preconditions, of justification."[37] The "christ-making" also has profound implications for the Christian community: it is a "hospital for the incurably sick" to care for the poor, sick, depressed, and weak.

Many of these groundbreaking results and insights have been incorporated into the Lutheran-Catholic Joint Declaration on Justification. Article 15 wonderfully summarizes this outlook: "Christ himself is

---

35. Pannenberg, *Systematic Theology*, vol. 3, pp. 215-16; in this context Pannenberg makes an approving comment on the Mannermaa School approach, while acknowledging that this view is an alternative to the prevailing trend in Luther research.

36. This is clearly spelled out by Luther already in his 1519 Sermon on Twofold Righteousness (included in the *Formula of Concord* [Solid Declaration, Article III, "Righteousness," §32]).

37. Pannenberg, *Systematic Theology*, vol. 2, p. 218.

our righteousness, in which we share through the Holy Spirit in accord with the will of the Father."[38] Behind this convergence is a mutual Bible reading in which many of the insights discussed above helped shape the received doctrine:

> Justification is the forgiveness of sins (cf. Rom. 3:23-25; Acts 13:39; Luke 18:14), liberation from the dominating power of sin and death (Rom. 5:12-21) and from the curse of the law (Gal. 3:10-14). It is acceptance into communion with God: already now, but then fully in God's coming kingdom (Rom. 5:1-2). It unites with Christ and with his death and resurrection (Rom. 6:5). (#11)

Under the subheading "Justification as Forgiveness of Sins and Making Righteous," the document says: "These two aspects of God's gracious action are not to be separated, for persons are by faith united with Christ, who in his person is our righteousness (1 Cor. 1:30): both the forgiveness of sin and the saving presence of God himself" (#22).

To clarify my intentions here, I am not saying that Catholic, Lutheran, and Orthodox soteriologies have given up — or should give up — their distinctive features. What I am saying is that much of the problematics attached to traditional positions, mostly going back to the time of the Reformation and Counter Reformation, are historically conditioned and no longer form an irreconcilable obstacle to dialogue and joint ventures. Even more importantly to my argumentation in this essay, what I see emerging out of these ecumenical conversations is a revised view of justification among the advocates of the New Perspective and current constructive theology of salvation.

6. Last Words: The Continuing Ecumenical Task

Intentionally, the task of this essay has been limited and partial. My main goal has been to attempt to construct a doctrine of justification

---

38. The Lutheran World Federation and the Roman Catholic Church, *Joint Declaration on the Doctrine of Justification* (Grand Rapids: Eerdmans, 2000), #15 (the document is also readily available on the Internet, e.g., http://www.vatican.va/roman_curia/pontifical_councils/chrstuni/documents/rc_pc_chrstuni_doc_31101999_cath-luth-joint-declaration_en.html (accessed 11/8/2010). For a detailed discussion, see Kärkkäinen, *One with God*, pp. 99-108.

in which, through the work of the Holy Spirit, there is "real" participation in the life of the Triune God who, as the faithful Creator, justifies himself and renews creation. This means that the contextual nature of the traditional Protestant doctrine of justification had to be exposed in order to make its role relative. Fresh insights into the inclusive, comprehensive nature of justification as an important metaphor of salvation have offered the positive materials for such a constructive work.

Much had to be left unsaid in order to make the short essay manageable. As mentioned above, there was no opportunity to glean insights from the rich harvest of Spirit-Christologies. What was established, however, was the need for an "objective pneumatology," which would help Western theology regard the work of the Spirit as equal to, although different from, that of the Son in all works of creation, salvation, and final consummation. Part of this "big picture" is a much more detailed account of the trinitarian ramifications of a pneumatological theology of justification. Although I have tried to frame my discussion in a trinitarian way, space limitations have not given opportunity to do justice for example to the necessary trinitarian discussion of "atonement," especially the cross. As is well known, the theology of the cross too often suffers from a "trinitarian anemia," as it were. That conversation, however, has to be left for another occasion.

In another essay recently I have tried to be more specific about the "global" implications of the revised view of justification for the needs of our pluralistic world.[39] In that essay, I also tried to draw conclusions from the work of many theologians, both Lutheran and others, regarding the integral relation between justification and justice. This has to do with the blurring of the separation between forensic and effective justification ("declaring" and "making" righteous, respectively) which has too often blocked the way for Protestants to appreciate the importance of the fruit of salvation. Granted that behind this distinction there has been the legitimate fear of "works-righteousness," it has also led to such a separation between "justification" and "sanctification" that not much incentive for the discipleship and following of Christ in everyday life has been provided.

Now that Pentecostal theologians such as Macchia have offered highly useful insights into the doctrine of justification — which, after

---

39. Veli-Matti Kärkkäinen, "The Lutheran Doctrine of Justification in the Global Context," *CMT* 38 (2011): 4-16.

all, is also their traditional way of speaking of salvation — the ecumenical world should join hands with them to highlight one aspect of soteriology badly in need of revisiting, namely, empowerment and gifting. In other words, the Pentecostal emphasis on "Spirit Baptism" as a distinct but not separate act of empowerment by the Holy Spirit could provide a template for a more robust link between "making righteous" and "making empowered," including the various gifts and energies of the Holy Spirit.[40]

More work towards the communal implications of the doctrine of justification, focusing on the idea of the "ecstatic" existence in Christ through the Spirit, should be attempted.

---

40. For a highly important work in this respect, see Frank D. Macchia, *Baptized in the Spirit: A Global Pentecostal Theology* (Grand Rapids: Zondervan, 2006). Important insights can also be found in Steven Studebakker, "Pentecostal Soteriology and Pneumatology," *JPT* 11 (2003): 248-70, and Amos Yong, *The Spirit Poured Out on All Flesh: Pentecostalism and the Possibility of Global Theology* (Grand Rapids: Baker Academic, 2005), pp. 81-120.

Towards a Theology of Togetherness — Life through the Spirit

Graham McFarlane

1. Introduction

It is a world of strange ironies: the tutor who first taught me to think in a way that would subsequently lead me into a career in systematic theology through his seminars on discourse analysis was to become not only a colleague but a confidant, a friend, and a fellow theological entrepreneur in seeking to unite New Testament studies and systematic theology. Ironic, too, that a growing tension emerges today between a world gifted by the Spirit and that demonstrated on streets throughout the world — whether in Arab uprisings or in civic unrest within English society — as people take out their frustration and anger on political and commercial institutions — close, very close, to where Max has spent almost all of his professional life teaching, mentoring, and inspiring. A deep irony, too, in timing: social unrest, on the one hand, and the reflections of a systematician on the contribution of a New Testament scholar in the field of pneumatology, on the other. What unites these disparate musings is the fact that we are privy today to increasing demonstrations of human alienation — of humans *not* being together. What we see on our own screens in our comfortable homes or experience more closely to home are the outworkings of what Scripture describes as "sin," or put more contemporaneously as the lack-of-human-togetherness. What I want to do in this offering to Max is unpack some of these disparate insights and draw them into a theology of human togetherness, or put more bluntly, a theology of at-one-ment that makes space for the ongoing reconciling role of the Spirit in the work of Christ on the cross in the here and now.

At the heart of the Christian evangel is a transforming invitation to a completely different way of living. If we take seriously the teaching of Jesus then his own response to how we "inherit eternal life" must contour how we perceive this call and respond to it. In Luke 10:25-28 we are privy to the typical encounter that takes place between the religious elite and any perceived threat. The hubris of the lawyer tests Jesus' mettle with the ultimate question — how to gain "eternal life" or, in more contemporary language, how to get "saved." Interestingly, Jesus responds with a highly political answer: eternal life and the way to eternal life is a life of togetherness with God, neighbor and self.[1] To illustrate this we are given the parable of the Good Samaritan. Here we encounter an alternative approach to community — a self-sacrificial form of relating where true togetherness is demonstrated in the startling action of one human being towards another. In it we are offered insight into the way the Father gives up his Son to the world in order that the world would be saved. All this illustrates a human togetherness formed from a divine initiative. The scandal of this evangel, in turn, is that it transcends both the solipsism of individualistic notions of salvation and the hegemony of nationalist religion, both forms of exclusivism, in order to reach out to "the other" — the neighbor — with the invitation to belong, to be social, to participate in a "law" which leads to community. It is a call to be together. Here is an offer of reparation, of salvation, within which we find the seeds of social — not merely individual — togetherness, initiated through the neighbor-love of God, as Father loving his creation, as Son rescuing it and as Spirit making this gift of togetherness possible in the here and now. It is a radical and perichoretic action designed to bring about togetherness. As such, then, in order for us to appreciate fully what God has done in Christ on the cross — the means by which the Father and Son establish at-one-ment — there must also be in place a definite hope that what has been achieved is an actual experience for those who aspire to it. Such a hope is empowered by an eschatological dimension where such togetherness already exists because of the at-one-ing work of Christ: what waits to be experienced in its fullness is, at the same time, also realizable in some form in the here and now.

---

1. Scot McKnight explores the grammar of this Christian doctrine from both biblical and theological perspectives in *The Jesus Creed* (Brewster: Paraclete Press, 2004).

2. A Contemporary Problem and the Gospel

This is indeed "good news" not merely to the individual to whom modern soteriological models pander but more positively to those seeking a polis — a relational expression of Kingdom living — that accommodates both God and neighbor. It is against this backdrop that current sociological insights render a stark reminder that we are very much far from achieving this hope. Take, for example, the growing wave of unrest rippling across certain nations of the world. If society can be understood as the "factory" that provides us with meaning it would appear that its production line is breaking down. So much so that those who are excluded from the modern polis, whom we might call modernity's *neighbors,* are forced to live in parallel universes to those around them. Thus Camila Batmanghelidjh writes concerning the civic unrest being experienced by English society, "How, we ask, could they attack their own community with such disregard? The young people would reply 'easily,' because they feel they don't actually belong to the community. Community, they would say, has nothing to offer them. Instead, for years they have experienced themselves cut adrift from civil society's legitimate structures."[2] The prescient nature of such comments captures the reality of the "other," the "neighbor" for whom there is no "togetherness" and from whom both status quo and *hoi polloi* turn a blind eye. Sure, we do not read "Samaritan" but Batmanghelidjh captures the essence clearly when she goes on to say, "The individual is responsible for their own survival because the community is perceived to provide nothing. Acquisition of goods through violence is justified in neighborhoods where the notion of dog eat dog pervades and the top dog survives the best."[3] Nothing has changed: in Jesus' time the assault on the neighbor and her obvious plight consisted in ignoring her with plausible religious reasons with little comeback. More recently, today's political turning of the eye results in riots. As Batmanghelidjh concludes, "the lawlessness is, suddenly, there for all to see. Less visible is the perverse insidious violence delivered through legitimate societal structures."[4] Whilst the cultus of Second Temple Ju-

---

2. Camila Batmanghelidjh, "Caring Costs — But So Do Riots," *The Independent* 218 (09 August 2011): 13.
3. Batmanghelidjh, "Costs," p. 13.
4. Batmanghelidjh, "Costs," p. 13.

daism created an ethos in which neighbor love was diminished to kinsmanship, the political ideology of modernity leaves the individual to create his or her own world. This modern counterpart is fed by a belief in democracy that believes in the "individual's ability to influence the conditions of their own lives, to formulate the meaning of 'common good' and to make the institutions of society comply with that meaning."[5] These institutions, of course, work both to keep the inhabitants of society in place and to empower a ruling elite (religious or political or both) to determine where this society will go. They serve a social-order-building established not on togetherness but on deeply held beliefs concerning segregation (them/us), alienation (top dog/underdog) and repression (submit/be damned). In turn, dogma — secular or religious — consolidates such belief endorsing it with gravitas and kudos. All serve one end: the constant undermining of the hope of as well as disruption to human togetherness. Indeed, it is not too far off the mark to say that it is the problematic of "togetherness" that impacts and critiques us in all levels of our personal and social existences. It critiques, on the one hand, any religious ideology that excludes the "other" and reflects its own neighborly bankruptcy and any political agenda, on the other, that creates "waste products" incapable of ever belonging or contributing. Each, in its own way, demands a proper theology of togetherness. Only with this can the individual hope against religious hubris or the mob hope against political hegemony. It is a transcendental without which hope is vacated of any real meaning. And for it to succeed its potency rests on an eschatological fulcrum — that what we hope for is already achieved and therefore achievable.

This is the Christian gospel: that in Christ there is no room for any form of human alienation. Here is the "space" in which "church" is called to operate. Not a call to withdraw from its world and abrogate any prophetic authority to speak into the chaos around it. Nor a mandate to create parallel religious worlds that collapse as the paradigm on which they themselves have been molded, namely modernity, itself folds.[6] The problem for both is a political one — an evangel-call for the church to become that alternative society expressing the Kingdom of

5. Zygmunt Bauman, *In Search of Politics* (Cambridge: Polity Press), p. 106.
6. Whilst dated, the following speak into the current state of affairs with precision: Andrew Walker, *Different Gospels* (London: SPCK, 1993); Stanley Hauerwas and William Willimon, *Resident Aliens* (Nashville: Abingdon Press, 1993); and Richard Middleton and Brian Walsh, *Truth Is Stranger Than It Used to Be* (London: SPCK, 1995).

God — a *factory of meaning* where neither individual nor collective are burdened under false hope, whether consumerist or religious, and where togetherness is not only promised but is achieved.

Such a hope, clearly, is a high one but it is also a *Christological* one. It is a hope founded on the life, teaching, death, resurrection, ascension and glorification of Jesus Christ. In him we find a life centered on total obedience to God and love of neighbor. Indeed, as Hooker points out, it is Jesus who straddles both the world we hope for and the one in which we find ourselves.

> Christ stands over against Adam as the new head of humanity. It seems that there are in Paul's view . . . two spheres: . . . the sphere of humanity "in Adam" — which includes everyone; and there is the sphere of those who are "in Christ," who have been 'incorporated' into Christ. . . . The two spheres . . . must be seen not as touching at their edges, but as intersection; Christians live in two spheres at once. But the reason why it is possible to move from one sphere to another . . . is that Christ himself shared the condition of being "in Adam"; the new humanity was created within the circle of the old.[7]

It is here we affirm the unique work of Christ on the cross — that by virtue of being Son of God and Son of Man he alone is able to deal legitimately with our condition before God on our behalf. And if we can translate this back to Jesus' own answer as to how we inherit eternal life — that is, "get saved" — then here we see the only authentic human being, Jesus Christ, loving God with all his heart, mind and strength, even to the point of going to the cross in obedience to the Father's will as the only way the power of sin could be broken and the love of God be demonstrated to such an "untogether" world. This is the great power of the Christian gospel — an evangel in which God deals with God on our behalf. Yet to stop here is to do serious damage to the gospel. Inheriting eternal life, according to Jesus, also demands engagement with our neighbor. And to do this demands a pneumatic dimension — where life through the Spirit is hypostatized and earthed in forms wherein neighbor is reconciled with neighbor and togetherness may be demonstrated *en carne* in the here and now as an anticipatory expression of what is to come in fullness. As Christ's death on its own is a groundless hope — "under normal circumstances, this death would be yet another

---

7. Morna Hooker, *Pauline Pieces* (London: Epworth Press, 1979), p. 43.

reaffirmation that the hopes he aroused were groundless, that any other way of life has no possible future"[8] — and is given power through his resurrection, so too the hope of togetherness is empty without resurrection hope. The imperative towards togetherness rests on both the presupposition of the cross and the empowering of the Spirit. The heart of the matter is that we cannot separate atonement from ecclesiology and pneumatology without rendering the narrative of the gospel devoid of any real hope. The work of Christ, who reveals the togetherness of Father, Son, and Spirit in their redemptive action towards a messed-up humanity, is endorsed by the Father by raising the dead body of Jesus through the agency of the Holy Spirit.[9] This becomes the foundation for all future notions of togetherness — that this same Spirit shall take what has already been accomplished through Jesus' physical existence and replicate it throughout those who faithfully place their hearts, souls, and energy over to the Father and love their neighbors as they have been loved and love. It is pneumatic love, made real in the humanity of Jesus, which fulfills the Law. This is the triumph of the Father.[10]

3. Making Some Space

It is here we locate the significance of current pneumatological studies in the most recent decades to which Max has been a significant biblical contributor. Such studies have opened new windows of perception regarding not only *who* the Spirit is but also *what* the Spirit does and therefore what life in the Spirit may look like. The potency of such studies resides in the way they furnish theological reflection and cre-

---

8. Adam Kotsko, *The Politics of Redemption* (London: T&T Clark, 2010), p. 202.

9. Colin Gunton describes "the ministry of Jesus as that of the true Israelite who did the will of his Father because the Spirit maintained him, *as Son*, true to the Father from whom he came and to whom he was to return." Colin Gunton, *The Christian Faith* (Oxford: Blackwell, 2002), p. 106.

10. Robert Jenson, *Systematic Theology* (Oxford: Oxford University Press, 1997), vol. 1, p. 48. I am indebted to Andrew Stobart for pointing this phrase out to me. See: A. J. Stobart, "A Constructive Analysis of the Place and Role of the Doctrine of Jesus' Resurrection within the Theologies of Rowan Williams and Robert Jenson," unpublished PhD thesis (University of Aberdeen, 2011). Andrew was also a student of Max and myself and continues the legacy of biblically informed and applied systematics he first encountered at London School of Theology.

ativity to create the space — the eschatological space[11] — necessary if redemptive hope is to be fed and established. With the modern, secular notion of hope came a sense that "liquid individuals seem to have no hold on the present in a way which makes them capable of acting creatively towards the future."[12] It has proven to be bankrupt. Unlike its modern counterpart the hope offered in the gospel is no chimera, a vacuous desire impotent to deliver what it promises. Rather, its potency to deliver is grounded in the life, death, resurrection and glorification of Jesus Christ whose dying on a Roman gibbet lays foundations for togetherness, not only with God but also for the hope of human relational integrity and friendship.

How? If we push this notion of Christ being "in Adam" — that collective humanity to which we all belong — we begin to see how this mode of being offers us a glimpse into life in the Spirit. And it is here that my systematic theology and New Testament studies dialogue. Whilst for Max research covers life after Pentecost, my own interests originate in life before Pentecost, and in particular how the Spirit relates to Jesus in the economy of salvation. With nineteenth-century Scottish theologian, Edward Irving, we engage with questions necessary for any theology of togetherness where the hope of reconciliation, forgiveness, and neighbor-love are a possibility. For Irving, the kind of humanity the Son of God assumed in incarnation was not one instantly perfected when union between divine and human occurred. If so, there is no hope for sinners to change since this kind of union is not ours to enjoy. Nor was it perfected prior to life in the womb, as though Jesus' mother, Mary, was somehow sinless and thus passed on to her son a sinless humanity. Again, little hope for those of us who have not undergone a virgin birth. Rather, the force at work in Jesus' humanity was neither his own self-will nor his own divine nature. It was, for

---

11. Human relationships do not happen in a vacuum — they happen in the "space" of time, history, culture. Thus, for human relationships to be-at-one there needs to be an actual space-time-historical context in which this happens. Secondly, the only grounds for actual togetherness is the belief that Christ has done all that needs to be done in order for this to happen. However, this is a hope we wait for in anticipation of its full realization. Any "togetherness" experienced in the here and now is a derivative of this future hope.

12. Poul Poder, "Bauman on Freedom — Consumer Freedom as the Integration Mechanism of Liquid Society," in *The Sociology of Zygmunt Bauman: Challenges and Critique*, ed. M. Jacobsen and Poul Poder (Aldershot: Ashgate, 2008), p. 207.

Irving, pastorally and soteriologically necessary to demonstrate that Jesus was truly human, that he never sinned, because he lived life *through* and *by* the Spirit.[13] Only this particular relationship between Son and Spirit provides the hope necessary to subsequent disciples of Jesus that they, too, may know what Irving described as "holiness in the flesh."[14] It is a pneumatic empowering based on the experience of Jesus himself.[15] As Jesus was "in Adam" and overcame Adam's sinful nature through the Spirit, so those who are "in Christ" receive the Spirit and as such participate in the hope established by Christ's death, resurrection, and glorification to the right hand of the Father on high. This is no ephemeral hope — it is established in the here and now both by Christ's once and for all death and the Spirit's ongoing appropriation in the lives of believers today.

What does this mean for a theology of togetherness? On the one hand, it is all too easy to reduce atonement thinking to a private/public transaction between the believer and God. To do so may well do justice to western theological tradition but it fails miserably in light of the full demonstration of God's love shown to us in Christ, on a cross, in an empty tomb, with a seated victorious and omnipotent Savior. Why? Because it fails to link the death of Christ with life through the Spirit and in so doing facilitates a theology of independence that reflects more the mores of western modernity than a New Testament ecclesiology of togetherness through the enabling gifting of the Spirit and his gifts. Without a pneumatic foundation to our understanding of atonement we are left with the possibility of togetherness with God — Christ has dealt with the Father's response to sin and there is now no condemnation for those who are in Christ Jesus — but it fails to offer an equally substantive foundation for human togetherness. It lacks any underlying rationale for human togetherness — we are simply saved "to get on with it."[16] Consequently, this state of affairs is reflected in our versions

---

13. See Graham W. P. McFarlane, *Christ and the Spirit* (Carlisle: Paternoster, 1996), pp. 139-40.

14. Edward Irving, *Christ's Holiness in the Flesh, the Form, Fountain Head, and Assurance to Us of Holiness in the Flesh. In Three Parts* (Edinburgh: John Lindsay, 1831).

15. Edward Irving, *The Collected Writings of Edward Irving in Five Volumes*, ed. G. Carlyle (London: Alexander Strahan, 1864), vol. 5, p. 126.

16. Indeed, we could argue that the removal of the imperative to neighbor love as an intrinsic salvific element creates a vacuum that has to be filled either in legalism, activism or materialism. Each is the manifestation of *self-interest* and not neighbor love, the

of church where all too often, wittingly or unwittingly, we create insidious communities that either ingest the individual demanding she become like the status quo or communities that vomit out individuals who do not conform to the norm.[17]

On the other hand, a theology of togetherness requires some *ontic* ground upon which future relating can take place with confidence. A one-dimensional understanding of the work of Christ — one lacking any pneumatic dimension — provides assurance of togetherness with God but not necessarily with neighbor. And since, for Jesus, eternal life is manifested in loving one's neighbor as oneself, this neighborly togetherness requires an equally robust foundation. Indeed, without such all we can hope for is some kind of patronizing or condescending attitude towards "the other" as an object of salvation and possible future member of our own version of the panopticon rather than a togetherness that does not require the neighbor to give up her personal identity — perhaps even his collective identity.[18] "Rather, it is a willing-

---

drive towards self and away from neighbor. Religion, then, only consolidates what is already there in the deeper recesses of the human spirit. Gregory A. Boyd, *Repenting of Religion: Turning from Judgment to the Love of God* (Grand Rapids: Baker, 2004) is interesting for his pastoral insights on this dynamic.

17. See Zygmunt Bauman, *Life in Fragments: Essays in Postmodern Morality* (Oxford: Basil Blackwell, 1995), where Bauman describes such communities as *anthropophagic* and *anthropoemic* respectively. See, too, Claude Lévi-Strauss, *Tristes Tropiques* (London: Penguin, 1992 [1955]) pp. 287-88: "Above all we should realise that certain of our customs might appear, to an observer belonging to a different society, to be similar in nature to cannibalism, although cannibalism strikes us as being foreign to the idea of civilization. I am thinking, for instance, of our legal and prison systems. If we studied societies from the outside, it would be tempting to distinguish two contrasting types: those which practice cannibalism — that is, which regard the absorption of certain individuals possessing dangerous powers as the only means of neutralizing those powers and even of turning them to advantage — and those which, like our own society, adopt what might be called the practice of anthropoemy (from the Greek ἐμεῖν, to vomit); faced with the same problem, the latter type of society has chosen the opposite solution which consists in ejecting dangerous individuals from the social body and keeping them temporarily or permanently in isolation, away from all contact with their fellows, in establishments specially intended for this purpose. Most of the societies which we call primitive would regard this custom with profound horror; it would make us, in their eyes, guilty of that same barbarity of which we accuse them because of their symmetrically opposite behaviour."

18. Jeremy Bentham, *Panopticon; or, The Inspection-House* (Gloucester: Dodo Press, 2008 [1791]).

ness to embrace a stranger as representative of herself instead of treating her as an unwanted peculiarity constantly out of place."[19]

4. Why the Gospel Works

What Bauman and others are unable to do, however, is offer sufficient grounds for establishing a way of relating that is both truly inclusive and achievable. Indeed, it could be argued that the whole notion of community itself implies alienation — of not belonging, of not being together — since to be in community with some is to be out of community with others. The genius of the Christian gospel is that it contains what is necessary to bring about togetherness whilst safeguarding individual identity. On the one hand, because of the work accomplished by Christ on the cross, the Spirit transcends the various expressions of human collective identities (there is neither Jew nor Greek, male nor female, bond nor free in Christ, Gal. 3:28) and thus can bring about unity since all are *in Christ Jesus*. On the other, the particularity of Jesus, seated at the right hand of the Father, safeguards each particular person, for it is on the template of the humanity of the Lord Jesus Christ that the Spirit works in and through each subsequent believer. Colin Gunton moves this towards a theology of the mundane — thus, concerning baptism in the Spirit he writes, "it is the gift of life with others. Because the Spirit is the one who perfects all the creation, his work is centered on enabling the ordinary, and especially ordinary life in the human body, to be what it is made to be."[20]

5. We Can Identify Two Important Insights from This

Firstly and most importantly, we affirm that the presence of the Spirit is as much a gift to us as the reality of salvation through Jesus Christ. He is, as Pannenberg and Welker put it, "the field of force"[21] — an apt

---

19. Niclas Månsson, "Bauman on Strangers — Unwanted Peculiarities," in *The Sociology of Zygmunt Bauman: Challenges and Critique*, ed. M. H. Jacobsen and Poul Poder (Aldershot: Ashgate, 2008), p. 170.

20. Gunton, *The Christian Faith*, p. 156. What Colin describes as "the gift of life with others" is very much a theology of togetherness.

21. Wolfhart Pannenberg, *Systematic Theology* (Edinburgh: T&T Clark, 1991), vol. 1, pp. 235-36; Michael Welker, *God the Spirit* (Minneapolis: Fortress Press, 1994), pp. 239-48.

Towards a Theology of Togetherness

metaphor for the dynamic of togetherness. For in the reality of human brokenness both in its own alienation and in the various forms others take in response to such mess we are unable truly to overcome the obstacles, undo the damage, recollect what has been said and done. The true condition of sin is just too insidious. We cannot undo its consequences. It can only exist in fragmented forms of personhood and sociality. Only a power greater than the problem can do this. Such is the gift from our Neighbor — the Father who sends his Son in the empowering agency of the Spirit to bring us together as they are together. And if the original recipients refuse the gift then the divine drive towards togetherness demands the net be thrown wider to include those who live at the very edges of neighborliness — first to the streets and lanes, then to the highways and hedges — because there is an imperative to be fulfilled: "that my house may be filled" (Luke 14:15-24). This is the quality of togetherness the gospel demands and which the Spirit empowers. It reaches out beyond the status quo, to those initially invited and embraces — actually demands the presence of — those who have been discarded by the factory of meaning, whether the cultus of Second Temple Judaism replete with dead men's bones, shining like white-washed tombs (Matt. 23:27) or contemporary forms of religious and social existences that are exclusive, self-justifying and domesticate the very means of transformation and togetherness.

Secondly, we can locate the Spirit's specific role in atonement: the Spirit is the one who brings into reality the gift of togetherness accomplished on the cross by the Son both in relation to God and in relation to neighbor, as in Ephesians 2:18. The curse of alienation — of non-togetherness — has been lifted through the cross (Gal. 3:13-14). Something real has been broken and something objectively real has taken its place and the Spirit can now apply to those who live in faith with Christ. Thus

> Due to his obedience to God's will and his commitment to serving others, Jesus did not shrink from the cross (a type of death upon which the law has pronounced a curse) when his life of obedience and service led to conflict with the authorities; instead, he remained obedient to God, continuing to seek the promised age of redemption for others and their deliverance from their present plight of "curse," which was due to their sins.... The deliverance sought for others when he went to the cross became a reality when

he *had become* a curse, that is, when he was raised by God *after* giving up his life on the cross so that through him the blessings promised through Abraham and the gift of the Spirit might now be given to both Jews and Gentiles.[22]

This is the perfecting work of the Spirit[23] — to bring into reality "a new objective situation, namely, the end of exile and the construction of a new kind of temple, indwelt by God's own Spirit. The cross saves, not by bequeathing an example, but by bequeathing to the church the same power that enabled Jesus to lay down his life for others: the Spirit of self-giving love."[24] The cross achieves a realizable eschaton[25] wherein the faithful realize in each of their lives, through the Spirit, what is already real, Christ's victory over sin, law, and death, and in so doing participate in the Father's Kingdom.

6. Conclusion

The Spirit's role in atonement is such that:

a. We receive power to become children of God by virtue of the redeeming work of Jesus Christ achieved through his faithful obedience to the Father's will, his love of neighbor and his own vision of the Kingdom which took him to a Roman cross where he died, was buried, was raised to life and ascended to the ultimate position of authority, next to God the Father on high.

b. This power enables us to live by the law of the Spirit of life in Christ Jesus — to be "in Christ" and to be "like Christ." It is an existence demonstrated in reflecting divine togetherness as it is worked out in human will and loving relation.

---

22. David Brondos, "The Cross and the Curse: Galatians 3.13 and Paul's Doctrine of Redemption," *JSNT* 81 (2001): 3-32, esp. p. 25.

23. See Part 3, "The Perfecting Cause: 'And in the Holy Spirit,'" in Gunton, *The Christian Faith* (Oxford: Blackwell, 2002).

24. Kevin Vanhoozer, "The Atonement in Postmodernity. Guilt, Goats and Gifts," in *The Glory of the Atonement*, ed. C. E. Hill and F. A. James III (Downers Grove: IVP, 2004), pp. 200-201.

25. John Milbank, *Being Reconciled: Ontology and Pardon* (London: Routledge, 2003), p. 59, talks of the aporia of finality re forgiveness, that without a hope that is already real there is no real substance to the gift of forgiveness. All that exists, in effect, is an "illusory *eschaton* . . . because its finality is a chimaera."

c. The Spirit gifts each participant in this new polity with unique contributing faculties that bring to birth the possibility of equality and establish an alternative "factory of meaning" — the Kingdom of God — with its own political and economic values and currency — where there are no outsiders but all are one in Christ.

d. The Spirit makes possible a realizable eschaton where what is already real in Christ is given substance in the here and now in the Church as a guarantee of what is to come.

e. The impossible possibility, the gift of true forgiveness,[26] becomes a reality in the lives and social intercourse of those who follow Christ. Any notion of "indebtedness" disappears in a relationship that moves from servant to friend, slave to co-heir. John 15:15, Ephesians 2:5-6, Colossians 3:1, Romans 8:17 — each signifies a new political reality wherein what Christ achieved on the cross, by resurrection, ascension and glorification is to be understood within the context of "covenant" where social intercourse — togetherness — is valued to the degree it manifests being "faithful" (covenant) and not "successful" (consumerist). The values of the former will reflect the politics and economics of togetherness best summarized in Micah 6:8: "He has shown you, O man, what is good. And what does the LORD require of you? To act justly and to love mercy and to walk humbly with your God." In essence, it is to love God with one's entire being and relate to one's neighbors, to love them whether near or far, as we love ourselves. This is the parallel community we are called to be through the Spirit. This is life together empowered from on high: costly, since such at-one-ment is achieved in the sacrificial death of God's own Son; dynamic, since its effect is to birth an alternative factory of meaning, the church; effective, since its victory is assured and its end achieved: a life of togetherness, of Father, Son, and Spirit; of the man, Christ Jesus seated with God above all other forms of power; and of a people dragged from the highways and byways of planet earth and discipled into living a life of togetherness.

---

26. Jacques Derrida, *On Cosmopolitanism and Forgiveness* (London: Routledge, 2001), argues that true forgiveness is an impossibility due to the fact that once forgiveness is offered one enters a polity and economy of "sovereignty" where there can be no equality. It is my argument that this very real economy is overcome only in the sacrificial death of Christ for us and the subsequent full adoption of those who put their faith in him which annuls any economy of sovereignty and replaces it with equality and mutual empowerment.

Creative Reason and the Spirit: Identifying, Evaluating, and Developing Paradigms of Pneumatology

André Munzinger

Max Turner's work has inspired scholarship to be sensitive to the liberating, empowering, and creative work of the Spirit. This is true not only within New Testament studies but also within systematic and practical theology. At the same time, what characterizes his writing is his adherence to the academic virtues of rational, reflective and critical thought. Spiritual life will not lose but gain significance, if it is firmly grounded in reason — that is how I would interpret the impetus of his work. How do these two quite different emphases — on the one hand pneumatic creativity, and on the other hand reasonable reflection — go together? Is there an interpretative paradigm which allows for each of these, in some respects countervailing forces, to be given their own weight? In the following paper I aim to firstly follow up recent discussions on the paradigms of pneumatology in order to secondly introduce a new perspective developed by Eilert Herms on the old but major paradigmatic discussion in systematic theology. This concerns the debate between theologies orientated towards revelation (Karl Barth) and experience (Friedrich Schleiermacher). Finally, my aim is to use the work of Herms as the backdrop for further differentiations with regard to the possibility of evaluating and developing pneumatology. While it is inevitable that we interpret reality in certain frameworks of thought, I will argue that the interpretative development of any such paradigm is in itself a creative process and can be linked — if some critical conditions are attended to — to the creativity of the Spirit. The main goal of this article is therefore to map the terrain of the interrelationship of Spirit and mind with reference to recent interpretative paradigms in systematic theology.

1. Paradigms of Pneumatology

In the mid-1950s, Karl Barth expressed his vision of the future orientation of dogmatics in general, and the development of his theology in particular:

> Today I would speak more of the Holy Spirit. Perhaps I was too cautious. You students should not make that mistake in your polemical writings! . . . A good theology can be based on any of the three articles of the Creed. You could base it on the Doctrine of the Holy Spirit. . . . I personally think that a theology of the Spirit might be all right after AD 2000, but now we are still too close to the eighteenth and nineteenth centuries.[1]

Since Karl Barth is generally identified with work in Christology and trinitarian theology and far less with pneumatology, this comment may be surprising.[2] Nonetheless, the spread of Spirit-theology at the end of the twentieth century confirms Barth's prediction in terms of the significance of pneumatology for the development of theology. Horst Georg Pöhlmann has compiled recent pneumatologies and made a point of comparing traditional and more innovatively orientated pneumatologies as well as secular concepts of spirit.[3] Although he has done an admirable job of documenting the wide-ranging interest this topic has generated, his depiction of the Pentecostal and charismatic as well as Anglo-Saxon debates is limited. Nevertheless, any attempt to classify the stark differences is a complex exercise. How can the Spirit-teachings of the likes of Friedrich Schleiermacher, Karl Barth, Wolfhart Pannenberg, and Amos Yong be compared?

The adjectives "high" and "low," which are used to classify approaches to Christology, could serve as a means for making pneumatological distinctions: *On the one hand*, then, those which could be called "high pneumatologies" may be identified with the attempts which un-

---

1. Karl Barth, in *Karl Barth's Table Talk*, ed. John D. Godsey (Edinburgh: Oliver & Boyd, 1963), p. 27.
2. Even research dealing with Barth's pneumatology has been set in a Christological setting. E.g. John Thompson, *The Holy Spirit in the Theology of Karl Barth* (Allison Park: Pickwick, 1991).
3. Horst Georg Pöhlmann, *Heiliger Geist — Gottesgeist, Zeitgeist oder Weltgeist?* (Neukirchen-Vluyn: Neukirchener Verlag, 1998).

derstand the Spirit in a Christological and soteriological setting. The Spirit is introduced as the solution to the difficulty every dogmatic conception faces: bridging the gap between the second and the third article of faith, the gap between the Christological center and its soteriological, ethical, ecclesiological, as well as eschatological implications. In this type of Spirit-theology the differentiation between the divine and the human spirit is emphasized. Moreover, pneumatology is presented as an alternative, relational perspective on dogmatics and contrasted with a traditional, rational approach. This broad description is of course somewhat indistinct because it fits pneumatologies which have been developed in the wake of Karl Barth's work (Colin Gunton for instance) as well as in light of the Pentecostal and charismatic movements (recently by Amos Yong).

On the other hand, a keen interest in "low pneumatologies" is evident. They are orientated towards the doctrine of creation and argue for continuity or even an identification between the divine Spirit and the spirit of life. These interpret the Spirit, for instance, in mystical frameworks (Thomas Merton), in the context of liberation theology (Gustav Gutiérrez), or that of the natural sciences (Wolfhart Pannenberg). Again, however, this classification, if pressed for details, is not adequate for understanding these elaborate and innovative positions. For instance, Pannenberg follows T. F. Torrance in relating the Christian teaching of the Spirit with modern field-theories in physics (of Michael Faraday). In understanding God as such a dynamic field, however, he remains firmly indebted to a trinitarian structure and an eschatological framework.[4] His work displays elements of both "low" and "high" pneumatologies.

Another type of classification has been developed with regard to precisely these problems raised by Pannenberg and his incorporation of the natural sciences into a theological framework. Wolfgang Vondey has argued that the problem with large parts of the "renaissance in pneumatology" since the middle of the twentieth century is the fact that it has "remained indebted to Newton's philosophy of nature and ignored the implications of the most recent scientific revolution."[5] He defines this as the paradigm shift which replaces Newtonian physics with Einstein's theory of relativity. Whereas scientific circles have de-

---

4. For an overview, cf. Geoffrey Wainwright, "Geist V," *RGG*[4], 3:570.

5. Wolfgang Vondey, "The Holy Spirit and the Physical Universe," *TS* 70 (2009): 5.

bated the structure of these revolutions, theologians, according to Vondey, "have said very little about the impact of these paradigm shifts on religious thought."[6] Pneumatology after Einstein should, however, be located in a different cosmological framework, which Vondey marks with the concepts of order, rationality, relationality, symmetry, and movement. "The contemporary task," as Vondey concludes, "is to understand the Spirit in the physical universe, rather than the metaphysical; in time, rather than the eschaton; in space and matter, rather than the supernatural; in movement, rather than in presence."[7]

Notwithstanding the argument that theology is interrelated with cosmology and that this intricate relationship is often neglected to the detriment of the clarity of understanding our "world," Vondey's position needs to be questioned with regard to his own neglect of the interpretative issues involved. He seems to assume that understanding the concept of the Spirit is a question primarily of the paradigms of physics rather than hermeneutics (and attempts to strip "physics" of "metaphysics," which in itself is highly contested).[8] The major difficulties of translating between the cultures of the natural sciences and the humanities are not even mentioned. Moreover, the term and concept "paradigm" itself is not straightforward and requires closer definition. Thomas S. Kuhn's use of the term — which is influenced by Wittgenstein, who in turn refers to Plato — suggests that paradigms offer certain standards of thought and action which can be revolutionized in and through a change in methodological, conceptual, and metaphysical presuppositions.[9] Kuhn was, however, interested primarily in the hard sciences and was intent on pointing out differences from the humanities.[10] Whether one agrees with Kuhn or not, the link between physics and pneumatology is mediated by complex interpretative pro-

---

6. Vondey, *Spirit*, p. 4. He cites William Lane Craig who laments that theologians still think and work in the perspective of Newtonian physics and without any clear understanding of the "philosophy of space and time" (p. 4).

7. Vondey, *Spirit*, p. 36.

8. For an in-depth analysis of classifying spirit-language, cf. Matthias Petzoldt, "Gehirn — Geist — Heiliger Geist," in *Die Wirklichkeit des Geistes: Konzeptionen und Phänomene des Geistes in Philosophie und Theologie der Gegenwart*, ed. Ulrich H. J. Körtner and Andreas Klein (Neukirchen-Vluyn: Neukirchener Verlag, 2006), pp. 1-18.

9. Cf. Hans-Joachim Waschkies, "Paradigma," RGG[4], 6:920-21.

10. Cf. Thomas S. Kuhn, *The Structure of Scientific Revolutions*, 3rd ed. (Chicago: The University of Chicago Press, 1996), pp. 164-65.

cesses and methodologies in both of the disciplines involved: theology and the natural sciences.

Hence a third and final type of classification is to be introduced, which is the paradigmatic approach to philosophical methodologies. It has not been applied to pneumatology directly, but will offer the ability to structure further debate. Jürgen Habermas (in line with Ernst Tugendhat) differentiates three paradigms of philosophy which are described on a historical trajectory:[11] While philosophy since Plato was orientated towards understanding "being" ("das Sein"), Enlightenment and Idealist philosophers shifted their whole enterprise towards the transcendental question of "consciousness." Finally, the "linguistic turn" has, according to Habermas, superseded the first two paradigms. These paradigms are defined correspondingly as "ontological," "reflexive" and "linguistic" manners of thought and are presented in a chronological order, as a type of evolutionary process in clarifying the foundations of possible knowledge: In the *first*, "ontological framework," truth is associated with the unchangeable and the necessary, and the structures of being itself express themselves in our knowledge. However, questions regarding this priority (of being before knowledge) paved the way for the *second* paradigm: The self-relationship of the knowledgeable subject opens a new approach to an inner world, which is given priority over the objective world. In the wake of this model it is postulated that theoretical judgments about the world and its truth can only be made by means of a theory of consciousness. At last, a *third* paradigm has been developed in which the monological approach to reality, displayed in the theories of subjectivity, has been starkly criticized. With the focus on the research in language, Habermas argues, the intersubjective relations and societal patterns have been found to be the formative influences in structuring approaches to knowledge, truth, and reality, and these intersubjective relations are formed by the language we use.[12]

Numerous questions need to be raised with regard to this division of the history of philosophy. The concept of such a stark development in philosophy is more than contested. The major paradigms described here are *at present* still the object of intense debate. In the existential and phenomenological traditions the question of understanding "being" is

---

11. Cf. Jürgen Habermas, "Metaphysik nach Kant," in *Nachmetaphysisches Denken: Philosophische Aufsätze* (Frankfurt: Suhrkamp, 1988), pp. 18-34.

12. The only rational access to these relations is through our language.

still prominent. At the same time, important philosophical and theological positions (following for instance Fichte, Hegel, or Schleiermacher) are still heavily influenced by the idealistic, transcendental tradition of understanding subjectivity as a fundamental anthropological category.[13] Peter Dews has rightly argued that a new paradigm in philosophy cannot simply ignore the questions and issues of the former paradigms. One paradigm cannot fully replace another. Rather the same questions appear "in an altered form, as a fundamental tension with which our thinking is confronted."[14] I would suggest that a synchronic differentiation of these approaches is more appropriate than a stark diachronic analysis of philosophical method.[15]

This synchronic approach offers the means of classifying the following three very different approaches to systematic theology. And in developing this line of thought, I will argue that this classification provides a structural advantage. It offers more differentiated frameworks of thought than the qualification of "low" and "high" theologies, and does not fall into the trap of identifying the methodologies of the natural sciences and the humanities. The structural gain of this approach becomes apparent in three basic methodologies in theology. So for instance, Ingolf U. Dalferth from the University of Zurich and the Claremont Graduate University (Danforth Professor of Philosophy of Religion) is keen on deconstructing theological programs which are indebted to a theory of subjectivity as developed in German Idealism.[16] In contrast, his own program is indebted to a mixture of the analytical

---

13. "Subjectivity" as developed in German Idealism is not to be confused with a subjective or relativistic perception of the world. It denotes a universal cognitive structure of the constitution of reasonable beings.

14. Peter Dews, "Communicative Paradigms and the Question of Subjectivity: Habermas, Mead and Lacan," in *Habermas: A Critical Reader*, ed. Peter Dews (Oxford: Blackwell, 1999), p. 113. He is, however, concerned only with "the tension *between* subjectivity and intersubjectivity."

15. Cf. the exemplary manner in which Herbert Schnädelbach argues such a case ("Phänomenologie und Sprachanalyse," in *Die Öffentlichkeit der Vernunft und die Vernunft der Öffentlichkeit: Festschrift für Jürgen Habermas*, ed. Lutz Wingert and Klaus Gunther [Frankfurt: Suhrkamp, 2001], pp. 243-67).

16. "Subjektivitätsstrukturen sind ein wichtiger anthropologischer Phänomenbestand, aber nicht die fundamentale Begründungsbasis und das letztgültige Plausibilitätsforum aller philosophischen und damit auch religionsphilosophischer Argumentation" (Ingolf U. Dalferth, *Die Wirklichkeit des Möglichen: Hermeneutische Religionsphilosophie* [Tübingen: Mohr Siebeck, 2003], p. 425).

and hermeneutical philosophies of *language*. Eilert Herms, from the University of Tübingen, has also been highly critical of giving the subjectivity theories too much weight. He has, however, been forceful in his own phenomenological approach, which bases epistemology and action-theory on fundamental *ontology*[17] and qualified realism.[18] Quite in contrast to both of these approaches, Ulrich Barth from the University of Halle (who is *not* related to Karl Barth) has developed a concept of religion which is inextricably linked with precisely such a theory of *subjectivity*, based on the Idealistic endeavor of establishing a transcendental foundation for knowledge.[19] In this sense, I have interpreted the classification of Habermas synchronically and used it to understand the starting points of these leading theologies. But what influence does this have on pneumatology?

In what follows I will first take a step back from these three different approaches and argue that their contentions can only be understood within a deep divide in continental theology between dialectical and liberal traditions — acknowledging that these are not to be understood as homogenous schools of thought. In the light of this significant division, the work of Eilert Herms, and particularly his pneumatology, will be introduced and assessed as an attempt to bridge this gap — so that the focal point of the interrelationship of "subjectivity," "language," and "being" can be revisited.

2. Bridging the Divide between the Theologies of Karl Barth and Friedrich Schleiermacher

At the core of this fierce theological battle lies the contested issue of how to describe the relationship between divine revelation and human reason. Or put simply: Where does theological thought begin: with God or with the human subject? A correspondingly undemanding but not particularly convincing answer is: Barth starts with "God" and

---

17. This term is notoriously difficult but in the following it is used as a formal concept for understanding the question of our finding ourselves as beings for whom "being as such" remains a question.

18. Eilert Herms, "Schleiermachers Erbe," in *Menschsein im Werden* (Tübingen: Mohr Siebeck, 2003), pp. 200-226.

19. Ulrich Barth, "Der Weg zur absoluten Reflexion im nachkantischen Idealismus," in *Gott als Projekt der Vernunft* (Tübingen: Mohr Siebeck, 2005), pp. 309-38.

Schleiermacher with the "human subject."[20] More precisely, Christoph Schwöbel has argued that Barth has rejected the modern inversion of the order of "being" and "knowing."[21] In that sense, it can be stated that while Barth follows an "ontological" ("theo-ontological") approach, Schleiermacher builds on an "epistemological" foundation. Naturally these terms require closer definition. For the moment it is remarkable that while two of the major paradigms of philosophy which Habermas identifies ("being" and "subjectivity") become apparent, their synchronic interrelationship remains highly contested.

Stereotypically, those orientated towards a Barthian theology argue that any other foundation than one which we might also call a "top-down-approach" diminishes the validity and exclusivity of the Christian revelation. This broad depiction can be illustrated well with the contention that Barth had with Schleiermacher. He accused Schleiermacher of thinking from the human subject, portraying this as an identification of anthropology and pneumatology.[22] In contrast, those who follow an epistemological or subject-orientated theology question the possibility of such a "top-down-approach." They argue that human knowledge of God will always remain just that, namely human. To deny this in an attempt to disregard the role of the human subject in theology will only lead to the mere *appearance of objectivity*, of reflecting on God's revelation in an unmediated manner.[23] It has been put forward that Karl Barth's work enhances the illusion of dealing di-

---

20. Cf. Dirk-Martin Grube, "God or the Subject? Karl Barth's Critique of the 'Turn to the Subject,'" *NZSTh* 49 (2007): 308-24.

21. Christoph Schwöbel, "Theology," in *The Cambridge Companion to Karl Barth*, ed. John Webster (Cambridge: Cambridge University Press, 2000), pp. 17-36.

22. "Als ob nicht eben das tief Problematische bei Schleiermacher wäre, daß er . . . 'vom Menschen her' gedacht und geredet hat! Als ob ausgerechnet der Heilige Geist ihn dazu ermuntert hätte oder irgend jemand dazu ermuntern würde! Als ob Pneumatologie Anthropologie wäre" (Karl Barth, "Nachwort," in *Schleiermacher-Auswahl*, ed. H. Bolli [Munich: Siebenstern, 1968], p. 312).

23. "Der Ausdruck 'Schein der Objektivität' ist von Konrad Stock übernommen, der damit dem Konzept Karl Barths widerspricht, der versucht das Geschehen der Selbstoffenbarung Gottes in einer Weise zu begreifen, die strikt das unvordenkliche göttliche Faktum ihres Geschehen-Seins . . . beleuchtet und demgegenüber die damit gegebene Erschließung einer neuen, inhaltlich bestimmten Daseinsgewißheit im Selbstgefühl der Person — man muß schon sagen: hartnäckig und prinzipiell vernachlässigt" (Rainer Goltz, *Das Werden der Gewissheit: Eine Untersuchung zum protestantischen Verständnis von Offenbarung als Grund des Glaubens im Anschluss an die Theologien von Barth, Ebeling und Herms* [Leipzig: Evangelische Verlagsanstalt, 2008], p. 301).

rectly and immediately with the wholly "Other" and some have dismissed Barth's theology as a whole due to this problematic theo-ontological starting-point and criticize him heavily for not clarifying his epistemological foundation.

Eilert Herms, in contrast, has attempted to bridge the gap between the dogmatics of Karl Barth and Friedrich Schleiermacher, between the "Otherness" of revelation and the experiential anchoring of Christianity in a theory of religion. According to Herms, revelation is not a peculiar phenomenon to Christianity or even to religion in general. Rather it must be seen as an anthropological constant: Every new insight is the result of an experience which in turn, he postulates, is linked to a revelatory moment. Our existence is constituted and determined by experiences in which reality is disclosed to us — Herms refers to these as "disclosure events."[24] The passive voice is important since for Herms the source of disclosure does not lie in human reason, rather it is found "outside" of that which is at our disposal. That is *not* to say that every revelation is of the same nature and content — and certainly does not mean that every revealing experience is of religious significance. For Herms those revealing experiences which have existential consequences and which are constitutive for our beliefs about the origin, constitution, and end of the world are of a religious nature.[25] The Christian belief is but an example of these experiences, albeit in his view the only true one.[26] How does his concept compare with Karl Barth's?

On the one hand, there are major differences compared to the Barthian position considering revelation: Karl Barth decidedly states that only one revelation exists.[27] Revelation is everything but religion,

---

24. Eilert Herms, "Offenbarung," in *Offenbarung und Glaube* (Tübingen: J. C. B. Mohr [Paul Siebeck], 1992), p. 177.

25. Herms's position is not entirely new. It is comparable with that of Ian Ramsay and has been pursued by Christoph Schwöbel. Herms differentiates his concept from Ramsay's however in showing that Ramsay uses the term for those "Erschließungsgeschehen," which are characterized particularly as *religious situations*. In contrast Herms thinks the term "revelation" means all those events, which concern the personal existence as such (Herms, "Offenbarung und Wahrheit," in *Offenbarung und Glaube,* p. 284).

26. Truth in this sense cannot be developed in a neutral or abstract manner from one's world-view and religion. Compare his concise argument in Eilert Herms, "Wahrheit — Offenbarung — Vernunft," in *Phänomene des Glaubens: Beiträge zur Fundamentaltheologie* (Tübingen: Mohr Siebeck, 2006), pp. 96-115.

27. "Es gibt nur eine Offenbarung" (Karl Barth, *Kirchliche Dogmatik* [Zollikon-Zürich: Evangelischer Verlag, 1970], vol. 4/1, p. 47).

and revelation is the incomprehensible "Other."[28] Herms questions this position, which differentiates revelation as a supernatural message from all other normal human insight. In fact, Herms criticizes in an equal manner both those who are fundamentally critical of revelation (particularly empiricist positions), and those who depend on a positivistic understanding of revelation. According to Herms, all reasoning can only take place as the result of revelatory experiences. He develops a differentiated and detailed theory that locates revelation on the horizon of interpretation in general, and hence prepares a level playing field for the interrelationship between faith and reason and between religious and secular worldviews. In this sense Barthian theologians still interpret Herms as watering-down the "top-down," "God-rather-than-the-Human-Subject" position.[29] And indeed, in contrast to Karl Barth, Herms does not reject the inversion of the Enlightenment because he does place an epistemological question at the forefront of his theory of revelation.

On the other hand, the gravity of the differences between Karl Barth and Herms can be questioned. Herms agrees with Barth in placing revelation at the center of Christian theology, and in explaining revelation as the only way to receiving and understanding the gospel. Similarly, he claims that the Christian revelation is special and true (because, as will be shown, its content is unique). Like Barth, Herms sees this center not as an active pursuit, not in an intellectual ascent, but as a passive experience, constituted by a reality outside of our own activities. Herms speaks of the radically passive and external constitution of this revelation[30] and Barth expresses his sentiment in similar terms when he postulates that truth comes toward or to us in revelation.[31] In sum, for Herms it is important to demonstrate the theological continuity between Karl Barth, Friedrich Schleiermacher, and Martin Luther. He posits that they all stress the difference and discontinuity between the event of revelation and our reflection of it.[32]

---

28. Barth, *Dogmatik,* vol. 1/2, pp. 327-28.

29. Cf. Christoph Kock, *Natürliche Theologie: Ein evangelischer Streitbegriff* (Neukirchen-Vluyn: Neukirchener Verlag, 2001) for the difficulties of the Barthian tradition with Herms.

30. Herms, "Theologie und Religionswissenschaft," in *Phänomene des Glaubens,* p. 460.

31. "Dieses Zu-uns-Kommen der Wahrheit ist eben die Offenbarung" (Barth, *Dogmatik,* vol. 1/2, p. 329).

32. Herms, "Ganzheit als Geschick," p. 181.

His fundamental theological and epistemological concept is then developed pneumatologically. Herms expounds his understanding of revelation — as a foundational experience of all humans — within a trinitarian framework, in which the key link is the Spirit. In this sense, his whole concept of revelation can be identified as pneumatologically inspired, since the third article of faith is the entrance point for his dogmatic concept and for his philosophical framework. In order to explain this entrance point, Herms differentiates starkly between the declarations *(Aussagen)* of the gospel and the events which they refer to *(Geschehen)*.[33] In the tradition of Luther, he refers to the events of God's acting in creation, in redemption and in consummation and their significance is communicated in and through the Spirit.[34] It is then the Spirit which reveals the meaning of the cross, by showing the depths of the powerless human position due to sin and death and by helping out of this despair (Rom. 8:26).[35] How does this take place? Again, Herms uses his formal concept of revelation to explain this process. As noted above, he argues that revealing experiences in general constitute our self-assuredness, our certainty about the world and our commitment to our own truth claims ("Gewissheiten"). Revealing experiences are constitutive for any understanding of reality and they come in the *form* of such certainty. Human interaction depends on a belief system with corresponding commitments. The Spirit's revelation gives a new *content* to these foundational experiences; it allows for a new certainty about the world, about God and about oneself. The revelation of Christ through the Spirit gives us a new emotional basis for a new cognitive certainty about the basic orientation of life.[36] Herms describes this as the certainty of being loved and of wanting to love.[37]

This concept is an incisive suggestion of how the stark differences

---

33. Herms, "Fundamentum fidei," in *Phänomene*, p. 83.

34. The point is that the object of faith is also its basis: "Der einheitliche Gegenstand des Glaubens ist also nichts anderes als dasjenige, was zugleich der Grund des Glaubens ist" (Herms, "Fundamentum," p. 85).

35. Eilert Herms, *Luthers Auslegung des dritten Artikels* (Tübingen: J. B. C. Mohr [Paul Siebeck], 1986), p. 64.

36. The change or the sanctification process comes through the transformation of the content of certainty: *"inhaltlichen* Wandel der *Selbstgewissheit"* (Herms, *Auslegung*, p. 68; cf. pp. 77-80).

37. This love according to Herms — again in his interpretation of Luther — is not the result of a human act but a positive and certain emotion.

between two major theological traditions in theology can be bridged. Coming back to the first typology of pneumatologies at the beginning of this article, Herms can be seen as developing an intermediate position between what has been called "high" and "low" pneumatologies. On the one hand, he asserts the belief that there is an absolute qualitative difference between Christian spirituality and all other certainties, commitments, and belief systems. On the other hand, he focuses on portraying this difference as being one of content and not of the form of revelation.

3. A Spiral of Creativity: Reason and the Spirit

There are, however, two major questions with regard to the mediating suggestion that Herms offers. First, his hermeneutical and epistemological approach needs closer scrutiny. This contention is concerned with showing that in order to develop a pneumatology we need to understand not only the experiential dimension of revelation but also the interrelationship of "language," "subjectivity," and "being." The second question arises out of the hermeneutical argument. It questions the pneumatology of Herms and underlines the pneumatological significance of the creative powers of reasoning.

I will first address the hermeneutical issue: Herms insists that revelation is a completely passive experience and strengthens his case with arguments from the phenomenological tradition.[38] His point is that basic life-orientating certainties are not the product of an active, constructive pursuit of knowledge. On the contrary, the formative experiences which shape the content of a vision of life are "given" ("vorgegeben") in a pre-reflective manner and cannot be directly influenced by cognitive decisions.[39] Hence the basis of belief-systems, and in turn of action and thinking, is an immediate, passive self-awareness or self-consciousness (following Schleiermacher's terminology). However, this terminology itself requires precise definition. Ulrich Barth has argued that with regard to newer psychological insights concerning emotions,

---

38. Herms hence attempts to combine an ontological anchoring of experience with its subjective interpretation, and both these aspects are in turn phenomenologically linked to a theological premise. Cf. Herms, *Philosophie,* pp. 412-16.

39. Herms, "Offenbarung," p. 170.

it is not plausible to differentiate between passive immediacy and active reflection in a manner in which the latter builds on the former.[40] Rather a complex process needs to be envisaged in which experience and reflection are integrated and are complementary to one another. While "experience," with its various nuances of "feelings," "sentiments," "apprehensions," and "impressions," cannot be identified with the act of interpretation, the two operations are intertwined. Apprehensions and sentiments include a reflexive dimension, and interpretations may be rooted in what Ulrich Barth calls "passive syntheses."[41] The line of argument which follows on from this differentiation is that our interpretative and reflective capabilities are involved in all of our experiences, even experiences of the divine.[42]

But what does Ulrich Barth mean when he speaks of an interpretation process? He differentiates five connotations of the term:[43]

First, "interpretation" denotes the fact that an understanding of reality is based on models. These will necessarily vary but not inevitably contradict each other. Alternative models may be stringent on their own rational terms, because each is based on a different interpretation, without necessarily negating another approach.[44]

Second, he points to the constructivity of knowledge: In reaction to the claims of logical positivism, it has been shown that not only completed theories, but even the most basic scientific descriptions of mundane reality represent highly complex mental constructs.

Third, the insight that all knowledge is bound to an individual

---

40. Ulrich Barth, "Was heißt 'Vernunft der Religion'? Subjektphilosophische, kulturtheoretische und religionswissenschaftliche Erwägungen im Anschluss an Schleiermacher," in *Der Gott der Vernunft: Protestantismus und vernünftiger Gottesgedanke,* ed. Jörg Lauster and Bernd Oberdorfer (Tübingen: Mohr Siebeck, 2009), p. 200.

41. Barth, "Vernunft," pp. 202-3. See also the discussion in Volker Rabens, "Power from In Between: The Relational Experience of the Holy Spirit and Spiritual Gifts in Paul's Churches" (pp. 138-55 in this volume).

42. While ecstatic spiritual experiences may have very little immediate reflective activity, for them to have any significant effect on a worldview or on character-formation they require reflective, mindful appropriation.

43. Ulrich Barth, "Theoriedimensionen des Religionsbegriffs: Die Binnenrelevanz der sogenannten Außenperspektiven," in *Religion in der Moderne* (Tübingen: Mohr Siebeck, 2003), pp. 29-88.

44. The example he gives is related to the theory of light of early modernity. Here the corpuscular theory of light (Newton) is first viewed in opposition to the wave front theory (Hugyen's). They have, however, in the long run proved to be compatible.

perspective of the world is emphasized — an emphasis which has a long tradition in philosophy. Every perception and cognitive operation depends on a certain position and location in the world.

Fourth, the dependence on speech is stressed. As mentioned with respect to Habermas, the "linguistic turn" in philosophy, visible particularly in the analytical and hermeneutical traditions, has shown that thought requires symbolic representation. As a consequence, the question arises whether languages and systems of representation are compatible with one another. The issue at stake is that no language can adequately represent the scope of any other language, and that no language has the ability to represent truth as such.

Fifth, and in close relation to the fourth point, interpretation denotes the traditional hermeneutical task which concentrates on the interpretation of signs.

Each of these connotations may be more or less significant for the interpretation of religious experiences, and in each case, their precise interrelationship requires close analysis. In any case, it is difficult to comprehend how a concept of revelation can be developed without understanding the mediating operations of reason in and through the "subject," which in turn depends on the molds of thought provided by the "language" of his or her environment. In that sense I would disagree with both Karl Barth and Eilert Herms who implicitly suggest that an experience of revelation can bypass these mediating instances of reflection. On the other hand, this constructive activity is not arbitrary. A process of understanding between various subjects or language groups will only make sense if they are interpreting the same reality, the same existence, and are speaking with reference to the same "being." Our reflective abilities must not be identified with a form of relativistic nominalism.[45] In sum then, all three paradigmatic terms which Habermas put on an evolutionary trajectory must be aligned synchronically and understood as being in a constant process of correlation. "Being," "language," and "subjectivity" are all three foundational modules in a theoretical endeavor of understanding ourselves in our world.

Second, a pneumatological controversy with Herms arises: If reflective capabilities are always involved in understanding revelatory experi-

---

45. In other words: reality can only be interpreted in certain perspectives and constructs. These are, however, more or less adequate, authentic, and right or true, since these interpretations do not operate in a vacuum.

André Munzinger

ences, reality is consequently interpreted within the confines of models, schemes, languages, and symbolic worlds. But the manner in which these confines are filled, constructed, and shaped is itself the result of a highly creative process. The creative force within this interpretation process should not be, as Herms suggests, contrasted with the experience of revelation. On the contrary, the creativity of reason itself can be understood, I would argue, as a significant display of the Spirit.[46]

Placing creativity at the center of the work of the Spirit requires further clarification.[47] For one, it needs to be established that this emphasis on creativity makes sense of the biblical tradition. There may not be any major discussion with regard to an argument that places creativity at the heart of a Judeo-Christian understanding of God, the creation of the world and humankind (as created in his image to create for himself). There may be, however, more misgivings about identifying the process of creative reason with the Spirit's activity, because this could be misunderstood as claiming the Spirit for reason *per se*.[48] This hesitation can be countered with two significant points with regard to a theory of creativity.[49] For one, there is the observation that creativity is contingent upon personal and societal freedom or, put negatively, creativity is often mitigated or blocked. Secondly, creative acts are ambiguous in the sense that they can be instrumentalized or misused. Spiritual creativity is understood when developed in response to these two hindrances.

---

46. With the term "creative reason" I denote the mental faculty that is able to generate conclusions (about causes and effects) on the basis of reasons and hence makes comprehension possible. For an excellent introduction see Wolfgang Welsch, *Vernunft: Die zeitgenössische Vernunftkritik und das Konzept der transversalen Vernunft* (Frankfurt: Suhrkamp, 1995).

47. "Creativity is the ability to produce work that is both novel (i.e. original, unexpected) and appropriate (i.e. useful, adaptive concerning task constraints)." For this definition and an overview compare: Robert S. Albert and Mark A. Runco, "A History of Research on Creativity," in *Handbook of Creativity*, ed. R. J. Sternberg (Cambridge: Cambridge University Press, 1999), p. 3.

48. This is the direction Gordon D. Kaufmann takes (*In the Beginning . . . Creativity* [Minneapolis: Fortress Press, 2004]). However, he is right to point to various dimensions of creativity (from the beginnings of physical life to the various degrees of symbolic and cultural focusing and framing of that life).

49. Creativity as such is a well-worn term but I do not agree with those objections that estimate it being overused and overstretched, as Hartmut von Hentig suggests. However, he is right to be skeptical about the material definition and instrumentalization of creativity, as the above definition of Albert and Runco may suggest (*Kreativität: Hohe Erwartungen an einen schwachen Begriff* [Munich: Hanser, 2000]).

The *first* problem — creativity and its dependence on freedom — is dealt with in the Christian tradition in the context of soteriology, the teaching of liberation in light of the appropriation of the Christ-event. Applying this liberating experience to the problems of creativity means understanding it as the restitution of the ability of mankind to co-create. Matthew Fox argues pervasively for connecting soteriology with this liberation of human creativity as the locus where the divine and the human spirit meet.[50] In this sense, terminology associated with "sin" would be understood as estrangement from oneself, others and God, and identified with the lack of connectivity to one's creative life-force. Liberation and salvation are then interpreted as a return to and the renewal of originally intended creative abilities — to be authentically in touch with the hope, trust, and love that the Spirit gives. The important insight here is that hope, trust and love are essential elements in the ability to deal with the contingencies of life. Only if "reality" can be trusted, can one be creative in dealing with life's vicissitudes.[51]

Hence a fundamental problem associated with creativity requires a soteriological answer of some sort. The Christian tradition offers such an answer: Here soteriology is the "starting point for an epistemological revolution, a *conversion of the imagination*,"[52] and this implies an existential, liberating force which makes creativity possible.[53] This soteriological point, however, still does not differentiate the qualities of creativity.

Hence I turn to the *second* of the aforementioned problems, which explains that creativity is essentially ambiguous. Fox argues that inquiring into the obstacles that prevent creativity, *"is to reveal the*

---

50. Matthew Fox, *Creativity: Where the Divine and the Human Meet* (New York: Penguin, 2004), pp. 88-117.

51. For a more detailed analysis of these thoughts compare André Munzinger, "Gewissheit der Liebe: Paulinische Impulse zur Fundamentaltheologie mit Blick auf den Umgang mit Kontingenz," *EvT* 68 (2008): 192-208. In this sense I presuppose a world-view which is associated with the Enlightenment's shift from actuality to possibility, against Karl Barth (cf. section 2).

52. Richard B. Hays, "Wisdom According to Paul," in *Where Shall Wisdom be Found? Wisdom in the Bible, the Church and the Contemporary World*, ed. Stephen C. Barton (Edinburgh: T&T Clark 1999), p. 113.

53. Clearly this argument requires a refined look at exegetical differentiations and alternative soteriological themes, such as justification. But I would argue that creativity as a significant soteriological topic has been ignored to the detriment of understanding salvation *and* creativity.

André Munzinger

essence of who we are and who we are becoming or failing to become," because creativity is central to our nature as human beings.[54] And it is correct for him to posit that the fear of unharnessing creative powers particularly in education processes has had detrimental effects on the development of individual freedom. At the same time, Fox does not reflect on the ambiguous nature of creativity. The unleashing of creative intelligence for instance, which came as a result of the productive insights of the Enlightenment, of the industrial and technical revolutions and of the development of highly differentiated societies, has had vast transformative effects on eco-systems, human thriving, and societal integration. These effects, however, have not all been beneficial to humankind or to nature. And it has become paramount to understand this ambiguity which lies at the heart of creativity itself. In this sense, education is not only necessary to open up creative mindsets, but it is also quite significant for comprehending the effects and goals of creativity. In short, an ethos of creativity is required. On a general scale this ethos could be described as the edification of the community in which one lives or of the natural habitats in which communities exist — which is the ecological system of the earth as a whole.[55] But can we be more precise?

The Apostle Paul offers keen insights into both the necessity and the possibilities of discerning the truth of revelatory and soteriological experiences.[56] In his letters he admonishes the churches to learn to discern independently (for instance Rom. 12:2; 1 Cor. 2:6-16). This discernment is possible insofar as the believers are allowing themselves to be-

---

54. Fox, *Creativity*, p. 121.

55. One of the most substantial innovations that the work of Eilert Herms offers is the description of the intricate interrelationship of dogmatics and ethics in a formal sense. That is to say that any belief-system (dogmatic) has a teaching on the formative elements of how our world came about (creation), what goal, if any, this world has (eschatology) and how these goals can and will be achieved (soteriology). These beliefs are the foundation for their ethics, which are a theory of how individual action is linked into culture and society as whole. Ethics in this sense is always an extrapolation of a reflected world-view (dogmatics). I am developing this concept in a research project on the intercultural significance of the work of Eilert Herms; cf. as an introduction: André Munzinger, "Deutungshoheit der Religionen? Weltanschauung und Wirtschaft im Horizont globaler Institutionen und in Auseinandersetzung mit der Ethik von Eilert Herms," *ZFWU* 11 (2010): 35-49.

56. Cf. Andre Munzinger, *Discerning the Spirits: Ethical and Theological Hermeneutics in Paul* (Cambridge: Cambridge University Press, 2007).

come part of the dynamic of love. Soteriology is not a clear-cut, abstract concept which can be identified without taking part in this transformative process. It is, at best, itself ambiguous and fraught with shadings of liberation. Discernment, I would argue, requires becoming sensitive to this ambiguity and implies looking out for the contextuality of creative reason.[57] Its use depends on its orientation. The key elements of this orientation are the goals with which we are creative, our motivations, intentions, and power interests.[58] If creative reason is to be genuinely communicative and not solely instrumental, these power interests require redirection. Here then we have a connection between salvation and discernment with regard to creative reason. Reason is not in and of itself creative. Creativity is not *Spiritual* per se.[59]

However, this line of thought may be questioned: Is it not a circular argument if the Spirit is needed to understand the Spirit, if Spiritual creativity is required to develop a pneumatology? This circular movement is indeed a result of the above argument. Nevertheless, I would suggest the picture of a spiral is more appropriate — a spiral in which knowledge is developed in the consciousness of the need for continuous correction. If Eilert Herms argues that revelation is linked to human experience, the creativity of reflecting and constructing our understanding of the world should not be seen as the human counterpart. Rather, experience always requires interpretation. This interpretation has creative elements, and creativity is one of the central elements of biblical tradition. Not every interpretation need be or can be identified as a manifestation of the creative Spirit. On the contrary, the paradigms of understanding reality have vast qualitative differences. In other words: To develop and establish an authentic, accessible paradigm within which we interpret the world requires a creativity which is in tune with the liberating power of the Spirit of life.[60]

---

57. Amos Yong integrates such a discernment process with regard to a public theology and with regard to other religions; see chapter 6 in his *The Spirit Poured Out on All Flesh: Pentecostalism and the Possibility of Global Theology* (Grand Rapids: Baker Academic, 2005).

58. Cf. Anthony Thiselton, *The First Epistle to the Corinthians,* New International Greek Testament Commentary (Grand Rapids: Eerdmans, 2000), p. 1055.

59. All creativity is spiritual in the sense that a person's spirit is necessarily involved, but not all creative spirits are necessarily in touch with the divine life-force.

60. To put it very simply, liberating, Spiritual creativity will be orientated towards letting others be and become who they are, developing my own and their full potential;

André Munzinger

4. Conclusion

The first step in this article was to establish the vast diversity of pneumatologies and to ask how they can be classified. Three suggestions for making such a classification were identified and discussed. Only the third paradigmatic approach, I suggested, offers a way forward. Its distinction between the philosophical foundations of "being," "subjectivity," and "language" makes sense of three general orientations in present systematic theology. However, its structural gain only comes into effect when these paradigmatic approaches are taken synchronically and not as an evolutionary replacement in which one paradigm negates the approach of the other. Indeed this article argues that the stark differentiation between these three models needs to be translated into an exhaustive methodology in which all three dimensions of "language," "subjectivity," and "being" are correlated — although this article has not itself been able to realize this correlation.[61]

In order to substantiate this line of argument, I introduced the work of Eilert Herms who has bridged the gap between the Barthian concept of revelation and an experiential orientation, which Schleiermacher's work exemplifies. Herms argues for the wholly "Other" of Christian revelation, but embeds this in a formal concept of experience. While this suggestion offers an incisive development in theology, it does not integrate sufficiently the role of "language" and "subjectivity" into the interpretation of reality. The ability to relate to reality depends on the individual perspective, the constructive use of models and the objective function of language. In short: understanding, establishing, and developing pneumatology require the powers of creative reason. At the same time, this creative process of interpretation and reflection can itself be seen as a Spiritual exercise. Since creativity needs to answer difficult questions with regard to its being contingent on

---

cf. John Macquarrie, *Principles of Christian Theology*, 11th ed. (London: SCM Press, 2003), pp. 113-15; Munzinger, *Spirits*, ch. 4. Of course this requires more reflection.

61. A forthcoming article of mine will argue that "being" cannot be understood without the subjective and intersubjective interpretation processes located in our minds and in our common language. It is key, however, that the mediation processes of "language" and "subjectivity" should only be seen as limitations on asking questions about the nature of our "being," not as an excuse for ignoring these questions. I aim to show that this type of correlation of these three paradigms can be found in the works of Schleiermacher (particularly his *Dialectics*).

personal and societal freedom as well as to its inherent ambiguity, it depends on a concept of discerned liberation. Being creative in defining the paradigms, models, metaphors, and symbols of our world implies being prone to mistakes, misuse, and misunderstanding.

Charting the deep waters of pneumatological paradigms is fascinating; making sense of their elaborate differences is more than challenging. To meet this challenge two avenues of research require more thought: firstly the intricate link between liberation, discernment, and authentic creativity needs to be studied at length; secondly, addressing the first issue will require a better understanding of the correlation of "language," "subjectivity," and "being" in the process of interpretation.

List of Publications by Max Turner

Books

Jesus and the Four Gospels. Amersham: Hulton, 1983 (with Douglas R. de Lacey).

The Expansion of Christianity. Amersham: Hulton, 1983 (with Douglas R. de Lacey).

Linguistics and Biblical Interpretation. London: SPCK, 1989 (with Peter Cotterell).

Power from on High: The Spirit in Israel's Restoration and Witness in Luke-Acts, Journal of Pentecostal Theology Supplement Series 9. Sheffield: Sheffield Academic Press, 1996 (reprinted, with corrections, 2000).

The Holy Spirit and Spiritual Gifts — Then and Now. Carlisle: Paternoster, 1996 (revised 1999); US-edition: *The Holy Spirit and Spiritual Gifts in the New Testament Church and Today.* Peabody: Hendrickson, 1997 (revision of the 1996 edition of above).

Baptism in the Holy Spirit, Renewal Series 2. Cambridge: Grove Books, 2000.

Edited Books

Jesus of Nazareth: Lord and Christ — Essays on the Historical Jesus and New Testament Christology. Carlisle: Paternoster, 1994; Grand Rapids: Eerdmans, 1994 (*Festschrift* for I. Howard Marshall; ed. with Joel B. Green).

Mission and Meaning: Essays Presented to Peter Cotterell. Carlisle: Paternoster, 1995 (ed. with Antony Billington and Tony Lane).

Between Two Horizons: Spanning New Testament Studies and Systematic Theology. Grand Rapids: Eerdmans 2000 (ed. with Joel B. Green).

List of Publications by Max Turner

Journal Articles

"The Significance of Spirit Endowment for Paul." *Vox Evangelica* 9 (1975): 56-69.
"The Concept of Receiving the Spirit in John's Gospel." *Vox Evangelica* 10 (1977): 24-42.
"Jesus and the Spirit in Lucan Perspective." *Tyndale Bulletin* 32 (1981): 3-42.
"Spirit Endowment in Luke-Acts: Some Linguistic Considerations." *Vox Evangelica* 12 (1981): 45-63.
"The Significance of Receiving the Spirit in Luke-Acts: A Survey of Modern Scholarship." *Trinity Journal* 2 (1981): 131-58.
"Jésus et l'Esprit d'après Luc." *Hokhma* 26 (1984): 18-46.
"Spiritual Gifts: Then and Now." *Vox Evangelica* 15 (1985): 7-64.
"Ecclesiology in the Major 'Apostolic' Restorationist Churches in the United Kingdom." *Vox Evangelica* 19 (1989): 83-108.
"Atonement and the Death of Jesus in John — Some Questions to Bultmann and Forestell." *Evangelical Quarterly* 62 (1990): 99-122.
"The Spirit and the Power of Jesus' Miracles in the Lucan Conception." *Novum Testamentum* 33 (1991): 124-52.
"The Spirit of Prophecy and the Power of Authoritative Preaching in Luke-Acts: A Question of Origins." *New Testament Studies* 38 (1992): 66-88.
"The Spirit in Luke-Acts: A Support or a Challenge to Classical Pentecostal Paradigms?" *Vox Evangelica* 27 (1997): 75-101.
"Tongues: An Experience for All in the Pauline Churches?" *Asian Journal of Pentecostal Studies* 1 (1998): 231-53.
"Interpreting the Samaritans of Acts 8: The Waterloo of Pentecostal Soteriology and Pneumatology?" *Pneuma* 23 (2001): 265-86.
"The Charismatic Movement and the Church — Conflict or Renewal?" *European Journal of Theology* 10 (2001): 49-65.
"The Work of the Holy Spirit in Luke-Acts." *Word & World* 23 (2003): 146-53.
"'Trinitarian' Pneumatology in the New Testament? — Towards an Explanation of the Worship of Jesus." *Asbury Theological Journal* 57/58 (2002/2003): 167-86.
"Approaching 'Personhood' in the New Testament, with Special Reference to Ephesians." *Evangelical Quarterly* 77 (2005): 211-33.
"Human Reconciliation in the New Testament with Special Reference to Philemon, Colossians and Ephesians." *European Journal of Theology* 15 (2007): 37-47.

Book Sections

"The Sabbath, the Law, and Sunday in Luke-Acts." In *From Sabbath to Lord's*

List of Publications by Max Turner

Day: A Biblical, Historical, and Theological Investigation, ed. D. A. Carson (Grand Rapids: Zondervan, 1982; reprint: Eugene: Wipf & Stock, 1999), pp. 100-157.

"The Spirit of Christ and Christology." In *Christ the Lord: Studies in Christology Presented to Donald Guthrie*, ed. H. H. Rowdon (Leicester: IVP, 1982), pp. 168-90.

"Prophecy and Spiritual Gifts Then and Now." In *Christian Experience in Theology and Life*, ed. I. H. Marshall (Edinburgh: Rutherford House, 1988), pp. 16-54 (with D. Mackinder).

"Prayer in the Gospels and Acts." In *Teach Us to Pray: Prayer in the Bible and the World*, ed. D. A. Carson (Exeter: Paternoster, 1990), pp. 58-83 and 319-25.

"Ephesians: Introduction and Commentary." In *New Bible Commentary: 21st Century Edition*, ed. D. A. Carson, R. T. France, J. A. Motyer, and G. J. Wenham (Leicester/Downers Grove: IVP, 1994), pp. 1222-44.

"The Spirit of Christ and 'Divine' Christology." In *Jesus of Nazareth: Lord and Christ — Essays on the Historical Jesus and New Testament Christology*, ed. Joel B. Green and Max Turner (Carlisle: Paternoster, 1994), pp. 413-36.

"The Spirit of Prophecy and the Ethical/Religious Life of the Christian Community." In *Spirit and Renewal: Essays in Honour of J. Rodman Williams*, Journal of Pentecostal Theology Supplement Series 5, ed. M. W. Wilson (Sheffield: Sheffield Academic Press, 1994), pp. 166-90.

"Mission and Meaning in Terms of 'Unity' in Ephesians." In *Mission and Meaning: Essays Presented to Peter Cotterell*, ed. Antony Billington, Tony Lane, and Max Turner (Carlisle: Paternoster Press, 1995), pp. 138-66.

"Modern Linguistics and the New Testament." In *Hearing the New Testament: Strategies for Interpretation*, ed. J. B. Green (Grand Rapids/Carlisle: Eerdmans/Paternoster, 1995), pp. 146-74.

"The 'Spirit of Prophecy' as the Power of Israel's Restoration and Witness." In *Witness to the Gospel: The Theology of Acts*, ed. I. H. Marshall and D. Peterson (Grand Rapids/Cambridge: Eerdmans, 1998), pp. 327-48.

"The Challenge of Personhood: Towards a Theology of Personhood." In *Christian Life & Today's World: Not Conformed but Transformed*, ed. A. Robbins (Bletchley: Scripture Union, 2002), pp. 47-63.

"The Churches of the Johannine Letters as Communities of 'Trinitarian' Koinōnia." In *The Spirit and Spirituality: Essays in Honour of Russell P. Spittler*, Journal of Pentecostal Theology Supplement Series 24, ed. W. Ma and R. P. Menzies (London: T&T Clark, 2004), pp. 53-61.

"The Spirit and Salvation in Luke-Acts." In *The Holy Spirit and Christian Origins: Essays in Honor of James D. G. Dunn*, ed. G. N. Stanton, B. W. Longenecker, and S. C. Barton (Grand Rapids/Cambridge: Eerdmans, 2004), pp. 103-16.

"Early Christian Experience and Theology of 'Tongues': A New Testament Perspective." In *Speaking in Tongues,* ed. Mark J. Cartledge (Milton Keynes: Paternoster, 2006), pp. 1-33.

"Luke and the Spirit: Renewing Theological Interpretation of Biblical Pneumatology." In *Reading Luke: Interpretation, Reflection, Formation,* ed. C. G. Bartholomew, J. B. Green, and A. C. Thiselton (Milton Keynes: Paternoster, 2006), pp. 267-93.

Lexicon Articles

"Holy Spirit." In *New 20th-Century Encyclopedia of Religious Knowledge,* ed. J. D. Douglas (Grand Rapids: Baker, 1991), pp. 400-404.

"Holy Spirit." In *Dictionary of Jesus and the Gospels,* ed. Joel B. Green and Scott McKnight (Leicester: IVP, 1992), pp. 341-51.

"Trinity." In *New Bible Dictionary,* ed. I. H. Marshall, A. R. Millard, J. I. Packer, and D. J. Wiseman (Leicester: IVP, 1996), pp. 1209-11.

"Holy Spirit." In *New Dictionary of Biblical Theology,* ed. T. D. Alexander and B. S. Rosner (Leicester: IVP, 2000), pp. 551-58.

"Languages." In *New Dictionary of Biblical Theology,* ed. T. D. Alexander and B. S. Rosner (Leicester: IVP, 2000), pp. 627-29.

"Spiritual Gifts." In *New Dictionary of Biblical Theology,* ed. T. D. Alexander and B. S. Rosner (Leicester: IVP, 2000), pp. 789-96.

"Ephesians, Book of." In *Dictionary for Theological Interpretation of the Bible,* ed. Kevin J. Vanhoozer (Grand Rapids: Baker, 2005), pp. 186-91.

"Utterance Meaning." In *Dictionary for Theological Interpretation of the Bible,* ed. Kevin J. Vanhoozer (Grand Rapids: Baker, 2005), pp. 828-33.

"Divinity of Christ." In *New Interpreter's Dictionary of the Bible,* ed. K. D. Sakenfeld (Nashville: Abingdon, 2007), vol. 2, p. 150.

"Ephesians, Letter to." In *New Interpreter's Dictionary of the Bible,* ed. K. D. Sakenfeld (Nashville: Abingdon, 2007), vol. 2, pp. 269-76.

"Semantics." In *New Interpreter's Dictionary of the Bible,* ed. K. D. Sakenfeld (Nashville: Abingdon, 2009), vol. 5, pp. 161-64.

Review Articles

"The Anointed Community: A Review and Response." *Evangelical Quarterly* 62 (1990): 253-64.

"'Empowerment for Mission?' — The Pneumatology of Luke-Acts: An Appreciation and Critique of James B. Shelton's *Mighty in Word and Deed.*" *Vox Evangelica* 24 (1994): 103-22.

List of Publications by Max Turner

"Every Believer as a Witness in Acts? In Dialogue with John Michael Penney." *Ashland Theological Journal* 30 (1998): 57-71.

"Readings and Paradigms: A Response to John Christopher Thomas." *Journal of Pentecostal Theology* 12 (1998): 23-38.

"Receiving Christ and Receiving the Spirit: In Dialogue with David Pawson." *Journal of Pentecostal Theology* 15 (1999): 3-31.

"'Universality?' A Response to the Responses of Menzies and Chan." *Asian Journal of Pentecostal Studies* 2 (1999): 297-308.

"Does Luke Believe Reception of the 'Spirit of Prophecy' Makes All 'Prophets'? Inviting Dialogue with Roger Stronstad." *Journal of the European Pentecostal Theological Association* 20 (2000): 3-24.

"'Revival' in the New Testament?" In *On Revival: A Critical Examination*, ed. Andrew Walker and Kirsten Aune (Carlisle: Paternoster, 2003), pp. 3-21.

"James Dunn's *Baptism in the Holy Spirit*: Appreciation and Response." *Journal of Pentecostal Theology* 19 (2010): 25-31.

"Levison's *Filled with the Spirit*: A Brief Appreciation and Response." *Journal of Pentecostal Theology* 20 (2011): 193-200.

List of Published PhD Dissertations by Max Turner's Research Students

Bennema, Cornelis. *The Power of Saving Wisdom: An Investigation of Spirit and Wisdom in Relation to the Soteriology of the Fourth Gospel*, Wissenschaftliche Untersuchungen zum Neuen Testament 2.148. Tübingen: Mohr Siebeck, 2002.

Chae, Daniel J.-S. *Paul as Apostle to the Gentiles: His Apostolic Self-Awareness and Its Influence on the Soteriological Argument in Romans*, Paternoster Biblical Monographs. Carlisle: Paternoster, 1997.

Clark, Andrew C. *Parallel Lives: The Relation of Paul to the Apostles in the Lucan Perspective*, Paternoster Biblical Monographs. Carlisle: Paternoster, 2002.

Elliott, Mark A. *The Survivors of Israel: A Reconsideration of the Theology of Pre-Christian Judaism*. Grand Rapids: Eerdmans, 2000.

Fatehi, Mehrdad. *The Spirit's Relation to the Risen Lord in Paul: An Examination of Its Christological Implications*, Wissenschaftliche Untersuchungen zum Neuen Testament 2.128. Tübingen: Mohr Siebeck, 2000.

Heliso, Desta. *Pistis and the Righteous One: A Study of Romans 1:17 against the Background of Scripture and Second Temple Jewish Literature*, Wissenschaftliche Untersuchungen zum Neuen Testament 2.235. Tübingen: Mohr Siebeck, 2007.

Munzinger, André. *Discerning the Spirits: Theological and Ethical Hermeneutics in Paul*, Society for New Testament Studies Monograph Series 140. Cambridge: Cambridge University Press, 2007.

Neagoe, Alexandru. *The Trial of the Gospel: An Apologetic Reading of Luke's Trial Narratives*, Society for New Testament Studies Monograph Series 116. Cambridge: Cambridge University Press, 2002.

Petrenko, Ester. *"Created in Christ Jesus for Good Works": The Integration of Soteriology and Ethics in Ephesians*, Paternoster Biblical Monographs. Milton Keynes: Paternoster, 2011. (PhD begun under Max Turner and completed at Durham University under the supervision of James D. G. Dunn and John Barclay.)

Rabens, Volker. *The Holy Spirit and Ethics in Paul: Transformation and Empowering for Religious-Ethical Life*, Wissenschaftliche Untersuchungen zum Neuen Testament 2.283. Tübingen: Mohr Siebeck, 2010.

Strauss, Mark L. *The Davidic Messiah in Luke-Acts: The Promise and Its Fulfillment in Lukan Christology*, Journal for the Study of the New Testament Supplement Series 110. Sheffield: Sheffield Academic Press, 1995.

Tilling, Chris. *Paul's Divine Christology*. Wissenschaftliche Untersuchungen zum Neuen Testament 2. Tübingen: Mohr Siebeck, forthcoming 2012.

Weatherly, Jon A. *Jewish Responsibility for the Death of Jesus in Luke-Acts*, Journal for the Study of the New Testament Supplement Series 106. Sheffield: Sheffield Academic Press, 1994.

Wenk, Matthias. *Community-Forming Power: The Socio-Ethical Role of the Spirit in Luke-Acts*, Journal of Pentecostal Theology Supplement Series 19. Sheffield: Sheffield Academic Press, 2000.

Index of Authors

Aaron, D. H., 98
Albert, R. S., 350
Allen, D. M., 214-15, 217, 220
Allison, D. C., 207
Altmann, W., 306
Anderson, K. L., 76
Arand, C. P., 317
Attridge, H. W., 221, 224-25
Aune, D. E., 231, 239, 241, 243

Baer, H. von, 267
Bakken, K. L., 313
Barrett, C. K., 54, 105-6, 114, 124, 127, 129, 132, 136, 168-70, 212, 272
Barth, K., 309, 337, 343-45
Barth, U., 141, 342, 348
Batmanghelidjh, C., 325
Bauckham, R., 36, 54, 76, 101, 177-80, 183-84, 187-88, 191, 234, 239
Bauman, Z., 326, 331-32
Beasley-Murray, G. R., 106, 234, 239, 240, 272
Belleville, L., 272
Bennema, C., 14, 39, 45-46, 87-98, 100-102, 104, 106, 108-9, 111-13, 159, 161-63, 166-67, 176, 219, 271-72, 361
Bentham, J., 331
Berger, K., 139, 142-43
Berger, P. L., 141

Best, E., 177, 191, 193-95
Beutler, J., 94
Blenkinsopp, J., 23
Bock, D. L., 21, 36, 39, 56, 67-68
Bonney, W., 106, 111
Borgen, P., 260
Boschki, R., 144
Bousset, W., 196-97
Bovon, F., 37
Bowlby, J., 144
Boyd, G. A., 55, 331
Braumann, G., 54
Brondos, D., 334
Brown, R. E., 8, 13, 105-6, 114
Brown, T. G., 88, 91-92, 99
Bruce, F. F., 122, 128, 225
Brueggemann, W., 208
Buch-Hansen, G., 88, 100-102, 104
Buckwalter, D., 40, 47
Bultmann, R., 105, 121, 143, 145, 154, 191, 271-72
Burge, G., 104, 271-72

Cadbury, H. J., 72, 80
Caird, G. B., 239
Calvin, J., 2
Campbell, C. R., 116
Campenhausen, H. von, 300
Capes, D. B., 192

Index of Authors

Caragounis, C. C., 116
Carson, D. A., 95, 104, 113, 115
Casey, P. M., 257
Chadwick, H., 289, 301
Chae, D. J.-S., 361
Chester, A., 184
Childs, B. S., 211
Clark, A. C., 361
Coloe, M. L., 88, 93
Colson, F. H., 249-50, 256, 258-59
Conzelmann, H., 71-73
Cotterell, P. xix, 356
Craddock, F. B., 57
Cranfield, C. B., 168, 170
Crump, D., 88, 92
Cullmann, O., 111
Culpepper, R. A., 57, 106
Cunningham, S., 54-55

Dalferth, I. U., 341
Davies, J. A., 174
Davies, W. D., 207
De Lacey, D. R., 356
Deissmann, A., 197
Derrida, J., 335
Dews, P., 341
Dodd, C. H., 71
Dunn, J. D. G., 1, 9, 13-14, 36, 46, 104, 123, 155-56, 168, 176, 182-83, 185, 187, 191, 196-97, 211, 220, 222, 247, 264, 267-69, 308
Dyrness, W., 304

Ebeling, G., 279
Eddy, P. R., 54
Edwards, M., 301
Elliott, M. A., 361
Engberg-Pedersen, T., 144, 146, 148, 156, 170, 174, 176
Erlemann, K., 148
Ervin, H., 2, 104
Evans, C. A., 56-57
Evans, C. F., 60

Fairbairn, D., 290
Fanning, B. M., 116

Faraday, M., 338
Farelly, N., 97
Farrer, A., 274
Fatehi, M., 183, 219, 361
Fee, G. D., 7, 156, 173, 180-82, 185-88, 190, 192-93, 197
Feldman, L., 256, 262
Fitzmyer, J. A., 37-39, 122, 168
Fletcher-Louis, C. H. T., 246
Forbes, G. W., 60
Forsyth, P. T., 274
Fox, M., 351-52
Frend, W. H. C., 300
Frey, J., 148
Fuller, R. H., 78

Garrett, S. R., 57, 59
Gause, R. H., 234, 236, 242
Gaventa, B. R., 123, 130
Gielen, M., 155
Gieschen, C. A., 246
Gloer, W. H., 108
Godet, F., 274
Goldingay, J., 24, 42
Goltz, R., 343
Gould, G., 285
Grässer, E., 218, 224
Green, J. B., 40, 56-57, 83, 85, 133
Grogan, G., 22, 28, 34
Grube, D.-M., 343
Grudem, W., 278, 282
Guelich, R. A., 281, 283
Gundry, R. H., 235
Gunkel, H., 138-40, 143, 145, 150
Gunton, C., 328, 332, 338
Guthrie, D., 221
Gutiérrez, G., 338

Habermas, J., 340, 342-43, 349
Hacking, K. J., 55, 68
Haenchen, E., 48
Hägerland, T., 88, 94-95, 104
Hamilton, J. M., 88, 100, 104
Harstine, S., 106
Hauerwas, S., 326
Hawthorne, G. F., 274-77, 279-80, 283

Haya-Prats, G., 267
Hays, R. B., 351
Healy, M., 185
Hebblethwaite, B., 274
Hedlun, R. J., 119, 126, 128, 130
Heider, G. C., 73-74, 85
Heliso, D., 92, 147, 149, 361
Helleman, W. E., 254, 261
Hengel, M., 72, 146
Hentig, H. von, 350
Herms, E., 336, 342, 344-47, 349-50, 352-54
Herms, R., 239
Hinde, R. A., 144
Hoehner, H. W., 193
Holladay, C. R., 247, 249, 255, 257-62
Hooker, M., 327
Horn, F. W., 139-41, 144, 200
Hurtado, L., 179-81, 184-85, 187-88, 213, 247

Irving, E., 330
Issler, K., 276

Jenson, R., 314, 328
Jeremias, J., 78
Jewett, R., 156, 171, 173
Johnson, L. T., 198
Jonge, H. J. de, 276-77

Kähler, M., 82
Kamppuri, H., 317
Karris, R. J., 54, 61, 66, 70, 83
Kärkkäinen, V.-M., 304, 310, 312, 320-21
Käsemann, E., 119, 132, 168, 171, 271
Kaufmann, G. D., 350
Keener, C. S., 88, 91, 93, 95, 100-101, 104, 108, 271-72
Kelhoffer, J. A., 38
Kelly, J. N. D., 292
Kiddle, M., 242
Kilpatrick, G. D., 79
Klein, G. L., 43
Knierim, R. P., 159-60
Knight, G. W., 204, 209
Kock, C., 345

Koester, C. R., 221, 223, 225
Kolb, R., 317
Köstenberger, A. J., 95, 104, 272
Kotsko, A., 328
Kruse, C. G., 38
Kuhn, T. S., 339
Kümmel, W. G., 72, 271
Kysar, R., 88, 92, 104

Ladd, G. E., 73, 233
LaFollette, H., 144
Lane, W. L., 219-20, 222-23, 226, 283
Lee, P., 236
Leisegang, H., 268
Leith, J. H., 302
Leroy, H., 111
Levison, J. R., 4, 88, 95, 97, 99, 104, 146, 148, 156-57, 160-61, 163, 165-67, 176, 204, 210, 212, 360
Levi-Strauss, C., 331
Lincoln, A. T., 191-94
Lindars, B., 214-16, 222-23
Lohse, B., 317
Longenecker, B. W., 88, 199, 268, 358
Longenecker, R. N., 77
Luckmann, T., 141

Macchia, F. D., 309, 311-14, 318, 322
MacDonald, N., 185
Mackinder, D., 358
Mackintosh, H. R., 274
Macquarrie, J., 354
Maddox, R., 54
Mahé, J., 293
Makambu, M. A., 88, 99
Mannermaa, T., 317-19
Månsson, N., 332
Marcus, J., 278-79, 283
Marcus, R., 248
Marshall, I. H., 37, 38, 56, 57, 198-99
Martin, T. W., 148
Martyn, J. L., 113
Mathewson, D., 234, 239, 243-44
Mayo, P., 242
McFarlane, G. W. P., 330
McGrath, J. F., 184

Index of Authors

McGuckin, J. A., 301, 312
McKay, K. L., 116
McKnight, S., 324
McQueen, L. R., 229
Meeks, W. A., 246, 257, 260
Menzies, R. P., 2, 6, 14, 16-17, 42-43, 46, 59-61, 88, 100, 104, 267-68
Metzger, B., 56
Michaels, J. R., 115-16, 241
Middleton, R., 326
Mikulincer, M., 144
Milbank, J., 334
Minear, P. S., 53
Mittelstadt, M. W., 54-55
Mittmann-Richert, U., 80
Moessner, D. P., 60
Moltmann, J., 303, 313
Morris, L., 73
Mounce, R. H., 232
Mounce, W. D., 198, 206
Munzinger, A., 141, 173, 351-52, 354, 361
Murphy, F. J., 244

Neagoe, A., 361
Nicholson, S., 185
Nickle, K. F., 57-58
Nolland, J., 56-57, 131
Norris, R. A., 295

Oberdorfer, B., 141, 348
Orr, P., 144
Ortlund, R. C., 195
Owing, J., 107

Pannenberg, W., 305-8, 310-13, 315-16, 319, 332, 337-38
Pao, D. W., 270
Parratt, J. K., 125
Parry, R., 185
Parsons, M. A., 108, 123, 131-32
Pattemore, S., 235, 239
Patterson, S. J., 81
Payne, D. F., 42
Pearson, B. A., 174
Penney, J. M., 68, 360
Pervo, R., 209

Pesch, R., 38, 124
Peterson, D., 80, 358
Petrenko, E., 361
Petzoldt, M., 339
Pfleiderer, O., 147
Poder, P., 329
Pöhlmann, H. G., 337
Porsch, F., 87, 89, 104, 271
Porter, S. E., 116, 201, 216
Pretlove, J., 88, 95, 104
Price, R. M., 285, 294

Rabens, V., 99, 102, 144, 146-47, 149-50, 153, 155, 157, 161, 163-64, 166-67, 200, 211, 348, 362
Rahner, J., 111
Rainbow, P. A., 190
Räisänen, H., 11
Ramsay, I., 344
Ridderbos, H., 106
Rissi, M., 220, 227
Ritter, W. H., 140
Rosner, B. S., 359
Runco, M. A., 350
Runia, D., 259, 261
Russell, N., 290, 299, 358

Saarinen, R., 317
Sanders, E. P., 309
Schäfer, P., 45
Scherer, H., 150
Schlier, H., 217
Schnackenburg, R., 106, 142
Schnädelbach, H., 341
Schneemelcher, W., 209
Schneiders, S. M., 88, 94, 100-101, 104
Schütz, F., 54
Schweizer, E., 79, 267, 269, 271
Schwöbel, C., 343
Scobie, C. H., 123
Scott, I. W., 185, 260-61
Sellers, R. V., 286
Shauf, S., 121, 123
Shaver, P. R., 144
Shelton, J. B., 359
Shults, F. L., 186

Smalley, S. S., 233, 235-36, 240-41
Stacey, D. W., 171
Stanton, G. N., 81, 88, 199, 268, 358
Stecher, L., 144
Stein, R. H., 36, 41, 278, 281, 283
Sterling, G., 174
Stobart, A. J., 328
Strauss, M. L., 270, 276, 362
Strobel, A., 81
Stronstad, R., 2, 68, 267
Studebakker, S., 322
Stuhlmacher, P., 168
Sweet, J., 236
Sylva, D. D., 83

Tannehill, R. C., 21, 56-57, 125
Tanner, K., 310
Taylor, C., 74
Taylor, V., 274
Tengström, S., 3
Terian, A., 249
Terrence, 197
Theissen, G., 140-41, 143, 172
Thiselton, A. C., 148, 171-72, 353
Thomas, J. C., 243
Thomasius, G., 274
Thompson, J., 313, 337
Thompson, M. M., 88, 94, 99
Tiede, D. L., 255
Tilley, T. W., 197
Tilling, C., 184-86, 190, 362
Towner, P. H., 204, 206
Trebilco, P., 199
Tuckett, C., 44
Turner, M., 16, 18-19, 22, 35, 38-39, 41-43, 46-47, 52, 68, 81, 87-88, 95, 97-100, 104, 124-27, 129, 132, 138, 146-47, 151, 155, 160-61, 197, 201, 205-6, 213-14, 266, 268-72, 277
Twelftree, G., 120

Vanhoozer, K., 334, 359

Vanhoye, A., 227
Vondey, W., 338-39

Waaler, E., 185
Wainwright, G., 338
Walker, A., 326
Wall, R. W., 201, 205
Walsh, B., 326
Walton, S., 79
Ware, B. A., 275-76
Waschkies, H.-J., 339
Watson, F., 181
Weatherly, J. A., 362
Wedderburn, A. J., 167
Weinandy, T. G., 288-89, 291, 296, 299
Weinrich, W. C., 136
Weiss, H.-F., 220, 223-24
Welker, M., 332
Welsch, W., 350
Wenk, M., 362
Wesley, L., 69
West, C., 312
Westermann, C., 42
Wilckens, U., 71-72
Wilhite, D. W., 209
Willimon, W., 326
Winston, D., 253
Witherington, B., 67-68, 122, 131
Wojciechowski, J., 95, 104
Wolter, M., 119, 150
Wolterstorff, N., 201
Woods, E. J., 60
Wrede, W., 197
Wright, N. T., 207, 309

Yong, A., 322, 337-38, 353
Young, F., 291, 294, 301

Zehnle, R., 73-74, 85
Ziesler, J., 176
Zimmermann, R., 232
Zyl, H. C. van, 73, 80

www.ingramcontent.com/pod-product-compliance
Lightning Source LLC
Chambersburg PA
CBHW032148010526
44111CB00035B/1247